CRONUS' CHILDREN

Yves Navarre

CRONUS' CHILDREN

Prix Goncourt Winner 1981

Translated by Howard Girven

JOHN CALDER · LONDON
RIVERRUN PRESS · NEW YORK

First published in Great Britain in 1986 by
John Calder (Publishers) Ltd
18 Brewer Street, London W1R 4AS

And in the United States of America in 1986 by
Riverrun Press Inc
1170 Broadway, New York 10001

Originally published in French as *Le jardin d'acclimatation*
in 1980 by Librairie Ernst Flammarion, Paris

Copyright © Librairie Ernst Flammarion, 1980
Copyright this translation © John Calder (Publishers) Ltd, 1986

British Library Cataloguing in Publication Data
Navarre, Ives
   Cronus' Children
   I. Title   II. Le jardin d'acclimatation, *English*
   843'.914[F]   PQ2674.A88

   ISBN 0-7145-4013-7
   ISBN 0-7145-4014-5 pbk

Library of Congress Cataloging in Publication Data
Navarre, Yves 1940—
   Cronus' Children.
   Translation of: Le jardin d'acclimatation.
   I. Title.
PQ2674.A88J313   1986   843'.914   86-4860
ISBN 0-7145-4013-7
ISBN 0-7145-4014-5 (pbk)

Typeset in 11 on 12 point Baskerville by Margaret Spooner Typesetting, Bridport, Dorset
Printed in Great Britain by The Camelot Press, Southampton.

'For Henri, our Cronus, that god we never speak of, time is inaugurated with his sons . . .'

Claire, writing to
her late husband

'As an inscription, I'll put "this is the story of a murderous father who could find no better way of killing his children than letting them live."'

Bertrand, to his brother Sébastien

'Today I can only give you this garden where we will always be growing up without knowing it, without wanting to.'

Letter from Bertrand Prouillan to his brother
Sébastien

1

July 9th. Ten o'clock in the morning. Henri Prouillan stands, hands crossed behind his back, his head tilted slightly, his forehead against the windowpane, behind one of the three French doors, the centre one, in the grand salon. He is looking at the Place d'Antioche, 75017 Paris, from his first floor. He is seventy-four years old. When he was a child, at this same place, he sometimes used to post himself in the same way, hands behind his back, head slightly tilted, his forehead against the windowpane. If he left a mark he was scolded afterwards. If they surprised him, he would close his eyes and wait to be snatched away from his post. The servants had the right to move him away but not to touch him. Henri, a little boy, the only son, was untouchable. Some servant or other would wipe the pane with a rag. Henri then went to his room. He had invented a way, his way, of slowly, cautiously closing the doors behind him, pivoting on the toe, then the heels of his school boots or his high evening shoes, turning on himself, elbow raised, holding the doorknob with his fingertips like a scorn or a favour. Suzanne, Suzy, jealousy, had just been born. Henri saw little of his parents. He sees them better, here, now. But they have been dead for fifty and fifty-one years, one after the other such a long time ago. Henri Prouillan smiles, very slightly to himself or to whomsoever, a smile onto the emptiness of the square. Formerly there had been a statue there in the centre of it, with cobblestones all around it, with cars, much slower, all of them black, and often teams of horses from the Grandes Glacières of the Porte de Clichy, making deliveries, coming and going all day long, on Boulevard Malesherbes, the Plaine Monceau, the smart neighbour-hoods without shadows.

This morning Henri Prouillan leaves a mark on the windowpane as his thoughts stray. With a quick gesture he wipes it off, steps back, wipes it again. From the bottom pane to the top one, he grew up. After that he grew smaller. He is shrinking. He is becoming stooped. He has an impression of coming apart. But he feels very much on his feet. Even now. And master. He turns around. The apartment's decor has not changed. A decor Cécile never dared touch. Probably because she did not know her husband's parents. This morning Henri Prouillan is alone. With his dog. Pantalon.

It is a poodle. For some years now Henri Prouillan has been taking him every six months to the veterinary hospital on the Impasse des Acacias, near the Etoile, and Dr. Bermann has been giving the animal a shot of Bogomoletz serum. In this way they have been prolonging the life of Wallou, son of Wagguy, grandson of Watou, nicknamed Pantalon, like his father and grandfather. This morning Pantalon III is lying near the front door, under the marble console. It is his place. He is waiting to be taken out. Bernadette has gone to the clinic. At breakfast Henri Prouillan thought 'Again! But why?' He did not say it out loud, out of fear. Bernadette is irreplaceable. With no place to go except the old people's home, she chose to 'spend her retirement' with 'Monsieur' and 'as long as Monsieur is here'. Sometimes when they have shared a day in good humour, she reminds her employer that she is six months older than he, and she too has a right to worry about her health. Henri Prouillan, pleased with Bernadette's repeated refrain, her amused appeal, merely answers, 'You don't have the worries I have. So make me a cake like in the old days.' But the cakes no longer taste the same. The apartment no longer shines.

Pantalon gets up by halves, front paws first, then the back. His master is in the hallway. He can barely see him, like a shadow, and by his scent. He lowers his head, puts out his muzzle, wags his tail. The act of getting up places him alongside the door, at the very spot where it will be half opened, a decisive move made from above, when his leash has been attached to his collar. He will be able to go out at last, holding himself in until he gets to the pavement, the first chestnut tree, always the same one for the last seventeen years. They can count. But not he. Pantalon no longer feels his paws and sees neither day nor night, scarcely a glimmer. Cécile was the only one who looked at him when she gave him a sugar

8

lump or spoke to him when she gave him a bit of cake. Bernadette talks to herself about him: the day Madame died (in hospital) Pantalon peed on Madame's bed (in Madame's bedroom in the apartment) 'and he didn't even know!' Bernadette talks alone, out loud in the pantry. It is her way of surrounding herself with servants, the chauffeur and housekeeper who have not been employed since Bertrand left, the third son and the fourth of the children, Luc, Sébastien, Claire and Bertrand, three marriages, a departure and for Madame the beginning of a slow agony. Henri Prouillan attaches the leash to the collar. 'Come on!' Pantalon licks his hand.

In the square, at the first chestnut tree, Pantalon doesn't even lift his paw. Henri Prouillan, distracted, pulls on the leash. Pantalon pees walking, slowly, swaying his backend, a stiffness in his paws. They do not take Pantalon out as much as previously. His nails have grown. That bothers him. Nobody notices. Not even Dr. Bermann.

Suzy, widow of the playwright Jean Martin, is coming to lunch today with her brother. It's an event. 'We see little of each other because we love each other too much.' Either one or the other, one of the two is always saying it to the other, the brother or sister, the survivors, are still here. They toss the ball back and forth, (Suzy always used to cheat at croquet, Henri wanted at all cost to win at tennis), like a confession, their confession. For a laugh. Or else to apologise. A whole life of apologising, by pretending to be amused. Henri Prouillan, member of the Academy of Moral and Political Sciences, a former minister, honorary president of the Economic and Social Council, has known three Republics, twenty-seven governments, has inherited a fortune, which he has protected, kept intact, and Suzanne, Suzy, seven years younger, who mocks him ('What were you *really* a minister of?'), glorious ('Jean had only one wife and some women. One stays, the others move on') and childless ('The Boulevard isn't supposed to reproduce. Or else it's only neglect on our part!'). Suzy operates the Théâtre des Champs, on the right bank, year in year out for good or bad. 'I'm condemned to succeed.' Henri has had no more news of his children. Henri and Suzy have an appointment this July ninth at 1 p.m., at 2 Place d'Antioche, on the first floor, there is only one door. Bernadette will do the

9

shopping on her way home from the clinic. She has taken out the silver service from the grand old days. Monsieur's sister, as usual, as soon as she sits down, will demand an unstarched napkin. 'I have tender lips.' Everything about them is decided, has been lived in advance, and yet! Monsieur's sister will come on foot, 'like a neighbour', from the Boulevard Haussmann.

Henri Prouillan pulls on the dog's leash. 'Pantalon! We're going to be late. It's a long walk.' He has just spoken to the dog, out loud. The sound of his voice surprises him. He has not listened to himself for a long time. Pantalon is deaf. He follows his master, in tow.

In the Place d'Antioche four identical buildings form a perfect circle. Buildings of carved stone, a ground floor with a small, half-moon garden, a noble first floor with small balconies and French doors, a third floor with only windows, and dormer windows on the roof, oval, circular, alternately the eyes of the servants and the view from the garrets. Bernadette lives in Claire's room now, in the apartment. So Monsieur can call her at night if he does not feel well, and vice versa as well, but this is never the case. Henri Prouillan leaves the Place d'Antioche. He will go up the Avenue de Wagram to the Avenue des Ternes. He is wearing a hat and coat. It is summer. The morning sky is grey, mild, the air heavy. Paris already has an air of being abandoned. Henri Prouillan knows that Paris well, emptying itself. The Paris of the corridors of power when there is talk of a change of government or of ministerial reshuffling. The fomenting Paris, of the majority, of the opposition. The Paris without a National Assembly, without a Senate, when there is enough time for intrigue and for decisions to be left hanging. Every year Henri Prouillan would send Cécile and the children to Moncrabeau at the very beginning of summer. And in the emptiness of the city, an emptiness created for the mysterious month of August, with no one but the artists left to believe in the moment of grace, he busied himself with all the contacts he had not been able to establish during the autumn, winter and spring, took time to watch over the management of his stock portfolio, had a traditional lunch at Taillevent's with his stockbroker on the first Saturday in July, and especially to love whomever he wanted loved when he loved, liaisons which alone stuck in his

10

memory and gave him certainty of, for once, having power. Those bodies he caressed, Jacqueline's especially, she a brunette, with her soft bosom, who on entering the empty apartment, which was indeed the moment for him: she would enter and he unbuttoning her blouse, would free her bare breasts. He wanted to see her now, just like that, going into the living room, chasing out of his mind the children's cries, their happiness, Cécile's looks and silences, with never a remonstrance. As round and smooth as the Place d'Antioche.

Pantalon stops, paws stretched at an angle, head lowered. He interrupts Henri Prouillan in his walk and thoughts. Pantalon wants to do his duty. By force and the end of the leash and collar Henri Prouillan drags him to the gutter. Pantalon has his nails filed a little on the pavement. Henri Prouillan turns his head. One does not watch a shitting dog. Henri Prouillan feels thrown into his thoughts. Then it is possible he has never loved? Has he for one moment, a single moment of his life, been capable of being loved? When? Hasn't he invariably been judged with contempt for being too favoured by life?

There is only one gentleman out who walks with a coat, a hat and a dog on a leash. A dog that walks even slower than the gentleman. At the newspaper vendor, there are the daily papers, the headlines, and the gentleman reads: 'The sea on fire', 'New accord with Israel', 'Capsule K2000 back to earth', 'A Surprising Yellow Bathing Suit', 'How to lose weight in just a few days', 'Special gardening-lawn mowers', 'The campers' anger', 'She kills her lover in front of her rival', 'The right to be rich', 'Land prices region by region', 'Exclusive: Claudine Sperza and her third husband!' Henri Prouillan wonders who this Claudine is. A television announcer? Henri Prouillan watches television but does not listen to it anymore. He lets himself be cradled by the garbled images of the present and thinks only about everything that in the past, extracted, could have inspired him to a new activity, at least one.

It has been a long time since Pantalon has had such a long walk. From time to time he wants to stop, as if by astonishment, worry or curiosity, but his master pulls on his leash. The smell of berlingot comes from the entrance of the United Stores. Cécile used to do all her shopping there. She

11

once had a ten percent discount card given to large families. It was her favourite store. She used to say that she found everything there, including friendships with the sales girls. And, in the household department up on the fourth floor was that make of bridge table she liked to give as a wedding gift to the sons and daughters of friends and relatives. 'It was the ideal present,' she would say, 'useful and beautiful, the first table for a young couple to own.' Cécile's habits were only attentions. Others took them for niggardliness. The idea of a bridge table as a wedding gift was her own idea and each time it was a surprise for her. The gift was practical, of craftsman quality, good-sized, impressive and the United Stores made home deliveries. Once a year, with the money from the ten percent discount, Cécile went shopping for the children.

Pantalon stops and lies down on the pavement. Henri Prouillan bends over, tries to lift him up to carry him in his arms across the Avenue des Ternes but he cannot. Henri Prouillan has no memory of ever carrying anyone, human or animal, in his arms. Not even Luc, Sébastien, Claire or Bertrand when they were small. Bertrand whose name must never be pronounced again. But Henri Prouillan has just thought of his son. So, with violence, and ill at ease in his coat, he forces the dog to stand up. His hat almost falls off. He takes it in his other hand. A red light. They can cross. Eleven o'clock in the morning, that morning. They will be a few minutes late. But you always have to wait at Dr. Bermann's.

Luc, the eldest? Henri used to tell him, as if to get rid of him when he would interject a question, a provocation, 'When in doubt, abstain.' Then with a smile, Luc answered, 'And you, when silent, all you do is abstain.' Sébastien and Claire, always on the same side, so often accomplices, had chosen to speak very little to their father, in revenge, like an appeal. Only sometimes, to show their presence, their aggression or respect, they would utter one of those witty remarks they judged unworthy of Uncle Jean, that creator of a thousand performances, because it was too fine or significant. Sébastien, shouting to the world, 'One cannot *be* sincere and *appear* to be sincere' and Claire, adding a postscript to a letter to her father, 'The worst jealousy is indifference.' That left Bertrand whose name must be stifled and not mentioned, and who, in the year he graduated from the lycée shortly after the third marriage in the family, Claire's marriage, had said to everybody at the table, during a family gathering, demanding silence, 'Doubt is all I have left, my one and only certainty. Can you understand that?'

Henri Prouillan and his dog Pantalon pass the window of Berthier fils, the caterer, who has regularly supplied the Prouillan family and to whose establishment had been confided, by tradition, the buffet and the luncheon for the three weddings, almost as if they were officials for the festivities, engagements and nuptials for Cécile and Henri. Henri Prouillan does not stop before the window. But he thinks about his past. He tells himself that nothing has ever truly begun, the fault of the school boots and the evening shoes, the fault of Suzy's birth, nobody's and everybody's fault, the faults we prefer not to talk about and that yet, without our admitting their origins, govern all these beings and all these lives. Pantalon sticks out his tongue, drools a bit. At the Rue d'Acacias, 'Hurry up.' Pantalon slows down. He does not want to hurry. The collar chokes him a little, the pulls on the leash are becoming more urgent. He would rather be back at home under the marble console, hearing the clatter of the plate being put on the floor, on the kitchen tiles when Bernadette serves him his pâté which she has put through the blender. He does not have any teeth left. But the master insists. Pantalon follows, walking sideways. Obstinately. This walk is too long.

The special odour of veterinarians' waiting rooms. An odour of fur, leather and disinfectant. Almost a zoo or circus odour. Henri Prouillan folds his coat and puts his hat on it. A lady is already waiting, with a basket on her knees with a cat inside that is moving, turning around and meowing. The lady speaks to the cat 'You know very well it's nothing at all . . .' Henri Prouillan holds Pantalon in front of him, at knee height, by the collar. With the other hand he pets his head, the sparse fur is close-cropped and curly. The lady says 'How old is your dog?' Henri Prouillan smiles, as if to hide a recurring emotion. 'He is very old, like me. He hasn't much longer.' The lady murmurs 'You mustn't say that, Sir.' And she begins talking to the cat again. Henri Prouillan leans forward and kisses his dog on the head. The lady tells herself that the monsieur is going to cry. A door opens. The lady rises. The cat wriggles in its basketwork carrying-case. Henri Prouillan is alone again with Pantalon and the waiting room odour. 'I . . .' Pantalon looks at him. Henri Prouillan repeats 'I . . .' But he does not find the necessary words. Pantalon lies down, curled up at his feet, as if under the marble console. Seated, bent over the dog, his elbows on his knees, hands joined with fingers laced in a fist, Henri Prouillan watches the animal. Pantalon III.

Bertrand used to say 'I only love us for the details of life, sometimes, and only sometimes.' Bertrand had a strange way of saying 'I . . . us,' showing that he was not accusing the group nor anyone exactly, but the whole family and he himself, inside it, giving or receiving, the son, the last son. The course of every worry, every scandal, he would impose silence, smiling 'I want to speak now. I listen, I listen to all of us all the time. Now I know that speaking is a way of listening. So I'm speaking!' So he would catch his amused, surprised, almost convinced family members unaware with all their references and assumptions. 'Yes, it isn't just for some little detail, some slight flash of wit, or a lovely turn of phrase or a joyous idea that I like us sometimes, but for a half-made gesture that doesn't go all the way, for a word aborted, a confession left hanging in the air, a look from you, Sébastien, or from you, Luc, when you lower your head, or even you, Mama, when you ask us not to criticise our parents, or you, Claire, when you decide abruptly to help Bernadette clear the table, or you, Papa, when we talk about vacations, or about trips, and you answer that we are free to do what we want. But we are neither free nor do we have wills of our own. So let's go to Moncrabeau. I've already said too much. I'm listening to you too much.' Bertrand's voice choking on the last word and the last word was always 'too much.' Not an exclamation. Henri Prouillan recalls it, word for word. It was shortly before the Fifth Republic. The former administrative staff of the RPF was meeting more and more often with that intense secrecy that marks the eve of a grab for power. What was historically supposed to be a surprise was not at all that to him, being in on the secret of tomorrow's potential ministers. In certain salons of certain houses where a post-war dustiness still held sway, the Companions of the Liberation were tallying up ten years of dirty tricks and impotence. They were also counting among themselves — a round number of governments to come. Pantalon has gone to sleep at his master's feet, his tongue hanging out of his muzzle, his need to sleep stronger than thirst. Henri Prouillan knows perfectly well that he had once led Bertrand just the way he leads his dog today. Just like a little (smile) and even a lot, (an urge to laugh or shout), the way he has led his life. It is probably for that reason, on this particular morning, at 11.30, in a tiled waiting room, windowless, with ceilinged daylight, in a courtyard covered with frosted glass, at the end of the Impasse des Acacias, that he remembers so many events, word for word. But now he is listening. A tear would save him. But he has been incapable of tears since Suzy was born. A boy does not cry. And a man who believes he is strong does not cry anymore. He must be careful not to wake Pantalon. Is he only pretending to be asleep?

Henri Prouillan begins thinking that he would never really belong to any clan or caste. Therein probably lies the reason for his lack of contact with his neighbours in the Place d'Antioche. That would be of no importance for Bertrand, if he was still able to speak in order to hear, to impose a silence so that he could say something. In that probably lies the explanation for the durability of an important person's power, for the public credibility carried down from Republic to Republic, from government to government right down to the triumph of the Resistance itself which set itself to governing, in a game of wartime mythologies, a competition of medals, a display of wounds and of sometimes unverifiable exploits. But today, a day in July, at the start of the eighties, at a time of crisis, when the vassals on every side do nothing more than scoff at each other, as rivals, even when neither the party in power nor the opposition has designated a programme of any consequence to the country, each being as conservative as the other, pale plotters fearful of a future which will be determined too much by the events of a recent past, '58, '39/45, '36, '39, '14/18 and, why not, the separation of Church and State. Henri Prouillan remembers a visit by the former Prime Minister Combes to his father one Sunday. The two men were shut up in the little sitting room used as a library. It was a winter day. There was snow in the Place d'Antioche and the few cars that passed left circular tracks, like rails of mud, in what had just been white and beautiful. On the windowpane of the middle French window Henri made haloes of mist with his finger and wrote 'No' then 'No' and 'No!' He had just heard the words once spoken to his father, between swallows of coffee, 'My dear Prouillan, ambition is only the art of knowing how to say No and No again. Always No. Everything turns out best that way.'

The door opens. The lady comes out with the basket carrier. She seems relieved and pleased. She thanks Dr. Bermann. Through a little dormer window the cat peers out, wide-eyed. Henri Prouillan raises his head and stands up. Pantalon stretches, looks vaguely at the cat in the carrier and at the lady's feet, at the doctor's smock. The lady goes out, a last salutation. Dr. Bermann approaches Pantalon, kneels down, pets him. 'So there you are? Everything's going to be alright, you know.' He gathers up the leash, stands up again, helps Pantalon regain his paws. A friendly pat on the dog's backside. Dr. Bermann looks at Henri Prouillan, 'Are you coming with us?' Henri Prouillan gestures no. He puts his hands in his jacket pockets. Bertrand used to tell his sister and brothers, 'When Papa makes fists in his pockets, it's because he's embarrassed and might give himself away . . .' Dr. Bermann pulls Pantalon, Pantalon turns his head. His master is not following him as he usually does when he goes to get the serum shots. The doctor mumbles 'At least say goodbye . . .' Henri Prouillan answers with a too clear voice, the voice that can say No, no and no, 'It's already done.' The doctor goes out with Pantalon, closes the door behind him. Henri Prouillan finds himself alone. Without even realising it he repeats 'Already done, since the beginning.'

Then, standing, his fists clenched in his pockets, three sons and a daughter in each fist, Cécile across his heart, Jacqueline and the others all around it, Henri Prouillan makes a circle of the waiting room. On a sign he reads 'The hospital will be closed from July 3 to August 17.' On a low table some dog-eared magazines. A telephone begins ringing. Nobody answers. At Moncrabeau three generations of Pantalons have chased cats, birds and rabbits. Sometimes the poodle would instinctively regain his love of chasing ducks and at the first passing flight in September, would excitedly throw himself into the pond at the end of the yard, panting, pushing his proud muzzle above the water and when he emerged dripping with mud, the human population would move away, laughing. The dog would shake himself. The first, the second, the third, nearly fifty years of history. A memory. Henri Prouillan checks that he has not forgotten his wallet.

Bernadette has not been warned. The appointment at the Acacias Hospital was made in secret and, a precaution, Henri Prouillan wrote in his appointment diary only the word 'duty'. Like a duty. An obligation. And the fear of supervision which for Bernadette is only orderliness and kindness. She looks through everything. Now, Henri Prouillan realises he had not foreseen his return to the Place d'Antioche and the continuation of this event, only the continuation, as if events have endings. Even more than thinking about what was happening in the next room, here he is worrying about returning home, about questions from the person who really governs his life while she pretends to remain totally in the background, who makes the decisions now by submitting to him, an automatic submission, every decision that has to be made. And lunch with Suzy is important. It has to be a success. On the occasion of these rare meetings, Henri always wanted to hold his own against his sister. Or is he, just now, in his anxiety, just avoiding reality? Henri Prouillan heads toward the door. Softly with his left hand he knocks as he has never knocked at any door before and so awkwardly that the knocks cannot be heard. But he feels easier, about himself and Pantalon. He knocks again, gives it up, steps back and goes to sit beside the coat and hat. No sooner is he seated than the door opens, Dr. Bermann comes back. An assistant follows him, crosses the room without a word and disappears through another door. The telephone rings again. She answers. Dr. Bermann stays a moment, silent, motionless, the collar and leash in his hand, the leash still attached to the collar. He smiles. Henri Prouillan puts his elbows on his knees, his head nodding gently and bites his lips. The dog is no longer lying there on the floor, between his legs. The great space between his legs. Everything has happened so quickly. Now he has to pay and leave, return home and carry on normally, explain, continue as usual, pretend to forget. He remembers his father showing him how to knot a tie, placing it around his son's neck, a brief, precise almost hurried gesture and his father pulling it and laughing. Henri Prouillan was eleven. That day, held at the end of a tie, Henri watched his father burst into laughter and did not understand the reason for this sudden joy. Vertigo. Heat. Henri Prouillan stands up, staggers a little as if drunk, or else it is only the odour of the waiting room, the absence of windows or Dr. Bermann's gentle and conventional smile mumbling 'He didn't realise a thing. I just put him to sleep.' Dr. Bermann holds out the collar and leash. Henri Prouillan takes them, the smooth, worn leather, still warmish, just an impression, while with his other hand he takes his wallet from the inside pocket of his jacket. Dr. Bermann makes a slight gesture of refusal. 'You can settle with my assistant on your way out.' Henri Prouillan gathers up his coat and hat. He feels loaded down, harnessed, the coat on his forearm, his hat, leash and collar in his left hand. Dr. Bermann says 'Do you want to see him a last time?' 'No.' 'Do you want us to call you a taxi?' 'No.' 'You did everything for Watou. He wouldn't have lasted the summer. What can I tell you, Monsieur Prouillan? That at the last moment your dog asked me to thank you for everything?' A smile from Dr. Bermann. Henri Prouillan repeats a third time 'No.' The two men shake hands.

Paying for the injection, paying for the incineration of the body, paying as one always does when one has the obligation and the means, paying to leave no trace, the secret of intact fortunes. Dr. Bermann's assistant puts the bills in the cash drawer, returns the small change that Henri Prouillan finds ridiculous, the change generally left as a tip in restaurants but which here must be taken back, as an acknowledgement of the event. The assistant tries to be friendly. 'Don't you have one of Watou's sons?' 'No,' Henri Prouillan answers, 'he was the last one.'

The Impasse des Acacias, the Rue des Acacias, it is nearly noon, the United Stores are closing their doors, it's lunch hour. A break. The coat is heavy on his forearm and the hat is useless. The sky has clouded over. It's going to rain. There is no more summer in Paris. Just a vague memory of spring. The collar and leash hang from Henri Prouillan's left hand. They are light. A void in the collar. And by fits and starts, each time he has to cross a street at the crossing, each time he has to look to see if the way is clear, Henri Prouillan takes a deep breath as if he feared a coming pain or breakdown. He was never able or knew how to let himself be moved at the right moment. The sorrows of life had always awakened in him too late when there was no one close to him who could explain or place them. That is probably one characteristic of upbringing, the true mark, everything that in a given milieu creates a delay between cause and effect, impression and emotion, speech and listening. Never let anything show.

On the newspaper stand the racks are covered with plastic. The headlines are blurred. For a fraction of a second, Henri Prouillan has the impression of not seeing very well. But he feels reasonably prepared for this route home, the route of drudgery. He did not want to see Pantalon put to sleep but he did knock at the door. Henri Prouillan wants terribly and so strongly to be comfortable with himself that he feels a doubt awakening in him like a certainty, Bertrand's message, an indifference akin to jealousy, Claire's message, a transparent sincerity, Sébastien's avowal, and from Luc the idea of a withdrawal that, having been accepted for so many years as natural and simple, now seems to have become ambiguous and even sensuous. All of that, a stock-taking, guides Henri Prouillan. He has just found his children. He tells himself not 'Found again' but 'Found,' as for a first time. Luc will be forty-nine this year, Sébastien forty-seven, Claire forty-four and Bertrand thirty-nine or forty? So many birthdays forgotten in order to arrive at that appraisal of it, the appraisal of the difference between what has been lived and the living itself, between what is only just lovable and the act of loving itself, which draws them, in a game of strengths and oppositions, unfailingly closer together. Henri Prouillan feels in himself that utter renewal, that healthy burst of energy that used to animate him on the eve of great decisions or daring manoeuvres. He tells himself that he sees 'Everything clearly from now on.' And he hears Cécile telling his children through thoughtlessness or fear of seeing them conforming to

19

their father's image of them, 'Everything is never too much.' Everything is never too much. Thank you Pantalon.

Bernadette is watching over the clafoutis as it cooks. She unmoulds the jellied duck, decorates the silver dish with olives and lemon slices. The clock in the hall leading to the pantry strikes half past noon twice. Two strikes, a minute apart, two, heavy and compelling. But the clock does not strike the way it used to. When it strikes the hours, it drags them out. Bernadette would have liked to 'stop that machine' but when she pretends to forget to re-set the mechanism, Monsieur, without a word, starts it up again. 'And I'm the one with a ringside seat, getting all that clanging in my ears.' Pantalon's pâté is ready. There is also an unstarched napkin for Suzy, an affectation. The tray for the coffee has to be prepared. And Monsieur's sugar-substitute tablets.

The Place d'Antioche. Henri Prouillan has only a few minutes to change. Behind the glass in the concierge's room, is the sign 'Monsieur and Madame H. Prouillan, first floor, main staircase' and the names of other neighbours, who pass are greeted, but never recognised. Since Cécile's death, seven years ago, nothing has really changed. Having gradually retired from all his duties, an academician by chance, obliged to retreat from activity, Henri Prouillan dared not change anything at all. Another time lag to avoid pain, even many pains. And there in the stairway, rid of Pantalon, his mission accomplished, he feels light, ready for everything. Ready to resume everything at the very beginning of everything. The feeling is both juvenile and vengeful, loving and deadly. A product that Henri Prouillan has reproduced. He has produced and they have reproduced. Where are they? What are they doing? What is left of all that was created when he was born? When they were born? His children? He would like so much to inherit from them.

Henri Prouillan enters his home, hangs up the collar and leash in the coatroom, in the corner to the left of the door. Alerted, Bernadette takes her employer's coat and hat. The collar is on the hook, the leash dangling. Henri Prouillan says only 'Pantalon was too old.' And he heads toward his bedroom looking at his watch. No more than a few minutes before Suzy swirls in. Henri Prouillan has just made a decision.

20

Bernadette verifies that the door is well closed. She hangs the coat in the closet and puts the hat on the edge of the upper shelf in its exact place so Monsieur would not yell 'Bernadette! Where is my hat?' Under the marble console is a great void. Bernadette would like to pet the leash but such gestures are forbidden. She says in a low voice 'And he did that to you!'

In the pantry Bernadette picks up Pantalon's pâté and throws it in the trashcan. She cries or she laughs. Sometimes Pantalon would come to sleep near her bed in Claire's room. Then Bernadette observed this body stretched out, this pet's body, all shaken in sleep by unknown, unimaginable dreams, interrupted barks, sudden tensing of the paws. And Bernadette would feel very comfortable like that, with Pantalon, together. The two of them.

Henri Prouillan sprinkles himself with eau de toilette, the same one that Suzy cannot stand because she finds it 'too dry and really cheap.' In the mirror above the sink he gives himself a smile. He has just made the decision of his life. He puts on a white shirt and knots the tie.

The doorbell. It is Suzy. She is early. 'I adore the month of July! There are almost no cars about. You can cross without even looking. Pantalon isn't here?' Henri Prouillan kisses his sister on both cheeks, as in the old days when they left each other to go to bed, each in his bedroom in the same apartment, more than sixty years ago. Suzy looks at her brother. 'You have a funny look about you and you're looking too well!' 'I have just made a decision.' 'What?' They go into the salon. Henri Prouillan puts his fists in his jacket pockets, smiles, avoids his sister's look and says very distinctly. 'A decision! The only thing we won't talk about today.'

Suzy sits in an armchair and crosses her legs. She shows her legs, all that is left that can be shown. She murmurs 'That's cheerful.' Henri Prouillan opens the centre French window. 'Yes, very!' Outside, there is a fine warm and sifting rain, a patter on the chestnut leaves, and a rising wind. Henri and Suzy snicker like children.

2

Two Portuguese and an Irishman for the maintenance of the
engines, a German who serves as both nurse and administrator,
two Venezuelans who take jobs everywhere together for
romantic reasons, and live in the same cabin, they are also the
only two real sailors, an American thrown out of Alabama, a
radioman, a Greek who can't cook, and René, the pilot of the
surveillance helicopter, all with an average age of a little more
than 40, with the official language an English that resembles a
Latin American pudding. Sébastien leaves the mess table. It is
the moment when they all begin nervously crushing their
cigarette butts into the coffee cups. The moment when they
put on a little mood music. The moment of burps and farts,
fun and card games whose winnings for eleven months now
have been going into a kitty to be used on the last day, the eve
of their separation, to have a wild time out and tutti quanti in
Oslo. In Overfjellet fjord, 300 kilometres north of the capital,
two methane and five giant, laid up, oil tankers have been
moored for almost two years. Sébastien is the skipper of the
watch crew. There are nine of them, and he is the tenth, the
skipper for all that. The contracts were signed for a year.
Winter went by in night, almost the whole time in night, and
without incident. It's summer now with the same sun at noon
or midnight. The men are more nervous. In twenty-two days
the relief crew will arrive. In twenty-nine days they will be in
Oslo. In thirty days Sébastien will be back in Paris for an
undetermined length of time. With no home and no one to
wait for him really. During lunch he surprised himself making
little bread pellets, from the Greek's pale bread, an action
which was forbidden and therefore irresistible in the old days
at the Place d'Antioche, when Claire, a little girl, used to say to
her brother 'You'll go to the Naval Academy, you'll be an
admiral and I'll marry you!' An action, a memory. Sébastien
bangs his cabin door, takes a clean sheet of paper, uncaps his

pen, scribbles on the corner of a magazine to make the ink run and begins to write.

'July 9. Aboard the *Firebird*, somewhere between Elseneur and the pole. Dear Papa, I am writing you from the country of the slalom, a Norwegian word, from *sla*: slope, and *lom*: trace. So it is a slope that is leading me back to you (after a long silence) so I can perhaps leave a trace (one is always afraid of dying). You see, I haven't lost my bad habits, particularly this one, and it's only the beginning of my letter, of using parenthesis, which you used to enjoy telling me were an impediment to style, which should be clear and distinct for more effectiveness. This concern of yours, which has become mine in the exercise of my profession (I am acting here as pater familias with nine crewmen, that is, I say nothing, so that I can rule, like you), I will try to forget for the purpose of this letter. Watch out, there will be lots of parenthesis and lots of bread pellets (I'll explain why on my return to Paris, the first of August, flight 713, via Amsterdam, I will telephone you on the off chance, but I prefer staying at the hotel. Merci).

'(2) I have given you little news for nearly two years now. Little, but for me that is none at all. Where does one draw strength from in life if not in confessing? I can only confess the break, the fracture in our relations, and the inevitable attachment which arises from this failure, like a chasm, a void, a vertigo. And here I am starting to write, in this letter in the way we used to talk, Luc, Claire, Bertrand and I, at Moncrabeau, on summer evening walks. We would have so much liked to meet some neighbours at the end of the paths we walked along, private property. But never. How is that possible? Nightmares are dreams one doesn't remember. I haven't dreamed for years. I don't remember anything at all. I feel solidly anchored and adrift at the same time (an allusion to this methane tanker where we all live like dogs, sorry Pantalon, and in which I'll have lived during eleven months for endless days, in perpetual night and then endless daylight again, no longer truly able to tell the difference between going to bed and waking up, being asleep or awake). That parenthesis was for less efficiency, therefore more real clarity and the expression of your son's precision. A son who is no longer of an age to begin life again and is content to let it pass with

24

schedules, controls, meals, just to carry on. Only the general disorder or the crises of others here keep me going. I've grown a Viking beard. I haven't looked at myself in a mirror for months. I am writing you to tell you I love you. Because I just thought of you. Very hard. Abruptly. Why?

'(3) Yes, why? And why so abruptly? These months of metal and night, granite and snow, and then, now, you come back onto the scene (a real *coup de theatre*, just like one of Uncle Jean's tricks, a stunt of hinges and oiled locks) and I say to myself, well, I haven't written him for a long time. So know, at first hand from my own pen, officially, that Ruth is still living in Toronto with Laura and Paul, that she isn't dancing anymore but is teaching dance, that Laura is engaged and that Paul takes drugs the way one takes drugs when you are going to be twenty. And so forth with these misunderstandings that Bertrand used to call mis-listenings. Bertrand whose name I put down here with fear and reproach. That should be our family motto. I am not attacking, I am writing you. The words are playing their own games of laughter, which are rhythms and resonances with me, all that was left to us children when we had to wait for you to sit down at the table in the evening (you were keen on this ritual, when the soup came, sit up straight) and, all together, all we could do was to be silent. I was thinking about that a while ago at the table, because of the bread pellets (once again, I'll explain, when I meet you, if I see you again, if I go all the way to the end of this letter, if I even send it) but also because the only Frenchman on the crew, René, from Pau, a pilot without equal, thrown out by his family, he too, had just hit the table with his fist. Just like you.

'(4) Setting the record straight. You wanted me to be brilliant, with a naval career. I am only guarding a cemetery in the service of the merchant marine. But the sea is the same for those who are sailors at heart. It is still the same for me as it was in my childhood dreams when I would tell myself about the streams at Moncrabeau, that they flow into the Baïse which flows into the Garonne which winds its way to the Gulf of Gascony. *They* were going around the world and not me. Even if I am drifting (double, triple images, guess, there isn't any real imagination, there is only listening, listening is enough, and it's wonderful), I have found my element and my continent. I am. I exist. You didn't create me. You have a second son, but you don't possess him. I haven't succeeded. But I have no accounting to make to anyone unless it's an accounting of life, to you. Why? Why did our great grandfather go to Paris, with a bad conscience against the dictates of fortune, as Bertrand used to say, the passive Parisian, as Bertrand would say? Setting the record straight. Why did you pursue Ruth with your affectionate hatred? As dancer, modern dancer, protestant, and what else? Even Mama didn't dare like her for fear of offending you. Offending is the word (is Bernadette still as afraid of you when she irons your shirts?). When Laura was born, you weren't pleased: you wanted a grandson. When Paul was born, you were too busy for his baptism. I am not made for writing, Papa, still less for writing to you. I claim only one thing. I am exemplary in that I have never submitted to the rules.

'(5) Yes, I love you. Love pours out. The secrets must come out. Setting the record straight. You wanted so much for us to conform and succeed that we are, scattered, all over the place, no longer anything but the success of deformity. Luc pulled through. But at what price? The last time I saw him he only talked to me about computers and programming. He had just calculated (on the night shift) the millionth decimal of pi, 3.1415926 . . . etc., a million numbers. What good is it? A single flash of humour, he wondered if he was going to find a publisher. According to him, a former Polytechnic student's record might lead to a corporate presidency. I hear him telling me "Between school friends, a little solidarity in success was the only subject that could hold our attention." Luc pulled through? Like me? Are you pleased? Luc hasn't seen his son in seven years. Add to that my eleven, soon twelve, fjord months and it makes eight. Anne-Marie seems satisfied with her second marriage. Her husband is assigned to Buenos Aires and Pierre, my nephew, my godson, no longer knows what name he bears. The importance of the name, you were so jealous when *I* was chosen as godfather and not you.

'(6) Yes, I love you. Come on, Papa, let us have it out. On her hospital bed, Mama seemed so serene, and suddenly, young, beautiful, a true little fiancée. Last year before leaving for

Oslo, I took a plane to Marignane, I rented a car and I visited Claire at her house, above Forcalquier. Even with the map in my hand I got lost. I expected to arrive for lunch, without warning, quite by chance, surprises have become so rare, and leave again late in the afternoon. I finally found the house. Three young people on the roadside pointed it out to me. They were Loïc, Yves and Géraldine. They didn't recognise me. They didn't even recognise me, Papa. The house is on the hilltop. All the doors were open. It was as hot inside, in the shade, as outside in the sun. I called out Claire, Claire! In a room, her bedroom that serves as her studio as well, she was sleeping on a mattress on the floor, stretched out on her back, her neck arched back, her mouth open, a mask over her eyes, earplugs in her ears, hands flat on the sheet at each side of her hips. Around her were white, virgin canvasses, neatly arranged tubes of paint, and a brand new palette.

'(7) She was naked. She hadn't simply taken off her sandals and thrown herself onto the mattress. I still don't know if it was just a stage setting (theatre!) but, on my knees beside her, I called out softly, very softly two or three times. I waited. Then I gave up. I left. I passed Loïc, Yves and Géraldine. In the rearview mirror I saw Yves looking at me. But too late. Marignane, Paris, Oslo, the little port of Dunn. And the fjord, my fjord. Setting the record straight: I want to know what is happening with Bertrand. There, Papa, that is what you did to us. I wonder why I'm writing you. Yes, I do know! Today you thought about us! There is no other explanation. Tear off a leaf that's still green and the tree trembles right down to its roots. And Bertrand, the truth? Our family is only a tree hung, suspended, ripped out and hung up. I will not send this letter. Affectionately. Your loving son. Sébastien.'

Sébastien folds the pages of the letter in two, then in four and slips the whole thing into an envelope, just in case, the temptation always present, to send this disorganised message, a forty-seven-year old child's anger. There is only one lie in this letter. It concerns Laura's engagement and Paul's drug use. Hypotheses. And that is only a paternal emphasis. Ruth writes Sébastien three times a year, sometimes four, and in English to show clearly she has returned home, once and for all, that she intends to give her children the religion of her

27

mother tongue, a revenge for another war, this contested marriage, 'Ecumenical and one of the first ones' Cécile used to say proudly, in a church, Saint Ferdinand's Church, 'according to the rules', and before a pastor. Ruth and Sébastien had made fun of this comedy at the time. They loved each other too much to suffer from it, to be swept away by it, conscious of the scandal each represented for the other, both seeking expatriation. They charged ahead. It was all just a joke, a momentum, a genuine encounter. Everything but a misalliance. Bertrand, on the flyleaf of the voluminous cookbook he had given them as a wedding present, had written 'For the better and the better. Love has no recipes. But cooking does!' But he had only signed with an exclamation point. He used to say that this was important. Ruth's letters henceforth, twenty years later on, are only inventories. Part of Sébastien's salary is paid directly by the British Petroleum Company into Ruth's account in Toronto for the children. The letters coincide with the quarterly payments. The last one is due. There will be an acknowledgement of receiving it that Ruth will adorn with commentaries to fill out at least two pages. Laura has a fiancé? Didn't Sébastien marry Ruth when she was Laura's age? Was not Paul caught with two marijuana joints during an identity check in the street? How many times in the early fifties did Luc, Sébastien and Claire at Moncrabeau drink until they could not find their way back and fall 'living drunk', they used to say, in a ditch or a haystack? Early in the morning Bertrand would always find them and bring them a thermos of bitter black coffee. He had his pockets full of sugar and would say to his elder siblings 'Will you take me along someday? Don't leave me alone!'

Luc married Anne-Marie a year before finishing at the Polytechnic. Claire, pregnant with Loïc, married Gérard, who was like her, a Beaux-Arts student. Gérard died in an automobile accident shortly after Géraldine's birth. Loïc was three, Yves two. Everything happens so fast. The Prouillans were in a hurry to be done with it. With what? And to leave. For where? Ruth was beautiful when Sébastien saw her for the first time at the Odéon intersection, with her knotted hair, in a summer dress like a great transparent shirt. She was coming out of rehearsal. She was on tour with the Paul Stewart

Company, Sébastien was supposed to see her again that evening on stage. A dance program, without music, with the only rhythms the foot-steps and the lighting. The hall whistled, booed, made jokes. But the company danced. Sébastien had a date with Ruth afterwards. These facts are not decisive nor even truly forgotten. In Ruth's obligatory letters there was sometimes a hesitation over a word or in some punctuation as if she were about to go onstage again. Every night is the first one if one can wait. Ruth is living now with Ron. Sébastien no longer telephones because Ron always answers first. The children are at college, skiing, in the Lake region or else they are out. Ron always answers in French, Sébastien speaks to him in English. Ruth is never there. He doesn't need to call anymore. On New Year's Eve Sébastien asked Alabama, the *Firebird*'s radioman, to send a message to Toronto. But the message did not get through. That night everybody was calling everybody else. 'Bad luck, next time, maybe next year!'

Sébastien recaps the pen, slips the letter he will never send his father into the copy of *Hadrian's Memoirs* in which Bertrand has written, another flyleaf, 'This book was stolen from Bertrand Prouillan. Please return it to him,' the same copy that Sébastien puts on his bedside table wherever he goes, as a souvenir, or as a discovery yet to be made, to be made in two words, the family's style. The essential part of his library is there. There is also a letter that Bertrand gave him the day he married Ruth and that he has never dared open and read. Just as Sébastien is leaving his cabin René was about to knock on the door. 'We're going to be late!' René and Sébastien use 'vous' together because they are both French. Because they do not want to tell each other their respective stories. Because they have to hold out for twelve months. Because Sébastien is skipper. But Sébastien without René is nothing. With him he flies, he flies away. He makes love to the fjord.

There are only three seats in the helicopter if one plans to bring back supplies, all kinds of package and the mail, on the return trip. Today it is the turn of Horst, the administrator, who must also bring medicines back. He sits behind, with René and Sébastien in front. The propellers' whistle, a vertical take off and the ballet begins, of waves, tides, wind, the sun, and this immense tongue of dark and green water plunging into the mountains and rock. Never seen twice in the same light, the same vision, the same act. The men are still, with the roaring of the machine, the view from above, the sea threading its way, the earth drawing aside. Around the *Firebird*, are the *Apollo VII*, the *Septentrion*, the *Newton*, the *Ambrasy*, the *Spirit II* and the *G.K. Hall*, emptied of contents, with high waterlines, seven abrupt black islands, the biggest oil tankers in the world, lying unused because no longer profitable. The pilot and two men of the original crew are dead, caught by a gust of wind, or a bad manoeuvre. Their helicopter struck the portside of the *G.K. Hall* headlong, like on a cliff. No search was made. It was winter, a dark day, night came so quickly, again, and there was a storm. The crew was replaced. Risks and death — everything has its price. Sébastien thinks about it every time, everyday, just as he thinks about Ruth when he sees the fjord, and the giddiness of their embraces when they were new, the obstinacy, rows and the conclusion. A separation.

The port of Dunn is on the other side of the mountain, to the south. Moncrabeau was also to the south of Paris. To get to Dunn you first fly over forests, steep, flanked, black and massive. The helicopter vibrates, shudders. Inside you feel that you are on a leaf, in the wind, for only an instant. Then, at its maximum height, a pass between two peaks and there is the descent, dizzying, slipping to the right, to the left, the machine spiraling in the air, the space, and the sky. Very quickly, far below, what is only a dot is being sketched clearly. Houses, churches, roads, cars, a jetty, a lighthouse, boats, human beings, the port of registry. Sébastien thinks about the letter, dashed out on paper, folded, sealed, abandoned. He has never sent his new address to Claire. It is not forgetfulness, or an oversight. He writes better by not writing. It is his way of thinking of others more often. With a letter before him, intimidated, he tells himself he could never have cheated when there was some point to it and he would never have known how. Before a letter, fascinated by the immensity of all that he has lived, the privileges, the expectations, the joys, the mockeries, a kind of dizziness seizes him making him measure the even greater space of his unappeased desires, of his unrealised dreams of encounters shattered by the

30

unexpected hazards of life, of the captivating family that makes you a captive, that becomes a totem, a tribal meal, a banquet of tenderness, and then the flight from it, a whole different life, only to be caught up again, bound hand and foot. The helicopter comes down near the customs hangar. René looks at Sébastien 'Well! Are you dreaming?'

Often, in November, December and January, after dinner, Sébastien would put on two pullovers, a parka, an oilskin overcoat, a pair of wool gloves and another of leather, a hoodshaped hat and, armed against the cold, without notifying the others, as the *Firebird*'s master, he would go up to the forecastle to see, to 'fore' see, to dream, to dream just a little. At 20° below zero the cold, in order to take hold, sets about it warmly. You do not believe it but it invades you, filters in and flows quickly into the veins, ice like fire, if you do not move. Sébastien would feel the night sparkling from every part, on each side and in the depths of the fjord, the snow night suspended on the fir summits, the night of white ink. Under the *Firebird*, a movement of the sea and the Gulf Stream stirred the waters, ceaselessly calling to a spring that would create itself under winter's threat, a summer that would come, fleetingly, scarcely perceptible, with the sun hanging up like St. Jean's Chinese lantern. And so forth, a foreign country, like an unalterable dream. And Sébastien, there, on that empty trashcan. On stormy days the sea would beat the walls and great dull noises would reverberate in the holds of the giants of the sea, rolling from the emptiness, echoes of a lost grandeur, a stupid century. Sébastien, alone, mocked himself then until he laughed, and burst out laughing. An icy laugh, puffs of cold in his mouth. A useless, lost, unheard laugh. Inevitably. The feeling made him burst out laughing. And then he would go back in, shaking with the cold, to drink with the others, and to talk of nothing, with them, of nothing in particular, and that did him some good. René, in his corner scraped out the pipe he never smoked but that hung from his jaw, to keep him calm and, he would say, to keep him from talking. Carlos and Juan, the two Venezuelans, bent over a game of chess, did not dare look at each other before the others, a discreet and persistent attitude that fooled no one, hiding their attachment to enjoy it more. Alabama would sing sometimes. He was off-key but it

31

was better than the recorded music. Stavros, the cook, seated, bent in two, would sleep with his forehead on the table like a schoolboy who had killed a bird. Oswyn, the Irishman, the two Portuguese and Horst would play poker. It was neither beautiful nor picturesque, not very ideal, the weight of time, that's all, and of life when it makes demands, and of happiness when it hides away in order to bounce back. Sébastien and his men were waiting for the end of their twelve month contract. Sébastien used to tell himself, 'It's the same prison wherever you are.'

Horst, René and Sébastien make a date to meet in an hour at the Lillehammer Bar, the port's only sailors' bar. At the Post Office Sébastien gets the mail sack and the packages. There is a package for René. With a Toulouse postmark dated July 2. That is all Sébastien will know of René. He has someone in Toulouse. And Toulouse is not far from Pau.

All that is false and all that is true. Everything that is not laid down has become suspect. Sébastien has a little time. The pavements astonish him, and the children playing ball, a little girl who looks at him, a woman at her window hanging up her clean washing. They too have lived through this same winter. A sudden whim, made without decision, and Sébastien goes into Dunn's only barbershop. The sole client. With a gesture he explains he does not want his beard anymore. An old man tilts him back in the chair. He closes his eyes, a pleasure. He will find his face again, and his image, clean, neat, in the mirror in a few minutes, the clipping of scissors, then lather and the razor shaving.

When he is raised up again, he hesitates, looks at himself. He does not recognise himself. And he recognises himself too well. More and more he resembles his father. The same nose, the Gascon beak, the same fold at the chin, and his eyes, neither blue nor black, drained of colour.

At the Lillehammer Bar Sébastien waits with the sack and the packages. Horst and René are upstairs. They are taking the opportunity to get one off. When René comes back down Sébastien turns his head, with courtesy, discretion. He drinks, puts his hands on the table, tries to distract himself. Unfailingly he meets René's look who tells him 'You know, all I did with the woman, was to look at her. Horst was waiting for

32

his turn behind the door, you understand?' then, with a smile, 'Shaved so close, you look like someone making his first communion' and again, 'This woman, I just looked at her, like you're looking at me now. The only difference is she's a woman and naked and I tell myself for a moment that she loves me, that she's waiting for me.' Sébastien does not answer. He drinks. René takes the beer glass in his hands 'Have you behaved so much better than me to keep to yourself like that?' René puts the beer glass down and orders another round. Elbows on the table he leans toward Sébastien and says in an undertone 'Nor have I, I've not lived better than you. I'm here just like you. We don't get the same salary, that's all.' The two men clink glasses. René raises his beer glass toward the ceiling. 'Obviously Horst with all the medicines he's got can dip his wick in any old come bag!' René wipes his lips, laughs heartily and looks at Sébastien. 'Does that shock you? But we're always somebody's whores.' Sébastien offers the package from Toulouse to René. René plays at being surprised, astonished. 'Some socks a few months late getting here. My mother doesn't see too well anymore for knitting.' He puts the package on the chair without opening it. 'We're talking too much. Let's drink!' He drinks. Sébastien strokes his beer glass with his fingertip. He rises suddenly, 'I'll meet you at the helicopter.'

An old post card bought at the Dunn General Stores and stamps at the post office. He sticks on the stamps. The card shows a forest, the sea and a mountain with a midnight sun. The colours are not very natural but the real thing, in reality, is still more beautiful and does not seem as natural as that, either. Sébastien writes first the names and address 'Laura and Paul Prouillan, 82 Amelia Street, Toronto, Canada M4X IE4' then the text: 'Don't forget me. Daddy.' This time Sébastien sends the message. The post card makes a little noise falling into the box. Too late. It is gone.

For the return Sébastien takes the back seat with the sacks, packages and supplies. René looks strangely at Horst. Jealousy? The take off. Some children wave. The little girl watches from afar. A pleasure boat enters the port. And very quickly, the ascent, the sky, as if they were going to rip it open, the pass, a membrane of rock. René makes two attempts, a wind blows from the north and they need more altitude. Sébastien closes his eyes. Like a leaf in the wind, and the letter to his father, the image of the leaf torn from the tree, the tree suspended. The next time hey go to Dunn will be the departure, for good. And life goes on.

3

'One lump or two?' Henri Prouillan looks at his sister. A ritual in the small sitting room at coffee time. Suzy smiles. 'It seems that these sweetening tablets also cause cancer, I don't know what kind of cancer. But you die of it anyway. So two tablets, three please!' Suzy is happy. Turning away, her brother holds the coffee cup out to her. She murmurs 'You'll never change. What good would it do? Lunch was delicious. A big success. Long live death by inches! Which of us will go first? We're still good for another twenty years! Tell me about your decision, I'll talk to you about mine.' A swallow of coffee, the cup held with the tips of the fingers. Henri approaches the French window of the small sitting room. It is no longer raining. An ambulance goes by without sounding its siren. He tells himself there is no one inside it, then out loud '. . . Returning from a delivery!' 'Returning from what?' Suzy asks.

What did they say to each other during lunch? Neither one knew anymore. Except for a remark, only, like a cue from Suzy, 'My poor Henri, we don't even know how to kill time anymore,' then, 'In the old days we could, but that was just youth. We were young, but old enough all the same. You're not listening to me.' Henri did not dare look at Bernadette. Bernadette, serving, was not looking at the dishes nor the plates not at the hands extended toward her, the wrists bent elegantly, covered with silver, ceremonial souvenirs, she was holding back the tears, the ones you cannot control, burning tears, all that for a dog. She had to serve in spite of everything and in the same way as always. Henri wondered who was terrorising the other, in this hypocritical everyday life, with steps muffled by the carpet and rugs, the servant's comings and goings. Each time she went back to the pantry, Bernadette took the opportunity to blow her nose, curiously secret about it, and without too much noise. In the corridor at the end of the meal while bringing in the iced cake from Berthier fils, bought on the way back from the clinic, Suzy's favourite cake, 'I'm not served like you are, dear Henri,' Bernadette had given the clock a good kick, a kick of rage. For the first time in this house, a rage. 'You might have warned me!' Bernadette always talks to Monsieur, but only in the corridors when Monsieur is not there, when Monsieur calls her or when Monsieur is waiting.

Suzy puts her empty cup on the tray. Henri has not drunk his coffee. He is standing near the French window, he does not move. He says, as if he were alone in a soliloquy 'I want to see them again . . .,' 'I want to get them together again . . ,' 'I want to ask them why!' Suzy, amused, waits for what follows. Henri stands still. With a move of his hand he pats his white hair, fine, rare, cut short. For a brief moment he holds his chin like an interrogation and, a final punctuation, with an unconscious gesture, he pinches his nose. Suzy bursts out laughing. 'You really haven't changed,' then, getting up, going to her brother, taking him by the arm and locking him against her, 'I frighten you because for me you are still little, fearful, hidden away. Who do you want to bring together? Your children? Why, then? Do you want to finish them off? To finish off your fatherly job? Say something, Henri, please, otherwise I'm going. It isn't raining anymore. I don't have anything to do? But then I'll have a reason to leave!' Suzy speaks very distinctly, a relic of the bad actress she was and of the great actress she would never be, enunciating 'We have nothing more to do? Then we have reasons for leaving! I have decided to sell Jean's theatre. It's that or revive *The Collision*, for the sixth time. We would celebrate the 3,500th performance. It seems there is still an audience for it. Especially when the Automobile Show is on.' Suzy lets go of her brother, takes a few steps, turns around. 'You aren't listening to me. I was supposed to sign the contract the day before yesterday. I waited for this lunch to talk to you about it. I don't want the decision without you. Especially as you're not involved in it.' Henri looks at his sister. 'Why do you always say my poor Henri to me, my little Henri? You can go to hell with your theatre, Suzy!'

Bernadette enters the little sitting room, takes the tray and goes out again. Suzy is looking for her bag, for her cigarettes.

Henri keeps watching her amiably. When she comes back from the dining room, he takes her by the arms. 'Your decision is made. You could never do without the noise of squeaking aisle seats. As you were saying a moment ago, there is always an audience. We are that audience. *The Collision*, that's theatre. It's well done. And it works. I would even say that each time I see the play, I find it more and more profound and more and more empty, more and more funny and more and more sad. I find a personal echo in it.' Suzy lights a cigarette. Henri tries to kiss her. She steps back. 'I finally know what you think of Jean's theatre.' A puff, a gesture, she smiles. 'I suspected as much but I wanted to hear you say it.' She goes into the living room, sits in Cécile's armchair to which in her final months they had to carry her, and there, she is silent. Suzy chose this armchair to be silent in. Bernadette brings an ashtray. The clock sounds three. Bernadette disappears. Suzy looks at her brother, 'Pantalon is gone?' Henri answers 'Yes. Since 11.00 this morning. And it cost me 250 francs.' Suzy puts her cigarette in the ashtray, crosses her hands under her chin, a sidelong look. 'You're not thinking about that, Henri?' 'Yes, I'm thinking about it.'

1928. Bernadette was twenty years old. An only daughter. Her mother had died in childbirth. Her father had hanged himself the year before on the lowest branch of the elm tree in front of their farm in Auzan, near Moncrabeau. Bernadette sees her father again, hanging, feet stretched, the tips of his feet almost to the ground. The man had calculated what he had to do well. That story Bernadette never tells, for it would not be listened to as she remembers it, as a deliverance, you might say a stroke of luck, a man's own choice, there, before his own home, before his farm. It was his elm. The rest of the story? A mother dead in childbirth, a father who hangs himself for grief twenty years later, a farm belonging to poor people, a gigantic elm, and Lucien, a day labourer, who comes for the grape harvests and disappears early in October, 1928. The day of Lucien's departure Bernadette was taken with vomiting. In Auzan the people at first pretended not to understand, but the women, as soon as Christmas was over, stood by Bernadette and the harvest child. Early in May, 1929, Bernadette brought into the world a little boy, on her farm and in her parent's bed. The women from the village, around her in the alcove, moved about as if in a church. Bernadette did not like those shadows. She slept, exhausted, worried and did not waken until late the next day. Night was falling. Waking up at nightfall, an omen, tormented her. The doctor was there. He gave her an injection and again she slept. The third day Aunt Augustine was seated beside the bed, clasping her hand tightly. 'Your little Colas is dead.' That story too Bernadette never tells for it would not be listened to as it was received, a deliverance for the near and distant relatives and for the people of the village, a deliverance, you might say, a similar stroke of luck. There was the curé for baptising the child, a man and a woman for godfather and godmother. Viewed from the bed, everything happened simply and without drama. No one had ever come to their home before. The father's sorrow had kept everybody away. Now it was crawling. They could scarcely move about. What an event. Two days later was the burial. The women got Bernadette up, dressed her in black and hoisted her into the same carriage as the little white coffin. The people followed on foot. Harvest sons must die in the spring. At the cemetery exit everyone filed by her. Standing, alone for Aunt Augustine had refused to stay near her, Bernadette had to clasp her hands, with all her strength. How strange all that was, a ritual. To defend herself against this comedy played out by those she would willingly have called guilty, Bernadette repeated smiling to everyone, 'But you know, I didn't know him,' 'You know, I didn't know him,' 'You know, I . . .' They thought she was crazy.

Now, Bernadette is waiting for Monsieur's sister to leave. But Suzy has begun to smoke. That's a bad sign. She is going to talk, talk more and they are going to quarrel while they laugh. At the end of the corridor, at the entrance to the pantry, there is a bench on which the children used to come to tie their shoes in the morning. Bernadette sits there. She tells herself that the pain she had not been able to feel when she lost Colas, she feels now because she would have liked to take out the dog one last time herself. Because it was she, and she alone, who took the dog out regularly. In front of 2, Place d'Antioche, she would like to see an elm tree. Early in July 1931, a car came and parked in front of the farm. A young man got out of it,

Henri, accompanied by a pregnant young woman, Cécile. They were coming on behalf of Augustine and the curé. Bernadette packed her bags for the evening and they came back to get her. So few things in her bags. They were taking her on trial. She would be given a definite answer at the end of the summer. And, out loud, on her bench, talking to herself, as at the cemetery exit, Bernadette repeats smiling, 'Then, is it yes or no?' They never told her. She stayed. She learned to read with Luc, to write with Sébastien, to be a mother with Claire, then she taught everything to Bertrand who used to tell her, 'You are the other teacher, the only one and the real one.' In 1950, on Monsieur's advice, Bernadette sold the farm to the mayor of the village. Of that invested money, nothing remains but the top of the elm tree, seen from afar when passing in the car. Bernadette would turn her head just the same. As she turns it today, listening for voices at the end of the corridor.

'At the Liberation you also held people on a leash, like Pantalon. You always claimed it was other people who did it. And Bertrand, how did you go about that? With what? By force?' Suzy refills her armagnac glass, lights another cigarette and in a calm voice quotes Jean: "I recognise a snob by the things he claims not to be snobbish about. I recognise a murderer by the way he doesn't appear to be one." 'Suzy, please!' 'No, Henri, let's talk. It's good for us. Are you afraid?' Suzy waits for her brother to take a seat in an armchair. Henri knows Suzy will not leave until he is seated and until she has spoken. In what she is saying, today, July ninth, twenty years to the day from Bertrand's return from Barcelona, in that relentless questioning voice, that neat hesitation that suddenly surprises you, there is a change of style, an impropriety. Suzy extends a glass of armagnac to him, 'Of the two of us, you are the only true actor. You can make fun of Jean's plays. But they made no victims. Thanks to them, a theatre hasn't been closed or won't be closed. My decision is made. Yours is too, I'm afraid.' Henri drinks a mouthful of armagnac and sits in an armchair, across from his sister, the glass clasped between the palms of his hands to warm the alcohol, a gesture learned from his father and grandfather, the summers at Moncrabeau, under the wisteria, well before the Great War. He used to listen to the people he would later be copying. Nothing has changed, in almost a century in this country, nothing outside of some troubled ideas, that extraordinary intellectuality of the dreamers of revolutions. The basic events are always the same. And the silences, the silent majority, protect the fortunes of gems, gold and stocks and always suppress the same misfortunes of the heart. Henri looks at his glass, smiles so faintly that Suzy does not dare speak. She says 'Sorry,' but so discreetly that Henri does not hear her. He is lost in his thoughts,wondering if they are the traits of one family or of every family, typical of a human race with no true identity which would be reproduced exactly like himself, heir to clothing merchants and business people from the Middle Ages which still endure. Often passing near the Hôtel de Ville, Henri looks at the equestrian statue of Etienne Marcel, a strange ageless name with no century, a statue no one notices and which, nevertheless, all alone, perhaps still governs in the reality of a society that only pretends to change. 'Henri?'

Henri looks at his sister. Suzy murmurs 'Anyway aren't you going to feel guilty? Think about your Air Liquide, your Royal Dutch, your Michelin, your De Beers, your Pinay income, your Engins Matra, your Elf-Aquitaine and your Française des Pétroles. You see, I know your portfolio by heart. Thanks for your tip on the Crouzet de Valence shares. A fine bargain for the long term. I made it. Thanks to you. But what is it, Crouzet, what do they make? Yes, I'm making fun of you, of me, of us. In this armchair, or in her life time, Cécile wouldn't say anything to you. I'm speaking in her place. We only know the art of speaking for others. It's our way of loving each other and especially of never seeing ourselves as we are. Today, Henri, I believe you capable of anything. I will leave here only when you have clearly told me your decision. Sometimes just speaking about these decisions is enough not to put them into execution. Speak.'

Bernadette says to herself. 'I'm never going out again. Before there was the dog, but now?' She undoes her chignon, grey, rebellious hair, pins taken out one by one, then she shakes her head like a young girl, a motion still fresh. In her life there had been no one other than Julien, not ever, is that possible? She smiles about it, her hairpins in her mouth, and redoes her chignon skilfully like Madame did when she fastened her summer hats to her blonde hair. Bertrand used to say 'Mama's under her parasol.' Claire called her 'Lady Butterfly'. Luc called out to his mother 'You're making a shadow around you.' Sébastien gave the edges of the broad brimmed hats, the ribbons and braid little slaps and Cécile, annoyed, would say, 'Stop, you're hurting me and you'll knock my hat off.' Bernadette remembers the barley water. That was well before the liqueurs and the marriages. Four beautiful children. The Prouillans. And she a second mother to them. Uncle Jean noted everything she, Bernadette, said. The result, in 1949, the day after the opening of *The Collision*, Monsieur and Madame announced to her before the children that she had 'an important role in the play,' that the review in the *Figaro* was 'good' and that they would take her to it. Then a lapse of memory. She had gone alone to see the play, to a matinée, at the end of the season. In an aisle folding seat. But between the comic servant on stage, who knew everything about everyone, who opened and banged all the doors, and there were a lot of doors in that sitting room, the only set in the play, between that servant and herself there was no relation in either voice or life. Bernadette had just discovered that for them she would always be a stranger whom they needed, a landmark, in servitude, for information or prey, as they chose, for all of them at the same time.

Henri is silent. He adorns his silence with that somewhat soulful smile, almost an irony, that Suzy knows so well in him. The smile of all his certainties, therefore of a terrible weakness. Suzy thinks 'terrible', thinks 'weakness' and remembers Jean's theory of adjectives and their use. 'They peg the great falsehoods onto the truth of words and make truth, like life, flee.' Jean also spoke of verbs and conjugations: 'The simple past is complicated, the imperfect carries its name well. There is only the present indicative that counts.' The idea of the absence of pure imagination, the only true imagination, of listening and looking, an idea that circulates in the family and often returns as a leit-motif, also comes from him. Jean Martin had qualities for which he had not been celebrated. His first plays, his 'pre-war' plays, (the critics, when out of ammunition, claimed it was '14–'18), were performed before empty houses and most of them were forgotten in drawers which Suzy dared not even look through. With *Hôtel de la Gare* and *Céline* in '47 and '48, *The Collision* in '49, the audiences changed their mind. Distraction was demanded. And for all that, without truly submitting to the dictation of predictable or fabricated successes, by a subtle lassitude mixed with a desire for an audience, therefore of love, Jean, for the love of Suzy and to gain the respect of the Prouillan family, especially of Henri, had written what he had to write so that he would be seen as a success, even as a conventional and (why not?) short term one. Without transition. He then became a success for which he was reproached in other ways. He told Henri, on the day that Claire and Gérard were married, 'Before, they didn't talk about me because things weren't working. Now they don't talk about me because things are going too well. In our country success is suspect.' Romain Leval had just killed himself. There were only two lines in the evening newspapers. Jean had added 'For Romain it was still worse. They attributed successes to him just so they could reproach him. Their law is murderous.'

Suzy crushed the first three cigarettes in the ashtray very cleanly, in the middle. The armagnac glass was empty. Henri, his hands flat on the arms of the chair, his head propped up as if on the verge of a siesta, looks slightly to the side of Suzy toward the square, his look lost and distant. Jean used to say of theatre critics 'They are dirty, in the proper sense of the term. They are made to do a pig's trade. Only in that do I respect them, unless they enjoy the dirt they do and the success they've given me, since *they* gave it to me.' Jean would have been happy to scorn his successes in a theatre that was no longer his, but had become the toy theatre of a bourgeoisie which can no longer recognise itself or wants to be able to say 'that isn't us' and laugh about it. In his plays Jean stopped at confessions, he had discovered the power of formulas. His theatre always stopped with the 'concernable'. The expression made him laugh. Him. He alone. For Suzy too. But Suzy did not want Jean's bitterness. And Jean no longer had the loving courage to explain to his wife that this bitterness was respectable and healthy. Before his accident in Barcelona, Bertrand, had met his uncle, alone. And Jean had been able, for once, to trust the young man who knew how to listen and to understand that a successful author could only be a failure at what he would nevermore be, he would be labelled, derided, enclosed in all sorts of scornful boxes. To please his brother-in-law, Henri would quote General de Gaulle's saying, 'Praise or blame, it still makes a name.' How right he was, this minister-of-what-ever-it-was whom power and a sense of the respected vacuum had led to the same kind of success, like a distraction from not taking the time to live, to listen, to look, to develop a real imagination. And all that, the lumber of an aging memory, the calm of a July afternoon (Bernadette, tired of waiting, began to do the dishes and put the silver service away), occupies Suzy's mind and confounds Henri. Jean used to say frequently of his brother-in-law 'Only silences surprise and convince him.'

Suzy would like to see Jean again, her Jean, to talk frankly with him, to start again at zero, or be able to question Bertrand and know what they said to each other, what they had shared, both as outsiders. Bertrand would have liked to love the one he loved. Jean was never loved for what he was. They both lost the power of speech. One, by living as he henceforth lived. The other, by dying without being able to become what he was. Suzy would like so much not to feel guilty for never helping either one or the other, nor all the others in her life. She played the first plays so poorly before empty houses, and later, as wife of the prominent playwright, no longer played the plays that were sold out 'three months in advance'. Today she finally feels inclined to talk about all that, but the other beings concerned are missing. There is only Henri left, and Jean used to say 'One can only have play acting relations with your brother. He's so afraid of himself he doesn't even sigh anymore.' Suzy smiles. Henri looks at her. Suzy murmurs, 'Do you remember Romain Leval?' Henri answers, 'No.' He pretends to search in his memory and frowns. There is something black and determined in his look that escapes both the question and the answer. Suzy adds, 'I have Bertrand's letters to Romain. You should read them someday. You would be proud of yourself.' Suzy sits in her armchair, remembers Cécile, rigid, in the same place, bald, having lost all her hair because of the treatments, refusing to wear a wig, knowing she was lost and smiling just the same. Suzy says more loudly, 'We won't stop brushing against one another, it's no doubt that which keeps us on our feet.' She feels as if she is quoting Jean. However the words are hers, born within her. She and Jean did everything to have a child. Henri looks at his sister. 'Excuse me?' Suzy gets up, goes to Henri, bends over, facing him, her hands on her brother's hands. 'You're playing, Riquet, with the idea of killing your children. And I *do* say you're playing.' Four o'clock sounds. 'I have also the manuscript of a play Jean wrote after Bertrand's trip to Barcelona. The play is entitled *Mortmain*. Jean asked me not to read it. I haven't read it but I have it! Do you want it?'

Suzy moves about in the living room, a space, a stage, a breath. 'The day of your sixteenth birthday I swore to you I'd never call you Riquet again. I was eight and had the illusion of you as an ideal brother. Now the game of ideals is revolved. The last of the revolutions. Is that the way you must be talked to? May I?' Suzy opens the three French windows, a rumbling is spreading from outside, a dull noise, continuous and warm. The storm is getting itself ready again, the smell of leaves and wet macadam. The stone of the buildings in the square is turning almost to pink. Paris in the summer has a disguised air about it. People begin to sound false. Suzy feels that she has never expressed herself so candidly, even if the words are pounding, against her will, even if some rhymes and cadences slip into what she is finally and heartily blurting out. Henri sits up in his armchair. He is listening. Bernadette comes to let them know that she is going to rest in her room and they can call her 'If she is needed.' She would have liked to point out that on a normal day, even at that hour, she would have walked the dog. She was expecting Suzy to say her traditional, 'It was delicious' about lunch, but Suzy had just now given her only a new, dangerous smile, never seen before. The French windows, usually closed, were open. Bernadette disappears. Suzy is happy to have expressed her satisfaction with the meal that way, with a smile, by avoiding an imperfect, 'It was,' and an adjective, 'delicious.' Suzy breathes, smiles, strokes the backs of the armchairs, the tops of the pedestal tables, the fireplace mantle and comes back to her brother. 'I have only one good memory of you, just one. It was going fly fishing.'

44

Suzy sits on the arm of Henri's chair, one of those armchairs in a vaguely English style, wide and comfortable, that Cécile had recovered every ten years in the same velvet 'almost exactly,' she would say, 'respecting the harmony.' In this living room, the wing-chairs, seats, lyre chairs and stools accent the decor, and are welcomed to give the impression of an ensemble, but everything makes one think that nobody has ever used them to sit in, even on visiting days or holidays. Jean used to say laughing 'Petits fours keep an entire inhumanity standing.' He would add 'Maliciousness as well, and worse still kindnesses. I listen, I watch. I am awfully like them, and like them I think I am better than the next, a neighbour, an innocent, a genius or an imbecile.' Henri looks at his sister, 'This fly fishing! Are you having some lapse of memory?' An elbow on the back of the chair, Suzy caresses her brother's forehead. 'No, Riquet, I have some presences, a presence, I have just thought of Jean!' She pinches her brother's cheek. 'And you didn't like Jean because he was Jewish and you aren't antisemitic, not at all, confess it!' She laughs.

Between the French windows, two chests of drawers making a pair, signed 'Gaillard,' but no one ever knew who this 'gallant' was. Bulbous, plump chests of drawers (from the period or in the style of the period? One of Sébastien's favourite parentheses) that Luc referred to as 'pot-bellied', that Claire called 'the twins', Bertrand would then say to Claire that this detail was 'revealing', and Claire would get angry in a nice way, affectionately, two identical chests of drawers. Suzy goes from one to the other, caressing the bronze on the left one, Mercury, and the bronze on the right one, Jupiter. 'I loved you at fly fishing. And in order to love you still, or if I have to worry about you, it's the same thing, I call up that memory, rather than another. Unless it were to be — how would you put it, do you at least know that, we've forgotten the use of the conditional, we've truly left Moncrabeau — the only forbidden thing we did together?' Suzy smiles as if she were making fun of herself. 'I suddenly feel fine. I'm putting it well, don't you think? It's nice. I'm breathing. You frighten me. Henri, look at me!' Silence. 'How could you say of Jean that he was the family's watchtower?' Silence. 'How could you lead Bertrand where you led him?

Wasn't that enough?' Henri looks at his sister, standing with the sunlight at his back, his arms crossed. Only then does he notice the colour of her dress, which is blue, and the absence of jewellery, bracelets, brooch, necklace, just her wedding and engagement rings. A small brilliant-cut ring, a gift from Jean who was keen to make it himself, for Jean was poor when Suzy married him. The Prouillans marry others, one does not marry them. They choose. A small, sparkling brilliant-cut ring. Henri undoes his shirt collar without untying his tie. It is beginning to rain again. A blast of the horn followed by the squeal of brakes. Suzy has not budged. She crosses her arms, lowers her head a little as if she were going to play with the patterns in the rug with her toes, as in the old days when the grown-ups' gatherings bored her. She was dreaming of her room. Suzy says in a low voice 'You used to come to get me on the sly, the days when Papa and Mama went to the solicitor's in Lectoure, or to the sub-prefect's in Condom. Quick, quick, you would tell me! I was never fast enough following you. I wasn't even allowed to bring one of my dolls I didn't like, they got back at me, they wouldn't offer me a thing, a sweater or a piece of chocolate. If I were barefoot, I wasn't given time to put on my sandals. "Let your hair down," And I let it down. At the side of the pond, there was the pontoon float, the flat bottomed barge and the walnutshell boat. Often Mama would say to visiting friends that it was just a decoration invented by our grandfather and that it was "idiotic going round and round on that stretch of water." But every year at Easter the caretakers would set to work stripping the paint, sanding down and re-varnishing our two little boats. By the first days in July they were there, ready for us, for forbidden expeditions. To tell you everything, Henri, since I feel like it, here and now, like telling you everything, another illusion, I sometimes thought Papa and Mama used to go to Lectoure, Castelnau, Larressingle or Condom to leave the possibility of drowning ourselves. When they came back, Mama had a curious way of asking us "Did you go out on the pond again?" Hardly a worry, almost disappointed. I'm not inventing. The child inside me still invents. I didn't used to make any difference between "*l'amour*" and "*la mort*". I still don't make that difference. You're smiling. I like you when you smile. I tell

46

myself you're sharing a little. Even if it isn't quite true. And that gives me strength. Strength to continue.'

Suzy takes her seat again in Cécile's armchair. She is again opposite her brother. Elbows on the armrests, fingers crossed under her chin, she continues, enunciating, in the present tense 'You used to brandish the oars like weapons. You left the short rod on the edge of the pier. You preferred the walnut-shell because "It's more difficult and the fish will be less afraid." You slip into the little boat. You secure the oarlocks and oars and carefully, as a precaution, you offer your hand, that's my version, how I remember it. You loved that walnut-shell in teak, a ridiculous, dear little boat which scarcely held us, with me rowing, you fishing, my knees locked against your open knees, face to face, guilty of disobeying you, because at the least move by one not balanced by a counter move of the other, we would have found ourselves in the water. Well, we never capsized. So we knew, once, how to love one another to the point of measuring perfectly the other's movements, even one's intentions. I loved you. You pretended not to notice. You fished with the tip end of the rod, hook and line, no bait, just the sparkling of the hook. That was casting. And here, now, if I approached you again, if I fitted my knees locked against your open ones, you would still pretend. You're not smiling anymore, Riquet, why?'

On the wall behind Henri is a clock with gleaming bronzes. The noise of rain outside. The clock has been stopped a long time ago, at noon or at midnight, the large hand covering the small one, a curious vertical. And, for Suzy, 'a long time' begins with the first memory. Henri leans forward, elbows on his thighs and places his hands on his sister's knees. 'Continue. I know what you're coming to.' Suzy smiles. 'The fact you're telling me that doesn't discourage me. You talk as you did in August of '39 when your friend Coulondre, your beloved ambassador, you would say, used to send those letters to you and his niece Cécile from Berlin, those alarming letters where the names of Hitler, Wilhelmstrasse and Danzig were coming back like the tolling of the knell. Those letters you used to read calmly out loud at Moncrabeau. You knew what you all were driving at. But you did nothing.' 'Don't start again.' 'That last war loaded you with honours from which

47

you are still living. What became of Serrac who used to bring you the messages from Coulondre? Didn't I see his name condemned on a notice at the 17th arrondissement town hall at the Liberation? A notice which you signed?' Henri rose. 'Suppose we separate now, Suzy, on a bad note as usual?' Henri undid the knot and removed his tie, 'You should be returning home. Houses are robbed in the summer, especially in the afternoon. You have phone calls to make for the theatre. Since you're going to keep it. Thanks to me, yes or no? Serrac died but I whitewashed Jean. The selection was not an accident.'

Silence. Suzy murmurs 'I'm speaking to you about today, Henri, you know it. You needed me to go fishing. You needed me to maintain our walnut-shell noiselessly with short strokes of the oar as near as possible to the edge. There, under the branches of the leaning trees, their trunks in the pond, you made the short rod snap. You whipped the air. The line mustn't get caught in the branches. You were an expert and as soon as the hook was in the water you started briskly again. Once in twenty or thirty times you would catch a roachfish or a bleak. Hypnotised, they leapt on the baitless hook for the little flash of metal. And you would throw them in the bottom of the hull, on to my feet, it was disgusting, wriggling, but I wasn't supposed to speak or protest. We would have capsized. Today I am speaking. I remembered our fly fishing during the meal by your looks and Bernadette's silences. Everything is reeling again here. You want to go fishing once more, "One last time" as you say so well when you speak in that assumed manner to hide a doubt that is obvious to me. Or blatant. Choose.' Suzy rises. 'Only this time I'm not rowing.' She takes her bag, gathers up her cigarettes 'You're not doing anything tonight? Neither am I! Then I expect you at my place at eight. That's an order.' She kisses her brother on both cheeks, 'If not, everything will capsize and I don't want that.' She heads toward the entry, her coat, her umbrella. She laughs. 'Moncrabeau is only a big farm with land around it and roots underneath. The roots hurt.' She looks at the hanging leash and collar. Then she turns to her brother. 'Think carefully between now and this evening. We'll celebrate Bertrand's birthday. We have so many things to say to each other. Here's

48

to fly fishing!' She closes the door behind her. In Claire's room, Bernadette, in Claire's bed, has fallen asleep. In her dream she sees empty pavements. In the middle of Paris, an elm tree.

4

Claire likes the middle of the afternoon. Everyday at about a quarter to four she leaves the studio that serves as a bedroom, goes out directly by the backdoor of this former barn attached to the house she made over for herself, and for herself alone, this is her place, on the level stretch of land overhanging the valley, bonechilling in winter, facing the spring rains, breathing in the smells of autumn or still dazzled by summer, the sun, that sword that seems to plunge down there, into limestone causse or mountain, on arid land, bare, trampled on by centuries of religious wars, where she watches for the mailman's yellow 2 CV. She knows the mail's delivery route by heart. The little car appears, a few kilometers as the crow flies, below in the valley, at the crossing of the national highways leading to Digne and Forcalquier. The 2CV stops almost everywhere, depending on the day, at Gardioles, Cortasses, Vignasses, then at the Sandrini's, hamlets or farms. The little yellow dot disappears behind a wall, a knoll, a clump of green oaks, in a hollow or along the Calavon, a dry river which, it is said, has dug itself a deep bed, a secret underground river. As if Claire were still expecting a letter from Gérard, stupidly dead at the wheel of his car, on a straight stretch, near Estampes, coming back from visiting the building site. That was in '62. Sixty-two. In numbers and in letters. Like on a cheque that no one will dare cash, a cheque signed, initialled, finished, done with. The insurance paid for the house. It is still paying the basic living expenses and a little for the studies of Loïc, Yves and Géraldine who has just, this year, left Sauveterre to join her brothers at college at Aix-en-Provence. Gérard. A stupid death does exist. Head-on, at dusk, with someone passing another car in the Paris-Provence direction, not respecting the white no-passing line, who is also dead. One day Claire met the other widow. She felt guilty, why? The other mother not knowing what to say, smiling, coming out of the trial, had stressed the fact that her husband 'fortunately had life insurance, if not . . .' The woman's smile was strangely unassuming. Two men. Head on. In '62. Near Estampes. A straight line and a white line. The night before the accident Gérard and Claire had quarrelled, the way people quarrel so they can love one another more, a quest and a search. Claire would have liked to have been able to say at least another word to Gérard. Perhaps it is a little because of that that she waits for the mail. That she still waits for the mail. That she waits for it more and more.

In the case of misfortune like this, one tells oneself in the beginning, and especially as one hears it on all sides, that nothing is lost. Words like fate, destiny, verbs like overcome, control, begin again, or those ready-made expressions, make a new life, erase but not forget, get back on the track. Worse still if one reacts without showing too much pain by clinging to life and one's children, with justifiable joy and the necessary care and smile, hearing, as Claire did 'It's incredible how courageous you are' or 'I don't know if I would have had your guts.' Courage and guts are not in Claire's nature. They are the performances others make you play in order not to do you any of those practical favours, of staying in contact, the strictly friendly and sensual, simple things, the surges of affection, or just being present, by which one could better face up to things. Claire often thinks 'one' as if this story were not uniquely her own, a broken, fractured life that must go on. And this idea alone, vague and nameless, gave her the strength for the smiles and gestures of everyday life, gestures demanded and expected by Loïc, Yves and little Géraldine. They are blond, all three, like their father. The true photo is there. That blondness like wheat that had surprised Claire for the first time in the Rue des Beaux-Arts. She was coming out of a gallery. He was going in. And each hesitating to let the other pass, in the momentum, had bumped the other. They were alike in their ability to break down all kinds of barriers and they had married very quickly, to escape more quickly still, he, his family in Valence, she, that Place d'Antioche which was being deserted by all. Luc and Anne-Marie, Sébastien and Ruth, and Bertrand who no longer came home at night, passed by during the day only to pick up clean underwear and leave dirty, sometimes torn, clothes which used to worry Bernadette. Bernadette would hide them from Madame. And for Claire especially, Sébastien and Ruth's marriage. Claire would have so liked to dress in black that day and wear mourning for her sailor brother. Claire admired Ruth. So it was she, the latter, who would always be there, where she, Claire, should have been, to please her brother, to marry him and leave hidden, stowed away, in a ship's cabin, an absurd, little girl's dream. Ruth had chosen Claire as a witness at Saint Ferdinand Church. Claire had worn the same pink dress she had worn for Luc's marriage. A little lower cut by the careful attention of Bernadette, that's all. Black, in fact, is worn inside oneself. For some it is a vivid colour.

For some time now Claire has forgotten to count the days. At the Place d'Antioche there were calendars everywhere. One-day-at-a-time calendars in every bedroom. And even on Henri's desk, near the parents' bedroom, that room wedged between the little sitting room and the boudoir used for dressing. Curious façade. Henri and Cécile's bedroom, the boudoir, the office, the small sitting room, the large living room, and the dining room, in a quarter circle, an unrestricted view of the square. And on the courtyard side, the three children's bedrooms, that angular corridor, a maze leading from the other side of the building to the pantry, the kitchen and the service stairway by which, later on, Bertrand used to escape. During the period of the marriages and the family going, the daily calendars were no longer kept up to date and, happy with all these disorders of the heart, Bernadette no longer even looked at them to tear off the useless pages when doing up the rooms. Sometimes Cécile would do it in Bernadette's place, until the day she withdrew from everywhere, the day of Bertrand's return from Barcelona. And, there on the plateau, like a warm spangled wind coming from the south, naked in that long white shirt buttoned twice at the bottom, Claire counts and recounts the days. The 2CV stopped at the Schulterbrancks', they will arrive. Claire counts: it is July 9th. The children will arrive tonight, late. They have passed their exams. The boys are studying law, and Géraldine is taking a degree in modern literature. They are coming up 'for the holidays'. Géraldine on the phone told her mother 'Loïc is bringing his girlfriend. Yves and I are not getting on. But as he's the one driving!' The 2CV is approaching the Sauveterre junction, it is shifting gears, always the same shifting, at the same place, at the same time, the same emotion: is he going to turn in? The 2CV pursues its route. There is no mail.

The mailman's name is Michel. He went to school with the children. He has the same accent. Like the oldest ones. But Géraldine speaks like her mother. One puts down roots as one can, or one makes do with what one has. That's the way Claire formulates it for herself. Shortly after Gérard's death, considering that staying in Paris was only a distressing flight, a flight in circles around a stupid death, she had chosen Sauveterre, for its modest price, the insurance premium, and especially for the countryside, as if in this place, at the edge of the Alpes-de-Haute-Provence, the sky was more immense than elsewhere and the horizon almost totally round. From the first visit, she felt herself conquered there, not by the region of gravel, terraced fields and hundred year old oaks, but by the feeling from the top, so very isolated from those people who were isolating her by treating her as if she were courageous and admirable. It was here. It is here. And it is called Sauveterre. Today the mailman did not stop. And then? Claire goes inside. She is going to write.

Alone in the house, barefoot, Claire undoes the buttons at the bottom of her shirt. She likes feeling like that, both naked in front and dressed. If her children were to keep an image of her, it would be that. Not nudity on principle, the ecological sloppiness, an antisocial attitude in the early seventies' style, but simply a state of body, like a state of mind for an immense sky in that place. Forcalquier, a name that cracks in the wind. Claire does not feel she has aged just as, sometimes, refuged in her studio to paint those still lifes so delicately outlined that one would think the canvases were still untouched, that Loïc calls 'Mama's moving life', she tells herself that neither does she have the impression of ever being truly young. Perhaps because in her family youth was considered a danger and all precepts and habits held growing up as their objectives. They had to grow up, to do everything like the grown-ups, as if they,

54

father and mother, uncle and aunt, had acquired a mastery over everyone and everything. It is easy to revolt and hurl anathemas of hate that have their origins in that same comfort and conformity as those they hate. That pleases the mobs who think of themselves as cultivated because they recognise in these violences, these condemnations, a nature identical to their own hypocritical silence. Claire and her brothers in the secret of their complicity, all four, because they were four, had chosen the only true method: the direct, daily one of exactly measuring their attachment to their parents, their dependency on the justly devalued nature of the principles the parents wanted inculcated in them, and on the other hand, profoundly, to dream about fleeing; the real detachment is scarcely possible except to the person who knows he or she is attached, how, by what means, even if never knowing why. During the early hours of the afternoon Claire tried to chase the image of her father, Henri, from her mind. He had come back suddenly in the morning, in memory of the day, like an unexpected visit, imposing himself. Claire had just re-membered the Barcelona episode. Already twenty years. Twenty years abruptly. A whole page of unavowed history. Claire had had her main meal, a glass of water, raw tomatoes, a piece of cheese and some fruit, without really being hungry because *he* was there and this father could come back and impose himself only for the denouement of a drama that no one wished nor wishes. Uncle Jean used to say 'You have to leave the final act to my plays. Only they have a beginning and an end. What we live through together doesn't really have a beginning and will never know its end. Especially if the idea makers, the sellers of new ideologies talk about them the way they do talk. Some theorize. The others thesaurize. The subtle game of making the other point of view heavier in order to flatter yourself. These are monuments and cities that can't be torn down any more.' Suzy would tell Jean, 'Stop it, the children can't understand you.' Cécile would ask 'Who will have more cake?' Henri would add, serving himself a slice, 'to please Bernadette and to celebrate your *bon mot*, Jean. You ought to write it down.' And Jean, pushing his chair back, with an elbow on the table, catching Bernadette's eye, would say softly 'It's already been done, Henri. The real truths are no

55

longer for my plays. The children have understood.' Claire reddened. Sébastien took her hand under the table. Luc laughed.

Here, now, Claire reddens at remembering the words, a personal album, whole speeches by Uncle Jean, by Cécile, by Suzy. Henri's greediness too when he wanted, and knew how to, interrupt the uncle's dangerous discourses during the dessert. The moment of anticipation. Awaited even more for Jean's cutting remarks than for the cake from Berthier fils, or Bernadette's home-made chocolate one, which Lord knows was good. Bertrand used to say 'Devil knows it's good!' Sometimes, during a silence at a meal at home with her children, Claire observes Géraldine who is watching Loïc who is watching Yves. And she tells herself that she in turn has been excluded, which is the worst kind of violence. She also tells herself calmly that Loïc talks like Luc, Sébastien or Bertrand. He says 'Moving life' for 'still life', which is the most often repeated example, when German or American dealers come to Sauveterre to buy his mother's pictures. Nothing really changes. And nothing changes even more obviously if there is a will to change. It is by using silences and odd looks that we can best modify a condition of rank, or caste or spirit. The spirit of an entire immobile society. Immobile and touching. And what is touched revolts against it. So the fear of modification inspires a charge of sentimentality in the critic. Claire tells herself that it doesn't take any time at all, that it escapes human time. The roots are too deep. On the bare earth around Sauveterre nothing really grows but those few oak trees, tawny in winter, sovereign in summer, which have a whole eternity before them. And she is nothing, only a mother who has come here, who has lived days and days here, driving the children to school, picking them up in the afternoon, preparing meals, putting things away, cleaning, waiting, marvelling with them when necessary, giving them this little as if it were riches, never speaking of Gérard and not even thinking about the problem of replacing this man, this husband, because he is there all the time, multiplied in the little blond heads, the mouths to feed, their nakedness observed by the mother at shower time. Watching Loïc and Yves grow, arms, hips, thighs, feet, sex organs, cheeks, and teeth, Claire has lived her love inside out. She was seeing Gérard as he was before, before and long before their encounter in the Rue des Beaux-Arts. She saw two of him in their sons, not truly one nor truly the other, sculpting the body herself from a first embrace, the glance of the first meeting, one, Claire, not making way for the other, Gérard, and vice versa. Then, often, moved, Claire would tell herself that these visions in time, in development, the differences in these beings, her children, were enough. That in them was even the true medium for a drama which would never be played as a drama, a source of happiness. 'What's good and beautiful about happiness is the shock,' Bertrand would say. Tomorrow the children will be here. And Loïc's girlfriend. Claire will button her shirts from top to bottom. Time has passed. It creates a sense of proprieties, immodest and sensual. And if the older ones sometimes, early in the morning, burst naked into the studio to bring a bowl of tea, Claire closes her eyes laughing. Delighted. She has seen him again. The unique one.

No letters in the mail. July 9th. An afternoon at Sauveterre. During these last years, at one time, one brief while, Claire participated in the meetings of feminist groups in the area. They liked her for her way of always speaking straight from the heart. She realised very quickly that the militant ones who were not mothers, but were beaten down by life, frustrated and vengeful in spirit, attached to men who were divided from them, were lesbians. Claire felt solidarity with neither one group nor the other. These meetings were dominated by the women she did not like meeting. Their speeches, armed, combative, were offensive only in the sense of armour and combat. How many times, deep inside, gripped with doubt, questioning herself on the urgency of this militantism, did she tell herself 'There is solidarity only in anonymity.' She was no longer quoting anyone. A gift for speech was born in her. It was fine. And good. She would go to meetings until the day when, thrust onto the speaker's platform, under spotlights, before a full hall, she had to talk about her 'identity as a woman'. Seated at first, with the obscene microphone in front of her mouth, hearing an echoing voice that she did not recognise, she explained, 'I have nothing prepared. Anything prepared is dead. When I paint a picture, I don't make a sketch,' then, after a hesitation, with her voice trembling, 'It isn't necessarily the one on the platform who holds the power. It isn't the one with the loudspeaker who brings the gospel truth. I am not a truth bearer. I have nothing prepared but an idea, such a small idea, more of an invitation. We are here, gathered to speak of our identity as women. And my identity as a woman is the right to emotion.' Silence. Claire stands up, the chair had fallen over. Without even bothering to pick it up, impatient, she had moved in front of the table and in her own voice, standing, with arms crossed, her heart beating, like the day when Uncle Jean had taken her for the first time onto the stage at the Théâtre des Champs, when the house was empty, and here the house is full, no difference, but vertigo, she had repeated, 'My identity as a woman is the right to emotion,' and then, without hesitating, with that strength inspired by the fear of lacking strength, she had added 'Now let's talk. Let's talk about this right.' And it was a failure. Women got up in the hall, a roving microphone circulated, a confused ballet. They all began attacking Claire, and Claire did not understand why.

One of the three, Yves, Géraldine or Loïc, was always telling Claire, 'It's great, Mama, because you don't hide anything from us.' However, Claire hides everything from them, everything deep inside herself. No mask. Claire does not disguise the truth, but contains it, curbs it for fear of directing or disturbing Gérard's children and especially of deciding for them, an illusion perhaps but it is worth the trouble of trying. Only Géraldine wonders why her mother loves her less than her brothers, but she wonders about it less and less because more and more she is growing up and she resembles her so much.

Claire puts the plate, silverware and glass from lunch in the sink. The kitchen serves as the family room. Claire bends over and drinks from the faucet. Her face, spattered, drips a little. A luxury in this house, running water connected with the Durance-Ventoux water system. Water is no longer a rarity. Claire goes back to the studio. Today she sees her father, suddenly, her father is here, before her, he hides, he hunts her down. Cécile's memory as well, she who used to come to spend 'only a few days to see the children at least,' every year the last week in June, 'and for the shrubbery in bloom.' They are all here, he and she, father and mother, the parents and all those women as well, in that banqueting hall near Rians, the hubbub. Claire recalls it. She still cannot formulate the why of that evening's misunderstanding. She had just spoken from the heart. That statement did not conform to the expectations of an audience who wanted to hear only the conventional, anticipated, predictable speech with no surprises, a shotgun volley of quickly forged platitudes for a cause that has henceforth been entirely given over to the sole idea of being a cause. The right to emotion was apparently too meager compared with the anticipated hammering of demands. And from general issues, which Claire raised in the hope of a lively debate, she a widow with three children, who had been given the responsibility of conducting it, she found that the women in the audience, who were all acquaintances, whom she often took for friends, were doing everything they could to tip it to the particular. Feeling strong in the solidarity, in the power from the cluster, in the security of the swarm, they began to ask those intimate questions that are usually suppressed at the more restrained meetings. The insidious questions burst out. 'Your father was minister of what?' or 'How much do you pay your cleaning woman?' Applause. Without losing her calm, with that certainty of honest doubt, and a living memory of a brother, Claire pointed out the absurdity of this attack. She says, 'I was almost late because I had to do the dishes first,' new applause, then 'So isn't there anything except drama and flashy gestures to make us applaud tonight? And if some of you are smiling because I say to get "us" to applaud, it's because I believe "we" must stop debating by playing with words, and simulating aggressions, by only dealing with the flashiest ideas, and by blaming the bourgeoisie for everything. There is no more bourgeoisie in the sense you mean it and no more proletariat in the original sense but simply seventy million average people. Don't you understand? I don't want to be right all the time. The heart's reason isn't a matter of will. It doesn't play. It gives itself. That's where my identity is. Let's talk please. Let's talk of emotion, about my and our condition.' Claire realised only then that she was speaking in public. How had she come to be there, up on the platform? Then she began to understand a little, just enough to regain control of herself and face the fact that she had committed the sacrilegious act of not playing their game of conventionality, of foreseen expectation, and of comfort, by refusing the microphone, by speaking in her own voice, by not giving the ready-made speech, by wakening in these women friends that 'spirit of reserve' or 'spirit of hesitation' of which her father had been so much the denouncer as well as the able agitator. Only insults followed, unfailingly related to the bits of gossip that had circulated about her, without her ever having suspected them. 'Other than being a brilliant success, what did your uncle Martin do with that phallocratic Boulevard trash? Can you talk about him?' or again 'Your pictures get big prices in other countries. When you have a numbered Swiss bank account, you can let yourself talk about emotion, it doesn't cost you anything!' False, all that was false. 'You have how many acres on your farm? Will you tell us? Even in '62 that was worth a lot of money.' And so on. From time to time Claire would look at her closest friends, Martine and Léa. All they did was smile and encourage her. Then, Claire, taking a moment of silence, measured the feeling of the hall and realising that she had the ear of each one, cried out 'Bourgeois I am. And I admit it. The battle begins there. First admission. I didn't choose to be born where I was born. I'm not reproaching that. I see no reason to fight against it. That's the issue.' Silence, suddenly they were listening to her. She continued in a voice a little less sharp, 'Don't be envious, my pictures sell badly. It isn't because they are sold abroad that they sell well. Ask the art dealers. They're the rich ones, not me. And the French dealers have to sell abroad because they maintain that nothing good can be created in France. We have lost confidence in ourselves. I bought Sauveterre with the money from my husband's death. I didn't replace Gérard and I still need him. Don't make me say, as you're already thinking, that my widow's condition is a privilege. There are too many things I miss. They are irreplaceable. I don't want nor can I simulate them with anyone else. I look at my children, especially my sons and that's enough. I won't tell you any of the things you want me to say, none of that stuff

60

they're making us say because it's 'the Woman's Year'. Making us talk is the fascism that invades our life everyday. We're not gagged anymore but made to talk. I know you're listening to me. We're really speaking about censorship, all the time. Censorship isn't about withdrawing speech anymore but forcing us to say what you want to hear, preferably to say the conventional thing. Why are we so reluctant to discuss that? An insult is not an argument. Why pursue me with pointless questions? Isn't my problem of identity in line with the set speeches? I don't want to go on repeating what we've been repeating for months and months with no other purpose than to pander to a misfortune that I reject profoundly in myself. You can spit on yourselves. Not on me. I am here, in the process of living one more emotion. It isn't a failure. It's an experience. I have never heard my own voice. I'm hearing it now. Only real politics have that tone I hear, that resonance, which you hardly ever hear in a set speech and through the loudspeaker. No. I'm telling you No. I like you. And I'm going to quit. You don't combat one intolerance by using an intolerance of the same kind. You don't break a dominant power by a domineering power. I have chosen to make myself very small, one of the little ordinary people, in fact I am one inevitably because I learned to read, to watch and live the way in which I learned, where I learned to be a little person. And very small and little, I have chosen to keep myself at the level of language and the words with meaning, of ordinary behaviour and everyday life. There lies my emotion, my identity, my effort. There I fight. Everyday for little nothings, of which I have the audacity to say they're essential. *That's* my emotion. My feminine condition. The condition that we constantly see as a tragedy and complain of in radical slogans, but in fact we love it. We've grown up with it. Gérard, I love him because he is within me and he has been multiplied. Nothing counts but this multiplication. Yes, I loved my kids' caca in their diapers. I loved wiping their bottoms, sitting up with them, worrying. I loved and I love being my children's maid. And my children pay me back because they are here, when they are here, because they speak to me, when they speak to me, because they are he and he is my man. Only one man. I am still below him, him, Gérard. And when I say "me",

I don't feel cut in two, "me" dash "e", as you made me say it, the first time I was with you. The idea was to seduce me. Only to seduce me. A fashion. A rite of passage. In fact, I am quite whole in my "me". When I bleed, I'm not ashamed, I'm living, I don't feel threatened, wounded, antagonised. No. It's the rhythm of my life. And when I don't bleed anymore, my children will begin living a life that they'll believe is different. And so forth. I say "I". I say "I, I". I had a brother who was named Bertrand and who was homosexual. When I would say "I, I this" or "I, I that" to him, he would stop me, pinch my arm and explain "I is enough, don't be afraid." There. Thanks, Martine, thanks Léa, thank you, everybody. I'm leaving you the platform and the microphone. This wasn't a political speech. It wasn't a plea. It wasn't to make Margot cry. It was me. For the first time. In public.'

Instinctively stroking her arm where Bertrand used to pinch her in the old days, Claire descended the platform, her mouth dry, suddenly beginning to tremble, gathered up her cloth bag, headed toward the exit, quickly, before the tears came, and heard a voice, 'Are you happy now? Have you had your say?' then another voice 'Leave her alone. She's got the right to speak too,' then there was a rumbling in the hall like a roar, and at the door, just at that instant, a gust, like a smell, a stagnant smell of angry women. What kind of anger? And why? Abruptly Claire did not care nor need to cry. She felt calm. Léa followed her out saying, 'You aren't going home in that state. Stay at my place tonight. The children are big enough.' Claire had kissed Léa, as if for nothing. Another of Bertrand's expressions, 'As if for nothing'. Bertrand, then, would head toward the kitchen and pantry to go out by the service entry, and meet Romain Leval, his Romain. Or another. Parallel stories. Identical stories. A single root, a human one.

No mail today, July ninth. Claire hears Michel's 2CV returning from its delivery. Maybe a letter tomorrow, but from whom? The time when Claire would subscribe to magazines to get at least something, regularly, is in the past. Past since the evening at Rians. Claire remembers the sudden attention of the audience when she had said 'man' and when she had said 'caca'. That's all. There were visits, Martine, Léa.

'You should come back.' Armed with a smile signifying neither defence nor ulterior motives, Claire was content to give them something to drink, to put on some music, never to say No, never to say Yes, to leave them to their speech, and perhaps in this way, in the long run, to make them worry about her more. Martine, Léa and the others did not come back anymore. Claire has been living at Sauveterre for seventeen years. She has not gone to Paris for five years. Since Rians. Since the 'Year of the Woman'. Paris is a habit that is quickly lost once one accepts that those who call it aggressive are in fact only people who feel attacked, and if one finally recognises that liberty is loving what one loves, nothing more, nothing less. Paris is a habit that is quickly lost, if one feels one will never lose it. It is enough to place the pedestal within oneself, so as to not look at it anymore, a monument to the dead. It is enough to understand that isolation is not the risk of solitude, but solitude the crowning of all isolation. That's enough for one day. Under the nozzle of the shower, Claire bursts out laughing. Coming back from Rians, she does not like driving at night, the white centre line sometimes would guide her. She was to have this feeling in the present and even in the future. Claire, all wet, leaves tracks behind her on the studio tiles. Tracks that dry and are erased almost instantaneously. With her short hair, brown body, she hears something like a voice, Sébastien calling her. But that day, no longer expecting anyone, with the mask over her eyes, the plugs in her ears because Loïc and Yves had been listening to pop music and she had not dared to forbid them, Claire had thought she was dreaming. That evening at dinner, Yves had said, 'I believe it was Uncle Sébastien. How old he looked.'

Claire turns her pictures to the wall, one by one, cautiously. She does not want to see them so that she can write. She cannot feel watched by them. A table near the window, the unimpeded view of the Lubéron, a slightly hard chair, the pen given to her by Bertrand, his last gift, before Barcelona. Claire gets settled. Her father is there. She must speak to him. She is going to write. She writes. It can't be pained. It is written. One does not decide to write. One writes. To cry or to laugh.

Title *The Appointment in Barcelona*. Claire crosses out the title and begins again *That Day!* with an exclamation point. Hommage to Bertrand. She crosses it out again, wrinkles up the page and starts again, without a title.

'This story burns my fingers. Not because I have lived it but because I am still living it, from so close, not knowing, not wanting to. From the opening of the text I intend to remove that literary style that surprises, impresses, holds the attention and makes a person able to think it is beautiful, unbearable, while it is not true. I want a truth here, mine, my version of the events that occurred in my family exactly twenty years ago, to the day, since Bertrand was returning from Barcelona and we were all together that night, July ninth, Luc and Anne-Marie, Sébastien and Ruth, Suzy and Jean, Pantalon, Bernadette, my parents, Gérard and I, to celebrate my brother's return and his birthday, twenty years old. And two times twenty, forty. We were all uneasy. Happy too. In the bedrooms the little ones were sleeping. Anne-Marie had put Pierre, three, in his father's childhood bed. Ruth had put Laura, two, in her father's childhood bed. I was pregnant with Loïc. He was born a few days later. My two sisters-in-law did not like each other very much. I have never seen two women related by marriage embrace one another from so far and look at each other so little. With her Lyon origins, still more passive than the Parisians, Anne-Marie had a way of carrying her arms and shoulders, with a tension in her jaw, her fine and determined lips would have made her ugly if she had not been beautiful. As for Ruth, depending on how much love one showed her, she had only, and above all, a grace that brushed lightly and faded away. Never the same, always changing, Ruth was amazing, from one moment to the next, fragile and determined. If I am stopping to portray these very lovely sisters, it is because they were supposed to be the sisters I did not have. When Cécile, my mother, was expecting her fourth baby, I was four years old, but I understood everything. The story of the doll in Mama's belly I knew was false. A doll is made of rags, nothing more. I would watch Bernadette pick out, categorize and iron what had been my layette, a pink layette, and keep aside, in the bottom drawer, at my height, the blue layette of my older brothers who were both going to enter Sainte-Croix secondary school in October. Like Papa. That pink layette that I watched, inspected between Bernadette's fingers, was really the proof of the coming arrival of a little sister. But it was a boy, Bertrand. Our departure for Moncrabeau that year was delayed, and the trip silent. It was a defeat and an exodus. Nothing in comparison with the awful surprise of the arrival of a boy. They were all disappointed, why? Bertrand, as a baby, did not cry. Would never cry. From him I keep the assertion, 'I didn't cry because I hadn't been born where I was wanted. Where I was wanted they were supposed to expect me. You were expecting somebody else.' I loved Bertrand right away and too much. I loved him the way you love at four years old, totally. And because he was unexpected, I felt less loving looks falling on him than had fallen on me, tender caring 'How pretty she is,' 'She's our daughter,' 'Come on, Claire, smile?' They demanded smiles of me. I used to give them smiles. Sébastien was always there at my bath time. Sometimes Bernadette would pass the washcloth to him. He wanted to see, to touch. It was nice. In turn, I was present at Bertrand's bathing. Bernadette would tell me laughing, 'You want the washcloth too? You're all the same!' The war and one more boy. Blue layette cleaned and ironed in haste. The smell of mothballs had imbedded itself. These details are important. The trip to Barcelona begins there.

'I'm not blaming, I am observing. I'm not composing, I interpret. Interpretation demands a total forgetting of the self for the benefit of the work. Now the work, our work, was murderous. The too abundant love I bore Bertrand, the baby, the child, always younger by almost four years than I was, it was only a little, a little bit of the little he was expecting elsewhere, there where one expects it, as if one could choose. My attentions angered him. He rejected me. Then, obstinately, I involved myself in everything going on around him, in bottles, diapers, potty, putting him in his cradle. I was there when he awoke, before Bernadette, like a little mama. But Bertrand would already have his eyes open. He was waiting without saying a thing and without ever smiling. I'd have so liked to surprise him still sleeping. But when he was sleeping, I was sleeping. We were on the same schedule. He used to wake up before me, that's all. He was born different. Or else we had

65

greeted him as a stranger, our silences and our disappointment rendering him stranger, compelling him to be different. Here am I taking all kinds of precautions as if I were feeling guilty, as if I wanted to throw onto the other members of the family the responsibility for a criminal act. It is nothing of the kind. Bertrand is still alive, he lives the way he lives and where he lives. But is that living?

'In the living room that evening, Ruth was holding my nephew, Paul, four months old, in her arms. While we were conversing about everything and nothing in particular, Anne-Marie and Cécile playing the perfect ladies, Henri, Jean and Luc talking about the future, Gérard, Sébastien and Suzy on the little balcony, by the middle French window, telling each other stories, watching for the arrival of Bertrand's taxi, Ruth was giving a breast to her son. A small, pink, nibbled breast. A breast that made one wonder how it could contain any milk. This had never been seen in the Prouillan living room. Moved, I went to Ruth and I caressed the back of her neck, my hand lost in her hair. It was a lovely moment for me. I, too, had a child in my belly. These little humans would devour us. It was so much lovelier than anything that could be said, anything we were saying to each other. So many babies in our respective bedrooms, asleep, and in our arms or belly, in the making. The true banquet was there, full of birthdays to come. Then, I noticed my father was no longer listening to what Luc was telling him of the offer that had just been made to him for an important position in the computer business. My father was looking at the Place d'Antioche, furtively. As when someone begins to blink his eyes, one counts his eyelid movements wondering where this nervousness is coming from. The press had been murmuring for some weeks that there would be a ministerial reshuffling before the end of July. And our father, alone of the signatories of the draft Constitution of the Fifth Republic not yet to have been given a portfolio, was well positioned, this time, to make off with a ministry. When the first government was formed at the end of '58, a ministry had been planned, to be called Action, and my father was supposed to have the National Education ministry. The General had rejected Action, probably for fear of being accused of reaction in the sense that, however unfairly, there is

66

always eternal opposition to all the powers that be, and had given National Education to the one who was supposed to have Action. My father found himself with a fine letter from his superior at the RPF who told him that 'waiting is also undertaking.' And now, two years later, it was true this time. It was not yet known which portfolio, but there would be one for Prouillan. My father was watching the Place d'Antioche. Luc moved away from him shrugging his shoulders. Night was falling. Gérard and I had suggested going to get him at Orly. But my father had said, 'No, he has to return alone. He is cured!' We were waiting. Paul fell asleep, his tummy full, in Ruth's arms, and with a modest gesture Sébastien covered his wife's breast, slipping his hand in her hair, catching mine. He kissed us, her as well as me.

'Someone said, "Maybe the plane is late." There is no one but Pantalon, the second, at the French window. Cécile told Anne-Marie to ask Bernadette to turn off the stove. My father said, "Bertrand had the best surgeon. There was another in Geneva. Bertrand chose." Luc, Sébastien, Ruth, Gérard and I looked at each other. Cécile lowered her eyes. Suzy lit a cigarette. Jean stood apart, against the bookcase, looking into his glass of port. My father had just put his fists in his coat pockets. Anne-Marie came back from the pantry and murmured, "What's happening?" No answer. We had just understood that, in our lives as respective couples, we had abandoned Bertrand to our father. Henri had just condemned our brother. Gérard murmured, "It's not possible." Then Luc asked "So they operated on Bertrand for a brain tumour, yes or no?" And Sébastien, "That's what you're telling us, Papa, say it again now, if you can. For us. I'm afraid." Cécile rose, into the small sitting room, or the office, she had disappeared. Uncle Jean turned toward the bookcase, his forehead against the books. Suzy crushed out her cigarette. Ruth kissed Paul's forehead. Henri joined Pantalon on the little balcony. Bernadette was waiting at the entry. The sound of brakes in front of the building. A taxi. We are there, standing, behind the French windows, watching. The taxi driver gets out, opens the trunk of the car, takes a suitcase from it that he places on the pavement, facing the entry gate to the building, near the chestnut tree. Pantalon, from the little balcony, his muzzle low, between the bars, recognises Bertrand, wags his tail. The driver opens the rear door and helps Bertrand get out of the car. Bertrand, his look dazed, in a white shirt, an open collar, his sleeves rolled up, almost stumbles on the curb, gathers up the suitcase, straightens up, is lost, and lets himself be handled. Instinctively, he extends some bills to the driver and the driver returns the change to him, picks up a bag, a coat, a tie on the rear seat, gives it all to Bertrand, slams the door, goes around the car, to the wheel, starts up, and he's off. We have not moved. The tie fell to the pavement. Bertrand was holding the bag and coat at arm's length. He turned his head toward one building, then another one, then a third, turns around, like a child on an empty merry-go-round. He did not know anymore. But he was here. Ruth called him, she was the first. Bertrand looked to see where these invisible distinct voices were coming from, our voices, and looked at the middle of the square. We did not budge. The last ones to come on the scene were first to shout out. They did not understand the story that was unfolding. They believe they can modify its progression. They call, like Ruth and Anne-Marie, relentlessly.

'Then Sébastien, Luc and I dashed down the stairs. Pantalon followed us barking. On the pavement we surrounded our brother. "Well, well," Luc said, "you musn't scare us like that," then Sébastien, "Come on, it isn't anything. We're all here. Papa is a bastard. You should have talked to us about it!" But when I kissed Bertrand I understood it was all over, for him. His cheeks were cold. He had no expression in his eyes and he screwed up his eyebrows. Pantalon had just pissed on the suitcase. Luc gave him a kick. On the first floor, the balcony French window was closed. There was a light in the parents' bedroom. Instinctively I looked all around the Place d'Antioche to see if "they" had seen us. And it was also probably because of that look, that later when I lost Gérard, I decided to leave Paris. Paris begins to look at you as soon as someone makes a wrong move. That night was really the last of our weddings, Luc, Sébastien and I. When one leaves everyone leaves. Now we had left Bertrand as a hostage. And Bertrand, paradoxically, in his weakness, was stronger than we. So? I see myself again with the coat, the bag on the stairs. Luc was carrying the suitcase, Sébastien was helping Bertrand climb the steps. Pantalon the second was waiting on the landing but he was no longer wagging his tail. Bernadette was holding out a glass of water and behind her, Suzy, Jean, Ruth, Anne-Marie. The parents were in their bedroom. I see Bertrand again, seated in the armchair, near the fireplace. He is looking at the hands of the clock, one over the other, vertically. We believe he is trying to smile. Only he does not see very well anymore. Sébastien pounds his fists alternatively into his palms. Luc bites his lips. He holds out the car keys and orders Anne-Marie to return home immediately with Pierre "Without waking him." On his knees in front of Bertrand, Gérard is trying to get him to drink a little water. But with a bump of his head, Bertrand spills the glass, like he used to refuse the bottle when I would play the little mama. I! I don't like these lines. Unfailingly I still recognise the family's style in them. Bertrand was saying as he looked at the commodes in the salon, "We aren't from the period, but in the style, like them. We'll never be able to be anything but what we are." Uncle Jean accompanied Ruth, Laura and little Paul. Ruth did not know how to drive. Sébastien did not want "his family" to stay there. Suzy went into the kitchen, with Bernadette. Several times the two women went into the hall with the gift boxes, the birthday presents they had to hide. A strange silence in the parents' bedroom.

'I see Bertrand again later that evening, that night, put to bed by his brothers, nude, in his bed in his room, like a dead man, but he was alive and staring at the ceiling. With a curt gesture Luc turned the photo of Romain Leval down on the bedside table. Sébastien, a few minutes later, put the little silver frame back in place. Bertrand, then, turned his head slightly. That was all that was left him. Uncle Jean went into the room, returned the car keys to Sébastien. Suzy stayed behind him, in the doorway. Jean murmured, "I'll speak to your father about it, tomorrow. But what good will it do? You should go home. That's what Suzy and I are going to do." Gérard was waiting for me in the hall. He was smiling wanly the way one smiles to keep from being furious. We were all leaving. Bernadette was saying, "Don't worry," "Don't worry," "I'm sure that," but she too knew it was all over for a brother. Pantalon stayed curled up under the marble console in the entry, his eyes raised toward us. We met again the next day. Never was the word murderer pronounced but we all had it on the tip of our tongues. Never one word louder than another. It was too late. The melodrama such as it was has been lived. One further way of performing a tragedy which, in fact, has played itself out. No showing off. I know today that happiness is only a shock. Bertrand was right. The heart's reason is right. In that, still more than in his sensuality, in the call of his sex toward his own sex, he was unacceptable. Wrapped up in our respective happinesses, marriages, pregnancies, births, first cars, apartments, vacations, our lives, these lives we had believed separate, we had just abandoned Bertrand to his father, our father, as in the prayer of the same name, an atheistic family who went to church to get married. I don't know how to write. I don't know how to paint. I will never know how. Those who do know will someday know nothing more than how to reproduce what they know.

'In the following days, Bertrand was present, took part in our family gatherings. Henri said nothing. The telephone rang continuously. They were calling the soon-to-be-named minister. Cécile suggested, and then decided, to take Bertrand to Moncrabeau and settle him there. "He will have everything. And he loves the house so much." Bertrand would watch her without really hearing her. Taking advantage of her husband's absence, Cécile said, "I didn't know," "Your father hides everything from me," "He believed he was doing the right thing," "I just didn't know!" The morning of July 16th Cécile took our brother away. Into his luggage at the last moment, I slipped Romain Leval's photo, some notebooks, letters, books and the issue of *Le Monde* with the next day's date, in which figured his name, Bertrand Prouillan, on the admissions list to the *École normale supérieure*. 73rd. Austerlitz station, we were there, all three, mutilated, Luc, Sébastien and I, to hail a brother's departure. We have never seen each other all together since. Never. For Gérard's burial, Sébastien was at sea and Luc in the United States for a training programme. We have never come back to Moncrabeau. Cécile is interred according to her last wishes in her family vault in Lectoure. On July 17th the make up of the new government was announced. There was a photo taken on the front steps of the Elysée. Our father was there, in the second row, between two heads, his look turned towards the lens as if he were looking at us, were looking at Bertrand. He was a minister for seventeen months.'

Claire places the pen down on the words she has just written. She gets up, goes out, the hard ground, the valley, the Lubéron, the sun is already aslant. She goes around the house once in one direction, once in the other. She has just written a letter. She has just written. But what good is it? She is naked. She forgot her shirt. One last time, naked, before the children's return. At each angle of the house she touches the corner stones, as if she wanted to define her territory, her Sauveterre territory. She has just been writing in the same way that she spoke that evening at Rians. And it is still like a gift for speech being born in her, a new language being forged, even if the style is from Antioche and from nowhere else. Only the expression counts, the plunging in. By circling the house she is also looking for her father's shadow and she no longer finds it. He is hiding again, the way he hid the evening Bertrand came back. Then, on an impulse, a sudden reversal, with a smile or burst of laughter, Claire comes back to the little table in her studio, slides the written sheets into the drawer which she opens, that she holds open against her belly, her flat belly. For one moment, while writing, she had felt pregnant again with Loïc and, taking a clean sheet, decided, telling herself that writing is above all an assault, she comes back to the page, to the ink and to the word, to write it and admit.

'Murder? There are no prescriptions for murder, in a family. Henri P. knowing he was going to become a minister did not want his son to create a scandal for him, or meet another Romain Leval. This son, strong, intelligent, athletic, my brother, got himself caught in the father's trap with the complicity of numerous doctors. He never had a brain tumour. He accepted going to Barcelona for the operation. The lobotomy done to him had the objective, in fact, of making him healthy to his father. Healthy, thus no longer homosexual. He returned home half deaf, half blind and empty. Emptied. He had just been accepted at the *Normale supérieure*. This story is true. Some dozens of boys and girls, the pride and fear of their families, have borne the brunt of these experiments in Geneva and Barcelona. These medical practices lasted only a while. But this while was far too much. I am writing these few lines for you Géraldine, you Loïc or you Yves, if you find them some day. By chance. Know that anything can happen. And I told you nothing when I gave you the impression I was hiding nothing from you. Bertrand is still at Moncrabeau. I love you. At Sauveterre, July 9th. I'm waiting for you. Claire.

In the downstairs room Claire sets the table for five. She always sets the table before preparing the meal. Then she peels the vegetables, cleans the lettuce, puts a chicken in the oven. And she goes to get dressed. In the studio, on the table, there is nothing more. She has put everything away in the drawer, and the pen too. She takes a breath.

Then, sandals in hand, she turns on the music, goes out, leaves the house with the doors and windows open. She will walk to the intersection of the two national highways. She will wait there. When she sees the children's 4L, she will stick out her thumb and hitch a ride. And the children will bring her back home, to their home, laughing. They too have passed their exams.

Bertrand used to say, 'There is only one between-the-wars literature, the one between today's war and tomorrow's.' How gentle is the slope leading to the highways' crossing. Seven kilometres, one hour. And the hillside in blossom. Claire is going to give her children a surprise. 'She has a sense of humour, mother does, don't you think?'

5

On Jean Martin's desk, inscribed in pen and violet ink in a full and open calligraphy on a piece of parchment, framed in a fine, black moulding and placed like a first communion photo, is a sentence by Flaubert writing to his friend Ernest Feydeau in 1839: 'The bourgeois hardly suspect that we are serving them our hearts. The race of gladiators is not dead, because every artist is one. He amuses the public with his death throes.' Often Suzy sits there, the desk turned toward the wall, with no other scene visible but the quotation and the wallpaper, the beige veering to drab from all the dust, which she had not and will never have the courage to replace. There are some untidinesses that must be left in their disorder and their own life. Like a small sigh from the past, and the breath of a coming day that has already come. On the desk there are also files, dictionaries, unfinished manuscripts, and those piles of sheets of paper held together with rubberbands, sheets on which Jean used to make notes, in his tight, continuous handwriting, as if paper had remained a rarity for him, no blank pages, and rubberbands that Suzy replaces when they get dry and break, weary of stretching to hold things together. On a blotter shortly before his death, Jean had written in pencil 'W.A.M. I wish so much that those who know me might really know me.' He would sometimes make notes like that, to be erased after recopying, for fear of neglecting that feeling of orderly harmony that was so essential to him, that came to life every time he read a sentence. 'Time,' he would then say 'does not exist. I know only the instant, that brief certitude that restores, exhorts, and involves you.'

Jean did not really like quotations. He only found them valuable if they were meant to fade away and not remain inscribed in the memory or knowledge. And if he was wont to quote himself, it was to scoff at himself. Jean made fun of 'cultivated culture'. However, the handwritten text is there, an exception confirming the sentiment, and on the blotter lay that sentence by Wolfang Amadeus Mozart, addressed to his sister from Paris, which as fate would have it, Jean had not time to recopy, stricken as he was, in a very few minutes, in the belly of the theatre, on that narrow, twisted staircase leading to the dressing rooms of the 'supporting roles'. A blood vessel had burst. Jean had just distributed the pay envelopes. The house that evening, a Tuesday in February, was one third full, with groups of convention goers. The set was only half paid off. There were too many characters in the play. Alerted by the theatre doorman, Suzy came running from Boulevard Haussmann. The ambulance was there. A doctor too. On a stretcher at the foot of the stairs, Jean, his eyes half closed, had feebly raised a hand that Suzy had grabbed, repeating 'No.' Jean had told her, pinching her cheek gently with his other hand 'Catch your breath. You're going to need it. The actors are paid. I'm going. That's all.' And as Suzy was bending down to kiss her husband, Jean had said in her ear, 'That's good, thanks . . .' He had just closed his eyes. The newspapers the next day wrote that he had died a few hours later at Beaujon Hospital. But Suzy knew that he had in fact departed the moment he said 'Thanks' and especially 'That's good.' Right to the last moment Jean had avoided the imperfect. Not for fun but sense of style. Jean did not like to say 'but' either. He preferred saying 'and'. Thus never would he say of Flaubert's sentence, in full view on his desk, 'It's useless but touching,' but clearly, like a simile, 'it's useless and touching.' A few days later, apologizing for not being able to attend the funeral service (a Minister of Culture, but which one? Malraux was dead, they were always changing just when one was beginning to know their names at least), had sent Jean Martin's widow a telegram worded like this 'I beg you Madame to excuse my absence due to multiple activities concerning my duties which are known to your brother. I will be represented by my personal secretary, Hubert Potron. I ask you to accept my condolences as well as the respect the loss of the unforgettable author of *Midnight Ball* and *The Collision* inspires. Your humble . . .' and a name, nothing but a name, that one was supposed to forget a few months later in favour of another passing name. Culture can have only ephemeral

74

ministers, Suzy, reading the telegram, had burst out in laughter, or pain. As Jean would have done. As Jean used to do when he would joke about imagining his own funeral oration, or writing it on the days after reviews appeared, the days following bad dress-rehearsals of his plays, his own obituaries that, amused, he would tear into shreds, after reading them. A few days after his appointment to the position of 'minister of what really' Jean had planned to send his brother-in-law a telegram, the text of which he had submitted to Suzy 'Bravo. Stop. You have acquired the right to be silent. Stop.' But Bertrand had just left for Moncrabeau, with Cécile at his side. Jean had not made his promised visit to his nephews and his niece. One act had been played, despite them all. Bernadette had told Suzy on the telephone, 'Monsieur doesn't come home anymore except to go to bed and he gets up in the morning just to leave.'

Another time, as Suzy understood quickly, Bernadette, who had not recognised the voice of Monsieur's sister, had asked, 'Is this Mademoiselle Jacqueline? Monsieur asked me to give you a message.' Bernadette's voice showed a slight scorn Suzy had never known in her. Suzy had hung up. Today, returning home, in the little apartment on Boulevard Haussmann, encumbered with objects that refuse to be remembered, with that living dust everywhere that speaks of absence like a presence, Suzy goes and sits at her husband's desk. The telephone is there. She wants to think. Before sitting down she seizes the armchair cushion, puffs it up with little pats, turns it over, puts it back and takes her seat, elbows on the desk, fists joined under her chin, her gaze at the level of the yellowed wallpaper. She has no more money. She will have to find some to revive *The Collision*.

For some years now, since Cécile's death, she has been going to her brother's, and more regularly. But Henri almost never comes to Boulevard Haussmann in return. And only then to stay a few minutes in the hall. He comes 'to call for' his sister to go to other theatres, other final dress rehearsals, to be still 'seen', the widower and former minister. There is always a 'taxi waiting downstairs' or 'We're going to be late.' Perhaps Henri does not want either to see the abandonment, the gradual decrepitude of that apartment which had only had some lustre during the lifetime of his brother-in-law who was not really called Martin, a pseudonym, a pen-name, but Lehmann, and he was not an Alsatian Lehmann. He had had to save the man twice during the war. Once from the deportation trains, a second time from suspicion of collaboration. At Jean's plays the Germans used to fill the houses that had been empty before the war. And Suzy had made her farewell appearance on the stage before them. Nobody was fooled. Nevertheless, there was a Jean Lehmann, author up to '39, a Jean Moncrabeau, (Suzy had told Henri 'That house is as much ours as yours,') from '40 to '46, and Jean Martin was born, with a new identity in '47 with the new successes. In the minister's telegram, there was a subtlety or an implied official ministry insult, with the reason he could not be elected to the Académie Française hinted at, a reference to *The Collision*, of course, but also to *Midnight Ball* which had played, precisely, during the war and which at that time had made people laugh. Jean, who used to mock the idea of entering the Académie, was regularly heard to say during the last years of his life that he was submitting his candidacy whereas he was not. They wanted to maintain a grievance, to safeguard a memory, but what memory? The wartime audiences for *Midnight Ball* also contained French theatre-goers. Suzy smiles at the empty spaces on the wall. She had sold her bracelets by the weight, her necklaces stone by stone, her buckles, watches and brooches. The Théâtre des Champs is still open. It is nice there even if others are scornful. Performances still take place. Olga, the most senior of the usherettes, has taken over the coatroom since she can no longer walk. And when the theatre is lit up, amid the noise of the arriving public, 'Ask for the programme,' Suzy unconsciously strokes the little engagement ring, the little diamond nothing bought at cousin David Stein's who kept repeating, 'It vill pring you hoppiness,' then after twenty years of marriage, the success of *The Collision*, a smile 'You zee, it prought you hoppiness.' Jean used to tell Suzy 'My cousin is slop-hoppy.'

Today, Suzy only has a short time to get ready. On the desk is a package and inside it a dress she has just bought in a Faubourg Saint-Honoré shop, a model she had been seeing in the window for three years, every year at sale time. A white mid-length dress in gathered chiffon, the bust studded with Tyrollean stones like diamonds, two sequinned straps and a rose at the waist. A short evening gown. Suzy will be able to show her legs. The dress is finally her's. It is good to give yourself a present, especially when you are afraid. The saleslady recognised Suzy when she came in the shop and told her, 'The gown is still the same price. But I can let you have it for 800 francs. That's nothing for a handmade gown.' It is the 'handmade' that persuaded Suzy. She scribbled a cheque 'Paris, July 11.' 'It's the ninth, madame, but that's alright.' A cheque with no funds. Suzy had just gained two days and her brother would be impressed. The dress is here, on the desk. Suzy is happy. Each day's memory is total and sovereign. She wants to be beautiful, in a little while. Henri will reserve a table at Taillevent's. Before, she intends to take him to the theatre, all lit up, and to show him from the empty stage what had moved Claire, one day, in an empty house, and also from where Romain Leval had seen for the first time a young man who had just taken his 'bac' exam at fifteen years old who was named Bertrand Prouillan. Suzy picks up the telephone.

'David?' The jeweller cousin has become administrator for the Théâtre des Champs. Often Suzy tells herself he robs her because she is not 'family', just as Jean never truly belonged to hers. Nevertheless there was a tie, a love and trust between Jean and herself, thirty-nine years of marriage and debts, nothing but debts. 'David? I'm keeping the theatre. We're beginning again. We have to sign with the actors tomorrow. I'll find the money for a new set. Ferrier will direct. Final dress the thirteenth of October. The thirteenth, I insist.' David burst into laughter. 'And the money, my dear Suzy?' Suzy answers 'I'll have the money tomorrow. I'm not fooled by your game. You want to buy the theatre. I know. Are you happy now? You can warn your bank so they don't have to be furtive any more. I prefer losing everything to finding myself an ex, and a widow at the same time.' Suzy takes a breath, 'You see, I'm in great shape. For a glance I could even fall in love. I won't be coming over as usual for dinner tonight. Give Luce a kiss for me and tell her I bought the dress. She'll understand.' David mumbles, 'You're sure that tomorrow you won't be telling me the opposite? If I came now, we could talk about it.' David no

77

longer says 'vill this', 'vill that'. Suzy, her voice high, settling comfortably in Jean's armchair, taking off her shoes under the desk, exclaims, 'You're the one with money, David. I gave you a good tip on the Crouzet and the Valence stocks. You made a good profit with it.' 'But . . .' 'I forbid you to say but. I'm asking nothing from you. This money, I'll find it on my own, as I usually do. Make the necessary calls. From the theatre if you wish so that you don't have to pay for them. Sign the contracts. Till tomorrow. You have my love.' 'Me too.' 'Louder.' 'Me too.' Suzy hangs up, takes a breath, smiles, leans over and picks up her shoes. She needs new shoes to wear with the new dress, if not, all the ones she has will look old. She does not want to look wrong. She will be perfect. Tonight.

Drama is when people who should not meet each other do meet. A celebrated and accepted formula. Full houses. Receipts. Real drama is when those who should meet do not. Only real family reunions. The houses are emptied then. Jean mocked our society's knavish ways. Suzy hurried over to the shoe shop on Rue de Miromesnil that was also advertising a sale. She tries on, she chooses, she hesitates, she places the shoes on the dress, she looks for colour, shape, and comfort. Actually she is thinking about Pantalon, about Bernadette, about the meal, her brother Henri's undone collar, about all sorts of unfortunate decisions, about Sébastien who no longer sends any news, Luc who never comes to see his aunt and yet lives just a short way from her, Claire who sends a greeting card every year with 'affectionate thoughts' and about Bertrand who does what ever he does at Moncrabeau under the watchful eye of Merced and Lucio's son, Juan, who it seems has married and has children? Suzy thinks about the money and the second cheque she is going to sign before leaving the store, for her luxurious pumps. Suzy is thinking 'Everything is in hock.' She smiles. The saleslady is pleased. 'Do you like these?' Suzy nods yes. She did not even look at the style chosen. She feels good inside. That's all. The white of the leather is almost the same as the dress. 370 francs. David Stein used to say to his cousin Jean, 'You will be rich only if you have debts.' Jean used to say about him, 'He sleeps like gold bars.' Jean would then kiss Suzy and murmur 'Keep me awake.

Away from your family, just like I want to keep you away from mine. There is only one unchanging and repetitious story — their comfort and conflict. Not ours. You understand?' Suzy understood a little only on the day of Bertrand's return, a revelation, and after Jean's death, totally. She comes back home with the dress and the shoes. The water heater has not been working for some days now. She will take a cold shower.

On Wednesday afternoons in autumn and winter, Suzy goes to the Saint-Ouen swimming pool, near the junction with the Autoroute de Nord. On that day of the week the children and especially the teenagers flock there. She arrives before they do, at noon, and in the deserted pool she swims one length, two, three, until she is no longer counting, until she feels fatigued, or numbed with cold, when she comes out of the water. She then rolls up in a bath towel, near a radiator at the door to the shower room and she waits until the covered pool is filled with cries and echoes, until the children, playing, are throwing themselves into the small pool or the large one, splashing, making waves, a wild shivering of the blue or green water, depending on the daylight diffused by the glass, an odour of chlorine that rises abruptly with the cries of the games, strong and heady. She is only an old lady who stays seated on the floor, on her towel, always near the radiator, almost against it, and who, knees folded up, arms hugging her legs, folded in on herself, in a black one-piece bathing suit and rubber swimming cap to keep from getting her hair wet and to muffle the noise of the place, the fracas that gets louder, on the children's Wednesdays, watches. She forgets, for the length of time of an afternoon, that she is not the same age as they are, the young girls whose curves, nascent breasts and long hair she admires and the young boys with little hair on their bodies very busy snapping the elastics of their swim suits, diving candle straight, in perilous leaps, belly flops to make a splash, the great game being to push the girls into the water and for the girls to let them do it. Then Suzy scrutinizes, observes, devours with a look, all that disorderliness tidying itself out into twos, sometimes in corners, behind cement columns, on the tiled benches or the balconies of the tiers, before the doors of the changing booths, with the furtive gestures, seized by emotion, that some boy exchanges with some girl, or some boy with

79

another boy. Suzy tries then to remember similar emotions as if a whole panel of her life had been subtracted from her, a subtraction to be found in certain families, the power of a father she believed she was in love with and who kept her apart from everything. The metro is direct from Saint-Lazare to the Porte de Saint-Ouen. On Wednesdays in winter the pool's swimming teacher greets this lady, an habituée, who spends hours watching and to whom no one ever speaks. He supposes her to be a teacher, who has no classes at that time, and is athletic since she swims before everyone arrives. A woman of that age is not a voyeur. Yet Suzy loves this place and these beings. She is bowled over by the dripping bodies of the young boys when they surge up from the pool, seize the ladder, spring for a better dive, frisk their bathing suits, sees the pleat of their buttocks, the small of their backs, the way they carry their shoulders when, little animals in the changing booths, they towel their shoulders to make themselves feel male. The girls mince about or plot, talk among themselves, choose between the boys, decide on one or another, mocking those who ignore them by calling them faggots. And the games go on. Until four in the afternoon when, on the pretext of smoking a cigarette, some boy or other on the first or second balcony stands in front of the half opened door of his booth and waits for someone to join him. A lovely ballet. They must avoid the employee who opens and closes the doors, passes back and forth, with a noise of clogs, giving a dull rhythm to the hubbub under the glass roof. Night falls quickly. Stairways are lit with fluorescent lights. Suzy knows that behind such and such a door is such and such a boy and girl, together. She likes that. Not so much for herself, but for them. She imagines the embrace. She has seen them up close, around the pool. In thought, she sees them still closer upstairs behind their door and she tells herself that nothing is so beautiful, as when every gesture has yet to be learned, when the excitement still has the taste of instinct. She says that afterward, later, nobody loves anybody, one can be left more and more alone in pleasures that become gradually more elaborated, in experiments more and more premeditated and dissected. Suzy goes there on Wednesday afternoons for the dawning of an emotion she had not experienced at the appropriate time, in order to find Jean again, the multiple swimsuits, multiple bodies, Jean multiplied, determined to make a child for him that she was never able to have. Suzy would like to start everything all over again. It's impossible. But she watches. And towards five o'clock she goes home, red eyed from the chlorine, her head vacant. She feels clean, scrubbed. She fixes herself bitter, black tea without sugar, that smoked tea that only she knows how to mix, and while the water boils, she telephones the theatre box office to find out the number of reservations for that evening. She becomes Madame Lehmann again, Madame Jean Martin. But in her head are first names: Christian, Jean-Luc, Josyane, Bob, Martine, Luc, Pilou, the first names of Wednesday's children. And she, a mother in love. From one year to another she sometimes sees the same ones again. She calls them all Jean. She goes looking for them at Saint-Ouen, in the north of Paris. She doesn't want to be seen again in the pools in the fashionable neighbourhoods.

Under the cold shower she tells herself that the return to classes this year is on September 11th, and the first Wednesday is the 19th. She will be at the appointment. Between now and then, there will be a dead beach, Paris in the summer, of which Jean used to say 'It's our secondary residence.' And those children she did not have and wants to see live, Henri has them and wants to kill them. The bourgeoisie is bourgeois only by contrariness. If they recognise themselves, as they really are, they kill. If they can pretend, they spare, spare themselves and hold on. This bourgeoisie that has become so petty, excels in making the dead speak and in not listening to the living. Jean did not like quoting but Suzy quotes her husband continually, like a call for help. She wished she were not the way she is, just as she used to wish she had not been what she was. She would like someone to push her into the water of the big pool and bang her against the walls of a booth, with bruises on her knees, their bathing suits torn off, coming too quickly and clumsily.

A collar hanging in a coat closet, a leash hooked to the collar, an empty place under a marble console, an ashtray filled with cigarette butts on a pedestaled table, a brother seventy-four years old whose glance is suddenly no longer transparent, but has an opacity of affectionate schemes when they become murderous again, murder, the idea of murder, in all that dust, and Bernadette's step on the hall rug that must always be put back in its place, parallel to the walls; Bernadette goes to rest in

Claire's room, and it will always be Claire's room, the favourite cake from Berthier fils, images superimposed on themselves, Jean's words and cousin David's amazement, the buyer, the complicity of a bank's senior officers, a smile from the saleslady at that shop in the Faubourg Saint-Honoré, she is happy, she has sold the unsellable, out-moded dress, the pretty lady dress; bad cheques, but Suzanne-Lehmann-Prouillan has been signing rubber cheques for years, the circulation of the Théâtre des Champs' treasury, bought by Jean in his wife's name with the money from *The Collision*'s success, a tragic circulation, because the more the money comes in, the more it goes out, the hole of debts digs deeper, threatens, another hole; and that doctor who told Suzy, shortly after Jean's death, 'You need to exert yourself, walk, take walks, go swimming. Do you know how to swim? At quiet hours the pools in Paris are deserted.' Strange words, quiet hours, striking hours, battalions of bodies, of cries, of children, friends, lovers; Suzy feels so little like a little, unworthy old lady, at sixty-seven years old everything begins again, everything always begins again when one can no longer calculate, count, accumulate; and today, July 9th, at the very end of the afternoon, Suzy comes out of the shower, takes off the rubber cap, with the images of the day, one image, only one: Bertrand painfully climbing the stairsteps, the Place d'Antioche, all of them around him, and Jean murmuring to Suzy, arm in arm on the pavement of Avenue Niel, they had decided to return home on foot, 'Your brother doesn't fool around with mortmain,' then, 'It is mortmain, the lord's right to dispose of his vassal's goods which are left when he dies!'

This play, *Mortmain*, Jean wrote in the months that followed. He would hide away from Suzy and not answer his wife's questions 'What's it about?' 'Are you sure you don't want me to read it?' Suzy knew Jean was writing about the visit he had not the courage, or the cowardice, to pay to his brother-in-law, that he was writing about Bertrand and the family, was writing about Bertrand and was suffering from inevitably making it into a comedy of manners. At the end of November with the play unfinished, Jean had told his wife, 'I have just stuck my fingers in a door that won't slam,' then, 'Sorry. That's the only way I can talk about it. Just remember that *Mortmain* is unplayable, true, unbearable, anything you want in "-able", hateable, scornable,

82

so very aimable. I don't know anymore. It's a failure. Here, you can read it.' Suzy had refused. Taking the notebook back, Jean had said 'you're right. There are only bad roles in this play. Especially Bertrand's.' Jean had just confessed. Suzy had kissed him. Jean, slipping the notebook under a pile of manuscripts, had murmured 'Mustn't touch real life anymore.'

Suzy gets dressed, in panties, panty girdle, brassiere, no, she takes off the brassiere, puts on the dress, keeps the merry-widow, like a charm, then the shoes, and seated before what was her dressing table and is now nothing but an altar for bills, papers, letters, bank statements, press clippings, invitation cards, which hide combs, brushes, conceal powder puffs, powder boxes, rouge, nearly empty perfume bottles, she arranges her hair. Nervously at first, then gently, her fragile, medium long hair that in the old days used to curl, and it wasn't as long ago as all that, at the nape of her neck. Suzy will be going out, she is going 'out'. The sequinned straps and the bust sparkle faintly. Grace Parker, at the time of her weekends in London for the creation and failure of *The Cannon*, the English version of *The Collision*, would have said of this sparkling that it was 'glittering'. Or, getting into her Bentley, late for the final dress rehearsal, saying to the chauffeur, 'Think of my poor nerves.' Jean thought that if nothing in these Anglo-Saxon trifles could be translated by words into French, nothing of the endearments skilfully placed in the text of his French play would be able to blossom forth in English. Suzy looks at herself one last time in the mirror crowned with various condolence cards, some several years old. She addresses David, saying 'You won't have the theatre,' Henri with 'you'll die in your money,' Bertrand 'I'll have your revenge,' and says to Jean 'how do I look?' She gets up, spins around, in the high heeled shoes, the elevation, the gathered chiffon billows or caresses, like the water in the deserted pool before the children arrive. Suzy has an impression of disturbing a flat surface, of making her own waves. She smiles to herself, it has been a good day and in prospect a proud evening. From her bedroom window she sees the Jacquemart-André museum, its shutters closed. Treasures are sleeping there too. In a drawer of Jean's desk is the manuscript of *Mortmain*. Suzy has never dared read it. She will read it when she comes home.

Suzy attaches the rose firmly in place, at her waist. A cloth rose in place of all the roses received. And the bouquets would always come from Jean, with a little card 'Your eternal lover.' The doorbell is ringing. Henri.

6

Luc arrived in Exoudun, in the Deux-Sèvres on June 29th. He is staying at his friends', Eliane and Antoine Duperin. Eliane was a friend of Claire's at the school in the Rue de Lübeck, Antoine, a classmate of Luc's, prides himself on graduating second to last, in 57th place. The house at Exoudun, on a height above the Sèvre Niortaise river, has never really been completed. Eliane and Antoine's children have left for England. Luc has come to spend two weeks as he does every year at his friends', this time accompanied by Christine, Christine Eulard, twenty years younger than he. She could be his son Pierre's fiancée, and Luc wonders sometimes how and why Christine has been able since January, to become attached to him, and above all when it all began. Christine has kept her studio apartment in the same building as her parents and has never brought the smaller personal belongings to Luc's place on the Rue Téhéran, almost at the corner of the Boulevard Haussmann. She brushes her teeth with Luc's brush. She does not intend to move in. Or else Luc has never done what is necessary, by making a gesture, a sign, or a word, to invite her to join him and live with him, as if there was a double fear, on both their parts. In Christine, it is a fear resembling indifference. She likes the silence in Luc, an appearance of insignificance that reassures her, and the representation of the father who has become a lover. In Luc, there is that fear of age, at forty-seven years old, that, he says, 'No longer is put into the heart's computer.' But he confides it only to those who can neither hear nor be concerned, and he has never said it to Christine. He wonders every day on waking up how this young woman still with the body of a young girl, with a degree in economic sciences, with a full course load at Paris VII, seductive, secret, independant, and thus subtly dependant, can love him, and because love is a very big word, quite simply, 'stay with him'. A story of a toothbrush not brought along.

When she left for Exoudun, Christine took along a small cloth bag that seemed empty. Luc said 'Is that all?' Christine answered, 'It is enough.' They show their affection for each other only in the silence of the nights. They say 'vous' to each other even when alone with Eliane and Antoine. This morning, July 9th, at breakfast, Luc was making toast, Eliane was putting the bowls onto the table, Antoine was opening a jar of jam 'made last summer'. Christine was sweeping last evening's dinner crumbs from under the table and between the chairs, and Christine had said, smiling, addressing Luc but also their hosts, an unusual event, a first immodesty, 'Last night, Luc, you called Bertrand several times. I felt that there were three of us. Is he one of your brothers?' Eliane had looked at Luc. Luc had forgotten to turn over the bread on the grill. Antoine had poured the boiling water for the coffee, drop by drop, into the filter, the good aroma of every morning. Christine had emptied the dustpan into the trashcan under the sink, standing very close to Luc, looking at him sidewise, murmuring 'Sorry.' Luc had told himself that Christine had just decided to leave him. Since Anne-Marie had left, the divorce, the farewells, Luc has been finding himself getting older and older, while his girlfriends, liaisons of a day or six months, younger and younger, as if the chance of those he met was decided to confuse him or worse still to humiliate him. Christine is too beautiful. At the end of breakfast Antoine had said, 'Let's hurry up, it's the big day. We have to see it!'

The same idea of humiliation is tied, 'bound' Bertrand used to say, to education. 'Education according to Saint Henri, pater familias, coîtus tragicus!' Luc did not like his younger brother's humour. As the eldest, he would gladly have opted for peace, accepting the paternal model as it was, but in his heart of hearts, allowing more latitude, amplitude, aptitude to react to events or simply to act, to discover life and live fully, while keeping one's own counsel. At that time Luc liked words in 'ude', especially habitude, sometimes servitude, when Bertrand would hum the words in 'ism', a fashion of the Rue d'Ulm which he dreamed of entering, communism, stalinism, immobilism, cretinism, romanticism. He was devouring Nizan. Uncle Jean used to make *himself* the hero of everything ending in 'able', affable, accountable, honourable, or even table, that table of which he became the hero at every family gathering. Luc recalled it all day. To the preceding night's sleep, agitated by Bertrand's impromptu return, is now added, by day, the sudden appearance, of the father's memory. What is he doing in Paris? What has he done since their last meeting in February, when Christine was waiting downstairs in the car, in the Place d'Antioche, listening to music?

At Moncrabeau, during the summers of their adolescence, Bertrand used to leave notes behind sometimes, that were always the same, a formula, while the others had gone to get a sweater for the evening walk. This note was worded thus: 'I am leaving before you, for I want to take a walk and meet someone.'

Today, in broad daylight, there are more than two hundred people at the excavation site at Bougon, men and women from every corner of France and Germany, geologists, archaeologists, astrophysicists, the curious, or neighbours like Eliane, Antoine, Christine and Luc. Since 1840 on this spot numerous vestiges of neolithic civilisations had been found and, in particular, a number of dolmens that, the whims and fantasies of the twentieth century having turned more toward space and its conquest than to the quest for our origins, have since given birth to every kind of explanation, about magnetic fields, extra-terrestrial beings, theories of all kinds. For two weeks, as a group, almost as a clan, tribally, they have been making picks from deer antlers and extracting stones from the rocky vein with these rudimentary picks. For two weeks, in teams under the leadership of the curator of the National Museum of Saint-Germain-en-Laye, they have been making ropes from braided creepers and ivy roots, laughing, and joking, and believing in what they were doing, every one of them. It was not playing at being boy-scouts but, more seriously, proving, acting in the way that their ancestors, the first humans, more than 5,000 years ago were able to do. Some were light hearted in their mockery as if they were on the verge of proving the opposite. They talked about the 'tall-story mythology' that applied to these Bougon megaliths. Neolithic men were perfectly capable of erecting such monuments themselves. To prove it, one hundred and seventy-three men and women, that was the number counted by the television reporters who had come to film the event, had just displaced over an area of several dozen meters a thirty-two ton block of concrete, a size similar to a dolmen table found on the tumulus site, the enormous mass placed on logs cut from trees which were themselves felled with simple flint axes. Eighteen hours. And it is done. A few dozen metres, an exploit like a new discovery and the group fell silent rather than crying victory, amid the humming of the television cameras, the exhausted faces, the sky grey, becoming stormy, an early nightfall.

Eliane, Antoine, Christine and Luc did not talk about the day to one another. They carried, slid, pulled, hoisted. They mixed with the group because they were neighbours from Exoudun. In Paris before leaving, Antoine had said to Luc, 'You're going to see what'll happen this summer. Too bad for the bridge games. For once you're coming with a fourth who doesn't want to be the dummy. Christine is okay. Keep her. Don't be an ass.' They say 'ass' to each other, between classmates, it makes them feel young. Eliane had said, 'It will be better than your millionth decimal of pi. Have you found your publisher yet?'

Eliane goes over to Antoine and takes his hand, a little girl's gesture. Christine looks furtively at Luc, but as Luc lowers his eyes, then his head, pinching his chin, she does not go up to him as she would have wished, a sudden urge, abruptly, which was almost an avowal. They want to leave, and they stay. Luc is thinking about something else. Christine has just seen Luc again, coming out of his father's apartment, flanked by this father Luc was hiding from her, and who obviously, on that evening in February, late at night, was taking the opportunity, by accompanying his son, to walk that old poodle, or perhaps it was just the opposite, with the excuse of walking the dog, becoming a pretext to stay longer with his eldest son. Luc had tried to give the impression that he was leaving alone, walking in the street. Monsieur Prouillan had passed the car, in a no-parking space in the square, 'but tonight we're taking a chance,' and he had returned home, pulling the dog by the leash. Luc had come back like a thief, the door slammed, the key turned, the motor starting up. 'Sorry, with my father it's always too long,' a furtive kiss, then, 'The dog's name is Pantalon, fortunately he was there,' and at the first red light, at the Rue de Courcelle, 'Everytime we needed to say something important, to the family, we would say it to the dog. Nobody would get angry. Everybody was informed. My brother Bertrand used to call that the Pantalon function. But sorry, you can't understand. You can but you'd need time.' A second kiss, less furtive.

Eliane has never really been Claire's friend. They knew each other because they went in the same direction together every morning going to the Rue de Lübeck, in their blue uniforms, white anklets, with modest hair braided or in a ponytail, which was required by the school, and coming back in the afternoons. Claire never confided anything. So Eliane had chosen never to say anything in return. And if she sometimes was burning to tell Claire something that had happened to her, she would do it in the third person. Claire listened then, distantly, pretending not to understand. She did not want a girl friend. She did not wish to become close to her. In that Eliane found her likeable. That way neither of them would ever be able to get angry. Since then they have lost touch. Sometimes Eliane asks Luc the news of his sister and Luc invariably answers, 'I don't know anything about her. We've stopped seeing each other but not stopped loving. That's been our pact since Bertrand's departure.' 'Why the departure?' Luc then makes a helpless gesture, or else a simple nervous gesture indicating he has nothing to explain. On one occasion only, Antoine had heard him saying very clearly, 'It will always be too soon to explain about my youngest brother's departure.' Eliane likes Luc only because he is Antoine's friend.

As for Antoine, he does not know what keeps him around Luc unless it's the fact that he owes his job to him. When Luc became general manager of the Paris branch of Control Data, FACC, the French Applied Computer Corporation, which had 49% American capital and 51% government capital, insuring the government's control in the interest of chauvinism, nationalism, it was in short, 'a French corporation!', Luc had asked him to join him as assistant general manager. Polytechnic alumni always make little cliques. Antoine, instead of keeping his distance and bearing Luc a grudge for doing him this favour, the usual scenario of appreciation, was quite satisfied and remains satisfied in filling his assistant role servilely. That's his next-to-the-bottom graduate side. As assistant, he has come to know Luc very well. Luc is incapable of understanding the lives of those outside his own life. Luc is incapable of listening to anything at all. The beginning of a sentence and right away his look teeters, is lost elsewhere in his calculations, his work, his projects, his research. Luc has totally surrendered to FACC's profit motivation. And each time Antoine observes his friend, consciously or unconsciously, he thinks of Anne-Marie whom Luc used to torment with repeated silences and of whom Luc had forged a strange and unjustified jealousy until the day when, with her back in a corner, totally miserable, Anne-Marie had sought happiness elsewhere, fully justifying his diffuse and harassing jealousy, confounding Luc, by leaving. Now Luc has been treating Christine for six months in the same way that he treated Anne-Marie and the others. Only Christine, with her attachment to the formal 'vous', the early stage of the relationship, placing herself skilfully out of jealousy's reach, has ensnared Luc. And Antoine thinks, as does Eliane, that Christine is finally going to win the game of the heart. Just as in bridge, she plays her cards marvellously, has a sense for finesses, bids, and makes her contracts.

Christine came down from the concrete block, the false dolmen, to pose with the others for a souvenir photo of the day, like a class portrait consisting of adults. Suddenly through the clouds, there is the beginning of sunset. Christine has knotted her shirt under her bust. She is in jeans. She has taken off her shoes and has hung them around her neck by the laces. There is one man smiling continually at her and another one who has just offered her something to drink. Eliane approaches her and says 'This is the most wonderful day of my life. What about you?' The two women look at each other. They feel Luc observing them from afar. Christine thanks the man who has just offered her the drink and murmurs to Eliane, 'Each time I have a date with Luc I tell myself it's the last time. And each time some little thing holds me back. I'm comfortable with him at night. Yes, it was a wonderful day.'

Christine smiles, takes Eliane and, for the group picture, both squat down in the front row, at Antoine's feet who waves to Luc to join them. Luc has sat down on an embankment at a distance. He is pouting the way one pouts at forty-seven. You appear to be thinking intensely then. Luc wants a drama but he won't have it. Christine says in Eliane's ear, 'I'll stay with him.' The photographer yells, 'Silence,' then 'Don't move!' The television cameras film the group photo as it is being made. Antoine says to himself that everyone who is not in the group will make fun of the group. If he is questioned for TV, he will answer, 'It's as important to know how we lived 5,000 years ago as going to the moon. It's the same conquest. And if you really want to know...,' Antoine imagines the reporter holding the microphone, 'If you insist, I'll say that from now on it's more important for us to know where we're coming from than getting lost in the dead-end of space. Even if the technological progress that comes from space travel is a real asset for daily life and improved communications. Believe me, I'm well placed to talk about it.' Eliane turns toward Antoine, 'Are you talking to yourself?' Antoine puts his hands on his wife's head, forces Eliane to look at the lens of the tripod camera behind which a man under a black cloth is moving, raising his left arm, brandishing a rubber bulb and crying, 'All together! Smile, please! Again!' Antoine says to Eliane, 'Yes, I was talking to my-self. I'm tired. A real fatigue.' Eliane raises her eyes to the sky. 'A real fatigue?' Christine looks at Luc, still off by himself, his head lowered, squatting, his forehead on his knees and his hands beside his feet, kneads the earth and claws it, hitting it with his fingernails. Christine tells herself, 'He's crying, but that can't be,' and then she smiles for the picture, pushing up her bust, grazing Eliane's arm, with a shiver, the little happiness of a mission accomplished, two weeks of group effort. Christine tells herself again, 'And if he is crying, so much the better.' Christine would like to mock the idea of tears that so strangely resembles the idea of jealousy, that jealousy that passes continuously in Luc's glance. She resembles Luc. They all resemble each other. They are all carved from the same rock. A new smile. A photo.

'Do you mind?' Luc lifts his head, there is a man, kneeling near him, a tape recorder slung over his shoulder, the microphone held out, and a cameraman two meters away leans over, adjusting the lens, the camera on his shoulder, curiously armed. 'Can you tell me what led you to participate in this Bougon experiment?' Caught unawares, flattered, Luc answers, 'I'm here only as a spectator.' He smiles nervously. 'I participated in the work but as a spectator.' He comes to life, trailed by the microphone, the camera aimed at him. 'I wonder if we haven't all been just spectators. Even if we behaved like actors.' The reporter looks at the cameraman, signals him not to stop and sits on the ground almost against Luc. 'Can you tell me what you're thinking?' And, laughing, Luc blurts out 'There isn't any thinking. How can I tell you about it simply? I came as a neighbour, as a vacationer. I said to myself: it's pointless. I think we all thought so, more or less. We did it for fun. As a challenge. I don't know. Perhaps each one of us has personal reasons or discovered them during these last days. Now we've done it. There are no more spectators no more actors, but real evidence, a fact, a proof, an experiment, it's up to you to decide. And since you're asking me my opinion . . .' Luc looks straight into the camera lens, 'I'll tell you that mankind suffers more from not knowing where it comes from than from not knowing where it's going. We've also lost the taste for effort. Effort turned toward our roots. Where the sap and the spirit come from.' Luc looks at the reporter, smiles, sighs as if mocking himself, 'What good is it taping me, you'll cut it out in the editing. How do you want me to explain thoughts for which we've lost the taste because we pretend to think? Shall I stop now?' 'Please go on.' Luc shrugs his shoulders, is distracted by looking at the post-photo group, now standing up, mixed together and Christine lost inside the group, where is Eliane, where is Antoine? Luc tells the world, 'What annoys me is that it all becomes a special event. That you were filming it as such and that you want to hear me saying things that I may not have even dared say to myself yet. We only rolled a stone onto some logs to prove that our grandfathers the apes, seized by the spirit, had been able to do the same thing. And that dolmen table, I'd like to know what it signifies, just like the family table, in the family when I was little. The answer to your question is only another question. I told myself during these days, doing what I did, that in all my life, I had forgotten the essential thing, the effort, the group. But everyone is leaving . . .' The sentence was left hanging. The purring of the camera. The cameraman signals that he only has two more minutes, with straight fingers, the middle and index like a V for victory. The reporter asks Luc, 'What do you do for a living?' 'I'm an engineer.' 'Can you tell us your speciality?' 'That's not important.' Luc rubs his hands, the earth, the dust, the blackened nails. The reporter says, 'Thanks.' He puts the microphone away, there is a clapping of hands before the camera, reel noises, end of the sequence. Luc rises. The reporter's smile is ironic or gratified, how can one tell? The reporter shakes his hand. 'We'll edit it inside. It'll go out early in the year on TF1. If you want to see yourself?' Luc thinks, 'Certainly not,' but does not say so. He wants to find Christine, Eliane, Antoine again and go home. Twenty years ago, it was twenty years ago. Bertrand. It was Bertrand's twentieth birthday. In saying, 'I'm an engineer,' automatically Luc looked at his watch, the hour was 6.13 p.m., and the date July 9. That birthday he has not forgotten. Anne-Marie is February 22, Pierre November 7, and Cécile? Sébastien? Claire? July 9th, that's Bertrand, a time that stopped, stopped time. How old is Suzy if he, Luc, is forty-seven? How old was Uncle Jean when he died? Uncle Jean who used to say of conjugations that people no longer know how to use 'the past perfect for the recent past and the perfect for the distant past.' So, to laugh, to make others laugh, at the end of the meal he would begin speaking only in the perfect tense so that everything in the life of that family to which he would have so liked to belong would become in the past, finished, cut off: 'We began to speak under the arbour and we saw ourselves as we had never been, beautiful and desirable.' Another word in 'able'. The circle laughed, except him, Luc, because his father was not laughing and because under the arbour and the wisteria they all brushed by one another but did not meet. At the first opportunity each would take flight by forgetting one of them, all prisoners condemned to life who are escaping. Christine takes Luc's hand. 'Alright, I'm here. You're looking pale.' 'I want to go home.'

Luc is driving the car. He does not like to be driven, even for a few kilometers. He dons his general manager glasses and looks so straight at the road ahead that one would gladly believe him to be totally indifferent to what is going on around him, to the passengers, and whether they are speaking or not. Christine is beside him. She has unknotted her blouse and rebuttoned it over her jeans. Often Christine mocks Luc in his driver's stance. 'Are you meditating? The more I look at you, your frontview, when tense, the more I tell myself you're cooking something up, deciding something, judging. It's premeditation.' Christine does not like playing games with words, but she knows that in her relationship with Luc only this game will allow her express what she is thinking or feeling without Luc getting angry. One day in response Luc spoke to her about fly fishing,

93

taught him by his father. 'It annoyed Bertrand. Claire used to break the rod tips. Like a madman Sébastien would take a small boat out just by himself, all alone, and row in circles on the pond noisily to frighten the fish. I was my father's only true pupil. The glint of the gleaming fishhook. As long as what you say to me has the excuse of being interesting, I listen to you, Christine.'

Christine sits up straight, her hands on her knees. She watches the road. On the backseat Eliane has keeled over onto Antoine who has lowered the window, his elbow on the door. He gets the air full in the face. Luc observes them in the rearview mirror, looks secretly at Christine and, thinking about the two weeks spent with the team, a game about which you have a good or bad conscience, a game of conscience altogether, he tells himself 'Once more we've lied to ourselves.' He stares at the road. A curve. The entrance to a village, the white line continues, speed limit 40 kph. Since Gérard's death Luc has been afraid of the sudden appearance of cars coming from the opposite direction, head on. His sister's bereavement reawakened in him a taste for conformity, an instinct and nostalgia, that makes him say to himself, as if he were making fun of himself, tree, trunk, stump, branches, leaves and roots, 'Keep well to the right.' Antoine leans forward, Eliane straightens up, Christine smiles at her three friends, the strangers, and herself a stranger, so many families, so many millstones and sagas, as many hopes gratified as hopes disappointed, all of the same nature since the very nature of the hopes given to families, these families, is suspect. Antoine asks Luc to stop in front of the local tabac, 'Only two minutes. For cigarettes and your newspaper. I asked them to hold *Le Monde* for you.' Luc will always be Antoine's boss. Antoine needs a boss. Christine looks at Eliane, 'Everything is for the best in the worst of all possible worlds.' Eliane smiles. Christine looks at Luc. 'Don't you think so?' Antoine has left the door half open. The metronome noise of the direction indicator, no parking here. Antoine is quick, running back, a Gauloise carton in his left hand, the paper in his right. Eliane mumbles, 'There's nothing to eat. But we'll manage.' Antoine throws everything into the car. 'Was I fast enough?' The ignition. The Duperin's house is at the exit of the village, after the war monument, '14–'18, '39–'45, Indochina and Algeria, the whole thing in bronze letters that shine in the headlights when turning

94

at night. At the end of the drive, the house that Eliane and Antoine have never finished, with undergrowth all around, cots, a single shower and unmatching chairs inside. Each year as they arrive Eliane says to Luc, in front of Antoine, 'We'll fix the house up only when we're sure we really love each other.' Pointing his finger at his wife, Antoine answers, 'In that case, never!' Then turning to Luc, 'Do you have any news from Anne-Marie?'

Under the door, a post card from England. Eliane picks it up, reads it and hands it to her husband. 'The children send their love.' Antoine looks at Luc 'And your son? Isn't he coming this year?' Luc answers 'No, not this year.' Pierre is twenty-three and has not written since last summer. Anne-Marie does not write anymore either. Sometimes Luc has news from Buenos Aires by way of Argentine clients who frequent the French embassy. Anne-Marie, in her role as wife of the perpetual First Secretary, excels in the art of giving receptions and of making a second marriage succeed, guilty of having failed in the first, and is entirely devoted to the fictitious jealousies of her Polytechnician. And no one is fooled. Luc tells himself he wants to leave Exoudun, to go back to Paris, to take the time to straighten up the apartment, also to file some pending records at the office, read a few books, who knows, he does not read anymore, and especially to abandon Christine, abandon yet another woman the way he knows so well how to do, for no stated reason, with no explanation and as quickly as possible. Luc likes only the state of rupture, the prelude to the state of loneliness. In any company, he only likes the perspective of the separation when each goes his own way and, to use his expression, 'takes over'. Once, on an impulse, with an avowal or a sincerity which surprised himself, he had said to the Duperins, 'What I respect in you is the length of time.' But the only respect of which Luc felt capable, when it came to his own life, was an intermittent respect for the refusal of any other person. Sharing the toothbrush annoys him. And so does that cloth bag in which Christine brought along only a pair of jeans, some underwear she laughingly calls 'contact clothes' and two blouses.

Then, alone, having provoked the break, Luc enjoys feeling abandoned. That brings back Anne-Marie's memory, a fixed image, the film of a marriage which he plays over and over again, that he knows by heart, a director guilty of too skilful editing, a doctored film. The jealousy which Luc has lived through, created in spite of himself, constituted an appeal, an invitation to emotional conflict. Luc had expected a violent response from Anne-Marie that had been given to him only when it was too late. Pierre was thirteen. Anne-Marie sitting on the edge of their marriage bed, had said 'That's it, I'm leaving tonight. Pierre has already left. He's sleeping at your parents' house. I'll get him tomorrow. Your parents know all about it. Your father smiled. Cécile didn't say anything. *They* understood you were playing me up too much.'

Eliane and Christine are taking their shower together. They have to economize with the well water. Antoine, in his undershorts is waiting, standing near the kitchen window. He looks at Luc, 'You still want to leave.' Without even realising it, Luc murmurs 'Yes, I'm leaving before you, because I want to take a walk and meet someone.' Antoine shrugs, crosses his arms, nodding his head. 'What you just said isn't like you.' Luc stands up, undresses and answers, 'It's Bertrand. Everything beautiful comes from Bertrand.' The women come out of the shower, naked, Eliane hiding behind Christine. Christine kisses Luc formally, looks at Antoine 'kisses them both'. Eliane says, 'And we're going to make dinner, as usual.' Antoine takes off his shorts and throws them on the floor 'Is that a reproach?' Christine answers for Eliane, 'No, an observation.'

During dinner, a plate of noodles with grated gruyère, the remainder of the gruyère, a perfectly dressed salad, from the bottom of the oil bottle, and fruit, each savours his own enjoyment, in silence. Either 'We did well not to go to the banquet,' or 'In the end that thing with the dolmen took our minds off things,' each of them feels incapable of finding the right words. Even bridge is mentioned but nothing in the conversation gets very far and gradually the looks converge on Luc, the men are on one side of the table, the women on the other. The post card from England is still on the table with the Gauloise carton and the issue of *Le Monde*, near the bread. To break the silence, or on an impulse, she no longer knows why herself, Christine places a hand on Luc's left hand, bending over the table, almost tipping over a glass, and says to him 'I love you. I want to live with you. Trust me too.' Then, Luc kisses Christine's hand. 'Sorry. I was somewhere else. I need to talk to

96

you. To all three of you. Twenty years ago I participated in my brother's murder. I was the only one my father forewarned. Bertrand used to have very severe migraine headaches, ever since childhood and especially after the death of one of his friends. We used the pretext of a benign tumour to have a lobotomy of the brain done which theoretically was supposed to render him compatible with our respective marriages and especially to avoid a scandal which my father needed, for him to become what he wanted him to be. It was July 9th, twenty years ago. Bertrand's return. I wish I really knew what we should all think about it today. My father most of all. Bertrand believed he had a lesion and had chosen the date himself, the day after the exams at the Rue d'Ulm. That's all. It's like the dolmen, the reasons are numerous.'

Silence. Antoine clears the table, the women do the dishes. Antoine comes back, sits, unfolds *Le Monde* and leafs through it. At page seven he stops, sees the list of promotions to the order of Chevalier in the Legion of Honour, in the name of services rendered to industry. 'Why Luc, you could have warned us! And how should we celebrate? And with what?'

7

Henri, suit, waistcoat, tie, cufflinks, eau de toilette from Mont-Saint-Michel, closely shaved, holds the front door half open and with the other hand holds out a copy of *Le Monde* to Suzy. 'Here. You can keep it. I bought several when I left the barber's. Look at page seven. You'll see your brother hasn't totally forgotten his children. At least one.' Suzy takes the paper, holds it with her fingertips. She wants to close the door. Her brother tells her, 'No, the taxi's waiting. We have a meeting with one of my lady friends. Then we'll go to Taillevent's.' Suzy looks at her brother. 'Mademoiselle Jacqueline?' 'How do you know about her?' 'Bernadette took me for her once on the telephone.' Henri raises his head, a little smacking of the lips and tongue, a brittle sound like a reproach, a trace of a smile, showing off, something Suzy had not seen in him for a long time. Henri, pinned down, says 'Just the same you're not going . . .' Suzy slams the door. 'The taxi will wait!' Henri just has time to pull his hand away. His sister's abruptness amuses him. Suzy places *Le Monde* on a hall chair. 'Give me your lady friend's number.' Henri shakes his head, takes a few steps. For the first time in a long while he goes into the living room, looks for the light, groping. Suzy tells him 'It's to the left. You have to get back into the habit. The shutters are closed to keep the room cool. Perhaps too because nothing here is fresh anymore. You see, I'm in good form.' Suzy lights the wall lamps on each side of the fireplace and also the floor lamp near the big leather armchair where Jean used to set himself up, with a board on his knees to correct his plays and only for correcting. The correction was still there. Henri mumbles 'Nothing's changed.' Suzy smiles. 'Right. Nothing. That woman's number, please.' Henri has stopped under the chandelier that Suzy no longer turns on because nine of the fourteen bulbs are burned out and she gets dizzy standing on the stepping stool. Henri murmurs 'Maillot 53.39.'
Suzy goes into the bedroom, leaves the door to the living

room open behind her so that Henri can hear. She grabs the telephone, the knotted, twisted cord, places it on the bed, sits down while being careful not to wrinkle her dress and dials 624.53.39, it is ringing. Henri appears in the doorway and stops there, his fists in the pockets of his jacke. Suzy looks at him, an affectionate look, then, 'Hello. Good evening, Mademoiselle. I am Henri's sister. Henri Prouillan, Suzanne Lehmann.' Silence. A voice at the other end of the line, an indistinct noise that Henri follows intently and recognises. He wished he knew what Jacqueline is saying. Suzy goes on calmly, 'Yes, I am Jean Martin's wife. Lehmann is my real name. And Suzy, my nickname. I'm calling you to cancel tonight's dinner. I have no excuse to give really. My brother has just arrived at my home. I would like to spend the evening with him, and with him alone. Just as you have wished to do for a long time, I'm sure. Am I mistaken?' Muffled noise, Jacqueline's soft voice, and Suzy's also soft, but the softness is fierce, vicious, if need be. Henri comes back into the living room. He hears Suzy resume speaking. 'I knew you would understand very well. We have no reason to meet. That's the nicest thing I can tell you.' Suzy listens to Jacqueline. Henri feels like running away as fast as possible but the copy of *Le Monde* stops him, on the chair in the hall, and he hears 'Henri asks me to tell you he will call you tomorrow. I'm not giving him the 'phone because he's hiding in another room. He feels like slipping away. How long has it been since he's given you any sign of life?' Silence. Answer. 'He has never lied to you, obviously? Neither have I. We would perhaps have benefited by meeting, after so long a time.' Silence. Jacqueline is speaking at length. Henri comes back into the living room. Near the leather armchair, on a low table, he recognises Jean's writing on the cover of a notebook, '*Mortmain*, a play in two acts, Jean Martin.' He takes the manuscript, opens it at random, but Suzy goes on talking and Henri listens. 'Thank you, Mademoiselle. May I call you Jacqueline? I am very happy to have spoken to you. We will always have the first word. A line of my husband's. If Henri doesn't call you tomorrow, for the second time in seven years, then don't wait any longer. It's the only way to get in touch with him.' A small laugh from Suzy. She listens in turn then she says, 'Thank you, Jacqueline. I kiss you.'

Suzy hangs up, leaves the telephone on the bed, rises, gives

100

herself a furtive look in the mirror, she feels beautiful and well. She comes back into the living room, approaches her brother, kisses him on the cheek and whispers into his ear, 'We can only love one person at a time. Tonight I want you to love me.' She takes the manuscript of *Mortmain*, puts it back in its place on the low table. 'This script belongs to me. Understand? Come on, let's go. I'm taking you first to my theatre. I have something to show you.' In the entryway Suzy checks to see she has not forgotten her apartment keys, her bag and some money. She opens the door, looks at the issue of *Le Monde*. 'What's so important on page seven for you to have several copies of the paper?' Henri says 'Nothing,' his voice a little too distant.

In front of the building, Suzy goes straight to the double parked waiting taxi, pays what is on the meter, making her apologies to the driver. 'We want to walk, it's so nice out.' The taxi leaves. Suzy takes Henri by the arm. 'We have all the time in the world. You might tell me my dress is pretty.' Henri puts on an accustomed, detached air. They walk in the direction of the theatre.

Suzy sees herself again, running, on the evening of Jean's death, along the same route. The theatre doorman had told her on the telephone, 'Come quickly, madame, Monsieur Jean has hurt himself.' On her brother's arm Suzy tells herself that wheels turn in both directions and stop, either one way or the other, any way at all really, quite by chance, and she would have liked 'to grow younger by one year every year' as Jean used to tell her every birthday. Suzy would have so liked to grow old with him. She clings to Henri's arm but it is in fact she who is guiding her brother. She says to him, 'Don't you find we look like a couple of old American tourists?' As usual Henri answers, 'Don't talk to me about them.' Then Suzy is quiet. Henri asks her 'Are you making fun of me?'

They come into the Place Saint-Augustin, pass by the Berteil shop window, the maker of Henri's felt hats. Suzy answers 'No, I'm just happy.' Here they are, arm in arm, brother and sister, who would believe it, a senior citizen miracle. The sky has cleared. A picture postcard sky and a setting sun. Suzy is thinking about her Wednesdays at the Saint-Ouen pool when the swimming teacher goes looking in his metal locker for the sign that he hangs on the two railings of the ladder to the diving

board, strings knotted on both sides and on which can be read
'NO DIVING WHEN POOL IS FULL'. It is generally around
3.30 p.m. when the bulk of the crowd is there, the little ones as
well as the big, crowding onto the diving board to leap, holding
their noses or diving head first, according to age and courage,
the bigger ones risking jumping on the little ones. Suzy sees, one
January Wednesday, a little girl they were reviving on the tiles
mouth to mouth. And those children who line up at the diving
board, pushing, shivering, bursting with laughter, they have
such beautiful teeth, until, at danger level, the swimming
teacher puts the sign up, then he has to chase away the kids
climbing over the sign. Then the other game begins. The
forbidden one. Suzy says to herself 'Like today.' Suzy looks at
her brother, 'You don't know anything about me really.' Henri
does not answer.

Then, along the Boulevard Malesherbes, a pretty dead
neighbourhood, like the stroll of a landlord and a perpetual
tenant, while Suzy thinks about Pilou. That's his nickname
'Pilou'! She wonders if he will come back in September, with
those almond green swimming trunks, so immodest, the
triangular beginning of pubic hair, that way that young man of
barely sixteen had of never looking at her, for some twenty
Wednesdays in a row while she, Suzy, was watching him, Pilou.
It's what, his real name? Pilou knows Suzy observes him. He
dives, comes out of the water, dives again, comes out again and
so on. He doesn't stop. And when, like a little girl, Suzy turns her
head so as not to burden the young man too much with her
stare, it is a sacrifice, because not only is she refusing herself a
pleasure but she also worries the young 'watched one', a massive
little being, muscled, his long hair wet and plastered to his neck,
who has an anxious way of watching without watching. Suzy
then tells herself that all Pilou's dives are for her and her alone,
the perilous leaps, the rolled bombs, or candlesticks. From her
post near the radiator, she watches him take his spring, she sees
him in profile, and marvels each time. It is as if all the children at
the pool were emerging, laughing and playing, out of her
womb, and Pilou the first, the very young man from last winter
who will perhaps turn into the young man of next autumn. Suzy
thinks 'perhaps' because the summer will 'perhaps not' return
her Pilou to her intact. Pilou who *never* goes into the booths and

whom she glimpses through the door of the 'Men's' showers, soaping himself, all covered with suds. And 'Devil knows' Jean had a puny physique, but Suzy did not think so. Love mattered and she stopped noticing. Now Suzy carries the image of Pilou, as she carried the image of Sylvain, Pipo and a certain Philippe. She tells herself Jean had been like them when he was sixteen and she would have so liked to take him in her arms at that age. It's good imagining just by watching the present. Suzy does not want to lose any of those dives dedicated to her, to her, the sister, fiancée, girlfriend or mother in the mind of the young man. The important thing is to be attentive. And to keep the image in the eye until September's goodbye, if goodbye there must be. Who is the voyeur of whom? Who is playing with whom? And Suzy on her brother's arm, they must now turn into the Rue Berlanger, soon at the theatre, she bursts into laughter. 'If you say nothing to me, my dear Henri, you will know me even less well.'

Suzy had exchanged looks with Pilou only on the first Wednesday. Since then he avoids it. They have never spoken to one another. Once they left the pool together, how soft and warm one feels at that moment as one goes out, especially in winter. Pilou had left running. Suzy sees Bertrand again, coming out of the river Baïse, the bathing place near Moncrabeau, naked, not covering his sex and throwing his aunt one of those kisses with his fingertips, violent and resonant for which he had a fancy and the secret. Jean used to say about this family's ways, 'It's only a drama folded up that won't stop unfolding. Listening to the music is enough. There is mine. Dissonant and in tune.' And in one of those letters that Bertrand had sent to Romain Leval, and which, by a provision of his will, were handed over to Jean, Bertrand had written 'My dear Romain. In hoping to live lovely days again, we forget too easily the happy day passing. I would so like to spend a day, one whole day with you. But, around me, they all say but. They hold me with that but, and I have chosen, as you know, not to flee, not to pretend, but, instead with *my* but, to be open and confront.' Suzy surprises herself at knowing these images and words by heart. The memory she did not have on stage she was to have then, in real life. Pilou, Romain, Bertrand and Jean, her men! Here is the theatre, the façade, the posters: 'Closed, re-opens in October', the date is not given nor the title. Suzy thinks 'It will be *Mortmain* and nothing else.' The doorman is watching TV. The stagedoor. He gets up, shakes hands with Suzy. 'Monsieur Stein just left.' He looks at Henri, greets him. 'We don't see you often enough at this door, Sir.'

Henri does not understand why his sister did not speak to him during the entire walk, why Suzy seemed so happy, so suddenly, why she is bringing him here, why Jacqueline, Bertrand? He was excited when he arrived at his sister's and wanted to tell her about Luc's promotion to the Legion of Honour. He had seen to it himself that the nomination did not remain for another year in the dossier of the present Minister of Industry and Commerce. He did what was necessary and had obtained a signature on what had to be signed. Honours have no other importance other than that there is a desire to give them by withholding them. Just as he thinks he has, by his family background, no influence except for some things in the present, to make things happen (he had not known how to love) and happen in a certain way — he had once had some power. Power. With Suzy still silent, clinging to his arm, as bent on not wanting to meet Jacqueline as getting lost in the apparently cheering thoughts of which she alone had the secret, he had remembered the subject assigned for his entrance exam to Sciences-Po. It was from Montesquieu. 'When in a country there is more advantage to paying court than to doing one's duty, all is lost.' There is no subject more dangerous because it has no wrinkles, nothing to seize hold of, and it is so obvious that it was called neither thesis nor antithesis and, still less, synthesis. Henri had remembered what he had written spontaneously, a rough draft, in the margin of a yellow sheet of paper, even before making an outline: 'Montequieu? smooth face'. He would therefore have to hold forth without going too far in the author's direction, taking a chance on angering those examiners who themselves had won their power by paying court and playing on the fact that each of them claimed, behind the scenes, to have done his duty. The subject was really the diplomacy of power, the art of creating a vacuum and never letting oneself to be situated anywhere. Pay court, or courts, and especially never take sides. Henri and Suzy were passing the window of the hatter in the Place Augustin. Henri had just realised that he had come out without hat or coat,

104

in a hurry, and happy because of the news in *Le Monde*. He was also thinking that Suzy had provoked him during the afternoon just so that she could conceal better, conceal everything as she always does, when evening comes.

Henri had passed his dissertation. He had composed it with the spirit of that Third Republic which, even in our own time, still underpins everything, more violently so because the underpinning is secret. In 1924, such attitudes were all the rage and were expressed in all kinds of hypocritical paradoxes that people rendered moral because they lacked the means to arm them politically, and differently. It was only a matter of proving in the preliminary exam the ability to adapt to the existing environment of politics, to take issue at the level of intentions and acts but above all not on the structural level. Into that dissertation Henri had slipped some perfectly smooth and yet flagrant thoughts, such as 'all the reasons for which we should rebuke ourselves are in fact all the reasons for which we like ourselves' or 'how does one manage so that sincerity is not taken for resentment and confession for vanity?' He was already saying 'we', and doubtless for that he passed with an honourable mention. He was saying it as well through fear of resentment and vanity, worry and a desire for power. He was already regulating his sincerity and the conduct of his pronouncements on the examples given by others and no longer on the image that he would give to others if he did not care about the resulting effect.

How cheerful Suzy had seemed during the walk, how pretty she looked in that white dress, with a fabric rose on one side at the waist, her purse in her hand. And how faded the purse seemed in relation to the rest, almost worn out. Suzy should have paid more attention to it. Henri had thought to himself with a feeling of happiness that he believed equal to, and of the same nature as his sister's that 'nothing has changed. And it's a miracle, even if France is living in political chaos.' He had then thought of Bertrand, so strong in not condemning, so convinced of the fragility of ideologies, who had chosen to combat everything 'in his heart of hearts' and 'in the bud' just as he had told him frankly about his sensuality: 'I have nothing to confess to you. Why would I confess to you something I don't consider wrong? I wish to live differently but in the same way as other people — don't get angry, you're one of them — who find their identity in indifference and make themselves the lackeys of established power. It is enough to feel the love another gives you and to love in return.' Henri had listened to Bertrand. He loved him in the way you can love an enemy. He also used to tell himself, an adage of good conscience, that Bertrand, by not voicing his desire to see society's structures altered, by asserting his will to be completely honest in his sensuality, would always have that benefit of the doubt of which every guilty person dreams when, at all costs, braving interrogations, trials and confrontations, he refuses to admit guilt. Not only did Bertrand seem more bent on belittling himself so that he could be at the Normale-Supérieure level than in caring about who knows what heights of learning and knowledge, not only did Bertrand not talk about either his intentions or his loves, but he would expound and justify his refusal to confess. Henri had a dangerous son. And sometimes when Bertrand would not show up at table for dinner, and stayed in his room with violent migraines, Henri would complain to Cécile, for the sake of form, but secretly he was pleased. There would indeed be some kind of guillotine for this guilty party for whom doubt was the only certainty, who inspired in Claire, Luc and Sébastien all sorts of 'You can't *be* sincere and *appear* to be sincere' feelings or say 'How do we know between the children and the parents, from us and you, what we inherit from each other.'

Henri had waited for the older children to get married, and for Romain Leval's suicide, which was prompted by the fear of being accused of corrupting a minor, before he attacked Bertrand. He had to be put back on the right track. Henri had known how to wait for the necessary moment. Having been dropped from the first government in 1958, they were duty bound to call him back at the first ministerial re-shuffle. Bertrand used to chase away Romain's memory by going out at night, every night. Henri had had him followed and he had been given the addresses of bars, baths, and told especially of parks and bushes in and around the edge of Paris, it always ended in vague places. Bertrand's face became gaunt. He had a hunted look about him. What he had just lost with the death of another being, Romain, twelve years his elder, he was seeking in the night and the confusion of furtive encounters under the double threat of the vice squad police and suburban hoodlums. Henri no longer dared speak to his son. All discourse had become pointless. Until the days in March when Bertrand was no longer leaving his room. Henri had visited him there, which was unusual, and, sitting on the edge of the bed, placing a hand on his son's burning forehead, had told him, 'You can't go on this way. I have something to suggest.' Undoubtedly, moved by his father's words and his gesture of affection, like a first gesture, finally, and a look too, one of those looks he had waited for above the cradle and was only made nineteen years later, Bertrand, moved, had listened to his father without suspicion. Today, so as not to feel guilty, Henri still tells himself that Bertrand knew, had understood, had chosen, had decided for himself, had taken the exam that he would pass hands down the first time, and then go to Barcelona for the scalpel's stroke.

Henri is not afraid of Suzy. She can do anything, say anything. Luc, Claire and Sébastien can attack. Henri has the certainty of always having acted out of love. A love turned entirely to himself. The stone can be cast at him. That insult would make him still more certain in his conviction that it was done for the love he felt and his desire to save a son. The surgeon in Barcelona was positive about the result and a cure. Henri smiles. At the foot of the staircase leading to the minor actors' dressing rooms, Suzy tells him 'Here's where Jean died. Come!' She takes him by the hand, pushes a door on which can be read 'SILENCE. NO SMOKING' and leads him into the wings. Behind the door, the lighting-board. Suzy lights everything, from left to right, from top to bottom, the levers are lowered one by one. In the theatre and on stage, wall lamps, chandeliers, footlights, spotlights, everything lights up, the theatre is flooded with light. Suzy takes a deep breath. The stage is still emptier than the house. The house decorated in red and grey velvet seems to look at the bare stage, the leprous back wall, the central door that opens onto the theatre's rear courtyard, conceived undoubtedly for an extraordinary bustle of scenery, belonging to shows in repertory. But Jean had a taste for single sets and for plays that would last the duration of a season, sometimes for two and often more. The scenery grew tattier by the day but the audience new at each performance did not realise it. Suzy takes a chair, places it in the middle of the stage and waves to her brother to go down to sit in the house. 'That's all, except for one little game, Henri. Which I want very much to play!' And she feels herself on stage, in performance, as in Bertrand's arms, coming out of the Baïse, or in Pilou's arms or Jean's. So many arms are coming out of her arms. She is in charge.

'Where,' silence, 'is,' silence, 'Bertrand?' Henri mumbles 'but . . .,' the start of a protest. Suzy knows very well where Bertrand is. Henri says nothing else. He sits up straight, elbows on the armrests, hands hanging. The fact that there's as much light in the house as on stage annoys him. He was expecting this question only too well. He would have preferred going to Jacqueline's, letting the two women meet and outnumber him, but giving himself up to neither one nor the other. It is Suzy's dress that has dragged him into accepting this evening's unfolding game, a white dress like the one she wore on his wedding day with Cécile. That day Cécile and Suzanne were both beautiful. Wedding days give women's faces and bodies more appeal and charm. When he was leaving the Saint-Ferdinand Church, standing at the top of the steps, they had to pose for the photographer, and Henri had hesitated between his wife and his sister. He had not realised then the love felt by Suzy and would feel only meagerly the unassuming, ever present love that Cécile was going to offer him. He would truly realise it only at that hopeless time when she would begin to lose her hair, during the final months, and make the first gestures of affection, but too late.

Henri closes his eyes. Opens them again. Suzy, on the stage, seated in the chair, her dress falling nicely on both sides, her hands crossed on her lap, her palms turned up toward the flies, sitting quite straight, waits for Henri to look at her to repeat even more distinctly 'Where,' silence, 'is,' silence, 'Bertrand?' and to add, in the same way, with the same caesuras, 'Is he still living?,' silence, 'and how?'

Henri looks at the empty seats in front of him, the orchestra boxes with those second row chairs that Jean used to call 'giraffes' and that had to be repaired so frequently. 'That's a good sign. They're laughing!' Henri, too, was in the second row, on the front steps of the Elysée Palace, en route for only seventeen months of office. Just long enough to make the necessary contacts with administration officials, a notch or two lower, who remain in office after the ministers and governments pass on. Just long enough then to enjoy his new functions, to pay off a few old debts without appearing to, and to hand out as many favours as he made splendid and incisive speeches. Just long enough finally to understand that in the game of portfolio distributions, you can win only once. It was 'the euphoria of the 60's'. You had quickly to relinquish the job to your successor, complete a few files and say to yourself, 'I'll have a minister's retirement.' So you remain a minister in people's minds because you have been one. You are one, even more one, when you have been one, than at the time you were one. Jean used to say of political men, 'They're only corpse worshippers. They have replicas everywhere. They reproduce themselves only in what is reproduced, identical copies, dead.' Henri sits up again in his seat. Memory is fleeting. You think it is failing and then it quotes to you precisely, spits in your face, and bursts out again, repeating what should have been listened to at the appropriate time.

Henri joins his hands, crosses his fingers under his chin. He looks Suzy straight in the eyes. The table is reserved for 8 o'clock at Taillevent's. When he left the Place d'Antioche, he had said to Bernadette 'Do you want me to turn on the television?' She still does not dare to do it alone. Bernadette answered, 'Thank you. No. I would just like to spend the evening in the living room, to open the French windows like Madame Suzy did this afternoon. It would please me just to be there. Especially today.' And Henri, *Le Monde* in his hand, had left quickly. The leash was hanging attached to the collar. Bernadette had closed the door so softly that Henri on the stair steps, hesitating, his step muffled by the carpet, hand on the railing, had not heard himself sigh.

On stage, Suzy murmurs, 'I love you, Riquet. You must listen to me.' Henri exclaims from the house, his voice clear, 'I'm listening to you, Suzy! Bertrand is at Moncrabeau and you know it. I also know that that is not the answer. I still know you are all accomplices, that you have left me alone in this affair. By reproaching me for taking responsibility, you have made me responsible. By accusing me of aggression, you have behaved as if you were the attacked. It's the inevitable role of the father, and of the elder brother. That's the way all of you, including Cécile, Bernadette and Pantalon, led me to do what I did. I don't like this stage production, here, now. I have never needed a stage to express myself. How do we know whether or not, Bertrand, incapacitated as he is, it's terrible to say but I happen to think it, isn't more in harmony with himself now than before. Just as I don't really recognise you since Jean's death. I have never seen you so good on stage. You are beautiful. I don't recognise myself either since Cécile's death. That was equally terrible but I began to really love her only when I understood that it was all over. There's an armchair at your place, in your living room, and an armchair at my place in mine. We have at least an armchair in common. Humour wasn't Jean's privilege. Humour is also enjoying being still. Are you happy now? I'm speaking to you. And you're wondering how you're going to answer back. You still believe you have to contradict in order to talk and just to exist. Just as Luc, Sébastien and Claire have chosen, by going away, to oppose my opinion. Back to you, Suzy, I'm returning the ball to you. The empty seats are listening. Don't you agree?'

For an instant Henri thought he would stop at the 'empty seats are listening,' as the end of his speech, but the exposed emptiness of the house had made him afraid, so he added the pointless 'Don't you agree?' This hesitation made Suzy smile. She crosses her legs, crosses her arms, pushes with her foot and rocks on the chair, oscillating, unconsciously playing with an equilibrium like Pilou when he takes his leap, springing a little, checking the flexibility and response of the diving board. There is the start of an echo, in empty theatres, the echo of plays that had no success, the echo of the wings laid bare. And in that position which is no longer that of a woman playing at being a woman, Suzy projects her voice clearly, the voice coming from the diaphragm, and says like a whiplash 'When everything is lit in this theatre, stage and house at the same time, each minute costs me a fortune. Nearly 800 francs an hour. That's expensive for a rehearsal. Unless we're playing the big confession scene, not the farewell scene, the big arrival one. Bravo, bravo Suzy! You can smile, my dear Riquet, I'm telling myself bravo. When you begin to put words, no longer in their usual place, everything becomes tempting, a new beginning to life, even if you say at first, in a small way, nothing but the opposite of what is said normally. I'm paying for the electricity at this moment. I'm almost paying dearly for having married a Lehmann. Suzy

110

Lehmann hyphen Prouillan, says to you: speak again, tonight I'm on offer. Nevertheless you can pay the bill at Taillevent. I'm offering you my dress. And my new shoes. You had a funny way of looking at my purse, at the corner of Rue Berlanger. So, since you owe me some fifty birthday presents, choose it in crocodile, a real crocodile so I can at least make a small stir when I go into the old folks home. That and Jean's manuscripts are all I'll have left. I'm not joking and you know it. If I sell the theatre, if I sell everything there won't even be enough to pay off the debts. They have just raised the rent at the Boulevard Haussmann, fifteen percent at one stroke. Rents are free to do what they want. Everything is free. Even you. You can leave if you want to, now. Maillot 53.39, it certainly won't be busy.'

Suzy stops rocking on the chair. She uncrosses her legs, sits up straight again, tips her face back, in the full light from the flies, and murmurs 'In the theatre you always rehearse in the dark. With one light bulb. Or two if the author wants to follow his script in the house. You rehearse in shadow. Did you know that? In fact the lighting is only set at the last minute. The director must take it into account. In the dark he must find the movements that belong to the light. And in this night the actors must also place their voices for broad daylight.' Suzy looks at Henri. 'It's what we've been doing for twenty years, isn't it?'

'In this house, the more you murmur, the better you're heard. It's a real house and *that* is our theatre. So you get a little dizzy.' Silence. Suzy strokes her arms, then in turn her wrists. She lowers her eyes. 'I have nothing more, Riquet. Nothing more to continue. I need money.' She looks at her brother. 'I want to continue!' She smiles. 'I want Jean's plays to be played. Tonight when I go home, I'll read the manuscript I took out of your hands a little while ago. Like my dress, the shoes and not the purse, I want something new, original, and not left over. *The Collision* is finished. It will be, I know, *Mortmain* and you are going to give me the money I need to produce this play. You want to know, you too, not why but how, how everything could get all rolled up so it never stops unrolling. That's Jean. You know it. Your little Jew will have the first word.'

Suzy rises. Henri has leaned forward, his forearms on the back of the seat in front of him. Suzy circles the chair, lifts it, whirls it around at arms' length, a curious *pas de deux*. Then she stops, sets the chair askew. Henri would like to get up, but if he gets up he is accepting. Suzy goes and leans her back against the rear wall of the stage, a brick wall, shreds of posters. She has picked up her purse. She has just lit a cigarette. She throws the purse on the floor in front of her, towards Henri. She seems far away, way at the back, Henri says to himself she is like an old whore who no longer expects to get a customer. He cries out, 'Are you finished?' Suzy answers, 'Speak normally. You didn't understand me then? It's the theatre that needs it. The idea that you'll be in theatre. I'll wait until it's full of cigarette butts around me for you to tell me yes. No more customers? You're the last one. Go on, Riquet. The ball's with you.' Suzy bursts into laughter and smokes making extravagant gestures.

Then Henri rises, turns his back to the stage, takes a few steps up the centre aisle, stops, hesitates, wants to face up to her, but no, he continues, head down, and with both hands pushes open the orchestra's double doors, and disappears. From the back of the stage Suzy waits for him. She does not need to see him to know he is going up to the foyer, walking alongside the bar, taking the stairway to the second balcony, stopping, coming back down, going from one end to the other of the semi-circular corridor, looking distractedly at the little frames on the wall between the boxes with designs of sets and costumes for all the plays created and produced by Jean. He is taking a walk. He is getting some air. He is reflecting and that's all the better. Suzy, from the Boulevard Haussman, would hear someone enter her theatre at night, could track him, keep an eye on him. But in a theatre emptied of its audience, there is nothing to steal but worn velvet, red velvet, that red caressed by footsteps, hands, looks and which has never seen any light but theatre lighting, 'the only kind perhaps for truly lighting life,' one of Jean's sayings. This colour, Suzy wraps herself in it with her look. She inhales its theatre scent. Autumn will start here too. And suppose Pilou were diving from the second balcony? She smiles. Almond green trunks. She calls for help to her men, a cigarette puff to one, a cigarette puff to the other, she is smoking nervously. Henri is behind the entry door to the balcony. He will come back. He needed to be above her to be able to talk back.

Henri comes back. He comes down the few steps of the first

112

balcony and stands, facing Suzy who pretends not to see him, turns her head to the right, to the left, as if there were people in the wings, so many witnesses ready to burst in suddenly, so many actors worried about missing their entrances. For Henri the sensation is strange. He has often found himself in front of an audience denouncing in his mind the lies in the political speech he was about to make, the illusion of promises, underlining in advance the danger inherent in the 'successful technique, when speaking to fools, slandering opponents and mixing issues.' But here the seats are empty. The empty seats are turning their backs to him. They are listening but they seem to be listening only to Suzy. How many times, before halls crowded with notables, bald pates, grey and white hair, sleeping or elegantly dozing, has the ex-minister, academician of the sciences called moral and political, assured of retirement and honours, been able also to point to the ravages of political chaos; to say that 'ideas are not independent of the men who bring them into the world', to suggest that 'ideologies are not the fireflies of History'; to stress, the day after some particular election that the results expressed more and more clearly 'the growing discredit of the major parties' political practices', a discredit in which 'the left appears to participate less, but that's only an appearance'; to hail the opening of the minor electoral rolls proving that more than two million French people 'hope to change the rules of the political game', to scoff at the ascension of women in governments and to exclaim that 'the image of the reassuring mother serves well in a period of crisis and concern'. Henri has never been listened to. The audience facing him would pull itself out of its torpor only to applaud on principle. So there was neither a new Right nor an old Left, only politicians attached to a game, outside of social reality and entirely devoted to whatever they considered essential, holding on to their influence, having nothing but influence. The 'more than two million French people' whom Henri cited as an example and who wanted 'to change the rules of the political game' were, if one realised it in advance, composed only of those intellectuals, who do nothing but conceptualise and who always retreated before reality. And so forth. Henri repeats to himself the subject he wrote about in 1924. 'When in a country there is more to be gained by paying court than by doing one's duty, all is lost.'

He must be having a laugh, Montesquieu, in his grave. Henri shakes his head as if he wanted to abolish his thoughts, his images. A man of the Right, him? No. A man of roots and of heritage? Yes. Today he says to himself that even when he was doing his duty, the others, by not listening to him, made him pay his court. Each time he took the risk of analysis and relevance, as well as the risk of predicting the crisis which could only succeed the euphoria, he was only playing the game of the well-meaning who denounce current events, make pronouncements only to obliterate reality without realising it, who underline in order to erase, who inform in order to deceive, and bury the truth. The celebration goes on. Bravo Etienne Marcel and bravo Suzy! Henri lifts his head again, puts his hands on the edge of the balcony like an animal that has just drunk, and murmurs, 'Ask me anything you want, Suzy. I'll give it to you.'

Suzy crushes out her cigarette butt with the ball of her foot, lights another. On her bare back, between the sequinned straps, she feels the cold of the bricks in the back wall. In a film, she once saw a woman rise from a table, her back marked by the pattern of the metal chair she had been sitting on. It was funny. Henri clarifies 'Anything. But I don't want your cousin managing the money I'll lend you.' Silence. Suzy smiles. Henri goes on. 'I only want the right to look. I have nothing against David. I trust him too much. And you too. You too, Suzy, don't I? Say yes!' Suzy mumbles 'yes' and, laughing, she begins to walk around the chair, another ballet. She is dancing. It's a little ridiculous, she knows. It's a good moment and she is living it without thinking about what she is doing. A need to move. She comes back upstage, leans her back against the wall again, two three cigarette puffs, she reflects, shrugs, raises her head, looks at the flies, the spotlights. There are still some drops hanging and in particular the backdrop, in black velvet which has not come down since Jean's death. They had placed his coffin there, almost where the chair is, and the passing mourners, in hommage, all came in through the stagedoor. Suzy looks at her brother, way above, overhanging, and points her finger at him. 'But tomorrow you won't let me down? You won't tell me you don't have any money?' Henri answers 'Promise.' He turns, climbs the steps of the first balcony. 'I'm coming.'

As soon as the first balcony door has reclosed, Suzy sits down on the chair, in a three-quarter position, an elbow on the back as if she were about to begin sobbing. This house, this theatre has just won another match, and she, inside it like a ball in an empty suitcase, an image from a nightmare, that nightmare she has when nothing is going well anymore. She is walking on a station platform, a suitcase in her hand, a ball in the suitcase that doesn't stop bouncing against the sides, and Suzy knows, in the dream, that Jean is waiting for her at the end of the voyage but there is no train, and there is only the platform, which is endless.

Henri tells himself, a secret confession, a rectification, that he has never known how to live through an experience except after he has lived through it and that in this way he is of the eternal Right, so little new, but especially tenacious. He says out loud, coming down the staircase leading to the orchestra seats 'We know how to live only after we've lived through something. That's what holds us from generation to generation. That's what condemned you, Bertrand.' Henri would like to feel proud of what he had just said, unheard.

A temporary set of steps, at the end of the centre aisle, a few steps up and the stage. Henri kisses his sister on the forehead. 'Don't be afraid. We're going to be ruined together.' Suzy rises. Henri follows her. One by one Suzy lowers the levers of the lighting board, it is night, little by little, she closes the electric cage, takes her brother's hand. 'Come, it's this way, careful, there are two steps, you have to turn left.'

From the doorman's office she telephones David. 'Luce? It's Suzy.' Silence. 'Yes, I bought the dress. We'll talk about it later. Will you just tell David to cancel everything and to make an appoint with Ferrier for a reading. I really am saying a reading. Yes, an unpublished play of Jean's. Tomorrow at my place. Thanks.' Suzy hangs up, shakes the doorman's hand and says to Henri, 'Let's go. I'm hungry.'

8

Eight p.m. Bernadette has finished putting everything away but that is just a manner of speaking. She says it to herself every time. She also used to say it to Pantalon rather than in the emptiness of the pantry or the kitchen. When everything is put away, cleaned, placed, scrubbed, clean, tidy, it has to start all over again. Bernadette used to say, laughing, when Madame reproached her for forgetting something, 'This house is like the Eiffel Tower!' Cécile never had the curiosity to know where this image came from. Bernadette, shortly after her arrival in Paris, Luc had just been born, had learned to read in an issue of *Illustration* in which an article was devoted to the 'Painters of the Eiffel Tower,' those 'itinerant acrobats' and 'lovers of the void' who 'as soon as they reach the top had to begin painting all over again at the bottom.' Some years later, on a Thursday afternoon, Bernadette had taken the three oldest children to visit the tower, and with orders to go up only as far as the 'second level and no higher', she had kept an eye out for the workmen suspended from the girders, as in the photos, but had not seen them. Perhaps they were all the way up at the top.

At this early hour of the evening, the French windows in the living room were wide open, all the lights were on, too bad, Monsieur won't be back for quite some time, Bernadette tells herself, everything is put away, that she is at the top, all the way at the top, and she never wants to start anything over again. You do not forget the textbooks in which you learned to read. Bernadette even has the impression of having read only one, that one. She takes a seat in Cécile's armchair. With an unconscious gesture she reaches to pet Pantalon's head, as Madame used to do, toward the end, without even looking at the dog, for the contact.

Bernadette feels good about being abandoned. If the dog is no longer here, what good is it going on? Didn't she hear Luc say in 1968, shortly before his vacation, at an animated lunch,

Sébastien passing through Paris was pounding on the table with his fists, and Monsieur seemed quite reassured, 'After all, what do they want to change? From now on the servants are supermarket cashiers.' Sébastien had called his brother an 'ass' and added, 'What's more, you're right.' And turning to the dog 'Isn't that so, Pantalon?' Bursts of laughter. This family's witness, Bernadette often had the impression of playing a more important role than the one which had in general fallen to her. When she used to serve the table, her arrival with dishes would almost always interrupt a conversation which, according to Luc, Sébastien, Claire or Bertrand, 'was off to a bad start' or 'would lead nowhere.' With a single look the children told her a sort of thank you for arriving at the right moment. And when Henri would ask dramatic questions about their quarterly report cards, about 'too poor results in French composition,' he would have preferred his children always to come first, Bernadette would stay in the corner of the dining room, with no reason for being there, to annoy Monsieur and to calm his ire. Even Cécile used to thank her. The performance of service. The servant in *The Collision,* also always entered when it was not necessary but she spoke too much, whilst in reality she, Bernadette, chose to speak by remaining silent.

Tonight the silence is even more respected and even more silent since Pantalon is no longer here, in the lighted living room, all opened onto the square, and takes a 'deep, dead lungful' as Bertrand used to say when someone would open the windows. Bernadette tells herself she is still playing a role even if the lyre chairs, the dagobert chairs, the wing chairs, the two sofas and the armchairs are empty. So many years spent 'watching out, watching over, watching kindly', Cécile's motto, to arrive at this point, with apparently no one to talk to anymore, with the forbidden memory of Moncrabeau, a name that must no longer be pronounced, since no one ever brings it up, since Bertrand stays there 'watched over, well-watched, guarded' by Merced and Lucio, Juan their son, a few months older than Bertrand, and Jeanne their daughter-in-law, Aunt Augustine's grandniece by marriage, and so on. Everything is bound together, everything holds, the gatherings, the servants and the served. In order to play out her role in this family, to play it fully, with sensuality, a revenge for the cradling she missed with little

Colas, remembering Lucien at the grape harvests, Bernadette has created for herself a fully formed skein of memories, always waiting and ready, always at hand, a strong memory of what is said and especially of what was not and of what remains to be said. Alone in the living room, making use of Madame's chair and unable to keep from feeling devilishly alive, seventy-four and a half years old, she speaks alone and to each of them. The living room is empty, at last she has the floor. The floor will be heard.

She addresses Cécile first, 'I don't like your calling the money you gave me wages. A wage isn't nice, Madame. It's punishment or an escape. Wages or baggage, I'm going to go away. With 71,712 francs and a savings account book you can go back to Auzan and make a little place for yourself. Do you hear, Madame? I'm speaking to you!' Bernadette turns her head in the direction of the fireplace, Sébastien often used to stand there, leaning on his elbows, feet crossed, as if on a courtesy call, 'And you? Where are you? I can't see a boat on television without thinking of you. When it rains in Paris in the winter, I say to myself there's a storm at sea. How is it, the sea, and what is it? You had promised to take me to see it at least once!' Bernadette lowers her eyes, looks at the rug between the pedestal tables. She murmurs 'Pantalon?' then more clearly 'Pantalon! Come on, we're going for a walk! You're going to tell me what you saw when they pricked you. Did you really fall asleep without knowing anything? I don't believe it. That must be terrible. Like when my father pulled the medal out of my throat that I used to wear around my neck and that I sucked all the time? A funny feeling. Like when Colas was born. Do you hear, Pantalon? Was it like that for you this morning?' Bernadette sits up again in the armchair, hands flat on her lap, and speaks to Claire, 'Put your feet on the floor, you're going to soil the sofa and your mother will scold me for it. Quick, go fix your hair, your father's going to be home, we mustn't make him angry. Recite the end of the poem, please, you always make a mistake, it's hard but you just have to think about what you're saying, go on, with me, "If we capsize, there's no coming back, with our oars, ready to turn, into the wind we tack," you see, it's simple when you hold on to the image. Imagine it's Sébastien saying it, this poem.' Bernadette smiles to herself and turns toward Luc. 'Look at me. Why do you lower your eyes to me?

119

You always make me feel guilty for the favours I do you. You leave me all alone, dear, if you don't answer me. If you call me in a little while, I'll come right away, theoretically because I am paid to, and in reality because I love you. And because at the beginning you replaced Colas. I secretly called you Colas. Were you listening? Well, raise your eyes, look at me now . . .'

Nothing to be done, Bernadette tells herself there is nothing to be done with these people and yet she is here, so she continues. She sees Jean. 'Stop smiling and taking notes, Monsieur Jean. Too much watching is not good. And too much listening. That hurts, you hurt yourself, it ends up going to your head. And it's by his head that my father chose to depart. He used to watch too much, listen too much. He'd lost his wife. He talked to her all the time, like I'm doing now. All he had left was the elm tree. And his sister Augustine, the day of the burial, had the branch he hanged himself on sawn off. Afterwards, *I* was there, alone with the farm, the tree and the cut off branch, a large supporting branch, so large and so beautiful that Madame Cécile the day of their first visit took it for a bench and sat on it while I went to get her something to drink. Water from the well. And at the bottom of the well I saw myself. I was as beautiful as that woman with the parasol was. Are you satisfied? Did you get everything down?' Bernadette laughs gently and takes Suzy as a witness, 'He got everything down! And if it's ever in a play, invite me, but in the evening. I would like to see a play at night. And the people who go to the theatre at night!' Bernadette hesitates. It's dangerous talking in the emptiness, but it's good.

That leaves the master. She begins speaking louder pointing her finger at random. 'Stop telling me the ironed shirt has a fold in the back! It's ironed by hand and when it's ironed by hand a fold is necessary for it to be perfect.' 'Stop pestering me with buttons not being sewn on. It had to be said! And the cufflinks no longer in sets, you should have put them away yourself! Rounding off to the penny? I don't like asking for little receipts at every store. Do your shopping yourself! You'll see, prices are exploding and I do my best. Yes, sir. You can make fists in your pockets, you're pulling your coat all out of shape. That's all. Everything you touch is out of shape,' 'Stop loving people only after they've left! At that game, I'm going to leave too. From Auzan to Moncrabeau there are some beautiful little paths, birch woods, poplars, all that with WARNING and UNDER REPAIR, that's from Bertrand. I'll bring him the leash and collar. That's proof of all you're capable of. You! Monsieur! Henri!'

Bernadette puts her hands together, fingers interlaced. She is delighted now. Nothing is said but everything is said. Monsieur had telephoned to that Mademoiselle Jacqueline after coming home from the barber's, did that mean dinner for three? But that Mademoiselle Jacqueline, who all the same left quite another perfume on the bath towels, had called back a few minutes ago, 'Did Monsieur Prouillan return home?' 'No, Madame. May I leave him a message?' Mademoiselle Jacqueline had hung up, not believing she was recognised, but the more the years go by, the more one remembers. The memory for voices is so much longer than for faces. Monsieur must have been alone with Madame Suzanne. So much the better. Bernadette points a finger one last time at her employer 'And stop believing you can do what you like! I'm not letting you do what you like anymore!' Bernadette rises abruptly as if wanting to hide from the others, those others with whom she had just surrounded herself, now upright, she goes straight to the balcony and stands there, hands grasping the railing, just as Monsieur had stood there the night of Barcelona, and in the empty square, there are no lights at the windows, only city lights, nothing else, she utters a 'Bertrand' then louder 'Bertrand?'

Eight p.m. Antoine says, 'It's crazy, we ate so early, we were dying of hunger. How about a game of bridge?' Eliane sets the places with the breakfast bowls, the sugar, spoons and the knife for the butter. When she places the knife on the table, Luc turns his head away. Christine approaches Luc, kisses him on the neck, looks at Antoine and Eliane. 'Suppose we go to bed early, once won't do any harm.' She straightens up and stays standing, her hands on Luc's shoulders. Luc looks at her, tries to smile. Christine says to him 'Don't you want to?' Luc does not answer. Without asking anything more Antoine goes to get the game board, places it on the other end of the table at an angle, installs the chairs, paper, pencil, one column 'them', one column 'us', and the two decks of cards. He mumbles 'We draw for the deal.' A ritual, each takes his place. Eliane facing Antoine, Christine facing Luc. Christine deals. The bids: Christine 'One heart,'

Eliane 'I pass,' Luc 'Four Hearts!' Antoine 'It's starting well. You open Eliane.' Christine smiles. Eliane throws out a five of spades. Luc lays his hand: fourteen points, two fifth trumps in hearts. Christine feels like saying 'And the slam, then?' But Luc rises, looks at his three friends. 'I feel like being the dummy just now. It's a sure hand. I'm going to get some air. I'll be back.' And in front of the door of the house, feeling oppressed, abruptly, he had never expected to reach the door of this house, this strange house, this strange district, the night bristling with hundred-year-old trees, he turns toward the southwest. He inhales, takes a breath, takes a few steps, lowers his head, gives the ground a couple of kicks then stares at the sky, the moon rising over the horizon of trees, and the southwest again. A voice rises in him that he recognises, a voice from before the second part of his life, his child's voice, his brother's voice, the voice goes out of him, despite himself, a nausea or a joy, abandoned, he calls 'Bertrand' then louder 'Bertrand?'

Eight p.m. On table seven at Taillevent's, a round table, the maitre d'hotel places a little square sign on which can be read 'Reserved.' That is seldom done but there are few reservations, in the July desert, and he might as well use the signs. The maitre d'hotel goes to the cashier, his mind at rest, 'Is it two or three for table seven?'

Eight p.m. Loïc's girlfriend is named Stéphanie. Claire understood immediately that it was not the young girl's real name. Dinner is ready. In the car coming back up to Sauveterre they all five laughed. Claire was in the back between Yves and Géraldine, Loïc was watching her in the rearview mirror. Intimidated, Stéphanie said nothing. Claire would have liked her to be prettier. Loïc had asked his mother 'Where's your sleeping bag?' Géraldine 'Are you a hippie? That's out of style' and Yves, holding Claire's hand, 'Watch out. You can get yourself raped hitchhiking.' So here they are all together again, with already for Claire, through Stéphanie's presence, the idea of a departure, then of two, then three. Claire would not want to be jealous of her sons' girlfriends. She controls her feelings and draws from them a sense of sensuality as inevitable. A mother is made only to be quartered and pillaged. Letting oneself be pillaged is not necessarily a game of masochism but simply a fact of generosity. Tonight Claire feels herself gnawed, taken, held, completed and more whole than ever. They are here, they are grown up, they are themselves, he, and she. They meet in the Rue des Beaux-Arts, they each hesitate to step in front of the other, and they bump. Claire wishes she were able to explain all that to her children, but she cannot explain by explaining, nor make use of reasonings that never contain the essential, the very nature of an initial surge, the rupture's unimportance revealed by an accidental death. Gérard is still here. Claire still has on the tip of her tongue that word of reunion and gentleness that would have erased the memory of the quarrel of the night before, the night before an accident that is just an item in the newspapers. There are continuities that escape destiny. Bertrand used to say 'The opposite of fate, a word used by fools, is fête, a celebration by eating, a superb word whose use must be protected.' Dinner is ready, the table set. Claire goes in, out, goes back into the house. She is afraid she has forgotten a detail, the bread, salt, bottle opener. Loïc uncorks the wine, the bottle between his thighs, he loves making the corks pop. Claire puts the napkins and tableware on for dessert. It is always Yves who cuts the tart or cake. Géraldine passes the plates keeping an eye on the size of each piece.

When Claire found herself alone at Sauveterre, she believed, in the mid-sixties, that her children would never be able to live or share any of the tenacious feelings that bound her, and still bind her, to their father. She was afraid of a conflict. She feared that they would not learn to read in the way she had learned, she had fears of all kinds inspired by the bad reports in the papers of events and scandals, having given herself over to a journalism devoted to emphasising threats rather than describing real life. Caught up in the general anxiety, in the anguishes of sleepless nights, Claire imagined that her children would leave her without a word, would take to drugs, would indulge in all sorts of strange practices, of phoney trips then in fashion, that they would become advertising and marketing victims. Until one day shortly after '68, when she realised that by no longer worrying about anything she could give neither shock value nor a sense of the forbidden to their juvenile displays, that so-called youthful exaggeration, totally self-involved, alienated, and which was shutting itself up, as in a prison, in the word liberty, confused with the word anarchy. Natural good sense would prevail.

123

Today, observing Loïc and Yves, Stéphanie and Géraldine, Claire tells herself that by not worrying about things, she has not shown herself to be reactionary, in the worn out sense of the Prouillans, but to welcome fresh air, the only true political principle. Getting out of the car, Loïc had said into his mother's ear, very softly, not to be overheard by the others and especially not by Stéphanie, 'She isn't pretty but I find a charm in her. I like the way she irritates Yves and Géraldine.' A few minutes later while the other three had gone up to the bedrooms, kissing his mother's hands, with a burst of laughter, Yves had confided to Claire, 'I saw Stéphanie's identity card. Her real name's Myriam. I warn you right off the guillotine's going to fall. Loïc will pay dearly for leaving me alone with Géraldine,' then, 'May I put on some music?' Géraldine had quickly come back downstairs, looking stubborn and indifferent, a look Claire recognised too well as her own. And in front of her daughter Claire had sniggered, a sniggering rather like in the days at Moncrabeau when their parents were leaving for Condom, Fleurance or Castelnau, paying duty visits to friends and neighbours. Bertrand used to say 'Long live liberty!' This word, at that time, had a sense that involved all kinds of restraints and disciplines. Claire sees Géraldine shrugging her shoulders because her mother has just sniggered, passing in front of her without a word. But once outside Géraldine smiles at her mother.

Here now in front of the house, dinner is ready, everything is ready. Claire watches Géraldine at the top of the hill, alone. She tells herself her children have had a narrow escape, and, a paradox, she would like not to amuse herself anymore with the feeling that their love affairs, in a new generation, have become again courtly, beyond Hurelevent, the little princes and little princesses of Cleves. The countryside is beautiful and spread out. The line of the Lubéron to the south is clear, like a black stroke outlining the sky, a limit behind which there would be only a great void and space. Claire takes a deep breath. It's the count-down. In three years at the most they will no longer be here, or worse still they will have multiplied. And she, Claire, will have to renew her face and some of her roots. But where, and how? Claire realises for the first time that, for her, Gérard died yesterday, only yesterday. She would have to admit perhaps that time had passed and that her mourning clothes, never worn, are now unwearable. The years of her children's growing up, a perfect, intact nucleus, were about to be succeeded by the years of dispersal, by crossroads, roads leading in all directions leaving her on the roadside, an image, a little image an instant later, Géraldine is now coming back down the hill, her usual round trip, pouting, Loïc pours himself something to drink, Yves puts on another record, Stéphanie cries 'I'm coming,' she's without anyone to give her a lift, to bring her back up to the house, to talk about sleeping bags, fashions, rape, with no one to play the adolescent game again. Claire is afraid of finding herself old, all of a sudden. She will have to let go. Vertigo.

Claire goes back into the house. Yves says to her 'What's the matter? All of a sudden you're pale.' Loïc takes her by the arm. 'Mama? Do you hear us?' She no longer knows which of the two is Gérard, neither of them obviously. Her sons seat her in an armchair near the fireplace. The chair where Cécile stayed during her last visit, saying 'From here I can see the foliage, thank you.' Brief, secret images, the only ones perhaps to indicate, to give the direction. Yves turns down the music, kneels before his mother. Without realising it, Claire tells him softly, pinching his cheek. 'You should shave before dinner.' Loïc holds a glass of water. 'You mustn't startle us like that, Mama. What happened?' Claire smiles. 'Nothing. I'm just happy. That's it exactly. It's the way it should be. It's inevitable.' Loïc kisses his mother on the forehead. 'Inevitable how, Mama?' Géraldine stands in the doorway. Stéphanie has stopped short, at the foot of the stairs and sits down on the last step. Yves looks at Loïc, Géraldine, Stéphanie and his mother. 'So? How inevitable? I've never seen you like this, Mama, say something.' Claire rises, smiles, rubs her arms, a chilly gesture 'Excuse me, it's the first time I'm asking you to excuse me.' To Stéphanie, 'You can't understand.' To her children, 'I'm afraid I've forgotten someone these last years. And it isn't your father. Your father, on the contrary . . .' She approaches the door. Géraldine takes her hand the way Yves did in the car. She looks at the setting sun, in the west. Over there. Far away. She murmurs 'I . . .' then, 'No . . .' and turning around to the inside of her house, looks at them all, her voice sharper, a diversion now, 'I want to take a shower, to fix my hair, make myself pretty. A little effort. For a change. I'm making a date with you for a quarter of an hour from now, right here. And we'll pretend that . . .' She smiles, strokes Géraldine's hand and heads for the studio, the last words punctuating her exit 'pretend that . . .'

Yves watches Géraldine, his look flabbergasted. Géraldine murmurs, 'You can't understand.' Loïc opens the refrigerator door, 'I'm hungry.' He looks at Stéphanie 'How about you?' 'Me? I'm wondering what I'm doing here. Is your mother always like that?' Loïc keeps an eye on Yves and Géraldine. They were going to exchange a smile and he surprised them.

The staircase, the little corridor, the door with the glass window, the studio and the canvasses turned against the wall, the mattress on the floor, the bedspread of blue cotton, very neat, not a wrinkle and the puffiness of the two pillows, one for Gérard, one for her, one pillow for her head and the other to lock against her belly all night long, some books in a pile around the bedside lamp, and the white wire that snakes over to the wall and plugs in there, the books recommended by Marc and Marguerite, her bookseller friends in Apt, those books she would like to read so lovingly but of which she only ever skims the first few pages, feeling in peril of abandoning the specific text of her own life and losing contact with it. Claire has just given herself a few minutes respite, because of a fear of saying too much, for everything becomes inexplicable finally, and family instinct is to explain everything, everything and too much, when there is no real choice but to be silent and hide things away so that you can still be on your guard. Claire often tells herself that, in the final analysis, as in a final recourse to grace, there are only two categories of human being: those who wait and those who can wait no longer. Those who wait can read, listen, endure the others, but they do not read for fear of losing that small hope for which they are always waiting. And those who do not wait should read, so as to be able to observe life through other texts, finding relevance in whatever poetry there is, in the mutilation of their lives, in their failures or even their egotism (and they are the ones who devour, criticise, judge, celebrate and attack), in love as well, and even in love by omission. Claire buys books, especially novels, so as not to read them. But they are here and in the secret of their uncut pages, they are ready to bear witness. They are here for help 'Just in case!' Claire has just said out loud,

'Just in case!' just as she called out her 'pretend that' when she left. Claire says to herself that the heart's reason is not reasonable. Once again you must definitely not explain things. Entering the studio she sees the bedside books, the table in front of the window, the closed drawer, with the written message from that afternoon. She has remembered, recalled. 'Tattle tale!' Bertrand used to yell at her when she went to complain to Bernadette about a slap or a brotherly insult. The text of a life bears with difficulty the insult of writing about it. One would have to classify, prune, re-write, and from only a single point of view see the past in a new light, like a sun rising or setting, and take your pick. Claire smiles at the thought.

In the shower she takes care not to wet her hair. She should get in touch with Martine and Léa and forget about Rians, visit the Schulterbranks, make new or re-make old friends and leave her children before they leave her. But drying herself with a bath towel, she shakes her head. Impossible. She rubs her legs. She sees Gérard again, crouched before her, herself naked, seated on the edge of the bed in Paris, and Gérard is telling her 'I love your knees.' 'I'm mad about your knees' or 'may I kiss them?' Claire could not bear and still cannot bear to be touched there. The memory, perhaps of Sébastien's hand under the table to make her laugh, the memory too of falling on the roadsides when she used to run after her brothers, around the house at Moncrabeau, her knees cut by the flints. Very gently Gérard would place his hands flat on the knees of the one he called his 'little warrior' and would tell her 'Don't move. Let me caress them. They're perfect.'

Claire folds the bath towel and quickly arranges her hair. Braids like the old days, very tight, that she puts into a chignon behind, and in front her hair is pulled back evenly leaving her forehead bare. She is going to speak to her children. She wants to be beautiful. Beauty is a help when one has to face up to something. Claire hums the *Bal chez Temporel*. She remembers the tune but not the words. Perhaps on that account she will never write the novel of her life. But now, another image, she sees herself again in the real estate agent's car, Madame Plomé, heading for Sauveterre, on the first visit, and the lady in question, with white hair, an old witch, between middle and old age, a nervous driver, the tires squealing on the turns, forcing

127

her Southern accent a little as if that would create more confidence, explaining that in the old days that was 'the main road from Forcalquier to Sault' and that often on the narrow curves carriages would collide. 'The horses would crush other horses. I have an engraving, I'll show it to you.' Madam Plomé could not know. Sauveterre is that road. And a while before in the backseat of the car, wedged between Yves and Géraldine, held by Yves, Claire had once again seen, not imagined, but really seen, the tangle of the harnessed animals, the horses pawing the ground and smashing against each other.

A dress, a real one with a belt, the waist emphasised, cut low, this beige dress that Claire had bought last year without knowing very well why, that she has never worn and that tonight has a role to play. Shoes, real ones, simple in white leather, it's the end of sandals at Sauveterre. A look in the mirror over the sink, a furtive look, Claire is afraid of not recognising herself. She is ready. As she goes by she turns a canvas around, then two, then three. After dinner she will begin painting again. But she knows that all that, a respite, is the expression of her fear of a commitment. They are waiting downstairs. They are waiting and they are hungry. A final pretext, to be her own secret, she opens the drawer of the table before the window, takes out a page of white paper on which, bent over, she scribbles without even thinking about it, 'Incapable of taking delight in what I have done, I can only torment myself with what I have to do. That's it, the inevitable!' With an exclamation point. Like Bertrand. Rightly so Bertrand, today, July 9th. Claire puts the scribbled page away with the other pages written that afternoon. She slams the drawer shut and quickly leaves the studio. On the stairs the hem of her dress tickles her knees slightly. She had forgotten this sensation.

They are all at the table, all four of them. Stéphanie is pouting. It takes time to become part of a family. Jean used to say, 'And it's always for ever.' Under the eyes of her children, their smiles, like in a game about to begin, for one evening more and for few others to come, Claire takes her place at the end of the table. On her plate is a small package. Géraldine: 'It's a present from the three of us.' Loïc jokes 'From "The Three of Us," the magazine for the modern couple!' Yves seated at a three-quarter angle in his chair turns toward his mother, stroking his closely shaved chin. 'We thought you'd need it.' Claire opens the package. A watch. Stéphanie says, 'It's beautiful.' Silence. Claire puts the watch on her wrist, says, 'Thank you,' then, 'Thank you very much.' Claire passes the salad of green beans around. 'The first of the season.' Yves holds the bread basket out to Géraldine, to Loïc, to his mother and to Stéphanie. 'Bread, Myriam?' The watch goes tick tock. Claire does not like that noise. But she smiles. Then she murmurs, 'A while ago I frightened you. I was afraid. I thought of your uncle. Not Sébastien. Nor Luc. I was thinking of Bertrand,' louder, 'Bertrand!'

Two o'clock in the afternoon, local time, 82 Amelia Street, Toronto. A brick building, third floor, the left-hand door, a doormat on which can be read 'Welcome'. Ruth is coming back up the stairs, the mail in her hand. She has just given four hours of dance classes, 'One, two!' 'one, two three!' the last classes of the year. For her students it is already vacation time. No matter how much she had kept time with her hands, her foot, signalled the accompanist to hit the notes harder on the piano, she could not in four hours, with four different groups, control a single ensemble, rhythmically. For Ruth begins every day the same way and without classes to take, they are frustrating. She does not remember a single day without dancing since she was six, when her mother took her to the Ellery Dancing School for the first time, hiding it from her father who was against it, against everything that involved nudity. Even classical dance for him was nothing but a striptease. Ruth smiles opening the door of her apartment and thinks that, after all that's happened in thirty-five years, her father wasn't wrong. She does not dance anymore. The companies engage young girls and abandon them as soon as they are no longer young enough. The younger ones quickly show up the older ones. Short of making a career as a soloist or being able, one in a thousand, still to dance *The Dying Swan* at 65, or older, and multiplying your farewells, there is no solution but to put yourself on the shelf before they do, to teach, to spot in others, always younger, the movements, agility and leaps that were distinctive in you, and that can finally be admired by admiring oneself, and can be seen being born. Then one is reborn.

The classes that day were disorganised. Boys and girls between twelve and fifteen years old, so inattentive, were doing anything they felt like with helterskelter individual rhythms. Ruth sums up for herself what she always thinks on the bad days when she has had no sway over her students, that she was made only for the company, for the group spirit, the line, the ensemble choreography and the blending of beings. An ambition still greater than being a soloist or a star. She places the mail on the kitchen table. Her friend Ron and her children Laura and Paul have, as usual, left the dirty bowls from breakfast, the sliced bread, of which the first slices have dried up, the soft butter in the butterdish, and even the milk. Ruth puts everything away, with her usual movements, into the refrigerator and into the sink. The silence in the apartment surprises her.

For ten years now Ron has been living with her, one night after the other. Ruth never dares question Ron for fear of putting him under an obligation. Perhaps, because of this, Ron stays with her, always passing through, as if on tour with the company when they used to dance together. He stays, on permanent tour, a home port. No luggage. Ron is going to be fifty. He seems to be twenty years less only when he does not smile, so he smiles all the time. Ron lives from one day to the next and he is always there. As for Sébastien, he would leave for entire months at a time, at sea, and would continually, on his return, whenever present or in his daily letters when away, make plans for the future. Ruth has opened the kitchen window, wiped off the table with a sponge, she sits down. She opens the mail. A letter from the bank, the quarterly dividend from the British Petroleum Company has been credited to her account. There is also an electricity bill, a postcard for Ron and a letter for Laura. A strange silence in the apartment. An empty silence which has just given birth in Ruth to an anxiety about Ron and, in a sudden flash, to a certainty about Sébastien's memory. One cannot live only from plans. The only thing that remains is what has really happened. Paul Stewart, the magus of the company, had the choreographic art of having his boys and girls, in groups of four or six, move on stage as if they had been dancing or were still dancing in the wings before and after. In his ballets the stage would become only a tiny part of the spectacle, that part that was paid to be seen. And yet in the wings nothing was happening more than in a normal spectacle. Because of that, as creator, illusionist, Paul Stewart had been booed and then celebrated, because he was apparently an innovator. But he had only invented this illusion, slight, fleeting and only too quickly he had done no more than copy himself. Pregnant with Laura, Ruth had left the company, her career interrupted, but when she was able to resume, it was too late. There is no one in the apartment. The letter from the bank has arrived. She must write Sébastien, and do it at once, as usual, so as not to have to think about it for several days, an automatic thing, for fear of a reproach that, gradually, in the bad way one deals with automatic obligations, is directed at oneself. In the drawer of the kitchen sideboard, some paper, a felt pen, an envelope. On the page Ruth writes 'Toronto, July the 9th, Dear Sébastien . . .' But she stops. July 9th?

She sees herself again, on a certain birthday evening, giving her breast to Laura. Laura was biting this little, hardly existent breast which nonetheless was giving milk. Anne-Marie was jealous. *She* had not been able to nurse her son Pierre. Claire, very round, encumbered by her belly, kneeling before her, was delicately touching Laura's forehead with the tip of her finger. Silence was the rule, a silence from everyone, observed by each of them, everyone, those rugs, those curtains, those dresses, those suits, those people, a terribly civilised spectacle. At the moment when Sébastien had, with a modest gesture, hidden his wife's breast, the nakedness reproached by every father, Ruth had realised for the first time that she had just entered a dangerous trap. By claiming to break away from that place and with her, all Sébastien had done was to drag her into it, and he too was playing the game. A charm interrupted. From the day they had met in the Place de l'Odéon to that day at the Place d'Antioche everything had happened. Ruth saw Bertrand again. Bertrand's return. It was over between Sébastien and her. At that moment, in reality, they had left each other, and if afterwards, together, they made the gestures of love again and said the necessary words for a few years, those gestures and those words were nothing more than a repetition, a performance. In the trap Ruth had just seen a capture, a being taken. She would not let herself be taken.

Ruth re-reads the beginning of her letter. 'Toronto, July the 9th, Dear Sébastien . . .' She tears the page up. What good is it writing him anymore? That date, after all, is supposed to mark the end to a reduction of her amorous sentence. She will not write anymore unless a quarterly payment is not made. She has nothing more to say to Sébastien. Just as she says nothing to Ron. She goes to check, in her bedroom, if her eternally-passing-through friend's things are still there. They are. Abruptly she understands the nature of the silence in the apartment. In Laura's room and in Paul's everything is in order, so orderly that they must have left. But where and for how long? For the summer? On the telephone, a small card, 'We'll be back,' written in French, on an instinct, a demarcation. Laura had signed 'Laura.' Paul had signed 'Paul.' They wrote the 'We'll be back,' one letter at a time each, alternately, like a game, so that she could not blame either of them for impelling their departure. That reassures Ruth. She smiles about it when she needed to cry. Without thinking, she opens the door, goes out to the landing. You never know. It's Bertrand she sees again, framed by Sébastien, Luc and Claire. She doesn't like that. She goes back in, slams the door, claps 'One, two!' 'One, two, three!' She goes to do the breakfast dishes. They'll be back.

Three o'clock in the afternoon local time in Buenos Aires. Anne-Marie sometimes thinks about the time difference. She says to herself, 'If I'm doing this, they're doing that.' This, that, she does not define. She thinks about Lyon then, about her childhood, her family, her brothers and sisters, but she seldom writes them and does not see them anymore when she goes back to France with the one she calls her 'new husband' without ever naming him. A contempt. Anne-Marie has decided to keep her distance and is doing so.

The end of lunch, on the terrace, on the top floor overlooking the Plaza Quevedo. Anne-Marie observes her husband in conversation with Rosendo Juarez, Julia Cristian and Francisco Ferrari, a conversation apparently animated, interesting, each making broad gestures, witty remarks, bursts of laughter. Anne-Marie serves the coffee 'Azucar?' They do not want the sugar she is offering, the silver sugar bowl, the matching tongs. Pierre, sprawled in an armchair, in short-sleeved shirt, white trousers, the ones for visits, and bare feet, he has just taken off his shoes mumbling 'After all, I am at home,' giving his mother a smile, a peremptory smile, followed by a wink. Pierre gets up, his hands in his trouser pockets, shoulders raised as if he were about to

132

announce once again, 'I'm off to play tennis.' He looks at his mother. 'What birthday were you going to talk about, during lunch? You didn't finish your sentence.' Anne-Marie does not answer and holds out a cup of coffee to him. 'No, thank you. I asked you a question, Mama. I'm waiting!' Anne-Marie observes Julia, Rosendo, Francisco and her husband. Then she turns to Pierre. 'I forbid you to speak to me like that.' 'And I forbid *you*, Mama, not to answer me. They're ass-holes. Your husband's an ass-hole. They say stupid-ass-hole things. It doesn't amuse me anymore. Or you either. Have you had any news from papa?' Anne-Marie turns her head. Pierre smiles. 'Suppose you were to write him? *I*'m going to write Henri. After all, he is my grandfather. He has rooms to put me up. Bertrand's room is free, isn't it?' Anne-Marie says nothing. She trembles a little putting the coffee cup to her lips. Pierre murmurs 'Watch out. You're going to stain your dress.' Bursts of laughter from the others. Anne-Marie puts her cup on the saucer and addresses Pierre with a lost, rebellious look. 'Put your shoes back on. And go away!'

Eight p.m. On board the *Firebird*, in the middle of Overfjeld fjord, in full sunlight, René has joined Sébastien on the navigation bridge. 'Can I talk to you?' René, abruptly, unburdens himself, tells his tale, he's been drinking. Sébastien does not budge, stands there, gripping the engine room telegraph. He would like to stand watch again, all full ahead! and with a single gesture command the seven giants, with a single command put a little activity into this cemetery. René says to him, 'The Arctic Circle is worse than the Equator. The suns goes down just to rise again a little while after. Can *you* put up with that? No night? And before, no day? I'm made for seasons, I am. I'm from Béarn. And you, from Moncrabeau, I know. I've known for eleven months. Bernadette Despouet is a vague cousin of my mother's. And each time my mother writes, she asks me to ask you if you're any relation to the Prouillan's, from Moncrabeau. Even in my socks, sent a while ago, there was a little note. Is it really you?' Sébastien murmurs 'Yes,' his voice neutral, then 'Yes, that's me,' smiling. René does not like that smile. 'And what's so special about them, the Prouillans, from Moncrabeau?'

Sébastien looks at René, for a long time, without saying

anything. René shrugs his shoulders, hits his hands with his fists. He goes out onto the port wing, looks at the sky, then onto the starboard wing, the sky again, and comes back to the shelter. He laughs. 'The Belgian Congo I liked a lot, except the sun used to set every evening at the same time. Hardly a few minutes difference in six months. That made you crazy. Always the same evenings. I was running a tugboat from Banana, Boma up to Matadi. I was the specialist of Hell's Cauldron, the big bend in the Congo, a hundred and fifty meters deep at that spot. A fresh water sailor. All done with. Since then I've recycled myself into whirlybird piloting. Didn't you know? There you are. I'm the kind who says everything when it's too late and regrets it later.' René extends his hand toward the bridge's only armchair. 'Don't you want to play at being commander? Take the place of the Pasha? No? You're dying to tell me to shut up, but you won't do it. I observed you well, this afternoon, at the Lillehammer Bar. Something is going round in your head. Today's not like the others. That's obvious at a glance. A ghost is passing. Isn't that so?' Sébastien tries to leave the navigation bridge. René holds him back, drags him onto the port wing, mumbling, 'I need to tell you things about me that are things about you. Sometimes, during this last winter, I'd come up here, at night, you understand? And I watched in the jumble of the stars, I know them only too well, my three favourites, the Kings of the Magi. I would wait for them there, very precisely there, above that peak, one, then two, then three, all in a line, like a sword. I was also waiting for the fourth. I have always waited for it. I'm still waiting for it. It will never come. And for good reason, the fourth King of the Magi left, but he never arrived. That's everyone's history. The history of people who know how to love. They leave. But they don't arrive. Don't be jealous, it's yours as much as mine, this story. You can't invent a star, that's all.' René crosses his arms, lowers and shakes his head. He laughs.

Sébastien, for an instant, thinks René is going to break down crying. He would like to go back to his cabin, shut himself in until dinner time, tear up the letter to his father, re-capture the postcard in the mail box at Dunn, slip his arm in, stretch his hand, take back the message, and especially no longer to give any sign of life to anyone, anywhere, ever. Ruth had a beautiful way, naked, of sliding over him. She would cover him.

Sometimes Claire used to do the same thing, as they ended up rolling in the grass, dressed, on the bank of the Baïse. René grabs Sébastien by the arm. 'In the beginning I believed it! I was on submarines. I remember a friar. He had come on board, for a week. Monseigneur. He was a simple curé but we called him Monseigneur. Like with deck swabbers, you have to say seaman's apprentice. And when Monseigneur laughed at us, in the crew's mess, he would say, not apologising at all, 'I like dirty stories too, and in heaven you won't have to look for me in the first row but in the back, on a fold-down seat.' René belches, wipes his lips. 'Sorry.' He laughs. 'And one day the commander invited us up to his place, in Lorient. A stereo set-up was his pride. He said he liked military music. After an hour, softly, all we were hearing were Hitler songs. Did you know him, this Uncle Pasha? And that friar? You dream, and then you don't dream anymore.'

René takes Sébastien's hand. 'And Manila Bay? When I start talking, it just goes on and on. I'm like General MacArthur, I shall return. There are some books you never get to the end of-You want a picture? It's like a woman who pulls away at the best moment. You dream of it all your life.' René lets go of Sébastien's hand, lifts his head up, hits the guardrail of the wing with his fist, goes back onto the bridge, staggers a little. 'And the water hyacinths, in the waters of the Congo, the floating islands, we had to avoid them. Not a minute's rest on that river. Tons of hyacinths. Watch out for the propellers. They called it the Portuguese concessions. I even learned to detest flowers.' He turns to Sébastien, points his finger at him. 'Have you seen them, the widows, at the Festival of the Blue Nets, at Concarneau?' Silence. Hiccough. He laughs. 'I've even seen, in the middle of a storm, an aspiring polytechnician call an officer, a real one, for help to stand the watch, he didn't know what to do. The aspirant in question only knew how to sing. He was afraid. He sang bass and alto, two voices. "O death where is your victory?" Do you know *The Messiah*? Handel? I do, since then.' René looks at Sébastien. 'Sorry. The girl at the Lillehammer Bar, even if I'd wanted to, I couldn't have. I've been too long at sea. Horst did the honours in my place. See you later, Monsieur Prouillan. From Moncrabeau. And don't forget, we haven't said anything!' He leaves.

Alone, Sébastien strokes the engine room telegraph, looks at the radar, the gyrocompass, the chart table and the helm. Nothing on this ship runs properly anymore. Everything has stopped. René had surprised him as if he had been caught in the act. He had taken refuge, here, alone, at the top of the *Firebird*'s superstructure, to dream of piloting again. And, alone, looking south he had just called 'Bertrand,' and louder 'Bertrand.'

9

Sometimes, around eight o'clock in the evening, Bertrand comes to watch television at Juan and Jeanne's, in the caretaker's house, a low house, on the side of the road leading into the village of Lestaque. The house seems to be all huddled up against the gate of the Moncrabeau estate the better to watch over whoever comes and goes. The gate is always open. 'Unjustly' says the father-in-law Lucio, 'since nobody comes anymore, or goes.' Each year, at the beginning of spring, Juan pulls up the weeds along the pathway leading to the big house, weeds the border, mows the rim of the embankments, digs circular strips around the young trees, prunes the dead branches from the older ones, gives a sort of facelift to the drive, the slightly sinuous access road of several dozen meters. One never knows, the others might come back. They are not coming back. Jeanne has seen them, reunited, only once, well before her marriage. She was visiting Juan, who called her his *'novia'*, secretly from Merced and Lucio who did not want this little French Girl for their son, *'pequeñita'*, who brings nothing with her and had been to school too long a time *'pere no sirve cuando se ha de laborar como laboramos,'* that's no good when you have to work the way we do. For a wedding gift, Madame Prouillan had sent a beautiful square table, from Paris, shipped by the United Stores, with folding legs, but what good is it — the house is so big — and covered with green felt on which Jeanne has never dared place anything for fear of leaving marks. The table is here, bare. Bertrand leans his elbows on it sometimes, watching television and distractedly, with his hand, strokes the top, as if he wanted to brush it, smooth it. This contact pleases him. There are two other identical tables in the big house. The father-in-law said it was for 'bridge'. Jeanne has never dared ask what 'bridge' is. Monsieur sent money, for the marriage. He was a Minister then, but hasn't been for a very long time. Juan and Jeanne saved the letterhead, with the message of congratulations: 'Happiness has no need of money, but money can contribute to happiness. Cordially yours, Henri Prouillan.' The money served to buy the cradle and buggy for their first child, six months later, Antonio. Then the second, José, 14 months after. Merced and Lucio, Jeanne and Juan, José and Antonio. At Juan and Jeanne's marriage, only Bertrand represented the family. During the entire mass he remained standing, even during the consecration. They had forgotten to seat him. Merced is in the village. Lucio, Juan and the children had left that morning, hurriedly. Jeanne prepared her family's dinner. She turned on the television set. Bertrand is not there. It's time for the news and weather.

After the men had left, Merced went immediately to see the mayor and inform him. 'He's escaped. It's serious. You have to call the *guardias*. He touched the *nines*.' Merced knows she is never taken seriously. She speaks as best she can, with the words she grasps, like she grasped her bundle, in the reception centre at Alscall, near Hendaye, in the August of '36, when Monsieur had come to choose them. Lucio and she had been married a month before, in the church at Palos de Moguer, south of Andalusia, near Cuelga, so early in the morning, with scarcely time for the benediction and exchange of rings, then, after church, the departure, not for a honeymoon but for a flight to the north, by the plateaux of Estrémadure, those of Castille, all the way to Navarre and to the frontier, some hundreds of kilometres on foot or hanging on trucks, while Lucio would sing, holding her by the hips *'el viento galán de torres prendiendola por la cintura,'* the flirtatious wind of the towers taking her by the belt. Lucio and she had not touched each other in any other way when Monsieur had approached, smiling, and had asked their names. Monsieur did not understand that, the flight before the embrace. He was choosing a couple, that's all. One day late, in Palos de Moguer, the *guardias* would have had Lucio before a firing squad. The workers of Corchotaponer S.A. de Lepe had just joined those from the pyrites factory and rebelled. They were being hunted.

That morning, when the men of the house had decided, without informing Jeanne, the eternal French Girl and *pequeñita*, to go beating the ground for Bertrand, Merced, for a brief instant, had hesitated, but the *guardia*, must be called, and she went to the mayor's, to alert him. The people on duty, in uniform, are all 'mala suerte,' they bring misfortune. They are armed for shooting, arresting, restraining. For some years Lucio has been trying to explain to his wife that everything has changed back there, 'al pais,' and that they could, if they wanted to, return to Palos de Moguer, if only for a visit. But Merced looks at the horizon to the south and, on windy, overcast days, towards the Pyrenees frontier. She tells herself that, on the other side, the guardias are still waiting and all that can only be a trap set again, which she has, and will always have, the impression of having narrowly escaped. Palos de Moguer, Alscall, Moncrabeau, that itinerary of life is sufficient. Employed by luck, that day in August of '36, loaded into the car of that smiling Monsieur who was trying to speak to them in Spanish, Lucio in front and she, in the back seat, hugging her bundle, feeling sick, it was the first time she had been taken such a long way in a car, inside, Merced remembers the green countryside, the hillsides, knolls, meadows, grass, flowers, and especially the villages. At the end of that road of stone, of sun, fear and thirst, was this country she was entering. The paradise that the curé at Palos de Moguer used to speak of? There was water, from rivers, water flowing and immense clouds, like other mountains, in the sky. When they arrived at Moncrabeau, Madame Cécile was in bed, even more smiling than Monsieur. Near her bed, a cradle and little baby, Claire. Merced repeated 'Clara'. Immediately they made her pronounce 'Claire'. It made Lucio laugh 'Clairuh!' There were also the children, Luc, Sébastien, little blond heads, less smiling, or a little intimidated. At the end of the road, there was happiness, and a whole family already multiplied. Another abundance.

The first night of their arrival was their wedding night. The bedroom was rudimentary. It has remained that way. In the house, by the roadside, on the second floor, in the rear room, a rather narrow bed, a table and two chairs. Merced kept the cloth from the bundle, and kept it as if it were something precious. Sometimes she goes to smell it, laughing and burying her face in it as if she were wiping away tears that would not come. The rivers at Cuelga no longer flow on the surface, the delta is silted up, the port is dead, Palos de Moguer is several kilometers from the sea. A memory. Another world. That night, the first night, exhausted, happy, with that happiness that one only lives afterwards, one can live it for a whole life, Lucio hung up the crucifix, a gift from the curé, over the bed, he undressed Merced and Merced let herself be stretched out on the bed. Through the open window, Merced remembers strange plant odours she didn't know, even the dew, in the morning, when she finally dared look at Lucio, naked, sleeping in her arms. Juan was born ten months later. And Madame, during the whole month of September, word by word, in order to teach her French, made her read entire pages from a book, *Colline*, by a certain Giono. 'Claire', 'colline', and 'Giono' were the first three words Merced learned in French. But to designate Claire, she used to say '*la niña*,' Luc and Sébastien '*los niños*' and the three together, to be French, '*les nines*'. It made them laugh.

Monsieur and Madame left again, that year, at the end of September, for Paris. Luc used to say '*I'*m going to go to school.' Sébastien, jealous, would be silent watching him. Claire did not cry. Madame Cécile found her daughter 'Calm and so sweet.' As for Merced, she used to worry but did not say so. She worried also four years later about Bertrand's silences and especially about the way he would look at her when she leaned over the cradle. Juan asked his mother to show him the '*nuñeca*', the doll. Merced would tell him it was a '*chiquito*', a boy.

Merced has just spent the day with Mathilde, the mayor's wife, in the kitchen on their farm, helping her prepare the strawberries for jam. Léon, the mayor, said to Merced, 'I'm going to go with them. Bertrand wouldn't hurt a fly. You know that,' and to his wife, 'Keep Merced until I get back. And above all don't let her go out.' Sometimes, all rotund, squeezed into her black dresses, Merced feels like telling her daughter-in-law, 'I was bonìta too, you know.' But she contents herself with smiling at Jeanne who believes for a moment that her mother-in-law is going to become friendly. Juan, that morning, had left with his shot-gun. Lucio, Antonio and José had followed him. He is the master, the son and fruit of the great voyage from Palos, through sand and fire, to Moncrabeau, its grass and spring water, a scent. For one day, Merced has become Mathilde's servant. Mathilde asked Merced, 'What did he do to the children that's so terrible?' Merced answered, 'He touched them. Antonio and José saw it all.' Merced does not pronounce 'saw' in the French way but in the Spanish way. Since morning the two women have no longer been speaking. They are working, in the odour of jam. Watching over the huge pots. From time to time Mathilde smiles at Merced.

Léon went to get his two assistants. 'Come on, that Bertrand has done it again.' The three men made the full circuit. From Boué, to Lapla, they went back up to Souléris, Maripouy, La Maurague, Gouaresse, Toulien, calling 'Juan!' 'Where are you?' until Léon said 'We're frightening Bertrand. We have to take him gently, he's a gentle soul,' then, 'They're going to have to put him away. A shame. He isn't bad. Since it happened.' The three men then headed toward Tourne, Joüeton and behind Le Matouret, at the washing shed, where they found Juan and his gun, Lucio, Antonio seventeen and José sixteen. They quenched their thirst without saying a word. It was noon. Each examined the area.

Often Léon tells himself that this countryside is dead, 'But it's good living here.' That does not even make Mathilde smile. They had a son. He died in Algeria. What the hell was he going to do down there? Dying for the pieds-noirs who were already buying up their lands, cutting the hedges, consolidating the fields, changing the countryside as they pleased and by force, and were overturning thousand year old traditions. At the first heavy storm, the waters, formerly retained by human, become natural, barriers of stones and bramble bushes, would take only a few minutes to reach the brook and river beds, when they used to take hours to move across the fields, poor pasture lands, impermeable, barely covering the silica and clay. There would be a tidal wave. At the first very heavy storm, the groundswell happened. The region was declared a disaster zone. Nobody said why. A son dead is over there, and the ones from over there are here, now, prosperous, proud of making this land produce. It used to produce enough before, in harmony with the elements. For that, Léon had agreed to be mayor.

Léon turned to Juan. 'Why did you bring your gun?' Juan answered, 'It's to scare him. My gun isn't loaded. You can look.' 'And what'd he do, that Bertrand?' Juan looked at his father, Lucio turned to José, José waved to Antonio to speak. Antonio said, 'It was late afternoon. At the end of the estate near Le Risqué. In a birch wood. I was returning from La Beaucette. I heard laughter. I approached. There were some kids, lots of

141

kids, seven, eight, ten little ones, boys and girls, all from Lasmatrix. The dark haired kids were the Garcias. The others, I don't know. They come to play there, often. There's a clearing. They make themselves huts. You chase them away but they just come back. They could start a fire, couldn't they, grandfather? Bertrand was there, in the middle. He goes there a lot, in the winter, for walks, alone. But now the kids were circling around him, yelling. A game, perhaps. I almost left. But I believed Bertrand was in trouble. The boys were flinging stones, pieces of wood. The girls were hissing at him like cats. That's it. Bertrand was sort of blinded, like blindman's buff. The children were tearing off his shirt, were digging and burying his shoes laughing. Bertrand, barefoot, bare chested, arms raised in front of him, was turning around because they were making him turn. He was laughing or crying, I don't know, you never know with him, and trying to catch one, or the other, bending over, furiously, in jerks . . .'

Antonio is silent, he leans over, plunges his head in the washing shed water, stands up again, breathes deeply, shakes himself and says to his brother 'Your turn José. You saw it all, same as me.' Lucio is proud of his two grandsons. *They* are citizens by birth. *They* speak well by birth. And they call him 'Grandfather'. No more need to go back to Palos de Moguer. Lucio smiles. Juan crosses his arms, standing, turned toward the south. He frowns. Antonio thinks he may have said too much in front of the mayor. José continues 'It was better than that, more than that. I couldn't either, I couldn't tell anymore who was attacking, if it was a game or not. Then the oldest Garcia made himself a headband, with a piece of the shirt and he began to dance around Bertrand, his arms raised, him too, as if he wanted to fly away, making loud noises with his mouth. Twice, three times Bertrand was bending over, he seemed to have been drinking but he never drinks, he could hardly stand up, like someone who's afraid of falling, two times, three, Bertrand almost caught the Garcia boy. I believe he simply wanted to tear off the headband. The fourth time Bertrand caught him by the arm. The Garcia boy struggled. The others were yelling, the girls shrilly. Tonio, at that moment, said 'Let's go,' to me but I held him back. After all, we've played with Bertrand, too. Not like that, but . . .' José stops. Léon looks at him. Juan turns around.

'No point in telling everything.' Lucio mumbles 'What are you afraid of? You used to go with Bertrand, too. He would leave his brothers to meet you secretly. We have to say it. It's the alcalde's right to know everything,' and to Léon, 'Isn't that so, Monsieur le Maire?' To his assistants 'Isn't it Robert? Isn't it Sylvain?' and to José 'continue,' to Antonio 'or you.'

Antonio lowers his eyes. José murmurs, 'Bertrand was afraid because the Garcia boy struggled. When he tried tearing off the headband, he hit him in the eye. The little one fell. The girls moved away. The boys jumped on Bertrand. Everything happened very fast. They tore his pants and undershorts, in a few seconds. Bertrand was hurt on the forehead and began to bleed in the eyes and on his cheeks. He couldn't see anymore. It all happened suddenly. Bertrand, in order to defend himself, caught the boys, and was biting their arms, their legs, their thighs. Then the kids got fierce. Kicking, throwing stones. They waved his pants, undershorts, and the rags of his shirt around. They cried 'bastard', 'wolf', 'animal', and 'arsehole' hitting him with dead branches. On the ground, all curled up on himself, Bertrand was protecting his head. It was only when the Garcia boy unbuttoned his fly and ordered the girls to 'get the hell out' and the boys to 'piss on him like me' that I leapt in, with Antonio. I knew very well why we didn't move before. Because it all happened so quickly. To keep something terrible from happening, you mustn't stop those games.'

José looks at his father, 'You must never surprise some children. And when I say "some", I'm also thinking about Bertrand.' José turns to Antonio. 'Children forget everything, except when they're surprised,' then softly, 'As soon as the kids saw us, they ran off yelling Indian war whoops. As soon as Bertrand heard us calling him, the two of us, Tonio and I, he crawled away, as if he was mad, toward the other side of the clearing repeating "No," "no," or rather, like this, "oon . . .," from the throat. A groaning dog. A moaning animal. We said to him, "It's us, don't be afraid." As soon as he stood up, I cried "Don't be afraid, Monsieur Bertrand," Tonio bellowed "Nobody saw anything! Come back!" Yes, I suppose we said exactly what we weren't to say to him. We said "tu" to him because we say that with him, but then we said "vous" to him because with him you never know. Tonio said we didn't "See anything." I was going to say it too. That's what made him run away. If we'd tried to control him, he'd have killed us. That's just it, we had seen him. It was us.' José wipes his mouth, his dry mouth, with a quick gesture, as if wiping away a kiss. Lucio approaches his son and gives him a little tap on the nape of the neck. Antonio avoids his father's look. Juan seizes his gun. Léon takes Sylvain and Robert to witness. 'Where do you think he is?' Robert: 'If he's naked, not very far.' Sylvain: 'It'd be better if he were here, old man Prouillan, instead of leaving his son with us as a hostage.' Juan looks at him. 'A hostage for what?' Robert laughs 'You're asking me? You're paid to keep him, yes or no? You should know.' Léon says calmly, 'I know where he is.' Silence. 'But before, I want to see the kids. Especially the eldest Garcia boy.'

At Lasmatrix, at the Garcia's, it was mealtime. When he saw them arriving old Garcia asked 'Is the hunting season open?' and to Lucio '*Que pasa?*' Lucio answered '*Nada*' and Juan '*Nado hombre.*' Mother Garcia gave them something to drink, bread and some lima bean soup. The children were there, at the table, the eldest boy, the younger ones and the three girls. Nothing could be read in their faces and their looks. For a brief instant Léon wondered if these children suspected anything, were playing a game or had not yet experienced that feeling of threat that leads big children to consider themselves grown-up and adults to grow old while being conscious of growing old. Léon remembered his own childhood, so many events of which he had been the minor hero and which acquired a reality and importance only later when his son in turn had created them. Everything that day was only a family affair to be dealt with within the family. Invested with his power as mayor, flanked by his two assistants, sure of the fact that Mathilde would keep Merced, moved by Lucio's joy listening to his grandchildren express themselves, still more attentive to Juan's silences, Léon was sure of what he must do. Everything would be dealt with at Lestaque, in Lestaque. The Garcia's oldest boy was leaning against the table, his arms crossed, looking very slightly stubborn. Several times his mother asked him to fill the glasses. He pretended not to hear. Léon, Lucio, Juan, Antonio, José, Sylvain and Robert, discreetly, would have liked to see a wound, a bite, a mark, a proof. The Garcias' eldest, like the others, was neither moving or speaking. Léon, waving to the men to follow

144

him, had simply said to old Garcia, out loud, without in any way attacking the children, 'They're good kids' and in front of the farmhouse, aside, 'Just tell them not to go . . .' then 'No. Don't tell them anything. Don't worry. That Bertrand is just lost,' and to the others 'Let's be on our way to Auzan.' Léon and Mathilde had bought Bernadette's farm for their son. The fields have lain fallow. The house is abandoned. Léon looked at Sylvain, 'Bertrand could only take refuge there.' Then Juan: 'you used to go there, to Auzan, when you were fifteen, with him. I saw you there. Say you remember.' Juan, his gun broken open on his shoulder, is content to spit on the ground.

Since two in the afternoon they have been waiting, under the elm, in front of the house. Antonio and José have stretched out on the dead branch, cut, like a trunk, its bark blackened by time and bad weather, the wood dry and rough, a supporting branch which had to serve as a bench. Lucio and Léon had almost told the youngsters not to stretch out there, at the same time. But at the same time, they looked at each other, and chose to say nothing about the memory of the hanged man. Juan hid his gun in the undergrowth at the entry of the drive leading to the abandoned farmhouse. Robert and Sylvain returned to Lestaque. 'He's there. You don't need us anymore.' Juan kept circling around the house. From time to time he approached the dormer window, near the door of the barn. The shutter has fallen. He gets a grip, hoists himself up, looks in and murmurs, 'Bertrand, please come out,' then louder 'Come out, please' or 'Don't force us to knock the door down,' then louder still, 'We're waiting for you, outside.' He threw his shirt through the window. Then, after circling the house again, he threw in his undershorts, taken off, given away. Lucio murmured 'Suppose we telephoned Paris? He doesn't budge from there anymore, the old man.' Léon did not answer. Several times Antonio or José got up. But their father waved them not to approach. The sun is setting. Clouds and red beams. The immense elm tree begins to shiver. Without realising it Lucio says, 'Maybe we ought to warn Jeanne. She has to wait for us . . .' Nobody is listening to him. He's speaking for his own benefit. Juan, in undershirt with his arms bare, sits on the ground, his back to the shed door. José says to his brother 'What if I gave him my pants?' Antonio smiled 'You don't have anything on underneath.'

Then Antonio gets up, takes off his pants, folds them, as if there were a crease, canvas pants, worn, patched at the knees, that he puts on in the morning when he lets out the animals. There he is, feet bare in his leather boots, bare legged, in his shorts, shirt hanging. Antonio heads for the barn. His father makes no sign to stop him. Antonio holds out the pants, folded, like an offering. Léon tells himself it all is a little like at mass, when he used to go, especially the silence. But here gestures are important. There is someone in the house. Juan rises, takes the pants. Antonio boosts his father up and Juan, hoisted, calls into the night of the dormer window 'Bertrand? Get dressed. Come out. There's only the four of us and Léon. We're thirsty, like you are. And we want to go back to the house.' Antonio trembles a little under Juan's weight. But he holds him, strongly, with his whole body, vertically, his father's shoes making marks on his stomach, the stone of the house scraping his shirt and back. Lucio and José have approached a few steps nearer. Juan, still balancing, throws the pants inside. 'Take these. We're waiting for you at the end of the drive. And if you want, we'll talk. Like we've never talked.' Juan jumps to the ground, gives some taps to his elbows and knees. Antonio takes off his shirt, shakes it and puts it back on. Léon says to Juan 'You're right. We're too close.'

At the end of the drive, all five sit on the embankment. As he passed, Juan threw some branches over the undergrowth, to hide the gun completely. Lucio, his head down, thinks about that birch wood, the trees that Monsieur had had planted in November of '39, with the string, in straight lines, and on more than a hectare, because Madame Cécile 'used to dream of having' those trees, at her home. Ten years later, smothered, some were dead, in the middle, creating a clearing, organising that natural disorder which the curé at Palos de Moguer used to say was the first proof of '*la obra de Dios*.' God's work. Lucio closes his eyes. God for him, is only the calm, when it returns, hardly at all the peace that leads to war. Lucio, for the first time, feels old. Since Madame Cécile accompanied Bertrand, no one from the Prouillan family has ever come back again. Monsieur sends the money they ask for, always sends back the profits from the sharecropped lands worked by Juan, 'as a gift for your services', pays the taxes, worries about the condition of the big house, from Paris orders the necessary work and pays. He pays. But in

146

his letters, always typed by someone else, he never speaks of Bertrand. It is Jeanne, in response, who writes to give news and make requests. Invariably she mentions, 'Your son is well and asks us to say hello,' a hint of irony or a wish to reunite the father and son. And each time Jeanne reads aloud the letter she has just written, each time the phrase about Bertrand comes up, Merced turns her head, gets up, finds something to do around the sink, Juan tightens his fist on the table, Antonio looks at his brother, José begins to whistle, goes to lean against the window, observes the road, the village, the clock tower, and Lucio wonders if he hates or if he likes the Prouillans. What happened twenty years ago? Monsieur Henri and Madame Cécile had tremendous children. Why did this one come back in that condition? An accident? What kind of accident? When Madame Cécile accompanied Bertrand, she gave no explanation. She closed the upper rooms herself, checking the hooking of the shutters, having dust covers placed over the mattresses and seats. Lucio remembers the noise of the bunch of keys, a noise that went, from door to door, from room to room, growing louder all along the hallways in the attic and on the second floor. Madame Cécile then said 'He will have all of the bottom of the house for himself. These keys, I'm entrusting them to you. Nobody else but you, Merced and your children will have the right to go into this house,' then when she was leaving, 'Two houses divide the spirit.'

Lucio still did not understand this last thing that Madame Cécile said. She had a funny way about her when she said it. Those people say things sometimes they do not understand themselves. And when, often, almost every day, Lucio sees Paris on television, he thinks maybe that's the division. And people, those people, go up there to suffer, rule, dominate and get lost. When he was still at Palos de Moguer, Lucio avoided Cuelga. It was already much too big a town.

Here, now, Lucio looks at the drive, and at the end of the drive, the farmhouse. He listens. He watches intently. It's taken hours and hours. He does not want to feel old. He wants, some day, to see Antonio's and José's children. He hears, in the back of his memory, a curious noise from a bunch of keys. He also sees that woman again, Madame, usually smiling but who so abruptly, returning with Bertrand, no longer smiled or else, had a set, vague, lost smile, like a smile of remorse that would never leave her lips, when she ordered Merced to unmake the beds, to put back the furniture covers, to put everything back to the sleep of shadow and night, sheltered against dust, whereas everything had been ready, polished up, aired, for summer. That summer. Twenty years ago. Lucio hears banging shutters and the noise of hooks, enough to harpoon the heart. She was no longer the same woman, and suddenly, had become one of those 'coups de théâtre' Monsieur's brother-in-law used to speak of. 'Theatre' or 'bridge,' what do they mean? Madame had become hard and her youth was gone. No more did any of her gestures speak of the past, of what should have been a happiness, even superficially. One family can not understand it all. And to see better, to see again, Lucio closes his eyes. The evening silence helps, too, and the noises of memory become clear. Léon leans toward Lucio. 'Are you sleeping, grandpa?' then laughing 'You're going to miss your Bertrand's exit.'

Léon, in fact does not feel like laughing. Night is falling. It is starting to get cold, a real cold. The cold of days changing to night when all the air begins flowing, irrigating, mixing, keeping itself going. Léon will never totally get used to being what he is, someone from Lestaque, the only one in Mathilde's life, father of a dead man and mayor of a revenge. If he says 'tu' to his Spanish people, he still does not speak, or not much, to the pieds-noirs. The exercise of his duties, with 173 persons registered on the electoral rolls, 52 of whom allow themselves to vote no against him. In the *Sud-Ouest*, only Mathilde reads it daily, the column 'two yeses, for one name.' She wants to know who is marrying whom. Even if she does not know the young people involved, she pretends to be interested. She is marrying off her son. Léon asks her every time, 'Anything interesting in the paper?' Mathilde: 'No. As usual.' They went to Toulouse twice, once to Bordeaux and once to Pau where they were presented with a medal, a 'war cross' with a 'Citation of the Order of the Nation' and a quick handshake. They had been put in a row, in a barracks yard. That's all for trips. Léon never showed Mathilde Prouillan's letter of condolence. He simply told his wife, 'The letter began with: my family and I, then I threw it away.' Léon looks at the Despouet farmhouse that was to become his son's farmhouse. Inside, there is Bertrand, another family, other people, a marionette animated from Paris. There must be sons from Lestaque everywhere in the capital, from Moncrabeau to that Place d'Antioche address engraved on the mail addressed to the city hall. Monsieur Prouillan votes by mail. And he is the one who sends the most money, to the school, for the Christmas tree, to the holiday committees, for the Feast of Saint-Jean. They owe the installation of the telephone system to him, and the public pay phone. He gave too for the church roof. He always gives, but he does not come anymore.

Seated on the embankment, hands joined, fingers crossed, in the silence and cold, night has fallen suddenly, as if the gigantic elm had thrown a shadow over the entire region, a shadow or ink, the black ink of official acts, city hall registers, births, marriages, divorces, deaths, Léon says to himself that he, Lucio, Juan, Antonio, José and the others, Jeanne, Merced, Mathilde, and the women, they all no longer exist in the minds of those people in Paris who just govern amongst themselves. The province would be forgotten. And yet it smells good. All you have to do is inhale. The smells of the grass and the bark are irreplaceable. *They* are here, listening is enough.

Léon sees Bertrand again, thirteen years old, stretched out, bare chested, in the barn at Auzan, on the beaten earth floor. He is smoking a cigarette. Juan, standing, behind him, leaning against the dry stone wall, one foot raised, knee bent, arms crossed. Juan was sixteen. Léon has just surprised them. 'What are you doing here?' Bertrand straightens up, 'Nothing, we're talking . . .' 'So get out, you're in my place here.' As they were leaving Bertrand had said, letting Juan pass first, 'Don't be angry Monsieur le Maire, *I*'ll never be in my place anywhere!' Those people always want to have the last word.

Lucio murmurs, 'Jeanne has made a birthday cake.' Juan rises and, from the middle of the drive, irritated by the way Léon had of looking at him, cries out 'Bertrand? That's enough!' Antonio is chewing a straw. José places a hand on his brother's knee *'Tienes frio?'* He said it in Spanish, to please Lucio. Antonio answers 'Yes, I'm cold. But not the way you think.' Juan gives a stone a kick, shrugs, shakes his head.

Juan preferred Luc and Sébastien to Bertrand. He especially liked Claire and used to stare at her when, standing at Lucio's

149

side, his father would go to '*Tomar las ordenes*,' to take the work orders for the day. Claire had that white skin that Juan could smell when close to her, which he remembers when Jeanne lifts the top sheet as her husband joins her in bed. Juan remembers summers, but not winters. The closing of the house stopped time. Juan dreamed of becoming Luc and Sébastien's friend, Claire's lover. But there had only been Bertrand interested in him and he sometimes invited him, 'Let's go to Auzan. I want to see the elm tree, to feel the house.' See the elm tree? Feel that house? Sometimes, at the bend in the drive, Bertrand would catch Juan's hand and squeeze it, a little pressure of the fingers, and then release it. Glances were afoot, and constituted the essential part of the walk. They were, in themselves, in the speech, and conversation, little secrets. Bertrand would watch Juan still more by not looking at him. Juan remembers feeling tracked that way many times, going and returning from Auzan, to 'see the elm tree' and 'to talk'. Inside, Juan holds intact, powerful, the stubborn feeling of those silences, Bertrand's obstinacy in not making that extra move feared and desired at the same time. All this is brutal, clean, observation from memory. Juan felt himself desired. Bertrand liked to see him walk, breathe, sigh or even be silent when he asked him an intimate question about Claire or the young girls of Lestaque. It was barely yesterday. Still, nearly thirty years have passed.

And Juan, there, in the middle of the drive, watches the door of the shed, the way he used to when Bertrand would not want to return home. Juan, at the time, would feel guilty about gestures not exchanged, received, given, guilty of what was not even admitted in words, grand moments of conniving and complicity, the intense flavour of days' ends. They were expecting Bertrand at the big house, for dinner. No delay should give away the secret of their walk. After dinner, the Prouillans would go walking, a family united, as far as Maripouy or to the birch woods. Alone, with his parents, Juan would hear them pass through the gate. Juan and Bertrand had held hands. That's all.

Sometimes, Juan feels himself entirely in that hand. Even though one day Lucio said in front of Merced who did not understand him '*Bertrand es una mariqua*.' A fairy. Even though Léon surprised them in the shed, although they were doing nothing but looking at each other, still, a distance was respected,

150

maintained by Bertrand and which Juan, sometimes, bowled over, wondered if it were not up to him to break, to make the other move, in response. And then the following summer, Monsieur's sister had come with one of her friends, Romain who was also writing for the 'theatre' and who had a 'fabulous future'. A fabulous future? Juan had seen Bertrand and Romain head for Auzan and the farm. It was over. Bertrand had just rendered him a freedom for which Juan was not truly delighted.

Here and now, Juan says to himself 'It's the last time and we're going home.' He calls 'Bertrand? You're going to be late!' Antonio and José look at their father. They do not understand. Léon helps Lucio get up. Night has never been so dark. If one looks at the sky, between the clouds, one can see the stars. The moon is rising. Under the elm tree, a house hidden away in the shadow. The door opens. Bertrand.

Bare feet. Antonio's pants falling above his ankles, Juan's shirt over the pants, not buttoned at the wrists or buttoned in front, Bertrand looks like a puppet. He leaves the shed door half open, seems to hesitate, sways slightly, from left to right, as if he were going to flee again to one side or the other of the house. But he raises his head, straight before him, inhales the wind, blinks his eyes as if he were still having some difficulty in adjusting to the night, the top of the elm, the clouds, sky, stars. He looks without really seeing. A wound stripes his forehead, the temple over his left eye is swollen, his arms and hands are covered with bruises, scratches, gashes in places, scabbed over. Only Antonio and José have approached, instinctively, unaware, side by side, as if to calm an escaped animal. Twice, Lucio has just thought of an animal, of a dog inhaling, and a hunted beast, recaptured which must once again be domesticated. Lucio says to himself, thinking about the Prouillans, 'We're cut off from them, but not them from us.' He turns to Léon. 'It's fortunate they have us, isn't it?'

Bare feet. Antonio's pants falling above his ankles, Juan's shirt support him by the elbows to help him walk, but Bertrand frees himself of their hold, and advances limping with his left foot. Juan, flanked by Lucio and Léon, waits until Bertrand gets to him. He grabs his hands, with both of his, two fists in his hands, forces him to open his thumbs, stretch his fingers, palms turned toward the sky, a way of calming his friend and tells him,

151

'Tonight you'll sleep at our place. Jeanne has everything ready for your birthday party. Come.' This time, Bertrand lets himself be taken by the waist. Juan puts Bertrand's left arm over his shoulders, his injured hand hanging on the strap of his undershirt. Lucio, witness, thinks of his loving gesture, when he held Merced, both clutched to the side or rear of a truck, a human cluster, exodus. And the men, in a cortege, return to the estate.

On passing Lasmatrix, on the hill, Léon hears the noises of sneaking steps, light crouching noises, behind the hedges and bushes. The children are there. A voice rises from the Garcia farmhouse '*A casa, niños! A casa!*' Bertrand drools a little, a dry drool from thirst. From time to time José, with the back of his hand, wipes his mouth, then wipes his hand on his trousers. Antonio mumbles, 'My knees are cold.' Juan tells him 'Go on ahead. Tell Mathilde and Merced to meet us at the house.' Léon adds, 'Tell them to bring the antiseptic, the surgical spirit and all the absorbant cotton we have.' Antonio leaves running, holding his shorts so that they won't fall down. Lucio smiles. José laughs. Juan says to his son, 'Help me.' José supports Bertrand on the right side. They carry him, sweep him along, bring him home. They are going faster. They are hungry. Bertrand frowns on seeing Antonio leave before them. From time to time, a word gets blocked in his throat, a word that comes from the heart, a spasm, a word in 'an' that Bertrand can not manage to articulate. After passing through Lestaque, in sight of the Moncrabeau gate before which stand Jeanne, Merced, Mathilde and Antonio, a light in the downstairs windows, the dull and articulated word passes Bertrand's lips 'Thank you,' then '*Muchas gracias.*' Lucio heard. José looked proudly at his father. Juan feels nude in his trousers. Bertrand's left hand clings to the strap of his undershirt. José, on his side, tells himself that those people have soft, white skin. He carries Bertrand and, for the first time, he is certain he knows him, and understands him a little.

They have seated Bertrand on a chair. Merced gives him a little sweetened water to drink, little swallows at first, then fully, holding the nape of his neck. Merced remembered this same head, in a cradle, under which she slipped her hand, shaping to his skull, grasping it. Forty years later, she is still here, she is beginning all over again, the same holding and the same sensation in the hollow of the hand, the same sweetened water, and same forgetting of the parents, the other ones, the real ones.

Then straightening up, she lets the men take over. She stays with Mathilde and Jeanne in the downstairs room. The table is set, the television is turned off. Juan takes Bertrand in his arms and carries him, a colossus, to the second floor, into his parents' bedroom. On the bed, Juan unfolds a sheet, all the time looking at the crucifix, not for God and his Christ, but simply for the calm rediscovered and the calm found here, in this house, keeping watch over someone else's house. The rebellion of the workers from Corchotaponera S.A. de Lepe and from the pyrites factory, in the long run, resulted only in leading him to work for other owners. The same faction. How do you claim something if the error is a thousand years old? Antonio and José undress Bertrand and lay him on the bed. Léon brings a basin of warm water and towels. Lucio hands out cotton soaked in alcohol, to each of them. It is the men who cleanse Bertrand's wounds.

Mathilde looks at Merced, 'And what does he do with all his time everyday, this Bertrand?' Merced turns around to Jeanne, Jeanne answers. 'We get the impression he's waiting. He reads but like that.' And Jeanne places her hands, flattened, right against her nose. She smiles. 'It isn't funny. He opens this book. Sometimes backwards. He holds it right up close making a face. He never turns the pages.' Merced looks at her daughter-in-law, wipes her hands on a dish-towel, then on her apron. She takes the apron off, hangs it on the wall near the sink and clarifies, 'Not only do *I* believe he reads, but he does everything, all alone. He makes his bed. He washes his shirts. Then he washes them again, for real, but he washes them. With soap. He rubs a lot. And he writes also. He fills his fountain pen. He empties it in the inkwell. He fills it again. He wipes the point. He opens the notebook, or he takes a sheet of paper. He doesn't write anything, but I'm sure he writes.' She pronounces 'fonetane,' 'inkwail,' 'dozen.' She has talked too much. She looks at Jeanne and Mathilde. She turns around. She runs the water in the sink. For nothing. She cleans up with a sponge. It was already clean. She turns her back to them. She is not crying, her nose is running a little, that's all. She remembers Cuelga, when she danced the sevillana, as a little girl. '*Los suspiros son aire y van al*

153

aire,' sighs are made of air and go into the air, '*las lágrimas son aqua y van al mar,*' tears are made of water and go into the sea, '*dime, mujer, quando el amor se olvida donde va?*' tell me, woman, when love is forgotten, where does it go? Merced wipes the end of her nose. It is always the same story, it is never the same story. Since Alscall nothing has happened, truly, it's all she wished. And Bertrand, Antonio has just explained to her, did not truly '*touch the nines.*' So?

Noises of steps, on the second floor, around the bed. José comes back from the big house with clean clothes. Léon, twice, comes down and changes the water in the basin, dirtied, with blood, '*sangre.*' Each time, Merced cleans the sink, then sponges it. Not leaving any traces. Mathilde says. 'I don't understand either why Bernadette never came back. Not even for a holiday.' Merced stands with her back turned, her hands resting on the edge of the sink. Jeanne answers, 'They are doing with her what they're doing with Bertrand. Each one is best off where he is.' Jeanne approaches her mother-in-law, from behind, undoes her chignon, her black hair, a few white hairs, and redoes it, a beauty. Then she bends over to check the cake, in the oven, and the flame, under the soup.

Bertrand has come downstairs again, with no one's help, clean, dressed. He enters first. The men follow him. Bertrand realises that the television is not turned on and is making no noise. So it's another evening. Merced leads him to his place, at the end of the table. But Bertrand waves her to sit there, in that chair, at his place. Merced does it reluctantly, watching Lucio. Bertrand takes a seat to the left of Merced. Facing him, Juan, Antonio and José. To his left Mathilde and Léon. Lucio goes around the table, serves wine to everyone. Then he takes a place, facing his wife, at the other end of the table, standing, and says, clearly, with the least possible accent, looking at José and Antonio and raising his glass, 'We owe everything to them but they owe everything to us. *Todo*!' Lucio hesitates a little, looks at Bertrand. 'Tonight, Bertrand, we're keeping you here. Two houses divide the spirit. To your fortieth birthday! To all of us!' They drink. Mathilde helps Bertrand raise his glass. Lucio sits down. Jeanne places the soup in the middle of the table. Lucio gestures her to bring a plate, a chair and take a seat, between Juan and Antonio, for the first time, with them, at their table. That's the way it is.

Jeanne makes herself a small place between her husband and her older son. She is afraid of touching the arm of one or the arm of the other. Mathilde rises. 'I'm serving everybody,' almost cheerfully. Merced, for the first time, presides at this table, facing Lucio. She does not dare place her hands on the table. She looks at Bertrand, the cut on his forehead, his temple bruised, the wounds on his hands. Mathilde serves Bertrand first, by instinct, or by habit, also by reticence, which she still practises in the village, since she refuses to talk about the Prouillans, those 'eternally absent' who 'think they can do anything.' Bertrand, with his soup served, in front of him, awkward with his hands and fingers, makes the soup bowl slide on the table, over towards Merced who draws her empty bowl away and holds it out to Mathilde. This move from Bertrand surprises everyone at the table. Never, since the beginning, since that first time, has Bertrand ever really been with them, at the same table, but always, alone, at noon, in the big house, his meal was brought by Jeanne, away from the others, and in the evenings at the end of the table sitting as close as possible to the television, with that napkin that Merced changed everyday 'Like in the old days, I'm fond of doing it.' Then Mathilde, worried, but amused too, serves Jeanne, serves herself, then Bertrand again. Then the men last. Mathilde sits down. No one moves. Bertrand looks at them vaguely, shakes his head slightly, tries to smile. Juan began to eat first, then Lucio. Then Léon. The others follow. With a cut on the thumb of his right hand, Bertrand has a hard time holding his soup spoon. Merced helps him.

Two helpings of soup. And two glasses of wine. Juan clinks glasses with Bertrand almost brutally. José says to Antonio, aloud so everyone hears, 'Do you remember the rabbit?' Antonio looks at him, surprised, 'What do you mean, the rabbit?' 'The wild hare you caught, at La Beaucette, by hand. Your first catch. You were seven. And *I* was jealous.' Antonio shrugs, avoids his brother's look. José smiles, addresses everyone, 'Tonio had hidden it in our bedroom. In a crate, during the day. And at night, he let him out, into our bed. *I* had the right to touch it. He petted it all the time, all the time.' Antonio mumbles, 'Stop your stupidity *de conejo*!' José looks at Bertrand, his bowl in front of him, his glass, then his grandfather. 'He petted it too much. Then on the third day it

155

died.' José gets up, gathers the soup bowls and spoons. Jeanne tries to help him. 'No, Mama, don't move.' José places everything in the sink, takes other plates from the sideboard. 'Tonight it's a celebration, we're changing three times. Like at the big house!' Cheese, salad, José serves the wine. He almost laughs, is amused, circles around the table, leans over, kisses Merced, gives a wink at Bertrand and, standing behind his grandmother, murmurs. 'It's also like the story of the Whites who leave some country or other in Africa, are pushed out by the Blacks. I read it. They leave in a great hurry, and with good reason. They abandon everything. An airlift. They return to their homelands. Some are killed. There were pictures in the papers. I saw them. Eight years ago. I was eight years old. And those colonists, yes, those colonists, they left their dogs and cats. The *dogs*, they died. No masters? No life! The *cats*, they took refuge in the forests. They defended themselves. Now, there are some magnificent cats in the virgin forests, back there!'

José goes back to his seat. A silence. He smiles at Bertrand. Bertrand looks at him vaguely, but looks at him better, a sketch. Antonio shakes his head and smiles at his brother. Under the table Bertrand's knees tremble. Léon asks Mathilde, 'How many jars of jam today?' 'Thirty-seven.' Juan looks at Lucio. 'Someday we should go up to Paris and bust their faces in for them.'

10

Table 7, at Taillevent's. The end of dinner, candied fruits, wrinkled napkins. For the n-th time since the start of dinner, a waiter approaches and with a measured, precise move, always with the same move, he covers the ashtray in which Suzy has just crushed out a scarcely lit cigarette by an identical ashtray, withdraws the whole thing, and places on the table the top ashtray, which covers it for an instant, is clean, and has the logo of the restaurant on it. Suzy does not like this restaurant, with its odour of impeccable woodwork, of discreet varnish, its swishing of good linen and quality fabrics. Its way also, in the placing and intensity of the lighting, or organising an ideal, a perfect intimacy, for the person who wants never again to be disturbed and to get his money's worth. Suzy hardly remembers the meal, the taste of the dishes, the appetizer, the main dish, the dessert, the savour of the sauces and creams. She has just treated herself to a grand dinner but what did she eat? She is obliged to think about it just to recall it. Obliged to make that tiny, little effort of memory which abruptly signals an absence of pleasure, the absence of celebration, of contact, and conversation. Henri and she have said nothing but conventional things.

From time to time, nervously, she would light a cigarette, only to crush it and put it out again with almost the same gesture, barely a puff or two. She has left a stub. A provocation. A game. The waiter, in attendance, as if on watch, would head for the table and replace the ashtray, his manner placid, automatically. The same thing with the sommelier and that bottle of château-Batilly '70, in bouquet and body leaving a slightly bitter after-taste, that the man had applied himself religiously to pouring into their glasses, scarcely had they moistened their lips in it. It had all been attentive and mechanical at the same time.

There are few customers. A table of Japanese. Three tables of Americans. An old man alone, in a corner, who never leaves anything on his plate. Suzy noticed him. Suzy also notices that no customer ever really looks at the maître d'hôtel, not at the waiter or sommelier, at anyone who serves them. They eat and live as if they were not being served at all, as if these people, dressed in the mourning clothes of their office, did not exist. Only serving personnel, however, tell the truth about the masters. On the other hand, the masters play with their misfortunes or their plots, and can offer only one truth after the other, truths of self-effacement, of ostentation, resignations or comfort. Never the 'apron's truth' as Jean used to name it. Jean would often say to his brother-in-law in order to isolate him in his defences, to put an end to a pointless quarrel 'I give back my apron.' It was the only efficient technique, he used to say, the technique of 'dish towels and napkins. With the dish towel, you can still hope. You can feel rage. With the napkin, you can no longer wipe. Even though it's only wiping one's lips of everything that's been said.'

Suzy takes a candied fruit, with her fingertips, and cracks it, a small dice of pineapple jam. Too sweet. A swallow of wine. She wipes her fingers on her napkin. Henri watches her. 'What are you thinking about?' Suzy answers, 'About Jean. I'm giving you back my apron. Do you recall?' Henri, seated slightly sideways, chair turned away, his right elbow on the table, plays with the paper stand marked 'Reserved'. Suzy observes him. 'And you? Who are you thinking about? It's dangerous thinking in a place like this. It shows right away.' There is a sweetness in Suzy's voice, which is almost sugary. What good is it still playing a comedy, or playing it again? Suzy reaches a hand across the table and places it on her brother's so that he lets go of the card holder. 'Please, Riquet, it's your turn to talk.' And, in a short transition, like a breath, using the minimum tone, her real voice rediscovered at last, despite the place, the hour, the automatons surrounding them, those serving and those eating, despite the stifling, the perfection, the ceremonial nothings to be repeated, all the while leaving her hand on her brother's, with light squeezes of her fingers, she murmurs, 'When I was little I used to think that everything good had no end. And afterwards? Tell me what happens afterwards?' For the gentleman on his own, at the corner table, Suzy's gesture is romantic. Suzy, feeling herself observed, withdraws her hand, smiles at the old man and lights a cigarette. She will smoke it, this time, right to the end. The maître d'hôtel approaches. Henri orders 'two coffees. A decaffeinated and a real one, please.' Suzy corrects herself. 'A decaffeinated and a double real one for me. Thank you.' And to her brother in the guise of explanation. 'I have a lot to read when I get home.'

Suzy notices abruptly that the gentleman at the corner table is no older than she is, no older than Henri. Between the two. From her bag she takes out her compact, opens it, looks at herself in the small, square mirror, at her eyes, especially her eyes, and observes also what is happening behind her, of which no one's the wiser, it is a habit. Shadows. In the wings of the tête-à-tête. She says to her brother, 'No, I'm not going to powder my nose. I have no need to be natural anymore. I was when everything was good. It's already too much. Or much too much! Like the farmers around Moncrabeau, when the rain they had expected so long finally came. It was always too much or not enough. Do you remember?'

At the name of Moncrabeau Henri lowered his eyes, brought his chair closer as if to face up to a possible attack and picked up the card holder again, elbows on the table. Suzy goes on, 'I *did* say Moncrabeau. I did well putting off Jacqueline, for we'd have been obliged to talk during dinner. Or after the sweets. After dessert. Watch out. I'm going to love you like we've forgotten loving each other since I learned that everything good had an end. Smile a little.' Henri looks at his sister, straight in the eyes. 'Please. Don't start all over again like this afternoon.' They bring the decaffeinated coffee and the double real coffee. They bring. They. Who?

Henri takes the small box of artificial sweeteners from the left pocket of his waistcoat. The old gentleman gets up. The maître d'hôtel pulls the table in front of him, with a deep bow. From a distance, the old gentleman salutes Suzy, but with a look only. What seemed romantic to him had abruptly become bitter, almost fierce. The gentleman in leaving no longer knows what to think. Suzy, by a look, wants to tell him not to worry. But he has already turned his back. The maître d'hôtel accompanies him out. The Americans at one of the tables burst out laughing.

Suzy drinks a sip of coffee, burns her lips, puts her cup down, 'What are you thinking about, Henri, tell me?' She smiles, sighs or breathes harder, her white dress, with the fabric rose at the waist, a protection from the other tables which are noisier. 'Well, Riquet, who are you thinking about? Say it! Twenty years ago, to the day . . .' 'Stop, my dear Suzanne.' Suzy leans toward her brother, 'Come on, say it. The error was in thinking, when we were children, that there were good things and bad things, good moments and others that weren't. Are you telling me to stop? I'm answering you not to go on this way anymore. I want to reach your conscience, whether it's good or bad. Your conscience. Aren't you going to say something?'

Two tablets in the decaffeinated coffee. No sugar for Suzy. They are drinking, both of them, with small swallows. Henri is thinking that he will not give the money. Suzy remembers Jean, quoting his friend Grick 'You never reach another's conscience.' Henri tells himself that at that moment his sister was almost touching when she talked about everything good not having an end. Suzy is thinking about the manuscript she is going to read when she goes home. She does not want routine success anymore, another revival of *The Collision*. The coffee is too strong. She crunches a candied fruit, a caramel-coated walnut. She shouldn't have. It's bad for the teeth, she has unpaid dental bills. Suzy's feet hurt. The new shoes. The dress is a little tight too. Another swallow of coffee. Poison. She won't sleep now.

Henri signals the maître d'hôtel to bring him the *addition* and, with his arms crossed on the table, with a dry smile, all benevolence, the benevolence of doubt, begins to speak with that jerky diction that used to characterise him when he spoke in public, at lectures, courses, conventions, inaugurations or banquets. 'At Moncrabeau? There's Bertrand. At Sauveterre? There's Claire. I never went back to Moncrabeau. I have never been to Sauveterre. In Paris, closer to your place than mine, there's Luc. When I call him at his office, he's never there. He's in a meeting. At home? It rings. It does nothing but ring. Finally there's Sébastien. In Norway. Do you know Norway? Sébastien doesn't sail anymore. I was proud of him, but only when he was sailing. My grandchildren? I give them to you. Pierre is the exact copy of Anne-Marie. Laura and Paul send me Christmas cards in English. Loïc, Yves and Géraldine write me only to ask for money. My children and grandchildren? I don't know them. I don't even recognise myself. With them, it's always too much or not enough. You see, I listened to you. The best death I can offer them is to let them live.' Henri empties the coffee cup at one go. The maître d'hôtel places the bill on the table.

Suzy crunches another candied fruit. She looks at Henri grappling with his wallet, 100 and 500 franc bills. 'Proud of yourself?' She leans forward 'And what about Bertrand?' She smiles, imitates her brother. 'Do you know the story of the minister who was a minister only when he wasn't really one, and then when he wasn't one at all anymore? Do you know France's history, since we were born? Well, we're still here. That's all. A Jewish story? Jean too is still here. He's listening at this moment. A true story? It's the story of a young man who ought to be blowing out his forty candles. He can't do it. He doesn't even know how to blow in front of him anymore.' Suzy blows on the table, in a circle, her hands flat on the tablecloth, elbows bent, like an insect. Henri pulls himself back in his chair. He waves to the maître d'hôtel to take the bill and the money away. The maître d'hôtel approaches. Suddenly elegant Suzy looks at him. 'The dinner was exquisite. And the candied fruits as usual.' 'Thank you, madame.'

The maître d'hôtel withdraws. The ashtray attendant approaches, an automaton, the usual gesture, and retires as quickly. Suzy looks at her brother. 'Did you see? That time he took a clean one and put down a clean one. Are you ashamed of me? Are you wondering if you'll be able to come back here? Am I right? Let's leave.'

She starts to rise. Henri catches his sister's left hand. 'No, that would be still worse.' 'Worse, is it? You're very pale, all of a sudden.' Suzy slips her hand under her brother's hands. She smiles. 'You see, we're still playing at which of us will place his hand on the other's hand. And which of us will have the last word. And which of us will leave first. By the effort of wanting to win by oneself, one loses by oneself. In your place, I'd even be afraid of losing Bernadette.' The Japanese get up, leave the restaurant. The Americans at one of the tables have ordered champagne. Henri withdraws his hand, crosses his arms on the table, pulls his chair up again, his shoulders slightly raised, his manner childish. He tries to smile, a little pout twists the mouth as he looks at his sister. 'I don't want to, Suzy, nor can I change. I don't want to change.' Henri hesitates. In a hushed voice 'I cannot nor do I want to bend over anymore. People have never

161

bent over me.' Silence. He smiles at his sister. 'Who is taking care of me? Who has taken care of me, ever?' Suzy answers, 'Me. At this moment.'

The maître d'hôtel comes back with the change, places the saucer on the table. Suzy looks at her brother, 'I should have made the boat capsize when we were fishing. I should have demanded my share of things when you took over the Place d'Antioche, and kept my share of Moncrabeau. I accepted money instead. And that money, I spent it, with Jean, to live and enjoy some pleasure. Well, we really did have some pleasure.' 'Don't talk like that.' 'Oh, is taking pleasure forbidden?' A waiter brings the champagne to the Americans' table, puts down the bucket, then the white napkin, the preparation of the cork. Suzy lights a cigarette. A puff, long, thoughtful. Suzy pushes aside the glasses and the cup in front of her, strokes the tablecloth unconsciously as if she wanted to define a territory. The champagne cork pops. Suzy looks at her brother. 'How about giving me a lighter. Mine is old. I can't manage to lose it.' She smiles. 'How about offering me some champagne. I'm not thirsty. But you have the money.'

Henri orders a bottle. A smile from the maître d'hôtel. Surprise from the wine steward who was already doing the wine cellar accounts for the evening. Suzy watches over the ashtray and holds it under her hand, her fingers spread like an octopus, cigarette between the middle and index fingers. Never has the neutral, flat, uniform odour of a deluxe restaurant seemed so strong to her, so compelling, so instantly unchanged. The useless odour of a play that's already been performed, but when, how? What is ever really played, what ever? So little compared with the scent of an empty theatre, a nervous, capricious scent, with rumblings from the pit, the call of the lights. At the Théâtre des Champs, they still sweep the wings, the corridors and the dressing rooms with saw-dust. Jean used to say, 'It's the forum of fools and the meeting place of rats.' With her other hand, Suzy strokes the tablecloth. Someone clears away, someone else, a waiter, another waiter who had not yet approached their table, or perhaps had approached but Suzy does not recognise him, there are others like that, all the others always, her whole life long, oh so many, pretending, knowing, thinking but especially not changing anything, just someone,

162

someone clearing away the glasses and the cups. A clean table. Suzy guards her ashtray jealously. She wants several stubs in it. At home, the water heater is broken. No hot water to take a bath when she returns. At the pool at Saint Ouen, my Wednesdays, at day's end, for the final shower before leaving, there is, there too, nothing but cold water left. The tanks have been emptied by the soapy fellows. You have to take a breath, dare to get under. The boys' showers are separated from the girls'. At that moment, with the women, Suzy feels terribly grandmotherish. There are no more affectionate looks to make her believe in a youth regained. Suzy is delighted. Henri has ordered champagne not by submission but as the elder brother. Trapped.

And Henri is thinking about this power of his that Suzy mocks or objects to, by asserting to himself that to have the gift to think about it, makes it unshakeable, so that nothing can weaken it. And he tells himself that under the threat of having to listen and be pertinent, he has only to maintain the misunderstanding, by 'mis-hearing' and 'mis-listening', verbs invented by the children of whom Henri became afraid, wondering which of them would be capable, not of disputing for its own sake an outdated anticonformity a sword thrust in the water, so much in vogue among some bourgeoisie, but be capable of a more basic outrage, a devastation of the heart and mind, that attack from within, which alone can destroy the family nucleus. And it was the youngest, Bertrand. Henri regrets nothing. He leaves regrets to people out of power, to the eternal non-attainers of responsibility, the only true upstarts. Suzy stares at him. She is waiting for a word or for a look from him, but behind his face, impassive, Henri gives no sign. He ordered the champagne to catch his sister in the trap of her insolence. In that, he is still maintaining the misunderstanding. That is the fact and the sensation, in the sense of the event, the sensory even of their lives, a series, nothing but a series of immobile violences. Let nothing show and order the champagne.

Henri smiles within himself, deep inside, lurking, lying in wait for his sister. He remembers, in amused thought, one of Jean's numerous sayings and says to himself, 'I recognise a bourgeois in the way he claims not to be one,' and 'I recognise a bourgeois in the way he never recognises himself.' Pleased with himself for the double recall, Henri gloats. Suzy can go on waiting for a sign or a word from him. But she won't have it. The misunderstanding must be maintained. The doubt also must be maintained, and to the imaginations of rogues or madmen, philosophers or politicians must be left only the option of rushing about in a vacuum, of denouncing this and that but unable ever again to announce anything positive, because they are worn out, tormented and destroyed by themselves, jettisoned by their own ideologies to the point of having to believe in a reflective and thinking Right, when the one and unique root of this so-called Right is precisely not being reflective and not thinking, or else thinking and reflecting in order to do nothing. Nothing amuses Henri more than those people who cause the Right, to which he belongs, to theorize, because they are incapable of uniting a divided and irreparable Left which, because of its pointless quarrels, has ceased to be unrestorable and so let itself be restored, a thousand shards that are gathered up by a shovel and held above a trash can, for a little while. Henri tells himself that this other Right has never been as strong as since the crisis, the economic war, the rise of unemployment, the strikes, the administrative aberrations and the social injustices. There lies the only distraction in his life since he has been shunted aside and kept in retirement. The Left still did not understand that the true Right was the Centre, the scourge's support, but not the scourge itself. Nothing really bends for it, neither in one direction nor the other. Bertrand had understood. Too bad for him. Henri feels like answering his sister by saying, 'Yes, Suzy, we're still here. That's our history of France.' But Suzy would take it the wrong way, would take it as an observation of inability, or a confession of impotence. The champagne bucket. The bottle. The white napkin. And for them both a cork would pop.

Suzy, facing the impassive brother whom she knows is tormented, so very evident to himself, determined to let nothing show, everything done for the sake of appearance, his senses, feelings, smells, thoughts, his touching, so that once again they are fly fishing, the hook gleams, the useless catches. You must above all not move. She detests champagne. She raises her glass to Henri, scarcely wets her lips and always leaves her glass full. Jean often used to mock her about it and would tell her, 'You behave like a night club hostess. You're right. Champagne only

164

consists of empty bubbles. That's why, in general, we use it to celebrate and rejoice.' Suzy remembers all that, very exactly, word for word, running like a brook, a stream, a river, an ocean. All flows towards a present. The present. Her present indicative. Her brother's conscience, when all is said and done about the day's events, is expressed only in the way he organises lulls in time, he excels only in this art of recovering silences, of waiting, of waiting until the dangerous outcries fuse, burst, amaze and are lost. The true conscience then grows weary of returning again and again to the assault. Jean, even more than his brother-in-law's Right, used to denounce the leftist theatre. 'Theses in lead boots that do nothing but convince people who are already convinced.' Jean would have so liked to find the way, the true one. 'The human way,' and that made him laugh. The cork pops. A little bit of foam. The waiter fills the glasses. Henri and Suzy clink their glasses. Suzy bursts into laughter 'To the institutionalising of our dead times!' 'I don't find that funny.' 'Then to Bertrand? I dare you.' They toast.

Suzy only moistens her lips, a small taste, bitter and fizzy, on the tip of her tongue. She puts the glass down, stares hard at it. Henri, on the other hand, drinks with small sips. White wines are forbidden him, but he drinks, conscientiously. Most often, in attacking others one only attacks oneself, in insulting, one insults oneself. Suzy forbids herself to submit to the law of this common morality, which she in any case doubts, from an excess of simplicity, or perhaps of clarity. She hesitates. She watches the little bubbles rising to the surface, bursting and renewing themselves. Jean used to say of these bubbles, 'They're the exact image of the audience for *The Collision*, the more they rise, the more they burst, and the more they come.' He would add, 'The tragedy of that particular champagne is that sometimes it doesn't go flat. You believe then, just a little, in spite of everything, in what you've created.' Suzy closes her eyes, her hands flat on the tablecloth. Henri has toasted. She has toasted, with him, and in Bertrand's name, a light clinking of the glasses. Suzy knows that by provoking her brother she is only provoking herself, and so forth. It is only the instinct of the old, those who were born that way, educated in advance, are strong from roots that are not even intrusive anymore, strong in confidence, but which have intruded into everything, have become subsistence.

They survive. The dead moments in time keep them alive.

Suzy opens her eyes again, bends her head slightly, a nice air about her. She no longer knows what she is winning or what she is losing, in playing in this way, in that way, by claiming not to play, in imagining she has touched the conscience of a brother who has always applied himself to not having one, apparently. What good is it talking, insisting, using stormbearing words, and certain names, that stab like shining metal. The dagger and the clouds, in thought Suzy has just given herself two images, to let time run on, a little longer, between them both, since they have just drunk a toast.

In a letter addressed to Romain Leval from Moncrabeau, Bertrand wrote in a postcript, 'I only like the sky when filled with clouds.' Everything, in memory, turns, drifts, slips, whirls, comes back as if to one point of departure. There was also a short poem by Bertrand, *The Gliders*. To Romain. Lying down, you and I. The hill is made of chalk. Lying, you beside me, I keep watch on the sky for gliders. They will shoot up there. At the chalk crest, there where the sky tilts, limits. One will shoot up, then two. And three. You will squeeze my hand. This dream I had yesterday. I am writing it to you in the future. The gliders' present is forbidden us.' Suzy repeats out loud looking at Henri, 'The gliders' present is forbidden us.' The maître d'hôtel approaches to serve the champagne again. Suzy places her left hand gently on her glass. 'No, thank you.' She looks at Henri. 'It was for the principle.' The maître d'hôtel refills Henri's glass. Henri has a satisfied air. 'What principle, Suzy?' A breath, 'You're worse than the people you expose. You're alone. Terribly alone. Like a little animal turning around on itself. He risks going crazy and he doesn't know it.' Henri drinks a mouthful. 'I don't like champagne either. It gives me that taste in the mouth that makes me speak with a bitterness I don't really feel. You're a shrew, Suzanne, my little Suzy. You have always been one. I love you anyway.' He raises his glass. 'To your solitude, all right? May it get better by not questioning any longer.' Suzy does not toast. She watches the bubbles in her glass. She repeats, in a monotone, scraps of words, 'The gliders' present is forbidden us. That's Bertrand. He was seventeen.' Henri points his finger at his sister. 'You are going to throw those letters away. You're also going to throw the manuscript of

Mortmain away. It's how much? I'll give you the money you need only for *The Collision*. I love my children terribly. You don't have any. How can you judge?'

The Americans at one table get up and leave the restaurant, a disorganised and noisy ballet. Then the silence of hangings, carpets and indirect lighting, the measured silence of the place, falls again, instantly. The maître d'hôtel has prepared the bill for the bottle of champagne and holds it ready, on a saucer. Henri leans toward his sister and murmurs, 'We will never understand why we are cut off from one another, and also terribly attached to each other, creating ties for ourselves. Only running away brings us together. *That* is the family that you don't have and of which I am the father. I was thinking about that, at Bermann's, because of Pantalon. Perhaps also because I knew I was going to be meeting you. You were once again about to judge this family that you don't have and that I do. This family that I can no longer bring together in joy. So I had the idea, it's true, of bringing them together, once and for all, in misfortune. But it's just an idea. Add up all the allusions of murder and there's no more humanity.' Henri raised his glass. 'To Jean, who never understood anything.' Suzy does not move. Henri brings the glass to his lips, a small face, with a slight smile of satisfaction and begins again. 'To Suzy, who never totally left the family and to Jean who never could get in!' The same gesture with a face like the beginning of a grimace, a small swallow this time, and with deliberation, 'To Luc's Legion of Honour, to Sébastien's immobile voyage, to Claire's still-lifes and to my favourite son's fortieth birthday!' He raises the glass a little higher. 'To David who will steal the money I'll give you and to Pantalon who has forgotten his collar and leash!' He drinks, puts the glass down, looks at Suzy, 'I love you, and you know it.'

Suzy rises. Her napkin falls to the floor. A waiter leaps forward to recover it. Suzy murmurs, 'You forgot Cécile.' The maître d'hôtel, at Henri's gesture, brings the bill. Henri takes out his wallet, the notes, pays, puts the wallet back into the inside pocket of his coat and rises in turn. He smiles at his sister, a smile that is perfect for awkward pauses. 'So, how much for all of it, the letters and the play?' Suzy passes in front of him, 'Bravo!'

167

11

The numbering of the letters is from the hand of Romain Leval.

No. 1   To Monsieur Romain Leval
                                                          March 27

Dear sir,

I am writing you at the Théâtre des Champs as my Aunt Suzanne advised. Advise is a very big verb when one thinks of the thousand facets of this woman whom I have sometimes thought I would have preferred to have as my mother. Subjunctive of an offeratory. She and I have come down, for a few days only, to Moncrabeau. We are theoretically supposed to celebrate Easter here. I do indeed write theoretically. My brother Luc was married last year at the same period. Cécile, my mother, remained in Paris as Anne-Marie is going to give birth any day now. My mother is going to find herself a grandmother, me an uncle and my father a grandfather. Thrust of the family sap. Sébastien is at sea until two days before his marriage next June 17th. Ruth is in Toronto, a round trip to warn her parents. I accompanied her to the airport. She was afraid, but a joy mastered her fear. A joy of the same nature as fear. As for Claire, for this holiday, and for the first time, she has decided to stay in Paris. I sense she is pressured by my elder brother's decisions. She, too, will get married, I'm sure, very quickly. That will be the third celebration. I surprised her with her boyfriend Gérard, in the street, but I didn't dare speak to them. Often, in the sensual subject matter of my reading, the couple in love embrace, a tender couple of heroes in love, I feel them giddy, abandoned in one another, a contemplation from which I am abruptly excluded. They go away. They sail away. And not me. I am one of those who is always on the shore or on the pavement. Gérard was kissing Claire on the neck. I will never know how to be giddy.

An engraving reigns, here, in the shadow of an often

uninhabited guest room, for my parents entertain little as if they were afraid, for us, of an outside world. I write indeed 'of an', and not 'of the', for that world is not truly one, judged in advance, a dangerous prejudice. This engraving, which no one has ever looked at up close, shows, in a bed of wild grass, two shepherds, naked. The first is stretched out on his back, his arms up, his hands crossed behind his neck. The second, lying alongside the first, close to him, turned toward him, leaning on an elbow, with his other hand is caressing his friend's forehead. I know they have just fulfilled their embrace. I feel they are kissing for one last time. It is always the last time when you kiss each other. It is, doubtless, like that when love endures an entire life. Now, in looking carefully at the engraving, one makes out in the background, behind the weeds not bent under the two lovers' bodies, something like the shadow and the gaze of a third, man or beast, charming, tragic, another shepherd. This engraving, I have never dared take down. That would have attracted attention. There are marks on the walls, here at Moncrabeau, when they change the pictures. This engraving, I did not dare appropriate it and keep it near me either. It would have made me noticed. I like those bodies of the same sex, that's where my emotion lies.

When I was a child, I used to climb on a chair to look at it in secret. I have never spoken to my brothers or my sister about it. This engraving was, and still is, my secret garden. Only once, Bernadette, our servant and friend, surprised me and said, 'What are you doing there? You should go somewhere else to play. Outside!' Those are the exact words. I am giving them away to you, just as I am giving you the garden in this engraving. It is time for me to let go of it and to live it. I was forgetting: under the engraving can be read *The Intrigue*. I don't understand it very well. Maybe I don't want to understand it. The evidence suggests quite useless bad times. In wanting, with all my body, to be one of the two lovers, it seems to me I'll never be anything but the third one who does not understand the exhilaration of the first two, and who, in love with one of them, is forced to play a role he does not like. A role whose pain is equal only to the others' exhilaration.

So I am alone with my Aunt Suzanne and for two weeks. When we got here yesterday, as usual, I went to see the engraving again and I thought of you, the other day. Uncle Jean had asked me to come by the theatre. He wanted me to meet you. I have told him something in confidence, a brutal trust, I wish to be myself. And he did, it's true, organise this meeting. In your first look I felt you had been informed. At the second, that I was too young and you were afraid. Ruth's fear. See above. This is quite a long letter but my timidity tells me to go this way and this way only, straight to the goal. Then, after seeing the engraving again, after thinking about you, I spoke to Suzanne about you. She told me: 'Write him. *I* can't understand. But *he* will.' It is one in the morning. I am writing you. I know my uncle is giving you a chance by lending you his theatre (at the end of the season, let's not be fooled, he said it himself in front of us) for the opening of your first play. So you are very busy. But I hope so much for a third look. Write me. I await you. Bertrand.

P.S. In the engraving, on the bent grass, the shepherds seem to be in a kind of shell. I don't want to look at it anymore. If you intend not to write me, write me to say so. That's funny.

No. 2.   To Monsieur Romain Leval
                                                      March 29

Dear sir,

I have not ceased, since I addressed my first letter to you, to recompose it in my head. Now, I have a real memory only for what has no importance, learning, the learning of diplomas and education. Let's laugh! I have read and lived it in so many and far too many novels and especially poems, I have just lived myself for the first time: the heart's memory is absence of memory, at the mercy of sensations. And I feel myself pulled in all directions. Please write me. Even if you're very busy, there is always the moment when you feel somebody is calling to you. Don't stop at your second look. The time for amorous gestures has nothing to do with human time, or not too much. These two days, since I slipped the letter into the mail box at Lestaque, I have lived like two centuries. Sensuality is on the lookout. This morning the sky is grey and soft. Everything is damp. Nature is swallowing everything whole. On the lake, below the house, there are mists I'd like to inhale, water in which I would gladly plunge risking the cold and the slime, if Lucio, our caretaker,

171

and his son Juan weren't there, on the shore, near the pontoon, sanding the turned over hulls of the two flat-bottomed boats in which we had, my brothers, sister and I, strange circling competitions. It's the vision of these boats, the water, the impossible river (this captive lake is so populated with fish that it shimmers from them, especially at night, when the moon rises) which leads me to write you again. Desire charges all symbols. This charge is a pleasure if one can devote oneself to looking, listening, letting oneself go, forgetting what one has learned, the seduction of philosophers, the barbarism of analyses and psychoanalyses, the intellectual distrust that leads the firm believer to spurn what comes from the heart.

I have the impression, at seventeen, flanked by my two bacs, in the curious way my mother has of always specifying them 'with honours in each' as if she were sucking a honey drop, of only having won some paper victory, with conventional dissertations, constantly solicited by two perfectly identical ideas. One is to defend blindly the conventional and smug family that produced me, to be in the faithful image of the success they wish for me. And the other is one of fleeing, disputing, moving about, moving the way they move, arguing and moving around in a certain milieu, with wisdom teeth you think you've already lost, with the certainty, your fantasies resolved, of being revolutionary, of returning to the fold and the warmth, of taking your place again in the social standing and the safety deposit box. I don't want anything to do with these two privileges. I saw you and, even before your first glance, I felt that you had the path to show me, the place of bent grass, too.

Back in Paris, I too, will be very busy. I must prepare the university entrance exams. But I confess, how do I do it in such a way that my determination is not taken for vanity, I am afraid only of not having on one hand the strength to play the little game of passing all those exams again, and on the other hand, the weakness of not living up to what the correctors expect from me so that they can give me the best marks. My body is ready. I don't even need to touch myself to come. Sometimes at night, as a dream changes sequence, there are always so many forests and trees in my dreams, I spurt, all alone. It would be nicer to come for and with the other person that I haven't met yet or whom I have only just seen, before his first and his second look. When all's said and done my first letter was timid. This one, the second, with the pressure off, has the naturalness of gesture. I saw you in the forest, last night, a forest on a theatre stage. It was a real forest in a real theatre, another play, ours. You dared not look at me, but you were thinking about that look. And I didn't hold back. It was good. I was all wet.

This morning, writing you, nature is swallowing me whole. I do not want ideas nor castes nor the compatible attachment nor pointless running away. I want only to read you and see you again. We will take the time that theoretically we do not have. And we won't be afraid since I am leading you astray. Just show me the path. I would like to kiss your hands. I come with each finger as I write you and hold this pen. Images don't scare me. They are obscene only to the eye of the shameful. So in order to defend a shame, they show everything. They forget nuance and sharing. I am excited by you. I want to come with everything, all the time and from everywhere. I too, must marry, wed the other person. In the eyes of the law, I'm a minor, but that is not the age of our bodies if they unite. An impossible marriage, in view of the rules of their society, but we will ourselves be the rule and not its decline. This avowal of my sexuality, a wicked word bristling with barbed wire, that I made to my uncle and by ricochet to my Aunt Suzanne, I will never make to Henri, my father, nor to Cécile. Confessing would be admitting a fault and those people, my parents, even if they are not practising, have a church in their heads, a church built on a synagogue. Fault, pardon, compassion, pity, charity, even the idea of a revolution are all their property. They take over everything and I do not want to be part of their propriety, even at the risk of awakening in them the murderous instinct for 'their' conservation. Bunch of conservatives! I don't want this argument any more. I feel myself already terribly reproduced by you. Waiting for your letter. And straight to the point, don't hold it against me. Our gestures and our looks will just be better organised in their disorder. I am waiting. I already walk around with and in you. No point telling you I love you. So I adore you. Bertrand.

No. 3.

Thank you.

Your note arrived this morning. Juan brought it to me. Our letters must have crossed. In the second you 'will see' Juan with his father on the bank of the pond. Juan is three years older than I. Often, in the summers as a child, I would leave my brothers and sister for him, and only for him. I admire him so deservedly that I have never dared more than words, with him, respecting what, by instinct, can not push him toward me other than with gestures. It is also, of course, a matter of class difference for, take note, I am my father's son and he is his father's. He used to go with me, on walks, and in secret from the others, but there was always his fear like mine, between us, fraternal fears like a curtain of night, and for both of us a sun on our heads. And it's he who brought me your letter! I thought there was a sign in that, a delegation of power. I say 'note' and 'your letter'. Your few lines are enough since you have answered.

I don't like your saying you are twice my age. You won't have to bend down to kiss me and I won't have to stand on tiptoe to return your kiss.

At the top of this letter, I wrote your address the way they do in official mail and that, being incisive, pleased me. But I am writing you at home, from now on. I imagine you living up at the top with no lift. As well as I can remember, at no. 5 of that street you have an unimpeded view of the Impasse des Deux-Anges. What can I do about it? What can you do about it? That's the way it is. But I'm leaving you for everything is already said beyond words. One thought joins us. Thank you for answering. I snap my fingers at your suspicion. Don't be afraid. Paris is big. Jean and Suzanne will keep quiet. People keep quiet backstage. I return very early on the morning of April 7 and, as soon as I have left my bags at the Place d'Antioche, I will take the metro. I will have to change at Etoile and at Châtelet, two transfers for two angels. I will bring some hot croissants. I don't expect another letter from you before that. You must devote your time to rehearsals of your play. Which means I will wait for your message, terribly. Look carefully. I am in the house. With you.

174

There is always a fold-down seat for loves yet to come. Until the seventh! Bertrand.

P.S. Having just finished Kant, Bachelard, Mounier, the dead luggage of my Easter reading, we need to write like this. A little love never hurts. A little love yet to come. It's me, yet to come, in three words. I only like the sky inhabited with clouds.

No. 4.   To Romain Leval
                                                                April 2
    Hello!
Yesterday, I took a turn around the property. The perfect, exact tour of the perimeter of Moncrabeau. I don't feel like a property owner. Yesterday, I went to look at the engraving again. It did not move me as strongly as before. Henceforth the emotion is within me. Everything gives way. This morning I helped Juan to put a second coat of varnish onto the bottom of the boats. And I liked the smell of it. Several times Juan brushed my arm. I thought it was you. He didn't pay any attention to it. Anne-Marie has brought a boy into the world: Pierre. Much love. Uncle Bertrand.

P.S. Have you read Nizan? What nostalgia for the Rue d'Ulm. He's sincere. Because of him I joined the communist party. But I returned my card before I got it. There are only two errors not to commit in this country, joining a party and quitting it. I don't like taking sides. I like sides to be taken. I will post this 'note' which has become a 'letter', at Lestaque where Suzanne wants to go to see Mathilde, the mayor's wife, to buy jam, preserves and some foie gras. She chooses too much each time. When she has to pay, she takes almost nothing, and the basket, on the way back, is light. Suzanne repeats to me then that their theatre is a 'holey basket'. I thought she was stingy. She is amusing, like Jean, comically courageous.

No. 5.   To Romain Leval
                                                                April 7
                                                              Midnight
Dear Romain,
    I will never forget this morning, our first morning. Paris, from now on, for me, has a skin, an odour and a touch. Forgive me, in

your arms, for coming so fast. I couldn't wait anymore. And that's nothing but a detail. You seemed so surprised that I'm feeling a little guilty about it, tonight. How do you take pleasure with the other person, come with him and at the same time? There is always one who does the talking and the other who doesn't. In fact, we forgot to eat the hot croissants.

In a little while, our second morning, I will slip this note under your pillow. The door will be open, you said, and you will still be sleeping since rehearsals last late at night. Your wakening will be mine. You will read this letter when I will already be gone. My day classes and your night rehearsals. It's lovely getting to know each other in the morning. Seeing one another and seeing mornings again. My father looked at me strangely at dinner tonight. I too am going away. River bank or river, I don't know yet. Bertrand.

P.S. I wasn't mistaken, the 5th floor has a view from above onto the Impasse.

No. 6. To Romain Leval
April 8, 4 p.m.

Dear Romain,
The idea of climbing the six floors even though you are not here, to write you 'till tomorrow morning', pleases me. I am doing it. I like your looking at me with your eyes wide open and your preventing yourself, sometimes, from touching me. Nothing is going too fast, ever. Even the Place d'Antioche is inhabited by you. I have never smelled the odour of the chestnut trees so strongly when they bud out. To my sleeping beauty, thank you. B.

No. 7. I did not come backstage to congratulate you. It was a success. You know it. You felt the house listening. That tore my heart out. This April 20 is a date for you, as well as for me. The key to your apartment is burning in my trouser pocket. I hold it, all day long. I'm warming it. I am going now to make a round trip to the Place d'Antioche to mess up my bed. I will come back early this morning. I want to breathe in the rising day with you. Leave the window open. I'm coming. Tibi. B.

No. 8. April 21
Romain! I'm beginning to understand why you were afraid.

176

The danger present in that third look, I'm living it now. Here I am riveted. The Paris sky has tipped from the Place d'Antioche to the overhang in the Rue Saint-Benoît. You're no longer suspicious either. You know now that I'm up to your height. The height of kisses. Age is not very important and I have carried you off. Everything binding you awakens in you the most candid tendernesses, the violent ones, which are the prelude to the most craven flights. Why *did* you say you could very well change the lock? You said it smiling. You even made it clear you 'were teasing' by pinching me on the cheek. I still have the pinched cheek from it, wondering if you had not just betrayed us by that, although everything is only just beginning. That's it, it's pain, the pain of love. I am not scolding you. I admire you. I wish you complete success for your play. I am leaving this note on your desk. I am not folding the page. This kind of message is not folded up. Nothing is folded. I am going out of here, now, from your place, distressed. Yes, I believed too quickly that it was our place. I am going out without turning around and without re-reading these few lines. I will double lock the door, put the key underneath and, from outside, will give it a push with my finger, like a kick in football. This key too quickly given, so strongly returned, will slide into your apartment, well inside it. See you soon. Don't disguise your voice if you call me at some distant time or soon, at the Place d'Antioche, Bernadette would recognise you right off. Or Cécile. Or Henri. You only have to be seen. May we very soon be locked in each other's arms. That's my anti-teasing operation. There, I'm the one showing you the way. Supertibi. B.

No. 9.   To Romain. The Gliders
Lying down you and I
The hill is made of chalk,
Lying, you beside me
Let's keep a watch on the sky for the gliders
They will shoot up there
At the chalk crest
There where the sky tilts
And limits.
One will shoot up, then two.
And three.

You will squeeze my hand.
This dream I had yesterday.
I am writing it in the future.
The gliders' present is forbidden us.

No. 10. I want to see you again. I know you will never dare call or even write me at the Place d'Antioche. Still, you dared do it, at Moncrabeau. So I will have received from you only one letter, the pleasures of the first mornings, that key, almost one night after the first performance of your play, then, nothing more. I know fear is in control. A fear, for you, of not finding yourself again the way you were before me. So, throw my letters away. And especially that poem I left under your door nearly a week ago. I would very much have liked to be able to get it back, as soon as I had slipped it under. That's the way of all poetry and especially of that one, mine, which sings. You are afraid of seeing me again because you are afraid of seeing yourself, in love, attached and bare. Let me tell you, strong in my seventeen years, soon eighteen, that what you fear, I have the instinct for not having yet learned to fear and I have the violent intention of never learning it. There is a grandeur in holing up, licking your wounds and starting again. There is a splendour in coming and coming back again to that terrain two lovers create for and by one another. Nothing, compared with that space, has really any importance, neither the period nor fashions nor sufferings nor wars nor anything. I am writing you in pure loss when I think about you in pure gain. Two men like us should be able to reproduce themselves strictly by their own company. I don't like the word strict. It makes the noise of a checking-room locker's key. And yet, that's where our truth and danger is, everything that should bring us together. Sometimes I go to the Rue Saint-Benoît, and from the far end of the Impasse des Deux-Anges, leaning back against the metal door of the playground for the Sixth Arrondissement's communal school, with arms crossed, I observe your window. Watch and wave to me! And if someone else approaches, don't worry. What I am suggesting to you has nothing to do with what you are demanding of yourself. I have the taste of you in my mouth, your geography on my fingertips and your astonished looks that still surprise me in my head. Are you afraid? So much the better! It is five in the morning. It's the

178

fifth of May. A Monday. For us both, it is still the beginning of the week. I love you. I will have just the time to stop by your place, climb the five flights, with life in the soul, and then go to the examination room at the Rue de l'Abbé-Groult (who was he anyway?) to breeze through my first entrance exam. I'll pass. More important is that I pass — with you.

In the evening two days from now, to celebrate the end of my exam, I'll go as an ordinary spectator to see your play for the n-th time. Love counts performances, passion doesn't. I will wait for you, after the show. I like to see the front lights turned out and the doors closed. I'll be there, a little way off, on the street, to the right of the stagedoor. I have seen your play from the first row in the orchestra, from the back of a first balcony box, from the very top, from the gods, and even from the front of the second balcony. I have seen it from everywhere, and especially lived it from within me. I must talk to you about it. I am jealous of the house, for it listens. About you, Jean said to me 'So?' I didn't answer anything. Suzanne finds me 'handsomer than ever' and that my 'cheeks are getting hollow.' Cécile bought me new pajamas, on sale, at the United Stores. Henri, when I was sitting down at the table, told me to wash my hands and to put on a clean shirt. Everything is you. And I am sure you would be still more afraid if I weren't telling you. Throw this headless letter away, I can no longer write your name without raging, away with the other letters. To be continued. The day after tomorrow? I know you will be here. We will walk in the street, for the first time, together, outdoors. Now, I have to hurry. They don't admit latecomers for the examination papers. In fact, by chance, I met another boy. It was crazy. I also saw a being at your window. It was a beasting. A word I give you between being and beast. Till Wednesday. Bertrand.

P.S. My dear Romain. In wishing to live more beautiful days again, we too easily forget the happy days that are passing. I would very much like to spend a day, a whole day with you. But, they all say *but* around me. They hold me with that but. And I have chosen, you know, not to flee, or to pretend, but, my own but, to unite and confront.

No. 11. June 26th of our Year I. Beginning tomorrow the days

179

will grow shorter. I really knew you would one day arrive here, at Moncrabeau. I am leaving this note in the secret and in the softness of your pillow: it's mine. I have discreetly slipped into your pillowcase mine from my bed. When you go to bed, look well, across from you, there is the engraving. You have thrown away my letters, about which I have my doubts anyway, but I sense you did more than read them. That is, if one can do more than read, ever. But anyhow, here you are. You are coming, invited by my aunt. For Cécile, you are Suzanne's lover, Jean's protégé, the husband's deceiver, and so they have invented the theatre that they've always liked around her. For Anne-Marie, all that counts is the baby and the phone calls from Luc. Sébastien and Ruth are on their wedding trip. Claire has left for Epidaurus and Delphi, alone. My father is staying in Paris until mid-July, time for scheming. When alone he dreams of changing himself so he can be entrusted better in the idea he's made of himself. On the back of this message, there's a map. Join me. You can't get lost. The sky is clear. The moon will watch over you. You will need about twenty minutes to meet me. The spot is called Auzan. I will be lying, under the elm tree, near the farmhouse. When you leave the house, on the stairs, walk next to the handrail, no squeaking. You'll see, it's fun going out without making any noise, to meet a place or a friend. In a very little while. With a little luck, little Pierre will cry in his cradle, for his midnight bottle, and this will cover your slipping out. I have waited seventeen years for this moment, seventeen years on active duty, as the military say, whether they've been in a war or not. And if I cry when you arrive, down there, under my tree, don't be mistaken about the tears. They will be bursts of laughter. Like shards of glass for tearing the black fabric of the shortest night. Hurry. It's crazy. It's good. You are here. At last.

No. 12. Too bad, read, Romain, read! I ache all over from loving too much and not knowing how to throw it away at the required time. As soon as the game of our meeting was won, I should have, by cynicism, the cynicism of break-ups, given you that freedom you believe is free and which is only fear of becoming attached to another person. Who has thrown you over before so that you are so fervent in not believing in yourself? I ache all over from loving too much and that has to cease. I am going to leave

180

my skin and my spirit here, my spirit before my skin. Someday, distraught by emotion, I will no longer find the way back. Why did you leave for Paris-the-octopus so quickly, without even informing Suzanne? That telegram you received, you sent yourself from Lectoure. It wasn't a 'phone call you had to make to Paris, for your play and its 'revival at another theatre in the autumn', but a blow, a simple blow, that you made yourself thinking you were hitting me. So long! I will never forget the curve of your back nor your bites and especially not that dull groan strangled deep in your throat when you fear making any noise because you're coming. I understood. Tonight, July 9th, I am eighteen years old. You chose the right evening. I am telling you good evening. Words bow and scrape when they're no good for anything anymore. I passed my exams. My father is staying in Paris. He is one of the drafters of the preamble to the Constitution of the Fifth Republic 'I have understood you!' Moncrabeau is emptied of you. The pain is deep. Tomorrow, I'm going to take a little turn around on the pond. Juan no longer speaks to me. Next. Tibi or no tibi. Bertrand.

P.S. You should read Diderot, London, Reverzy's *Le Passage*, Wolfe, Housman, Wallace Stevens, Juan Ramon Jiménez, Cavafy: can one only be devoured in that way?

No. 13.   Paris. September 13.
My dear Romain,
    I want to see you again. You want nothing more of this foul affair. Neither do I. I don't adore you anymore. Greetings and may we very soon be locked in each other's arms.
                                        Bertrand Prouillan

No. 14.   December 7. Midnight.
    I've had enough of waiting in front of the door, leaning continuously on the time switch for a little light. It's the first time in three months that you haven't been at our date. I'm afraid of the black, the black in my head. I have a headache. I am going home. See you tomorrow at the same time. Be on time. Not at all loyally, Bertrand.

My dear Romain,

I will not be at tonight's meeting. My mother has insisted I be present at dinner, with my father. He wants, she said, to talk about my future. You will notice I no longer say Cécile and I don't say Henri. I have stopped considering them as friends, and in this way give them back their characters of parents who renounce those who sneak out quietly, an abdication of human beings. My mother told me, 'You don't have the right to criticise us and, in particular, to look at us in the way you do.' I answered her that my look was 'an invitation'. She believed I was making fun of her. She repeated, 'You don't have the right to criticise us,' but not the rest. They don't want their children anymore when they begin to look at them. And abruptly, I told myself that I knew nothing about you, or not much. Nothing about your parents, your childhood, your life. The image I have of you when I close my eyes and think of you isn't always set into any features. Nothing caricatures nor even traces the urge leading me to you. My determination to safeguard the little that links us, a liaison, has no equal, in force or in conflict except that state of flight that compels you to doubt yourself, when you so obstinately claim to doubt me. When I imagine you, smells and tastes rise in my head and do me good. The odours of skin, folds, niches, mouth, and the taste of you, saliva, words, semen, the taste of looks, of your look when the fear of becoming attached hasn't yet become the upper hand. My attachment, and your flight.

I won't be there tonight. I have to go to perform 'my' play, in 'my' theatre and play 'my' role (of opposition, to be opposed) with my two leading stars, the heads on the posters. Those people are not beheaded, they do the beheading. They wait for the cue, and woe if it isn't returned to them, as if one must render them back this life they've given us. The cue is written. I don't like my mother's silences since your abrupt departure from Moncrabeau. She has since then, when she looks at me, a hard way of sighing while smiling, a sigh for the child who will not produce any children and a smile for the son who will never go nestle in any other woman's womb. Now, this sigh and this smile are in the same breath. I don't like my father's bitterness either. Shunted aside from the first government, he will not fail, soon or even sooner still, to accuse his own family and exercise, on them, the power which, justly or unjustly, has always escaped him. He is going to speak to me about it tonight. I have however torn up your few letters and there is, in my look, only an image of you made of odours and taste. So he knows terribly. He senses. Think of me, I'm thinking of you. I will come by tomorrow morning but for a few minutes only. I used to love the blue of the morning, before the family gatherings, when these performances did not yet exist. I inhale you. B.

No. 16. January 4th. Two weeks, that's long, without you! I believe my father is going to give up having us followed. Where we walk together, no one will ever be able to surprise us. Look well at the reproduction of the Carpaccio picture. At the bottom, on the left, there are two birds, side by side. You see them only if you look carefully. It's the first time I've written someone at *poste restante* to be collected. A pointless terror. I need you. I have a glider in my head. Stuck. Planted. And a dead pilot, at the controls. But a glider does not control itself. It's the wind that decides. Now, it's me who's afraid. Don't give up, I won't. My father can do nothing against us. B.

No. 17. January 6th. I was very little. And you, lying on your belly, on the ground, in some green place, of freshly mown grass. Little, very little I was going back up the length of your spine. Up to the neck. It was soft. I was walking on you and you were not moving. I believe you were sleeping under my step. What a walk! B.

No. 18. Just as in the trains: there will always be a first and a second class. There used to be a third, in the old days, with wooden benches. Poets still had their place. Our society, henceforth, cut in two, begins there. Do you know that as a drafter of the preamble to that damned Constitution of this n-th Republic, my father proposed modifying our national motto 'Liberty, equality, fraternity' to 'Equality, fraternity, liberty!' Nuances! He got himself laughed at. The General would have said to him, 'Alas, Prouillan, whether too late or too early, it is hardly the moment.'

I am speaking and I'm writing you in first class. I don't see my future. I have never seen it. The cradle's horizon is always empty. One doesn't choose one's compartment. But when you take my hand and when I lick your fingers, there is no more equality of class, only our fraternity, and liberty calls. I am growing up. I feel you growing. There are no more taboos, rancours, close surveillance, or dominating powers, but the time of our meeting, this tiny bit of road travelled together that annuls, erases all the rest. I can't believe they are throwing us so strongly against one another in order to think they're separating us from each other. If I knew at what time and what day you will go to get this letter, I would take up a post where I could see you, at least at a distance. I see you from that near just by thinking about you. I would never have believed that a speech of this 'sentimental' nature could flow from my pen. The ink, black, veers to the blue of the sky as it dries, and the more I fill my pen, the more the inkwell runs over. All that isn't sentimental but resentmental. Resentment is the respiration of beings torn away from one another.

Jean's silence, Suzy's feigned indifference, the deaf complicity of my mother who must see in me a revenge on the established order which subdues her and that she defends so as not to suffer too much from it, and the threatening determination of my father, all that, when all's said and done, doesn't frighten us. I have forced your third look. That's all.

If the danger of my father's threats separates us, and if these letters are sent to *poste restante*, its because we quite like this night of blackmail of which we are the object. Or we've learned from the worst killers that they never have the face for it. Like in your play? Throw away my letters, please. I note that if they are separating us, we are also separating ourselves. There is only the memory inherent in the ink that can make this become a written memoir. So many weeds are bent under so many voyeuristic looks. I love you, Romain, to the point of no longer loving you. I loved so much taking your feet, kneeling, at the end of your bed, as if I were going to lift you with an acrobat's lift, brandish you, at arm's length, straight up over my head, come whole out of the womb of my head crying to you to pull out of the glider, that dagger implanted in us. Save me! How can you go away! And how I want to hold myself close to you, closer and closer to you!

We are no longer free of our bodies. We no longer even know

their use. What morality had banished, shadow zones, the flailing spirit of the century has totally covered with shame, throwing the sensitive person back to the holes of forgotten dungeons and total blackness, black cells with no landmark, where you can only lose yourself by no longer moving. Here's my song of hope, a final recourse. The stratagem of my father, as much in his desire to possess absolute and fleeting power as in his determination to separate us, I a minor, you of age, is only a form of writing gone wrong. My father is playing with us. His political outlook, that rightly should be the field of our collective conscience, is made only for pygmies. Therefore we hardly notice their manoeuvres and their petty battles, which are not worth discussing, leave instead on the sweet grass that smells so good when freshly cut, the cadavers of those who want to be waist high to them. Romain, I want to be done with you. I want to finish with you. I am going to ask Suzanne and Jean to invite us to their place. Us. They'll tell us the day and time. Too bad if we are followed. I'm mad about you. Bertrand.

P.S. Perhaps it's up to me to save you from trouble but two beings will never make up a pair. Love badly viewed by others emphasises the differences and makes them unmatched. They are playing with our skins. Yet it was so simple when we were together. The few times. At night. By chance. Their chance.

No. 19. This February 9th. Dear Romain. I waited for you at Jean and Suzanne's. I saw you arrive and leave again, on the boulevard. I was watching you. How grey and low the sky was. What happened? If you at least had a telephone, I would have called you. I would call you. Jean tells me that tomorrow you are leaving for London and Munich. That your play is going to be produced in those two cities and that you have a new play planned for next fall at the Théâtre de Lutèce. I'd have liked to read it. I know so little of you and that makes our separation still more painful for I interrogate and speak endlessly to you. Even during classes. And sometimes at the Place d'Antioche, more and more rarely, for he isn't there anymore for meals and I don't go home every evening, when I meet my father, we no longer speak to one another at all. He refuses to say hello to me. He believes he's doing the right thing. Claire and Gérard have decided to get married early in June. Ruth is expecting her first baby. When Anne-Marie does her shopping, she leaves Pierre with my mother who turns him over to Bernadette. And so on. They're proliferating. When they come here, the Martin-Lehmanns behave as they did before. As if nothing were different. Their smallest smile, for me, is one smile too much. They know. I think they want to see theatre everywhere when the theatre is already everywhere. I hope you have a good trip. Come back with soft lips. I am waiting for you. B.

No. 20. Romain. I will be before your door, tomorrow night, at midnight. This comedy has lasted long enough. It's other people's comedy, not ours. I want to see you again. I have met some boys, I do say 'some' boys. I know where to find them, all around your place. And everywhere. You just have to ask with a look. But there are no arms but yours, and no word to hold me upright but yours. So till tomorrow. Manage somehow. And leave the door open so I don't have to knock. Too bad, its stronger than us. B.

No. 21. March 11. Five minutes after midnight. Where are you? I am leaving. I'll come back tomorrow at the same time. I tried not to think about it, but I nevertheless feel watched, observed, followed, completely trapped by a father's surveillance, a midget in a killer's heart. Six after midnight. I'm stopping. I will kiss the door open before slipping this note underneath, for lack of slipping between the sheets of your bed, that ship. I will come tomorrow, at the same time. And day after tomorrow. And so on. Until you open the door to my kisses. Who is tapping on the glider in my head, if it isn't you, like the others?

No. 22. March 12. Midnight. I'll come back tomorrow. It was soft, the key, when you gave it to me. All warm and all hard, to the touch.

No. 23. March 13. This thing you would give up is nothing compared with what is taking shape. Risk is reasonable. The heart's reason inspires. Till tomorrow. I dare hope that, tomorrow, you'll be here, at last, at your place. Don't tell me you're hiding.

No. 24. March 14. When I go home from your place, my heart empty-handed, I cross the Tuileries, I stop in the bushes. The first person does with me what he wants, that is, what you want. I come very fast, closing my eyes and thinking of you. The animal is respectable. If he still hopes for another and someone he can become attached to. Till tomorrow.

No. 25. March 15. A few minutes after midnight. I just heard a step on the stairs. I thought it was you. I didn't dare bend over. It was your neighbour on the fourth. The light timer went out. I just soiled your door. Give it a wipe with a sponge. The animal is remarkable when it leaves traces where it loves. Tonight I return directly to the Place d'Antioche. Till tomorrow?

No. 26. March 16. I saw Uncle Jean this afternoon. Why tell him everything? Jean told me that, on his advice, you had left Paris for an undetermined period. But I don't believe him. What I did yesterday is beautiful. And I'll do it tomorrow night. Your door will be covered with it. I will come back every night. For that and also until your room is so full of messages you can't enter your place anymore, the day you come back if you ever come back. It's that, or nothing. More than ever, till tomorrow.

No. 27. March 17. I love this stairway. It erects me. I know you're in Paris. I feel it. Everybody I meet tells me. Till tomorrow?

No. 28. March 18. My father is downstairs. In a grey car. At the corner of the Impasse des Deux-Anges. A man is seated beside him, at the wheel. I recognised that man. He was on the other side of Boulevard Haussmann the day I was waiting for you at Uncle Jean's. It's the same one. Or do they all look alike when they have that death trade? I have neither the time nor the heart to leave the day's trace. Only this message. I will not come back anymore. I promise. You don't exist. You have never existed. It was neither really you nor I when we were together, if that's the version of things they want. But it was you and I, together, and neither of us wanted their interpretation of our relationship, I wanting the unique and the lasting, you no longer daring to share this desire for fear, so it seems, of something or other pursuing you. Steps on the stairs. I'm stopping.

Friend. A few minutes later. The people coming up turned around. When I came out of the building, I saw my father and the man, near the car, on the opposite pavement, at the corner of the Impasse. My father turned his head. I found him touching. He was wearing his hat, the grey felt silhouetted against the Paris sky. Then, I waited beside the door, leaning against the wall. I observed them until they left. My father, for his part, was looking at the wall, and the sign 'Post No Bills,' a public building, that school. I remember only one morning, with you, giddy, the day after your play's dress rehearsal, we were awakened by children's cries, the first recess of the day. Jean would make fun of me if he read this '*passé simple*' tense. This is my last letter. You can return home. You can love whom you love in passing and above all without ever having to stop. What I'm writing is cruel, I know. I would never have been so obstinate if I had not sensed, and felt melting in you, breathing, touched with my finger and tongue, our words, our words and our looks exchanged, your profound desire to stop with me, a desire which had, and perhaps still has, its equal only in my desire to stop with you. This is my last letter. You can return home. Live. Circulate. No longer fear for anything. Perhaps we will pass one another in life, in the street. Then please, only, return, from afar, the smile I'll give you. This is my last letter. I return to you what you believe to be your liberty and I take back what I don't believe to be mine. It's only a little tale of almost a year. They kept us from being together and, both of us intimidated, you by the failures you have already lived through, me by those I don't want to live, we didn't have the courage to take the risks. We've only played their game of prevention. When I write 'they', then I write 'them', I am putting my father in the plural for he has a singular something about him that he manages to reproduce everywhere, an immobility. The strength of men who believe themselves to be political is that they know how to be unchangeable. Yes, I loved him, a while ago, in his soft hat, turning his back on me. This is my last letter. I will not do stupid things on your closed door anymore. I will slip in no more notes. I will no longer be the house spirit of the Rue Saint-

Benoît. I will go to see your plays only as an anonymous and loving spectator. I will be the first to cry bravo when the curtain falls: you excel in living in your writing what you don't wish to nor can live in real life. It's the principle of all farewells. Our whole culture since the Century of Light has been built, like a house of cards, on this painful, and splendid, principle, which under the pretext of being human and of all humanity fabricates demi-gods of all kinds, from all milieux, from all causes, and in all artistic fields, so that everything is acceptable providing death sanctions love, and provided failure produces farewell. Everything beautiful, opera, philosophy, music, ideology, poetry, fiction, medicine, science, painting, architecture, everything is always marred. And in comparison, I *do* write comparison, with this principle, everything that succeeds is suspect, everything that lasts is sold, being destined for commercial, hence despicable, sale. We are badly made, and educated, collectively formed, only for the drama that must end badly. Our story, Romain, is surely more than just a small little tale of almost a year. This is my last letter. I observed my father and the other man for such long minutes. People passed, in the street. They went. They came. Some laughed without knowing. I at least took the time to wait by observing. I knew my father would not come to me. He only listens and understands silences from afar. Everything was said, in the drama, and the farewell. Were *you* too, at a distance, observing us? You were there, in one way or another, and for me in the best way.

It is three o'clock in the morning. I am writing you from a café near the Halles. I'll mail this letter in the Rue du Louvre. There is a post office open all night. One meets, I imagine, numerous fearful people there, anxious to send their messages. Yes, I want you to know as quickly as possible about my father's smooth look, under his hat, going around the car, taking his seat and making the door slam. I want you to know about the noise of that door, slammed in front of that building which was never really our home and which has always been only yours. I want you to know about the steadiness of my look when the man, beside my father, a colourless man, had trouble starting the car. He tried several times and became irritated. Impassive, my father looked straight ahead. I examined him. Then the car started up. From the exhaust pipe I saw fumes coming out in a cloud like you see sometimes in winter. Only then did I realise that it was cold and that I was shivering. Or trembling. I see you again, at Moncrabeau, putting on unusual airs and graces for my mother and Suzanne. I see you again in the barn at Auzan, gathering your scattered clothes. You had just made the decision to leave, the lie from Lectoure. I hear you telling me, on the way back to the house, as we were crossing through the birch wood, that you were 'never really young'. I see you again throwing that coin in the pond. But running water would have been needed for that coin to represent what we exchanged. I was born stagnant. I see you again blushing with happiness in front of Juan. I see you again kissing Claire after the theatre and winking at me as she returned your kiss. I see you again at the Place d'Antioche, at a family dinner, only once, and with reason. Suzanne was staying close to you, Jean was talking about your future. You brought it to my attention that the wall clock had stopped. With a fingertip you stroked the Mercury on the left hand chest of drawers, in the living room. I feel you, as I write you now, stroking me with your fingertip, quite occupied in the deep nature of your hesitation. I see you again, naked, from the back, closing your bedroom window, one morning, a unique morning, because the cries from the school recess were coming up to us, awakening in you the fear of a youth you had not known, and in me a fury for the one I knew too well. This is my last letter. I have lived everything, it remains for me to live, or to survive, poor me, rich with nothing, with my glider, well planted, in my head. And a glider is a motorless airplane that makes love with the wind. When there is any wind. This is my last letter. The wind has fallen. The glider has stuck. I kiss you everywhere that I haven't kissed you yet. I look everywhere we would have directed our looks together, at the risk of bad literature. But bad literature is other people who fear what the heart has to give. How angry my father looked and how determined to go right through to the end at the moment when the car finally started! He was tilting his head in my direction, slowly with that lost look, the look he has in front of Cécile, in front of the children that Cécile has given him, that look of being before a family, a faraway look, a kind of tenderness, but like a volley, with violence, a backhand. I would like to tell you everything that I could have and wanted to tell you, to listen to you endlessly as well, to discover in you that increasingly vast and inviolate terrain which is the other person if one takes the time to listen and share. But sharing is also ending. And here we are cut off from one another, as much by a father who cleaves the night, with a chauffeur detective at his side, as by ourselves. Have the door to your room repainted. That sixth floor was at a lovely altitude. Thanks for the unimpeded view of Paris. From the fashionable first floor at the Place d'Antioche nothing is seen. Everything is taken. Here's my last letter. It's finished for lack of paper. A letter written by fluorescent light and on formica. I feel a tiny bit drained from everything I have lived through since March 27th of last year, from everything I have wanted, written, said, listened to with you, from everything I have discovered, about the use of time, the use of body, abandonment, obstinacy. But when all is said and done about all the moments we 'spent together' I think you have never believed in the reality of my feeling of love and that you destroyed it, rejected it by seeing it as excessive, unequal, dangerous. You are a hesitant person. And I still love you in spite of it, without rancour, with serenity, and can tell you so. My intellectual studies with the Rue d'Ulm in mind, proved to me that many thinkers and artists, those my father thinks of as the 'parasites of society', those whom that same society has never been able to replace by anything better, have often, almost always, worn out their minds, their lives, and given themselves up to life, given themselves to death sometimes, or have died exhausted, in attempting the impossible: to reach the collective conscience, during their lifetime, to meet a little real-life love and especially to convince society by their sincerity. We always want the artist on show. We judge him on show, especially if he is not. I am not writing an essay, Romain. This time, I am abandoning you. The artist of our relationship, you persuaded me, placed me, held me in your mind, put me on show. The danger began there. In that fact. If you had understood me, felt me, embraced me, in full the equality of my sincerity, we would have run no risk. It is your hesitation to love me as I love you that alerted us and that instigated the pursuits, my father's pursuit. I will return home, in a little while, after mailing this farewell letter. I have lived a cycle with you, a whole lifetime. Just like some of my reading made me sick and at the same time cured

191

me of so many experiences. What good is the reproduction of misfortune? There will be no one after you, for me. There will only be my father if he wants to go all the way to the end of that look of his. A rupture. I give you the responsibility of telling Jean and Suzanne, and Claire as well if you meet her. Find the necessary words, I don't know them. In the bent weeds, I see myself in your arms and I am the watcher about to turn away. Once is enough. Farewell, since we must sacrifice to principle. Call me yesterday, as agreed. I adore you like you have never been adored. Bertrand.

June 17.
Dear Suzanne and Jean. Claire and Gérard's wedding, for me, was bereavement. I didn't show it. I smiled for the photos. I thank you for your company and for everything you could say by saying nothing. Holding a hand or giving a look sometimes is enough. Romain's death obsesses me. He is throwing himself, in my head, from that sixth floor, and there is a mark on the pavement at no. 5, rue Saint Benoît. Romain chose to be silent. I respect that silence. We must all respect it. I am a failure. A failed suicide. *He* had the courage. And I don't want to believe that the courage was again a hesitation. All that is false, is simply what is human, so little to do with the fact of a sexuality. I know Romain bequeathed everything to you, including the letters I sent him which he did not throw away. I also know you want to return them to me. I ask you to keep them and read them so they may be better erased from a loving and sincere memory. If that is possible. Thanks. I won't take an exam this year but I will be a student at the Normale next year, for Romain, for my twentieth birthday and for those who love. I will not condemn papa. I admire him as much as I fear him. He, too, loves in his way, he doesn't fool around with mortmain. How do you protect yourself from him and his love? Love to you. Bertrand.

12

'Those letters,' murmurs Claire, 'I read them. At your Uncle Jean's. Suzanne was present too, that afternoon, a few days after Barcelona. I was pregnant with you, Loîc. You were born the day after I read them. Figure it out. We're going to celebrate your twentieth birthday in five days. So it was five days after Bertrand's return. For his twentieth birthday.' Claire smiles, hums, then sings, 'If you ever come back to Temporel's, someday or other... don't forget those who passed by there...' She laughs. 'That's a good sign, I remember the words.' She lowers her eyes and sings again 'From an outdoor café beside the lake...' Silence. She looks at her children. 'The rest? It's a little la la di da, when you don't really know it anymore. But the important thing is remembering the beginning, the refrain, and a few words, at least. We all have a song hanging around in our memories. That one's mine. At the time I knew it by heart. Bertrand found it 'romantal and sentimentic' and used to sing it dumbly, with me, to make fun of me.'

Claire looks at her children, there is a silence, the meal's over, 'Yes, those letters, I read them. And I recall them, *them*, almost word for word. I wanted to understand, to know, to catch Bertrand again, to trap him. It was too late. Letter no. 1, Romain Leval numbered them himself, is dated March 27th. From Moncrabeau. In Paris two days before, Bertrand and I, the night before he left, went to see *Hiroshima mon amour* at the Georges V cinema. An afternoon showing. After the film Bertrand took my hand. "Let's stay." We saw the film three times in a row. He didn't let go of my hand until midnight when we came out. We returned home on foot, to the Place d'Antioche. He seemed shaken, moved. He would murmur, "It's beautiful," and then "It's beautiful because it's thwarted," and finally, "The nature of beauty scares me because it is always in conflict." I saw that film again, later, all alone, and another time with Gérard. I didn't understand right away what Bertrand meant. I grasped it only after, after your father's death.' Claire turns to Stéphanie. 'This is the first time I have talked to them the way I am talking. Don't be afraid of entering our family. Don't be afraid either of being called Myriam. I don't like my first name either but I am attached to it. A first name is a cocoon. You can't replace it.'

Loïc smiles. Stéphanie places her hands in her lap, like a little girl. She looks furtively at Yves who has pushed away everything on the table in front of him, his plate, glass, tableware and is seated, bent double, like an attentive schoolboy, his elbows spread out, his chin on his hands. He is clenching his fists. Géraldine is turned at an angle in her chair. Calmly she says to her mother, 'Describe Bertrand to us, please, mama. What was he like? Did you love him or were you fond of him? How is it you don't have a photo album? Why has grandfather never come here? Why did Sébastien not say anything to us or not recognise us when he came, last year? Why today, abruptly, this confiding in us, if you've chosen never to talk to us about all that? It's what, Moncrabeau? A big farm? Is the pond deep? Bernadette, how old is she? A hundred, since then? And your mother, why did she only talk about going home as soon as she got here? Why was she always giving us new, ugly flannelette pajamas that we were not to put on right away because they were brand new? We've always slept naked, like you. Was that shocking to your mother? What was she afraid of? Tonight, because you put on a dress, you look like her a little. Your mother never told us anything about herself and never asked anything about us.'

Géraldine looks at Loïc, 'Shall I go on?' then says to Yves 'Shouldn't I?' and to her mother, 'Tell me why we've never taken a trip with you. And Luc? And Ruth? Anne-Marie? Don't you ever write to each other? You know telephone lines don't pass very far from here. They could hook into the Schulterbrancks. Three or four poles, a wire, and they could call us. We could call too. It's like television. We'd have it. We wouldn't watch it. But we'd have it. The telephone wouldn't ring, but it could. I don't blame you. And if Loïc and Yves agree with me, we won't blame you for anything. Nothing but reality. Real life. Like in Bertrand's letters. It's crazy, being able to quote entire passages by heart from letters that have been read only because everything was done too late. Look at me, mama. That's the first time in a long time that I've called you mama and not Claire. Look at me. Yves and I are leaving tomorrow morning, on a trip. Loïc and Myriam will take us for the first few kilometers. As far as Italy. After that we plan to separate. Loïc keeps the 4L and Myriam. Yves and I will hitch-hike. We've bought everything we need. Everything is ready in the trunk of the car. We didn't know how to tell you. Loïc had planned to leave on the quiet, at daybreak. I'm not lying. You see the car outside? It's facing downhill. Last year, even then, we worked out how to leave without turning the motor on. Loïc was saying a while ago, when we were leaving Aix, that maybe that was the solution, and that with you it would be better, for one summer, to leave you with a bad impression. It's hard, but I understand Loïc. You have never been worried about us. Really worried. Yves did prepare a note. He's got it in his pocket. But *I* decided to warn you. There. It's said. Now talk to us about Bertrand. Did you love him? Were you fond of him? Did it matter? Which of you four really mattered? Sébastien? You *were* fond of him. A lot. But Bertrand? Speak, mama. We can very well listen to you, until we leave, when day breaks. Then we won't have to leave secretly, but only quietly, with a good impression. And with lots of images.' Silence.

Stéphanie rises, looks at Claire, at Yves, Géraldine, lowers her eyes before Loïc and tells him, 'I'm going to bed. Tomorrow morning, I simply want you to drop me as near Aix as possible. I'm not leaving with you anymore. I am not leaving with you three. I don't like your stories. Travel without me, you three.' She turns to Claire. 'Thank you, but I am fond of Stéphanie. Good night, Madame. Goodnight, Madame Géraldine. Tomorrow morning we will say nothing to each other. I did not leave one family in order to find another one.' Stéphanie crosses the living room, hesitates, smiles, then disappears up the stairway. Loïc did not make even the slightest gesture to stop her. A slight pout. He bobs his head. He looks at his brother, his sister, and mumbles 'Bastards.' Yves answers, 'Does that mean thanks?' Géraldine rises. 'I'm doing the dishes. Don't move. I want to do them all alone. It's up to you to talk. I'm listening.' The wooden floor creaks, upstairs. The noise of the bathroom door. Loïc rises, kisses his mother on the forehead, collects the dirty dishes and carries them to the sink, Géraldine puts on an apron whistling the *Bal chez Temporel*, while Yves empties each glass with a gulp, a wink at his mother. Claire doesn't move. She feels a little ridiculous in her dress. She murmurs, 'Bertrand was very tall, very handsome. Well, like everybody, he was young,' then, 'You're right to go on a trip.' She gets up. Yves puts on some music, softly. They are doing the dishes. Loïc sets the table for breakfast, Géraldine washes, Claire wipes and Yves puts everything in the cupboard, like before, during so many evenings, so many years, this habit of cleaning everything, putting everything away and setting the table for the next day.

Claire no longer knows if she should cry out or rejoice, speak or remain silent, weep or share her children's joy because they have created for themselves a night before the departure and they are jubilant, as she too has been jubilant, but so long ago, and only for Moncrabeau. The feeling was strong then. Claire used to vibrate with her whole body when she prepared her little-girl suitcase. Something was boring into her, from within, something spiral, burning and as she would choose her clothes to take along, her books, notebooks, adored possessions, her treasure, as she would place it all cautiously in her suitcase of stiff dark brown cardboard, bought at the 'travel' department, on the top floor of the United Stores, her throat would tighten. She was once again going to breathe the earth, the grass, the air of the footpaths and especially of the clearings.

Claire wipes the plates without realising it. She still does not know if she has to be worried or accept things, reproach or let it happen. She tries to remember another departure of emotion. With Gérard? But that was all the time. With him, every day was a voyage. And without baggage. That happiness, unalloyed, Claire finds no flaw in it. There is no succour to draw from it now. She wipes each glass by pushing the dishtowel right to the bottom. A door slams on the second floor. Yves shrugs. Loïc smiles. Géraldine cleans the sink. Claire says in a low voice, 'Thank you for the present. But it's a little cruel to give me a watch, with all its hours, minutes, seconds, the night before you leave.' Yves murmurs, 'Please, mama, don't say things like that to us.' Claire wipes the last glass. It is clean. She holds it out to Loïc for him to put away. It escapes her and breaks on the floor. Loïc clasps his hands. 'And one less!' Géraldine takes a broom, a

dustpan and quickly gathers the pieces of glass. She is afraid.
They are afraid. And so as not to say anything violent, so as not to
lose her patience before them, to protect the moment, and the
time remaining, the time before the departure, Claire goes out
of the house, waving to her children not to follow her, and goes
straight to the 4L.

She opens the trunk of the car. Back packs, brand new, well
placed against each other, stuffed with clothes, topped with
sleeping bags. It is touching. With the tip of her finger Claire
feels, strokes them, and when all is said and done, is amused.
Perhaps everything to do with her children is only an
entertainment, an entertainment on the margin of a drama, a
drama on the fringe of a society. Claire crosses her arms, shivers
a little. She does not like this moonlight, this night radiance, this
little wind flowing from the stones heralding the mistral, and
especially the sky full of stars. Loïc approaches her. 'Mama? This
time you're not so wonderful. You're hiding something from
us.' Claire does not answer. Loïc closes the trunk of the car, turns
the key in the lock, takes his mother by the arm and leads her to
the house. On the second floor a bedroom light goes out. Yves
and Géraldine are waiting before the door. Claire sees herself
again on Gérard's arm, climbing the few steps of the square of
the Saint Ferdinand Church. Worse than seeing herself again,
she feels herself on Gérard's arm, the same skin, the same
contact, the same gait, that way of walking, son or father, just a
tiny bit faster than she. That day, everybody was looking at
Bertrand and was thinking about the recent suicide of Romain
Leval. That day Bertrand was bearing a misfortune. That day
Bertrand had become an enemy. And when Henri finally told
her the real reasons for the trip to Barcelona, of the exact nature
of the surgical procedure, Claire had been content to keep
silent. Bertrand had stolen her wedding from her.

Claire, on the doorstep, sighs, takes a breath and says to her
children, 'Come to my room, we're going to talk.' On the stairs,
ahead of them, she stops, and turning around to them, she adds,
with no irony, as with calm recovered, 'Perhaps it's you who will
leave with a bad impression.' Two, three steps, she turns around
a second time. 'But only for the summer. That's what you said,
didn't you?' Entering her bedroom, her attic, studio, under the
glass roof, a transparent topping, reassuring, making this

197

room something like an open vessel, for Sébastien a place of stubborn silence, for Luc the white page of a letter, then Bertrand, Claire murmurs, 'Your summer will have no end.' Neither Loïc nor Yves nor Géraldine quite understand. None of the three dare ask Claire to repeat what she has just said. They feel guilty. This unusual feeling pleases them. It belongs to the feeling of leaving.

Loïc approaches the desk near the window. He tries to open the drawer, an unconscious gesture. Claire says 'No!' to him. Surprised, Loïc, his gesture interrupted, opens the window, and sits on the sill. His legs bent, his chin on his knees, hands on his ankles, he undoes his laces, lets his tennis shoes fall to the floor, takes off his socks and massages his feet. A distraction so not to answer his mother, a programme of activity so as to listen without participating, to receive without giving, to wait, wait for the departure. But no one is fooled. Loïc least of all. He says to his mother, 'As for my birthday present, you can give it to me when I come back. Better that way.' Claire answers softly, 'But I haven't bought anything. I thought I'd choose it with you.' One by one, Yves looks at the pictures and places them along the walls. Géraldine, seated on the floor, against the mattress, an elbow on a pillow, with the other hand puts the books in a pile. Claire stands in the middle of the room. She waits for all three to look at her. She waits. Then they look at her. She says then, 'Don't make me play the role of the loving mother. Don't make me say what disappointed mothers say when they cling to their children. Listen to what I'm going to tell you the way I'm going to tell you and not the way you want to hear it.' Géraldine looks at her. 'Then why did you put on that dress, tonight?' Claire strokes her arms, shakes her head slightly as if she wanted to undo her hair. 'I am perhaps just a little bit afraid of you. I was expecting everything but your leaving. Even if I've been expecting it forever. For twenty years? Do you understand?'

She approaches the window, bends down, gathers up Loïc's tennis shoes and socks, puts a sock in each shoe and places them on the table, noisily, almost comically, looking at her son. 'Do you understand?' And quickly, she crosses the room, heads toward the bathroom, taking off her dress. Yves, Loïc and Géraldine look at each other questioningly. The sound of the clothes closet door. Claire's voice: 'What size shoe do you wear now, Loîc?' Loîc does not answer. 'And you Yves?' 'Same as Loîc. I steal his shoes all the time.' Géraldine gets up. 'This is stupid. Let's leave!' Loîc signals to her to stay, his clenched fist raised. Géraldine throws herself on the mattress, her arms in a cross, her hair spread , and says very loudly, 'I know everything you're going to tell us, mama!' Claire comes back, naked under a man's shirt, too big for her, her work clothes when she paints, barefoot, and her face splashed, with water from the sink, what she calls her 'slap' when she is too hot. Géraldine sits up again, 'Sorry, mama.' Claire sits down near her, on the mattress. Yves takes a piece of paper from his pocket, unfolds it. He reads.

'Aix, July 9th. Dear Claire. Dear Mama. It's eeny, meeney, miney, moe that named me official writer of this letter and as I don't intend to put myself to the job several times, may as well tell you right off that the bags are packed, that we're leaving to see some countryside and that we don't know either how to tell you or how to make you like this leaving. May as well tell, also, that we are leaving without a penny, that it's so much the better, that we'll manage and that this winter at Aix gave us the idea, and especially the desire, to go to see what's happening a little farther on. At Sauveterre, we've had enough of gathering blackberries in blackberry season, linden in linden season, and so on, and especially of kicking pebbles. Don't be afraid. We won't catch cold, we'll be careful, etc., etc. And we'll come back with the first days of September. We will send postcards. Take advantage of this to meet other people than us, to paint nature with more vivacity than ever, and especially continue to expect nothing from us anymore. If you don't do it, it's at the risk of getting yourself scolded in turn. Even if you have never scolded us, which is the only reproach we could make to you. Read this advice well, our advice to you and your other population, the family you keep away from us. Having come out of you, one after the other, you have, when all's said and done about facts and events, a formula which is dear to you, and which has the Prouillan seal, which has put us in good condition to leave and make use of who we are. Papa agrees, I'm sure. And it isn't easy to say. So, no going backwards. Live each day, from now till our return, like one day more and not one day less. At breakfast, when you find this letter, don't cry, instead choose to burst out laughing. We will hear you from Digne or Mont-Cenis and we will know our reason is right. The heart's reason. Another Prouillan motto. I sign for the three of us. Yves.'

Yves tears up his letter. 'I don't know what I meant by one-day-less and one-day-more.' Little pieces of paper, like confetti that he throws in the air, that fall back to the floor. 'And you, mama?' He looks at Géraldine, 'have to sweep again.' He turns to Loïc. 'Aren't your feet cold?' He looks at his mother. 'When does the dealer come for the pictures?' He lowers his eyes, picks up the pieces of paper, places them one by one in the palm of his left hand, makes a ball of them and mumbles, 'Now if you were to give us some money, mama? We wouldn't spend it, but we'd have it.' Yves gets up, goes to the mattress, kneels before his mother, pinches her chin, kisses her on the lips, a little kiss scarcely touching, saying, 'Thanks in advance.' He gets up again, looks at Géraldine, Loïc, 'You could thank me too!' He goes to throw the little ball of paper in the toilet bowl. He pulls the handle. Noise of flushing water. In the mirror above the sink, he gives himself a smile: everything is turning out well.

When he comes back, Loïc kisses Claire on both cheeks, and stretches out on the mattress. Géraldine rolls up the sleeves of her mother's shirt. Claire lets it be done. Yves joins them, sits down cross-legged, near the bed. Claire says steadily 'Why so many precautions? Bertrand used to call that the principle of farewells. I don't want it. He didn't want it. But it's inevitable.' Silence. Claire picks up the second pillow and plasters it against her belly, the pain, the softness. Gérard is here as well. 'Listen to me carefully.

'I have no memory of ever leaving on a journey. My departures were always decided in advance. The object of the trip was always the same. Moncrabeau, it's something of a big farm, in which generations of Prouillans have lived, from their lands and the countryside, not caring to go up to Paris. Then they went, to the Place d'Antioche, where they put themselves on display. The house at Moncrabeau remained the same, with always too many bedrooms, and always too many keys. But the spirit of its inhabitants changed. Paris began to hold us like marionettes. There are in Paris, moreover, only people who've come from elsewhere and pull at their roots but never pull them out. From that was born what Bertrand called "the textbook provinces". If you don't understand, too bad. What I'm telling you isn't beautiful, but it's frankly true. The frankness of your leaving if you want to enjoy your trip.

'Here, at Sauveterre, I believed I was giving you something different. And all I did was make another little Moncrabeau, with linden trees, blackberry bushes and stones for kicking around. You can smile. That's it, the heart's reason, the only real one. We are made only to repeat ourselves in the same unadmitted affection, in the same need for money, and in the same desire to leave. Leave, because I never left. I have my doubts somewhat about how your journey will turn out, and the freedom you hope to find. When all's said and done about the facts and events, you can laugh, I adore laughing with you, you can go on and mock at everything, because I fashioned you, like they fashioned me. And whether you like it or not, you are from the same tree, the same trunk and the same sap. Look out. If you feel as if you're breaking off from the tree, it will only be a feeling. It's better to know that beforehand. I was thinking about it when the glass slipped from my hands: I have re-made with you what my parents had made with me and my brothers. We are incapable of difference. That's our only ability. And we have put down roots everywhere. Nothing will ever pull us up. We know how to talk about our dreams but we don't know how to live them anymore. Too dangerous. We know how to talk about justice, but we do everything so it is not just. Don't look at me as if I were performing a comedy for you. Your voyage begins here. The feeling expressed here is not a calculation, nor a performance, but an appeal.' Claire breathes deeply, sighs sweetly.

'Above the front door at Moncrabeau, there was an inscription, *Qui vivis pacem para bellum*. Luc, Sébastien, Bertrand and I, from the time we were studying Latin, were hooked on giving all sorts of translations to it. But we never felt that we'd found the right one. It probably means that the tranquillity of a place is a rampart against the tumult. Most often Bertrand would use the back door. He had a sense of humour. That inscription condemned us to a life of peace, out of the way, that we didn't want. Now I've delivered a life of peace to you here, out of the way, and soon you are going to tell me you didn't want it. Might as well say it before you do. Bad faith, or passion, makes people attribute to their adversary what is far from their feeling.

Mine is serene. I'm sorry. I can only reproduce myself in you. And let them, the Prouillans, be reproduced in you. If only Gérard had been here! You can go now. Go quickly.'

Loïc lifts himself up, an elbow on the other pillow. 'Stop, mama, I don't like that.' Géraldine looks at her older brother. 'But I find that very good.' Yves takes one of Claire's hands and kisses it, on the back. 'I'm thirsty. Don't listen to them, mama.' He leaps up, claps his hands 'I'm going to get something to drink!' A silence. Loïc turns his head. Géraldine lowers her eyes. They wait. Loïc sighs. Géraldine nibbles her lips. Claire murmurs, 'I don't like your remorse. Learn to express yourself honestly, at the appropriate moment. Learn that. At least that!'

Yves comes back with a bottle of water and some glasses. He serves Claire who says, 'Thank you.' Loïc who mumbles 'No' and Géraldine who places the glass on the floor. Yves clinks glasses with his mother. He laughs. Géraldine says in too soft a voice 'And Bertrand? What is he doing, today, at Moncrabeau?' Loïc answers, 'He's waiting!' Claire rises, goes to the window, furtively breathes the night, a sense of relief, turns around and says to them, 'Please, go right away.' She opens the drawer of the desk and, from under the pages that she's written that afternoon, she takes an envelope. Inside there is money. The cash reserve from which, for some years, Loïc, Yves and Géraldine have come to take a few notes, when they need them, because they don't want nor like to ask, just as Luc, Sébastien, Bertrand and she had for years pillaged Henri's wallet. Claire holds the envelope out to them. None of the three moves. 'Take it. This money has no importance except, for me to know that it will let you go farther.' Yves gets up, looks at Loïc and Géraldine. 'Do something, everything's worked out well.' He smiles, approaches Claire, takes the envelope and slips it into the back pocket of his jeans. Géraldine and Loïc are beside him, they too, abruptly, are happy. Up against the desk, near the window, surrounded, kissed, almost laughing again, Claire says 'I shouldn't have talked to you about Bertrand's letters. It's just a tiny, little story. He used to say so himself. But it's a little bit the story of all of us. Did you understand what I mean?' Loïc kisses Claire on the forehead, bending over a little, like Gérard when, with an identical kiss, on the night of Bertrand's return, he had indicated his desire to leave the Place d'Antioche. Loïc says, 'Even if we have understood, we wouldn't tell you.' Géraldine looks at her mother. 'A postcard a day, you'll see. It's Michel who'll have a good time!' Loïc takes his tennis shoes. Yves pinches his mother's left cheek. A little ridiculous in her too big shirt, Claire waves them to leave quickly. Yves asks 'And Myriam?' Loïc answers, 'She wants to leave as soon as possible.' They go out. Claire does not move. It's the best way.

13

Tonight Alabama is singing off key because he has not been
drinking. Oswyn has gone down to the engine room on the
pretext of checking the dials. Actually he wants to drink alone,
under the sea, under the waterline, thirty-four meters below,
down the girdered stairs. As he does every night, he has left with
his torch around his neck, an emergency lamp in one hand and
a bottle in the other. If he cried out from down there, he would
not be heard. The altitude of the 'empty boat' (that she, shitty,
empty boat) makes him, he's been saying for some months,
'dead drunk'. Tonight, Oswyn went down even before the card
game that Stavros, Horst and one of the two Portuguese had
suggested. Stavros is whistling while cleaning his nails. Horst has
sat down on the deck, taken off his socks and undone his belt.
He likes to get comfortable that way. And he has a great theory
about the ship's seating, the chairs and armchairs in which, he
says, 'time stops even longer.' He looks at the deck, fixedly. He
smiles. Maybe he's thinking about the girl at the Lillehammer
Bar. From his side, seated, with his elbows on the table, arms
bare, sleeves rolled up, his face in his hands, René observes
Horst as fixedly as Horst observes the deck. Carlos and Juan are
playing a game of chess. During dinner they insulted each other
in Spanish, spat out words 'cabrón' 'jipijape' 'hijoputa' 'puneta'
that none of the others understood, their own words, tearing
words like scratching slaps. Carlos and Juan look like each
other. They have the same wrinkles, the same hair on their
bodies, the same dimples, the same laugh, the same way of
spitting on the ground, and especially of keeping an eye on
themselves by not, apparently, watching out for the other's acts
and gestures as if a plot were always possible in the group. They
want to be a target. They have never known how to play chess.
They pretend. They think hard, each in turn, head in his hands,
each one lowering his eyes before the other, pushing the queen,
the rook or the bishop, any way at all, left, right, forward,

backward, as long as the others are there and until everyone has gone to bed. Then they find themselves alone again. Every next morning, someone always asks them who had won the night before. Carlos answers, 'Me.' Juan, 'No, him!' They smile. It's the only time they smile. And if you observe them carefully, sometimes, their knees, under the table, brush against each other, or their feet. They're playing, there. Very slowly. They are defending their terrain, in the very midst of the others' territory.

Stavros has finished cleaning his fingernails. Horst waves at Alabama to stop singing. He gets up, pot bellied, pants open, fills a glass of whisky and holds it out to Alabama who refuses it. Alabama begins singing again, even more off-key. It's a bad evening. Sébastien would like to speak to them, invent a game, find an idea, a distraction, use a single language other than their gibberish and make himself understood clearly to everyone. But to say what? The older of the two Portuguese is named Nelson. He has just made coffee for everyone. It's always him, making the coffee. His look is lacklustre, except when he scrutinises the sea, and a wedding ring that's too wide, and flat, is jammed onto his third finger. He is all the time trying to pull it off. The other Portuguese, Jao, is playing cards, alone. He's playing patience. Always the same. He has never got to the end of the game which consists of putting the hearts together first, then the clubs, the diamonds, and at the last the spades, because spades are unlucky. One day, counting on his fingers, he explained to the others that it came out 'only once in a thousand times.' He threw his hands in front of him, fingers stretched, laughing to show a thousand. Nelson forces René to drink his coffee. René looks at Sébastien. Sébastien has never smelled the metal smell of the *Firebird* so strongly. René mumbles, 'Have to find Oswyn. Or else got to take him his coffee.' Horst, seated on the deck, laughing, taps his head on the bulkhead. 'Eine kaffee, bitte, für Herr Oswyn!' Nelson knocks a cup over on the table. Stavros goes to find a dishtowel. Juan sneezes furtively. Carlos looks at him secretly. Alabama stops singing, takes his whisky and drinks it. Horst points his finger at him laughing still louder. Jao takes René to the lavatory. The first swallow of coffee has been fatal.

Nelson goes to put on some music to cover the general noise of the ship. Horst rises and mixes up Jao's cards. Sébastien closes his eyes, remains straight up in his chair, at the end of the

206

table, the place where he always sits, waiting, hands out flat. The odour of the metal is violent, dull, penetrating. It infiltrates, invades the body's terrain, stagnates and stops all thought. When a ship is under way, furrowing forward, that odour from long port calls fades, with the seaspray, the cries from gulls going from continent to continent, on the watch for the crew's garbage being thrown overboard. Only what is true is beautiful, the flight of gulls and garbage, crates pitched off the ship's fantail. Only what moves around is beautiful, what goes from one port to another and comes back to the port of origin. But they don't sail anymore. The smell is there, stronger still because Sébastien is closing his eyes. The odour is there, obstinately. In front of the buffet, organised by Berthier fils on the day of Claire's wedding, Sébastien again sees Bertrand go up to Ruth, kiss her almost on the mouth, with a sort of hesitation, awkwardly, a kind of desire, who knows? Bertrand, holding Ruth by the shoulders, as if he feared falling, had said to her, 'Did you see what I have in my head?' 'Please, Bertrand.' 'If you look carefully, Sébastien, you'll see a black butterfly. It fills up the whole space' and, clasping Ruth in his arms, 'un papillon noir!' He was laughing. 'You too, Sébastien, you have one. But it hasn't grown as fast as mine,' and then, moving away, pointing his finger at them, 'And don't say I've been drinking. If I drink, the butterfly turns faster and faster, and the glider sinks. Some images are not for laughing at. I'm going to open the French windows. It's so lovely out.'

Sébastien opens his eyes again. Bertrand was also afraid of everything that had to be planned in advance, that was grounded in fact or by principles. He used to open windows to clear all that away. The fjord of Overfjellet is nothing else but the pond at Moncrabeau, bigger and more beautiful. Opening onto the sea changed nothing. René comes back. He feels better. Jao has stayed behind in the lavatory to clean the seat and deodorize it. René wipes his lips, helps himself to the coffee, drinks it, hiccoughs, places the cup askew on the saucer, rubs his face, turns toward Carlos and Juan. 'Is your game exciting?' He says loudly to be heard by all, 'It's getting to be better, from one night to the next, because we're leaving soon. Can you understand, Nelson? Can you translate for Jao? And you lovers? *Ola, los novios, entendido?*' Carlos and Juan do not move. 'And you, Horst? When you come a little too fast, it's the same price, isn't it?' Horst smiles and looks at Sébastien. Sébastien murmurs, 'Please, René.' René says to Stravros, 'What was that, that you fed us tonight? Fish or meat?' He laughs. They laugh. Carlos and Juan have, slightly and simultaneously, turned their heads. If Sébastien leaves the wardroom, there'll be a brawl. Sébastien does not even dare close his eyes. René hits the table with his fist, bam, bam, faster and faster. He stops suddenly. 'What if we dressed up?' Sébastien repeats, 'Please, René.' 'If we talked to each other for once, it wouldn't be so terrible, would it?' 'Please René.' 'How about if we played at being a minister? I would make a good minister. That's it, I'm going to give audiences to you all! You still want to play the gentleman? Do you want me to be jealous?'

Jao comes back from the lavatory. Nelson holds a coffee cup out to him. Alabama takes his harmonica from the canvas bag from which he is never separated, dirty canvas, covered with grime, in which he carried photos and letters, mixed up together, and that novel by Wolfe that he has been reading for months and of which he says, to whomsoever asks, that he does not know if its 'fully true or totally rotten, like life, when you think about it.' Thomas Wolfe. The title of the novel is *Of Time and the River*. Sometimes, with the pages turned at the corner, Alabama opens the book at random and reads a passage, loudly so the others stop talking, so that the background music is turned down, or just to be carried away, to find again some mother-tongue words, descriptions of places from his origins, familiar people, and encounter events he would have liked to live and that he wouldn't even dare to believe in anymore. Alabama gets up and begins to play the harmonica standing behind René, as if to calm him. He plays. It resembles a polka. Abruptly a saloon atmosphere reigns, a festive air, a prelude to a movie shootout. Juan and Carlos look at each other. They scrutinise each other and it is rather like a first time in front of the others, an avowal or a provocation. Without looking down, with a precise and blind move, Carlos takes the bishop, places it several squares forward, a small, dry noise, claps his hands, rubs his arms, stands up and stretches. René says to him, 'Did you win? For once can we see it!' Carlos does not answer. Juan waves yes as he puts the pawns away. Alabama's polka becomes more and more rousing. Sébastien strokes his chin and cheeks, elbows on the table. He has found his smooth face again, that skin folding at the neck, under the ears, that little something that collapses and puts marks on a face, after the turn of a certain age, a lassitude that the beard was hiding. The barber at Dunn had made three attempts at it. Sébastien, shaved so close, feels naked sooner than expected. He looks at the others, bearded, ageless, and outside at that soft, summer night light, behind the mists of an evening that does not quite fall, with the rays of the sun, a velvet sun, bluish velvet. The fjord holds them.

Then, Alabama begins dancing, a walking circus bear, repeating endlessly, as shrilly as possible, the polka's opening theme. When out of breath, or as if determined, when he gets his breath again, he gives the impression that he is going to bite the harmonica. Carlos goes out without a word. Juan follows giving the others a vague wave of the hand. René hits the table with his fist. 'I'll get those fairies!' Horst looks at him. 'Jealous?' Alabama stops playing, wipes his harmonica on his shirttail, taps the top to empty it, and tosses it onto the deck on top of the sack, the letters, and the photos, one of which, a picture of a woman, is riddled with needle holes. But no one questions anyone. The silence has come back. Jao collects the coffee cups. Nelson offers a cigarette to René, Sébastien and Horst. Alabama rolls himself a joint. He will smoke it, alone, like every evening, without sharing it. And each one is listening, unconsciously, for a cry from Oswyn, a call from the bottom of the ship, as if that were possible, with so many bulkheads, nooks, ladders, gangways and doors. Oswyn, under them, at the bottom of everything, is drinking. And they, above, wait, observe each other, try to distract themselves, which renders all distraction impossible. In their cabin, Carlos and Juan undress. They are going to take their shower and go to bed in each other's arms on the double mattress they put down on the deck every night and that they slip, folded, every morning, under the bench of the single bed. That's the way it is. Fear and respect, the indifference and tenderness of each. It is the hour when, in the wardroom, Sébastien no longer has any escape: from thinking about what has happened in his life, from conceiving the yet-to-come as Bertrand used to put it.

'My desire for suicide is exactly equal to my instinct for preservation.' It was a Sunday, at the Place d'Antioche, a few days after Romain Leval's death. Anne-Marie was observing Bertrand the way one observes a stranger who has not yet given his name. Luc was smiling. He preferred hearing, in this statement, humour, only humour. Ruth was looking at her watch in order to leave as soon as possible. Claire was keeping off to one side, watching for a look from Gérard. Uncle Jean was savouring a cognac. Suzy was putting her bracelets back in place. Bernadette was cleaning a spot on the rug with a rag and some Perrier. 'The bubbles drink it up and don't leave a trace.' Pantalon II was waiting for his sugar. Cécile was holding Pierre in her arms, a full tummied and sleeping baby. Henri seemed happy, detached, elsewhere. They were all there. Bertrand had just said, 'Don't be afraid. My desire for suicide is exactly equal to my instinct for preservation.' It was the last meal of the Sunday before Claire and Gérard's wedding, the last of all those meals, the last of those obligatory family meetings, a year before the evening of the return from Barcelona. When he spoke Bertrand was looking at no-one in particular. A meeting of eyes would have stopped him. Each of them was waiting for a word from him, some kind of deliverance, a sign, a remark, so that the circle, in the silence and according to the principle of this family gathering, might close again truly and no longer put anyone in danger. Each one was thinking about Romain's death. Bertrand was convincing. 'I want to be what I am! And you take that for an insult?' Then 'My head is full of images. The taste for my own sex, I was born with it. I don't want your motionless time. That time strangles everything, will strangle us sooner or later. Too late to act. We are part of the stones, macadam, the sewers, monuments and the metal of safety deposit boxes. Does that amuse you? I know you're listening to me. Aren't they, Bernadette? They're listening! They're all very nice. We're all very nice. We speak like nobody else speaks. Especially you, Mama, when you don't say anything. It's the justice of the love we no longer feel for one another. We are too nice, and too nothing. And we are here. I'd do better to keep silent, isn't that it?'

Leaving the living room, Bernadette smiled, a rag in one hand, the bottle of Perrier in the other. It was the last gathering, the last real Sunday. In spite of everything, the Place d'Antioche smelled of growing trees. Some first communion boys were showing off their suits and armbands, the last armbands of first communicants, crossing in crosswalks, flanked by their families, on their way to other visits, which are also obligatory, to grandmothers who never go out but give a tea party. Henri without really answering Bertrand, had spoken twice. 'I helped too much. I made myself a slave of those I helped,' then, raising his eyes, his look faraway, 'What a great amount of thought for so little evidence of humanity.'

Sébastien sees them again now. Uncle Jean is getting up. 'They're waiting for me at the theatre to check the matinée receipts.' Suzy: 'I'll go with you.' Cécile returns Pierre to Anne-Marie. Pantalon barks. He has to go out. Bertrand shrugs. Ruth kisses him. Everybody leaves. Cécile gives Claire some 30 envelopes to mail. Invitations for the wedding. Claire mumbles, 'Again?' She looks at the envelopes, reads the names. 'I don't know these people.' Cécile smiles. 'They have to be invited.' Luc bends to kiss his sister. Bertrand observes them. Cécile clarifies, 'It's important for your father.' Henri has disappeared without a word. Sébastien approaches Bertrand. 'Do you want to stay with us tonight?' Bertrand: 'No, thank you, I have a date with someone. A date I can't break.'

Sébastien leans forward, unconsciously, as if he were going to kiss someone. René observes him. 'Something wriggling in your head?' He turns to Stavros. 'So what was it, fish or meat? Are you telling? I dare you!' They are all around the table, Jao, Alabama, Nelson, Stavros, Horst and René who draws his chair right against Sébastien's. 'If you don't say something to me, the evening is going to end in a bad way. We all want to know.' Sébastien looks at them. 'What?' 'I don't know. We don't know, but we do want to know! Go on, Alabama.' Alabama finishes his joint, a last puff, breathing deeply, 'We just wanted to know if you really were wishing to get stabbed by us.' Nelson translates for Jao. Horst repeats looking Sébastien straight in the eyes, 'That's it! So do you really want us to kill you, stab you or throw you overboard?' Sébastien mumbles, 'Is this a joke?' then, 'What's got into you?'

René tightens his fists on the table. 'We've all been talking for a few days now. You have a way of behaving without saying a word to us that we don't like. And a way of watching us without saying anything that gives us ideas.' René makes a face as if he were going to spit, gives Sébastien a tap on the shoulder. 'In fact, admit it, you're asking us to kill you.' He smiles. 'Today it occurred to us to take more notice of you and talk among ourselves. Even Carlos and Juan. The cowards, they left first because they want the world to be cooing together like doves. Yes, it occurred to us today that you've given us an order. Like a firing squad. But we won't do it. Because your look is asking for it. That's my opinion. We won't do it. We only want to know why.' Horst repeats 'why?' Alabama says 'Why?' Stavros looks at Sébastien, as if to alert him, and tells him, rolling his r's, 'I'm warning you, René gave a knife to Oswyn. Oswyn said he would wait all night down there. He's happy to take on the job.' Silence. The men look at each other. Sébastien would have liked them to all burst out laughing and for the whole incident to be reduced to a joke. But the looks are set, frank. These men really have decided something. Sébastien tries to get up. With a move of his hand René holds him back and forces him to sit down again. Horst mutters, 'We're not joking.' Alabama rocks on his chair, 'Funny.'

Sébastien does not remember ever being afraid, truly afraid. The sudden threat surprises him but it does not disturb him, astonishes him more than it worries him. René tells him, laughing, 'Behind your beard you were camouflaged. Without your beard you don't have the right to give us orders anymore. On the other hand, we feel like giving you a good clout. You're always behaving as if we were at sea. You treat us just the same. You're one of those who think we are still under weigh all the time, everywhere. But we're at a standstill. It isn't even a port call. The night that doesn't fall goes to your head. So papa was a minister? You'd hidden that from us? Horst says he saw a picture of your father with Adenauer. Is that true? And where'd that get us? There are only German shipyards working. I say everything is a mess. Your minutes are numbered.' Horst passes a bottle of whisky around. Everybody drinks. Stavros holds the bottle, spits in it, hands it to Sébastien. 'And don't act disgusted. Drink. It's the same spit for everybody.' Sébastien smiles, takes the bottle, drinks four, five swallows, Horst's voice, 'Again!' Six, seven. 'That's enough!' Sébastien places the bottle on the table. It is not a game anymore. He is happy. He looks at his men and tells them 'Thanks,' with no irony, for real, wiping his lips. Oswyn is waiting for him? The idea does him good. His thumb and index fingernails are yellowed, tarnished, smoky from tobacco. He laughs. Horst catches the bottle and empties it. Jao gets up to look for another. René begins to hit Sébastien on the shoulder, rhythmic blows, which get stronger and stronger as if he were trying to make him fall off his chair. On the other side of Sébastien, Stavros begins doing the same. A prisoner, Sébastien holds onto the table. They hit him from the left, the right, preventing him from rising. The others laugh. Even Jao who comes back, uncapping the bottle. René yells, 'Go and get the lovers, by force and in the raw, fast, they have to see this! Let them see an officer being beaten up.' Horst and Nelson get up. Alabama grabs the bottle from Jao's hands. With a leap Sébastien jumps up, knocking his chair over, and backs up, his hands tense, flat, in front of him. He does not remember ever tightening his fists, like Henri, in his coat pockets when everything was going badly. His father's image crosses his mind. Then Bertrand's face repeating, in the void, the words 'instinct' and 'preservation', that Sunday, a few minutes ago, the memory finds its way, goes ahead, shows him the way. Sébastien tenses his hands still harder, in front of him. The others approach and encircle him. Horst and Nelson come back pushing Carlos and Juan, before them, naked, they too jostled, but conspirators or crew, everyone must be involved, a factor of necessity. Sébastien wishes he were afraid. Another flashing image, Ruth, on the day she left, kissing him on the lips, 'You should have let me dance,' then, 'I had a dream, and you stole it from me. You're one of those who take and never give back.'

Horst, Nelson and Carlos block the three exits. René, Jao, Stavros and Juan keep out of arm's reach of Sébastien. Only the door opening onto release ramp 3, a steep stairway leading, through seven bridges, like a deep hole, directly to the engines. Horst points his finger, 'It's that way!' Alabama rocks on his chair. Juan leans forward, catches the harmonica and tosses it to him. Alabama spits in Sébastien's direction and begins playing a slow, serious tune, a funeral march or a song of disappointed love. Then Stavros spits in Sébastien's face. René spits in turn and says to Juan, 'Piss on him!' 'I can't.' 'Go on, I say, or else spit, you too.' Sébastien backs up, hears cries, raucus or gay, holiday cries, a holiday of which he is neither the hero nor the target, a holiday of fury, a reversal. René pushes him toward the ramp. 'Go on! We'll report you disappeared. We'll say you jumped in the water.' Everybody moves in. René says, 'And if you come back up alive you'll have the choice of the *Apollo*, the *Septentrion*, the *Newton*, the *Ambrasy*, the *Spirit* or the *G.K. Hall*! If you climb back up, we'll put you on top of one of the other carcasses till the day we get back. Understand? Go on!' Carlos, Horst and Nelson sock Sébastien and throw him into the stairway. From above, in the void, René opens his fly and begins pissing. Sébastien hurtles down the stairs. At the fourth bridge he stops. They are all pissing above his head. He hears them laughing. He is afraid now. He feels better. He wants to meet Oswyn. It's only a joke. They've been drinking. And not him. He was afraid when the men moved in towards him and hit him. René shouts 'And we don't give a damn about your service report to the British Petrofuck and Co.!' Silence. Night. Laughter. Then silence again.

Sébastien slowly descends to the bottom of the *Firebird*. In his dreams, often, since he has been at sea, he sees himself, very small, in his skull, descending to the bottom, all the way to the bottom of himself, his brain, medulla, spinal column. It is a dream caused by a fever, or from the ship's rolling. A heavy dream. Here, everything is real, cold, black. The fifth, the sixth, then the seventh bridge, Sébastien knows the *Firebird* by heart. And when he arrives, feeling his way along, at the corner of the gangway leading to the engine room, the spit is almost dry, and he wipes his face. A pain in the temple, he can no longer open his left eye. He licks the back of his hand, it's blood, his blood he tastes but he does not know from where he is bleeding. Sébastien calls, 'Oswyn,' then, 'where are you?' He advances, straight ahead, into the black. His shirt is torn. The smell of metal mixed with machines is even stronger. He bellows, 'Oswyn? Come here! And kill me!' And suddenly he falls, to his knees, exhausted, even though he was feeling stronger than ever, ready for anything. Nobody. There's nobody. It's a joke. And this is not a joke. Sébastien spits, into the black, in front of him, revenge. Then he holds his breath. He waits.

He had fallen as suddenly as if he had received a knife blow. He is the game, he knows it. This anger from the others has come entirely out of his own head and his dreams, provoked only by his attitude in the face of this life that makes him justify himself, have a power over others, a command that is even pathetic, a stubborn silence, putting everything into his expression so that he can dominate, protect his situation, but protect what? A father?

On the title page of the copy of *Hadrian's Memoirs* that Sébastien places, as a ritual, on his bedside table, underneath the words 'This book was stolen from Bertrand Prouillan. Please bring it back to him,' Bertrand had also written, but smaller and at an angle, 'the vivacity of a society, or what remains of it, is measured by its ability to be enthusiastic, to enjoy things, or both at once. A society entirely devoted to a spirit of caution no longer sparkles. Its sky is starless. Nothing is suspended in its space anymore. People can no longer contemplate. This book makes me enthusiastic.' And then in capital letters, 'NOTHING WILL EVER CRACK US.' Sébastien crawls in the night of the passageway. The idea of cracking crosses his mind. It comes from Bertrand, again. It turns about in his head, a black butterfly, and implants itself, a glider, in ages, in images of a living dead brother. A birthday present, twenty years after.

Sébastien rises, rubs his trousers and rolls up his torn shirt sleeves. He draws himself up. How could he let himself be pushed around? How could he ask Oswyn to kill him? How did he come to be here, down below? He yells, 'Oswyn!' Sébastien crawled the way he'd like to have seen his father crawl. Sébastien had just regained his feet and can stand erect, the way Bertrand had stood erect, in spite of everything, on the last Sunday that the family was together. You are always reliving the rôle of a father you want to kill and who is killing you. You are always imitating a brother who speaks up and then is not allowed to talk, for a fear of being either the father or the son, really, for fear of being anyone at all. And now there is the engine room. Sébastien yells, 'Oswyn! Where are you?' Silence.

The copy of *Hadrian's Memoirs* is also covered with notes, in pencil in the margin, 'Whatever is erased remains', 'One is always someone's landscape', a 'recourse to the sensitive, like a cry for help', 'he who writes actually reads: only reading is writing', 'each page, a hand-to-hand battle', 'truth is an outside chance', 'someone, in the wings, will never go onstage', 'we have even forgotten the taste of dishes, the sense of the meal', so many

215

notes, and also this: 'I don't want to look like myself anymore', that Sébastien, frequently, repeats to himself out loud, talking alone, exclaiming the sentence like a motto. But the years go by, and he looks more and more like himself. More and more he looks like his father, even in his fears when he doesn't yet know what they are or when they are born a moment too late. A torch lights up. Oswyn was there, crouching, very close to him. Sébastien, dazzled, raises a hand in front of his eyes. Oswyn says in a low, hoarse voice, his still drunk voice, 'Why did you want me to kill you, Sir?'

Sébastien bends down, tears the torch from Oswyn's hands and points it at the floor, at the dead bottles that Oswyn, surprised, knocks down with a gesture. They roll on the deck, all around them, the noise of empty glass, shocked by the metal. Oswyn tries to get up. He cannot. He lights the torch hanging around his neck, holds out a hand for Sébastien to help him. Sébastien hooks the lamp to his belt and pulls Oswyn up, drunken, a giant. And standing, laughing, after gently pushing Sébastien out of the way, the way you push a witness to watch a coming feat, Oswyn begins kicking the empty bottles so that they fly into pieces, chunks of bottle glass, bottle necks, breaking apart. He repeats flailing out again 'Alone, I want to be alone.' He, too. Then he calms down, hits his palms alternately with his fists, looks at Sébastien and mumbles in a broken voice, 'That's my graveyard,' then, 'that was my graveyard.' Oswyn then slips a hand into his back trouser pocket, takes out a switch-knife that he holds out to Sébastien, making the blade spring open. He gives it to him. Sébastien takes it. Oswyn ponders, 'You know Mame?' Sébastien does not know *Mame*. He gives a no sign. Amused, Oswyn shakes his head as if he were going to say something inevitable and unimportant, 'It's a musical.' A musical comedy. 'And in that musical, an old lady says to an older one: how old do you think I am? The other one answers: somewhere between forty and death.'

Sébastien backs up a step, crushes a piece of glass under his heel, closes the blade and takes the lamp in his hand again. Oswyn seems amazed. 'Don't you laugh?' Sébastien does not feel like laughing. He retraces his steps, faster, in the light this time. He hears, against the ship's bulkheads, the irregular bumping of the waves that come beating, here in the fjord, on

216

the immense, empty hull. He also feels a kind of pressure, a presence, a flow. You breathe better below the waterline. A rediscovered element. Better than topside, all the way topside. Oswyn follows Sébastien staggering a little, running his left hand flat along the passageway bulkhead. Sébastien thinks that Oswyn, 'is caressing the boat caressed by the waves'. He turns around, waits for Oswyn at the corner of the stairway, ramp 3, seven levels straight up. Oswyn grunts, his lips wet, and in his look that hint of mischief that makes him liked and always left alone, a tale of corners for him, of the smell of engines and the cemeteries of empty bottles. He joins Sébastien, takes him by the forearm and mumbles, 'Sorry, Sir, it was a joke.'

The giant goes in front of Sébastien. Between levels 5 and 6, crossing the waterline, Oswyn seems winded. The torch hanging around his neck swings right, left, with each pace, each step, lighting any which way, before him, like a ship rolling. Sébastien shines his lamp on each step ahead of them so that Oswyn can place his foot right and be sure of his balance. Sébastien knows he must not help Oswyn stay upright. He knows he must not touch this man. Level 4, level 3, level 2, a climb. In the stairwell, a smell of bleach. Jao has pitched buckets of it for cleaning. Oswyn grumbles, 'It stinks of being clean.' Sébastien, 216, 217, 218, stops counting the steps. He says out loud, a sudden thought spoken to Ruth, 'I won't let myself believe that I wanted the unhappiness of our separation.' Oswyn turns around, almost stumbles. Sébastien mumbles, 'Nothing. I was just speaking to my wife, OK?' He waves to Oswyn to climb the last steps. Oswyn laughs. 'During the war of Secession OK was the good report for no One was Killed. You know that, Sir?' At the top of the stairway, at the entrance to the wardroom, Oswyn blinks his eyes. It's still day light. He begins to bellow in Welsh, crazy words, thrown out, shouted, that Sébastien does not understand and can no longer translate.

The table has been cleaned, the chairs put back, the arm chairs lined up, the ashtrays emptied and lined up, at regular intervals, put back in place, the stools before the bar. The men have left. An odour of tobacco and alcohol dominates and competes with the smell of bleach. Alabama has left his bag, on the deck, with the letters, photos, the riddled photo and the harmonica. Alabama always forgets everything behind him, as if he wanted someone to pillage or search him. It's his way of calling. He would like someone to ask him questions and, as no one ever does, he plays or sings music, his music, his country's music. But where is Alabama?

Oswyn goes straight behind the bar. He takes a bottle, places two glasses on the counter, meets Sébastien's glance, puts the bottle away and withdraws the glasses. With a smooth gesture he strokes the counter, the whole length of it once, the whole length a second time, in the other direction, industriously. Oswyn has an intriguing way of smiling with his eyes. One would think, to watch him, that he was shining with happiness, ready to pour out the tears of a child upset by a dream or by his games. Tears that sting, burn and dig a furrow in his cheek, those tears one is never capable of, later. Now Oswyn is almost at retirement age. Where will he return and to whose home? And to do what? Sébastien places the switchblade on the table. He turns around, bends down, puts Alabama's paraphernalia back in the canvas bag, places the bag on the chair, tidily. He too is putting things away. He wants everything to be in order. Oswyn observes him. They exchange a smile, vaguely, amused, a smile of embarrassment or of complicity. Oswyn shrugs slightly, wipes his mouth, rubs his nose, puts his hands into his trouser pockets, comes out from behind the bar, clumsily, and heads for the passageway leading to the cabins. Sébastien observes him from the wardroom. Oswyn opens a door, disappears. A door is closed again in silence, as if everyone were sleeping.

But each one is listening, still observing. The silence and listening of the bulkheads, the ramparts, when each regains his bed, his concerns, his dreams, each watching and waiting for the others. Sleep is no longer possible on the *Firebird*. More than twenty-one days. And that silence, that order rediscovered, that neatness of the wardroom, with its sleeping decor, awaiting the events of tomorrow, the customary and the consequential, all of which now preoccupies Sébastien and worries him more than the threats, the dagger, and the night in the depths of the ship. It is the same order rediscovered when living at the Place d'Antioche when Bernadette had just finished dusting the knick-knacks, the chests of drawers and the bronzes, has shaken the rugs, put the armchairs, the pedestal tables back in place, forbidding the children to go in there as if only adults had the

218

privilege of moving them and bringing them alive, as if only Henri, the father, master, had the right to be the first to violate that space, the family's meeting place that he only fills with his silences or his sudden angers, but never with a gesture, between the two moods, a gesture of welcome, a simple touching gesture which would have suggested that he no longer wanted to be what he had decided he was, an only son, an eternal elder brother, the proprietor. Sébastien is surprised at the twists and turns of his train of thought, at the repeated presence, on this day, like an obsession, the knell of an anniversary, of this person, his father, who would never recognise himself as his son's memory portrays him, and of those others, the brothers, sister, brother-in-law, sisters-in-law, and especially Ruth, who were the family's actors, a simple and happy company until that day, the day of Bertrand's return.

For the first time in twenty years, with a strange realisation that it is day for day twenty years, Sébastien remembers that gesture he made when Ruth was giving Laura her breast, a prudish gesture which made him cover his wife's breast, not because the others were looking, but because a doubt had just seized him about the exact nature of his fondness for Ruth, about the role of mother he was making her play, tearing her away from her dancing and appropriating her to himself. Ruth had become the prey and he the proprietor. It was as proprietor that he had hidden Ruth's breast, which had made Claire smile. A few days later she was going to bring Loïc into the world. Claire had just smiled at the doubt her brother felt, a doubt which had its equal only in her fear of seeing the passion she shared with Gérard interrupted, in the same way as Luc seemed worried about Anne-Marie who no longer responded to his glances and stayed close to Cécile, imitating Cécile. Claire had just caught Sébastien in a blatant act of prudery. And Sébastien, observed and judged by his sister, told himself that everything would end between Ruth and himself, sooner rather than later. He knew that Bertrand was going to return home mutilated, diminished, that he too was a prey of them all. When families have no victims, they create them themselves. Uncle Jean had said, on that evening when Sébastien had come to tell him that Ruth was leaving, 'Prudish decency is the worst form of aggression. Take it as a joke if you don't want to understand me.'

Sébastien takes the switch-knife. He goes out to portside. The sun is finally setting. Sébastien makes the blade spring open and holds it out to sea, towards the west, towards the continent of the Americas so far away, and cries, 'I don't want to look like myself anymore,' and then, 'I won't let myself believe that I really wanted the unhappiness of our separation.'

Sébastien imagines that Ruth can hear him, that Laura and Paul are listening, that Ron, a little awkwardly, is staying out of the way. What time is it in Toronto, now? Sébastien looks at his watch. The crystal is broken. The spit has dried but Sébastien feels marked. He rubs his face, from top to bottom, his cheeks, his chin, his forehead. He wants to erase, rub away with his fingers and palms those scars that are not seen on the outside, but so clearly from the inside, the marks of hate and fear. A whole brotherhood can only express itself in that way. If only there were a little wood on board the *Firebird*, a bannister, a bench, a box, the hull of a lifeboat, but no, there is only metal, if there were only a tarp or a sail, Sébastien would stab it with the knife, once, twice, three times, and would strike repeatedly, the way one strikes in a murder of passion, a detail to explain mitigating circumstances. But nothing is mitigating anymore, ever. Sébastien strokes the blade with the end of his finger, makes a gash intentionally in his left forefinger and brings his finger up to his mouth, the taste of his own blood. How many times did Luc, Claire, Bertrand and he do this same thing, promising themselves, by this act, to accomplish nothing important but what would serve them all, and to determine their respective lives without their father dictating and resolving, ordering and driving them to despair? His finger in his mouth, the switch-knife in the other hand, Sébastien looks at the wounds on his arm. He laughs, he breathes, his nose turned toward the Americas. The sun is dropping. In the sky a purple light radiates and turns blue where it meets the mountains and rocks of the fjord. The mica sparkles softly. The sea is the same sombre green as the forests that drop straight down, steeply. The mineral tone of the sea shouts to the night as if one knows how to listen. Sébastien breathes Ruth's body. He runs his nose from her ankles to her knees, from her knees to her hips, from her hips to her bosom, from her bosom to her chin, and he places on the lips of the one who was wife, his wife, a submission, a kiss, lightly. Ruth looks wide-eyed at him. He cries out. Sébastien cries out, throws the knife into the sea, takes his finger out of his mouth, and hits his fists on the guardrail, with repeated blows, hard enough to break his wrists, a pain to chase away an image. Then he puts the two hands of his broken watch at the vertical of noon or midnight, like the wall clock at the Place d'Antioche. He must walk, now, and breathe a little.

He was expecting everything from this day, except this amorous state of deprivation so near to a revolt, this turning point, stirring up images from the past and placing them messily, in the most acute part of his memory, for a violent gesture, a confrontation, of a date and its significance, of a smell, a look, or an emptiness. Turning his back to the west and on the Americas, heading toward the east of the *Firebird* and its prow, Sébastien feels himself abandoning Ruth, Laura and Paul again. He is distancing himself from them. Penned in, he is going away. Moncrabeau also had strange limits. The limits determined by a grandfather who did not like undergrowth or untrammelled nature and who had had immense expanses of grass and lawns cleared, punctuated the horizons with paths lined with poplars, young elms, evergreens and laburnum. And beyond the paths, on all sides, even beyond the birch woods, one could only bump into the enclosure wall, without blemish, constructed at the end of the last century to endure for many more centuries. From the house or from the lake, one could dream and believe that this cleared space offered infinite ways for flight in every direction. But if one started running this way or that, the wall soon loomed behind the foliage of trees that had been selected, planted, placed with a purpose, in the shadow of which one felt constantly under surveillance. Bertrand used to say, 'These are our guards,' and claimed they had a way of shivering, in summer, or of creaking in winter, that signalled their desire to run away. One could only go out of the doors or the gates, by using the driveways. So there was no running away. Nothing but walks by the children, by the adolescents or young men themselves considered as property by the conviction of all the fathers in their society who, simply by claiming to have no titles, and to belong to no caste, were secretly defending the non-belligerent and vigilant silence of a 'France of the centre which alone won the Revolution and enjoys it like a cake that will never end.' From Bertrand again. Sébastien does not like this train of thought. He feels like a prisoner of his own mind. He will only have escaped, heavy with the weight of those thoughts, of those events, made vaguely happy by the memory of Bertrand's voice, of having at least voiced the truth a few times. But what was the point?

From the prow of the *Firebird*, Sébastien looks at the *Newton*, the *Ambrasy*, the *G.K. Hall*, further on at the *Spirit*, the *Apollo* and the *Septentrion*, black cliffs, tons and tons of floating metal, dead commerce. Very soon the sun will rise again. That will make one day less before leaving. The men, in a little while, will act as if nothing had been said, or done. In the night of the engine room, for a brief moment, Sébastien had wished that nothing in the incident were a joke and that a dagger had been planted in his abdomen. The ship is closed, like Moncrabeau. Sébastien looks to the left at his father, to the right at Bertrand. He feels boxed in. Before him the fjord twists and strangles itself. Behind, far away, Ruth is forgetting him, Laura and Paul are living another life, or even the same life. Nothing can really change family decisions. Impossible flights from reality repeat themselves. The first shock lies in admitting it. Bertrand's refrain: 'Only the shock of reality is beautiful and good in happiness.' Sébastien smiles to himself. In a while the men will also smile at him. He will send in good reports to 'British Petrofuck and Co.' Each will maintain his record for other jobs, in other places, always with the same load of ambition and disappointment. Family life, a loving or a rebellious condition, is only a perpetual repetition, it comes from conviction and hope. The hope of escaping it when you know you won't escape. The revolution is no longer where it is said to be. Romanticism is never where is promises to be. Each one's identity is only that 'right to emotion' that Bertrand spoke of to his brothers and to Claire, not to impose a rebellious state of mind, but to suggest a principle of action at a time when everything doomed them to submit to a ritual, to the rehearsal for a performance. They are both here, the father and the brother, because it is July 9th, because it is twenty years later, because they all knew what was happening, even Cécile, and nobody did anything about it. The butcher of Barcelona could take out a piece of brain in all tranquillity and, a year or two later, put down his scalpels and admit, that the practical result of his

222

work, was only to have sent cripples back to those families who would do everything possible to remain intact themselves or believe they were. They are here, Henri on the left, Bertrand on the right, characters for the day. They have come back. Only Claire seems to have lived the lesson of the 'right to emotion'. But only after Gérard's death. Sébastien leans over, on the prow, out over the sea. He likes this dizziness, just as he likes the silence in the passageway, the doors closed again, everyone in his cabin, even Oswyn, after the drinks and the fury.

With his whole body Sébastien feels himself in Ruth's body. He has entered her legs, her arms, her skull. He is she and she is here, in him, she is leaning over him, with him. She is he. She walks when he walks. She goes to bed when he does. She is the clandestine traveller no one can see. She moves when he moves and speaks when he speaks. Nothing really tears away this skin that has become his skin, even when Sébastien smiles or laughs, it is Sébastien who knows at the time that it is Ruth who smiles under similar circumstances. For seventeen years Sébastien had been wholly arrested in Ruth's body. When he is cold, he tells himself she's cold. When he moves his fingers, she is moving hers, the curious way she had of piano fingering in space, at a meal's end, at the Place d'Antioche, letting Sébastien know thereby that she wished to leave. During the first months of their separation, Sébastien and Ruth exchanged poignant letters, each taking the blame for the breakup, each amazed at the dizziness that had brought about their desire to separate, at the desire of each to give oneself to the other, a return to marriage, only to find in the end once again a feeling of distrust at the first meeting, a distrust that comes back, painfully, breaking whatever it is in the amorous spirit that had imagined it was sealed, united, joined together for ever and ever. Often Sébastien thinks, an image, that Ruth has become his pajamas. Pajamas he would never take off again.

Often, in other women's arms, stubbornly, obsessed by the idea of shedding this other presence, with an *amour fixe*, Sébastien tries to force an orgasm, for himself and himself alone. But then he hears in his head, because he closes his eyes, Ruth's soft panting coming in his place and before he does, holding back his own orgasm and making him impotent, still with an erection, who plunges but never attains the end, a sky

223

opening up, a cloudburst, and that silence afterwards, that sadness, that invites other emotions. Never that again. Ruth forbids it. What was the name of that woman he had met in the airplane, coming back from Marseille, last year, the day he went to Sauveterre, who, lying on the carpet in the silence of a room at the Orly Hilton, naked, on her back, unsatisfied, had said to Sébastien, in a raspy voice, stroking his forehead, 'You have a woman in your head! And she isn't close to coming out!' What was her first name? Sébastien, prostrate on the bed, humiliated once again, had put his hands up to his ears so as not to hear, remembering Ruth's gesture when she seized his face, standing on tiptoes, her arms stretched. She did not want Sébastien to hear what she was going to tell him. On Ruth's lips, deafened by his wife's firmly pressed hands, Sébastien would then read '1, 4, 3,' their number, 'I, love, you.'

And there, leaning on the prow, bent in two over the void, Sébastien plays with vertigo and the void. He repeats 'One, four, three,' then, 'I, love, you.' He gets an erection. He opens his fly. It is Ruth's hand working and holding him, movements that become less and less slow. He comes, into the void, another froth in the waves, looking at the end of the fjord. It is the only way he can come anymore. There. Forward. Alone. Aided. Inhabited. Everything really began at the time of the separation. Everything has really been beginning for seventeen years. Past the time of the first letters after the divorce, the times of emptiness for which one blames oneself, the omissions one admits, their correspondence becoming less urgent, less charged with regrets and therefore rarer, then nothing more. The quarterly payments and the obligatory letters. And although they were writing each other less and less, Sébastien felt Ruth slipping into him, or else he was dressing himself with her, as if he was afraid of forgetting her, some day, remembering only the sourness of other meetings. Uncle Jean had told Sébastien, 'Like your father, you're one of those who live only what they haven't lived. And I know, when I tell you that, that you'll never visit us again.' Aunt Suzy had made no comment. She only wanted to see the latest pictures of Laura and Paul. 'How they've grown!' It was a farewell. Bertrand, too, enclosed at Moncrabeau, abandoned there, prevents each of them from seeing each other. Sébastien closes his fly. It's his hand this time. Twilight, or morning, how do you know? the light is so soft. He heads for the poopdeck. Two hundred and seventeen metres of metal plates that shock and grate. He knows that as soon as he's naked, slipping into his bed, it will be Ruth, whole, once again, who is slipping into him, and is with him. Nothing. There's nothing to be done.

Footbridges, gangways, he's in the wardroom, then in the passageway. A door opens as he passes, it's René, who bends his head and says simply, 'Are you better? Us too!' He slams the door. Sébastien had neither the time to answer nor the time, looking at René, to have any response but surprise.

In his cabin Sébastien notices that Jao has been in, has prepared the bed as in an hotel, and put out clean towels, a service not given him for months. He is once again an officer.

After the shower, he dries off, dabs the wounds on his arms and hands with alcohol, puts a compress on his temple and eye. He throws the rags of his shirt away. He stretches out on the seat, picks up the copy of *Hadrian's Memoirs,* opens it at random and reads one of Bertrand's notes, in the margin, cramped writing, like a final message, 'I have a secret although I don't yet know what it is: they ask me to give, but never to receive.' Sébastien drops the book. He wants Ruth to sleep within him. He will watch. In the book is an envelope on which can be read 'To Sébastien Prouillan, in memory of the forbidden heart', Bertrand's message given to Sébastien on the day of his wedding. Bertrand had told him, 'It's for you, and you alone. Read it as late as possible. With us the latest is always too soon.'

14

Antoine puts away the cards and bridge mat. Eliane empties the ashtrays. Christine counts up the three games. Luc observes his friends, his arms crossed on the table, his back bent, his head shrunk into his shoulders. When distracted he plays badly, and knows it. Far from rebuking him or, between each deal, making remarks or, after each bid, reproaches, Christine seems to enjoy Luc's inattention. Antoine and Eliane are not drawing the right cards, rarely can they open, lacking the minimum number of points to bid, even for a pre-emptive bid. During the three games Antoine is content to smile and murmur sportingly, 'No cards for the innocent.' 'He does best who does best,' or even 'Oh sorry, forgive me,' a mocking humour not without a reminder to Luc of the way Bertrand used to have of putting an opposite word in place of an expected one. Bertrand used to call that 'sliding humour' and maintained that 'all dialogue begins in this way.' Across from Antoine, a good partner during the three games, Eliane amuses herself by never saying 'I pass' in exactly the same tone, during the bidding, and by never throwing out any opening card, in defence, without pretending to think deeply about it. Luc has arranged to be dummy. Christine would play the hand. It was up to Eliane to open. From bid to bid, there was nothing to be done, Antoine and she had no good cards. Christine and Luc had too many. Leading for three lively games.

Antoine says, 'It's as if we hadn't played,' then, 'A game in a vacuum' and, sitting down at the table again, across from Luc, speaking to Luc, 'Say it if you have something to say! Stop playing this comedy with us.' Antoine rolls up his shirt sleeves, rubs his forearms, gives a showing-off smile to Christine, waves to Eliane to sit beside him and bring the ashtray. The room smells of abandonment, like the house, the tenacious odour of closed shutters, of a second residence that no-one ever liked and only went to briefly. Antoine has just let himself be surprised by this strong smell that nothing can really disperse even if they stay a long time. For the record Christine announces, 'The first game was 14, the second 11 and the third 17. But we weren't playing for money.' She tears up the tally sheet, starts to get up to throw the little pieces in the trash can but Luc holds her back. 'Wait, please. Antoine is right.'

Antoine blushes like a child. Eliane sits leaning against him. She seems surprised. She looks at her husband, takes Christine and Luc as witnesses. 'That's the way I love you, Antoine. Like tonight. Like now.' She kisses Antoine on the cheek and tells him, 'That little hint of humour you had when I met you, I thought you'd lost it.' She smiles at Christine. 'He used to say of our marriage that it was only a funny story.' She looks at Luc. 'You're Antoine's boss, and then what? Does he owe you everything? He owes you nothing! We didn't have any good cards tonight, not even enough luck to defend ourselves properly. That puts Antoine in second place again. What I'd have given to beat you!'

Eliane laughs, shrugs pleasantly, gives Antoine a wink. 'Feeling better?' Antoine shakes his head, neither yes or no. Eliane says in his ear, in a voice loud enough for Christine and Luc to hear, 'You said what had to be said. Thanks.' She looks at Christine. 'It's up to him to say it, isn't it?' She holds out a hand towards Luc, flat on the table. 'So out with it!'

Luc has not moved. Eliane withdraws her hand sliding it on the table. Christine pulls back her chair, grabs a newspaper, unfolds it and, as if she had prepared herself all along, reads an article in a sharp, ridiculous monotone. 'The staff of this new magazine want to launch a monthly. Prior to its definitive appearance they recently put out an issue number 0. One object is to give information about the new actors, the new places to go, new products, problems . . .' Christine smiles and mumbles, 'Shall I continue?' Luc and Antoine exchange a look. Luc looks down. Eliane is proud of Antoine. Christine continues, 'Another objective of this magazine is to speak to a mature audience about what tomorrow's world may be like.' Christine laughs. 'Do you think it'll be for us?' and reads again 'less theoretically, the magazine will offer news reports, surveys, practical information, experiments in different life styles, photographs, classified ads or notices for "personal contacts", in short, everything for everybody, even for the established person with a thirst to know about the new winds that are already blowing somewhere else,' end of quote. Christine places the newspaper flat on the table, points to the article and says, 'That's it. That's what it says. It's funny, don't you think? What are experiments in different life styles? What does the new wind already blowing somewhere else mean? Where is it? And they don't say what they mean. It looks like a tease. Which wants a good kick in the backside?

Antoine, Eliane and Christine burst out laughing. Luc tries to get up. Christine, in turn, holds him back. 'No, stay, please. I read that article just for you. It's to laugh at what we're becoming. Please, Luc, talk to us.' Christine lets go of Luc's hand. Luc lowers his eyes. Christine slides her chair and goes to him. She stands close, looks at him questioningly. From the other side of the table Antoine mumbles. 'It's been a long time since I've felt so well.' He kisses Eliane on the hair, awkwardly and turns to Luc, 'What'd you tell them, on television? What were you thinking all day? What do you think about all the time? You hear, but you don't listen. Fortunately I'm here, all year long to listen in your place. You keep your place, I keep mine. I don't like you, Luc. You don't want to be liked. If I were at least sure you were listening, here, now.' He turns to Eliane. 'Aren't you going to tell me bravo?'

Antoine gets up, grabs the newspaper, wrinkles it up, makes a ball of it, goes to the fireplace, places the paper on the fireplace, on top of the twigs, the pieces of burnt logs that have been there since the Easter vacation. He lights the fire, stands up, rubs his hands. Then he heads towards the door, opens it, toward the window, opens it and rubs his hands again. 'We're waiting, Luc old man.' He comes back, sits on the table, up against Eliane, clasps her between his knees and in his arms, places his chin on the top of his wife's head. Eliane says, 'You're hurting me.' Antoine answers 'I love you.' Eliane mumbles making a face, 'It's the same thing.' They laugh, both of them, then Christine, then all three, then Luc, then all four. Luc takes Christine's hand and kisses it. Luc says, 'I have a family, in my head, that's posing for a photo. Like a class photo. But the photo can't be taken. Someone's always moving . . .'

Silence. Luc goes on, 'We all have a family in our heads. You

229

Antoine. You Eliane, And you, Christine. But in my family someone is always moving, in the photograph. Someone who wants to escape. Someone who doesn't want to pose. Bertrand used to claim "It's not wilfulness, but someone's always out of focus. And a person out of focus is wilfulness in motion." Bertrand used to say things I wouldn't even try to understand. He also used to say that "poetry doesn't use words, it creates them". He had trouble creating them, those words, in order not to use them. Like all of us. He would tear up his poems. Or else, if he were writing in pencil, he'd erase them, pretending to correct, and would invent others, comic ones. He would blow on his fingers then, as if he were blowing bubbles, and we would be quiet. Often he used to talk about a glider that crashed, in the summer of '47, at Saint-Cirice, not far from Moncrabeau. A black glider. Near the wreck Bertrand had found a glove. One of the pilot's gloves. He used to say, "It's the glove that believed it could command the wind." That was my brother. I didn't listen to him, really.'

The fire crackles in the fireplace. Air comes in, in gusts, from outside, laden with the odours of mosses and ferns. There is light too, from the moon. The house breathes. Eliane, under Antoine's chin and in his arms, holds her breath. Christine places her hands flat on Luc's hands. Luc hesitates. He finds that his voice is too easily able to evoke, the way that he does, the images and memories that he has been rejecting for years that have never ceased to harass him. All that is too true for comfort, a flagrant reality, too difficult an experience, to take its place in a pleasantly planned life, laid out in advance, the life of an engineer and an elder son. Luc remembers the day he was a witness at the marriage of Antoine to Eliane. He also remembers Antoine as witness at his own marriage, a few months later. He says, 'It's Anne-Marie who moves the most in the photographs. She never wanted to pose with us. She hadn't even left her family when she found another one and she was supposed to create a third. She never wanted any other child but Pierre. Often, to provoke me, or to show her love for me, in her own way, she would diaper Pierre and call him Luc. The day that Bertrand came back from Barcelona, when we, Anne-Marie and I, had left the apartment at the Place d'Antioche, I tried to take Pierre in my arms, he was sleeping, and Anne-Marie said to me, "I'm going

230

down this staircase and I'm never coming back up. You're like your father. I don't want to become like Cécile." There. In the photo, Anne-Marie is moving. She is descending the staircase with our son in her arms. That staircase is endless. For me, Pierre is only the age he was on that day. Do you understand, Antoine? And you, Eliane? And you, Christine? Don't look at me like that. This idea of a photograph only came to me late this afternoon, when you were all posing in front of the dolmen table. It's only an idea, but the good and indispensable thing about ideas is not only that they set our feelings but they also inspire them. I didn't believe Bertrand when he was explaining things to us.'

Luc smiles as if he were making fun of himself. Christine withdraws her hands, places them in her lap. With her look directed under the table, she takes off her sandals, rubs her feet against each other. Luc knows he has just lost Christine. She has either just given him up or else lost patience. Luc feels as well that after inviting him to talk, Antoine and Eliane are not listening to him either, and are thinking only about being left alone together, as if engaged once again. That's their way. They never put down roots anywhere. Even more softly Luc says, 'There's only one person who doesn't move in the family photo. That's my father. He stares at the lens. He watches me. He watches us. He is there, like someone observing a target so as not to miss it. He wanted us to succeed. Bertrand used to say, "Split up, quartered, our family is the colour of scarlet. Everything can only finish in blood. Just exactly the way everything began." I can see my father, *he* doesn't move. And I hear Bertrand saying "scarlet" pronouncing the word too precisely. Are you still listening?' Luc tightens his fists. Christine shakes her head. Her hair falls forward and hides her face. She stretches her legs under the table, she puts her hands on her hips. Bent double on her chair, she mumbles, 'Of course, we're listening.' Eliane raises her eyes to Luc 'We're listening.' But it's not true.

So Luc continues in the void, just for himself, furious at having started to talk like this, curious to get even by seeing how long they will insist on not listening after being caught out. Luc, however, knows the lesson of the void. The first to denounce are always the first to reveal themselves when the confessions begin. The knowledge of this is undoubtedly at the origin of all the abuses of power. Luc lives it and lives on it, it is the secret of his professional career. Antoine can mock him. Laughing, Luc looks at him, 'There's a dog in the photo. He moves because he wants to be taken out. And when this dog dies, they replace him with another dog, an identical one.' Luc laughs still louder, 'And there's a maid. She just passes through the photograph. She just passes through. She knows everything, but she does not judge anything. She doesn't even expect her wages. She's the only one who knows why she is there: she renders a service. She cleans. She puts things away. She sews. She takes the dog out. She goes out with the dog. She makes cakes. She cleans the shoes. She goes to open the door. She waits. Her name is Bernadette. Do you remember her, Antoine? Not even. She just passes through the picture. She is still paid for doing that. Shall I go on?'

Luc rises. 'If my father were to walk in, here, now, to kill me, I wouldn't be surprised. I even believe that's all I'm waiting for. Waiting is sometimes the only way to defend yourself.'

Luc goes to the window, 'I can only talk to you, Christine, by turning my back to you. It's my way of facing up to you. I can't help it. I'm a standard make like you. Very French and too bourgeois, it's all the same thing. Your look is judging me but you won't change me. Anne-Marie is lying crosswise in my head and she takes up all the room. Years go by. I have never been able to stop worrying about the mail. I am always expecting a letter to say that she's coming back. Like the perfume "Je Reviens". We've seen the commercial together at the movies. You took my hand at that moment. On the screen were various couples, very young, very beautiful, meeting in restaurants, in stations, in airports, in the street. And each time, the name of the perfume "Je Reviens". My hand was cold, wasn't it? You were always the young woman in those couples, but I wasn't any of the possible partners. Every morning when I shave myself, I have to look at myself in the mirror over the sink. I tell myself that every day I am losing more than Anne-Marie would recognise if she ever really came back. The approach of my fiftieth birthday. Something changed in the distinctiveness of the look. Anne-Marie and I were crazy about each other. A look from me made her blush then. I believed I was being avoided. Little by little she understood that avoiding things is impossible. The murder of one's father, the fine oedipus complex so much in style for a century now, is only one more way of strengthening the family as it is, in the sense that it is made and will always be made from itself.'

Luc hesitates. Christine does not move. Antoine makes a face. Eliane closes her eyes. So much the better. Luc goes on, 'And my family is exemplary in that it has no example to give about sharing. What is most alive about it is the way it is dying little by little in the shadow and the fear of no longer having what it has been, of no longer being what it has never been. Yes, Christine, I feel I've just lost you. Because I wish to lose you. There's no place for you. There isn't even any place for me. I owe you this admission: we have not existed for a long time. And we're here for a long time yet. We have proliferated ourselves in the false light of family ideologies and in the shadow of stock portfolios. Of suitable marriages. Of polytechnic schools. I love, Christine, but from a distance. I am held back. It is reticence. I was born with my future arranged in advance. I liked Anne-Marie because she was compatible with the idea of that arrangement. She was conventional and from a good family. I thought I'd escaped, with her, from the inside. Now I know that there is no way out in that direction either. Yes, I'm laughing. It's funny. We've all tried to escape the inevitable photograph, each in his own way. I just wanted mine to be ordinary. It didn't work out. Each one for himself. Each one in himself. And someone, for me, crosswise in my head, is still there.'

Luc turns around. Christine has risen. She is standing near the fireplace. She has just put on a log, there is a sudden blaze. Eliane frees herself from Antoine's hold, gets up, sits on the table, taking one of her husband's hands and placing it in her lap. Antoine mumbles, 'I'm dead. How about you? I don't feel my arms and legs anymore. Those logs were heavy. Sorry Luc. It was only a diversion.' Christine goes to the sink, fills a pan with water, lights the gas and puts it on the fire. 'Coffee for everyone?' Eliane turns to Luc 'And what about Antoine, in your story? Are you cutting yourself off from him too?'

Luc crosses the room, places a hand in passing on Antoine's shoulder, and goes near to the fireplace, his arms and fingers stretched as if warming his hands. 'When you start to feel certain that you're helping someone, the chances are that you're no longer helping him.' He shakes his head. 'I'm quoting my father, who in all likelihood was quoting his, and so forth. Even the idea of helping someone is a lie. No one puts himself out anymore. Better to say nothing. Especially if you're pressed. Especially if one can no longer do anything else. Every observation is taken for a complaint. And today, because it is today, because for twenty years my family has been posing for an impossible photograph, because nothing unites us except the observation that we've never really been together, and so I tell myself that at this moment Sébastien is thinking the same thing, that Ruth and Anne-Marie are thinking about us, that Claire is wrestling with a car accident in her head, that Bertrand knows exactly how to hold his fork in order to taste his birthday cake, that my Aunt Suzanne is stroking the pearl necklaces she no longer possesses by pretending to have taken them off, that Bernadette is waiting for my father to return, and that my father . . .'

Luc stops, his sentence suspended and mocks himself. 'Mustn't talk that way, must I? No one talks that way, ever. However, Eliane, it's what's burning my lips. It is also, Christine, what keeps me away from you. This distance entirely contained in you're saying 'vous' to me. Thanks to that, I've been able to live with you longer than with other women. I knew, even before our meeting, that no one, ever, would replace the first one. Anne-Marie is nothing extraordinary. Nothing. Neither am I. But she was the first and remains so. And don't tell me that confession is indulgent. I don't know a case where a person from the second or even the n-th meeting has prevailed over the first.' The water is boiling. Christine pours it into the coffee pot, instant coffee. She says, 'But you are my first, Luc,' then, 'I'll simply ask for a certificate like: I, the undersigned Prouillan, Luc, Henri, Joseph, born January 28, 1931 in Paris, 17th arrondissement, certify that Christine Euhart has loved in my service from January 27 to July 9 and that . . .' She burst into laughter. Luc kicks the firelogs, produces sparks.

Eliane gets up, goes to get the coffee bowls from the sideboard, the sugar and spoons. She comes back to the table, arms full, awkwardly. Antoine puts everything in place. There's something connecting about their silence. A complicity. Their looks meet and melt into each other. Christine observes them, the coffee-pot in hand. Luc's best friends could be everybody's best friends, and everybody's best friends are never there, really, as they should be, when they should be. One's own apparent happiness, even if it becomes obvious at moments, can never sustain the other, that of a friend, and invite him to live better. Christine tells herself that friendship, like happiness, has misled her world, with its funny ideas, its myths of changing times. She looks at Luc. 'You're right, no one puts himself out any more. To do that is to expose yourself to all kinds of ridicule.' She goes to the table, puts down the coffee pot. Then, in a pile of magazines on a chair against the wall, she chooses one that she leafs through saying, 'Since we got here, I've been digging around in the random pages of the papers to give me an idea of what we're all about. For lack of knowing who we are. Listen, I have another pearl for you. In seven sentences, each a heading, here is the summary of our present Head of State's thoughts. And it's not unrelated to your photograph, Luc.'

Christine reads, 'First sentence: we are at an important moment that I will compare to passing through a narrow tunnel.' Christine comments, 'We'll compare that, in the future, which will give us a better idea.' She goes on. 'Second sentence: We must not try to remain adapted to a world that has passed on. Third sentence: A society cannot live long without a collective belief. Fourth sentence: At the present time, the international political system is not heading towards a conflict.' Christine smiles, in an aside 'What is it heading towards then?' She reads, 'Fifth sentence: Pessimism can spring from a biological shortness of breath in the species.' Antoine shrugs. Eliane serves the coffee. Luc pokes the firelogs back onto the flame. Christine says very distinctly, 'Sixth sentence: We are moving towards a world without controls, whereas, in the past, they existed . . . With three dots, if you please. And finally, the last sentence: The consumer socity has devastated a part of our coasts, our mountains, and our cities. There it is. That's all there is to it. Everything isn't devastated.' Christine holds the magazine out to Antoine, 'Do you want to check? and to Luc, 'Do you want to read what's under each title?'

Eliane says, 'Let's drink the coffee. Tomorrow morning I'll make it real coffee.' Luc, squatting in front of the fire, is watching the flames, he hesitates, straightens, stands up and approaches the table. 'Tomorrow morning? I'll be gone.' He puts a lump of sugar in the cup, sips, 'I'm always leaving even before I arrive. Like at the office, Antoine. Doesn't that make you laugh? They take me for a workhorse. I am. Only because I don't think about what I'm doing, or when I do it. I am a perfect managing director. No more capacity for attention. The sense for reading cash-flow charts and making decisions, that's all. Profit decides.' He raises his bowl as if he intended to make a toast 'To our departures!' He drinks a sip 'To our respective lives!' He takes a spoon, melts the sugar, drinks again, 'To the scarlet family!' He wipes his lips with his hand and raises the cup still higher, 'To the Head of State and to my father! Thank you, Christine!' He empties the cup, places it on the table, slides it with a violent gesture in the direction of the coffee pot against which it breaks. Luc puts on an amazed look, 'Well, well, the cup broke, not the coffee pot! Strange, don't you think?'

Eliane puts a hand out to Luc, 'Calm down.' Luc turns toward Christine, 'To the biological shortness of breath in the species!' A pause, 'To those well-established people who thirst for the new wind that is already blowing somewhere else!' Antoine says to Luc, 'It's stupid to leave. There's only four days left. Surely Christine feels like staying. The place isn't so comfortable but . . .' Christine waves to Antoine not to say anything more. Luc leaves the table, heads toward the door and stands there, on the step, facing the night and the moon, facing the sombre foliage of the woods encircling the house. None of the undergrowth has been cleared away. Against the wall of the house are two deck chairs with torn canvases that have been waiting there, certainly a long time, for someone to repair them, restore them to use. At home in the Rue Téhéran, Luc, in his campside of a rented apartment, always throws away anything that is broken, when it gets broken, develops a hole, gets torn, when it does not work anymore. He throws everything away. Antoine and Eliane, on the other hand, keep things, but don't repair them.

Luc needs to go back to the Rue Téhéran, to be left alone, his head is confused. Solitary, isolated or self-isolating, the urgency of another person, unique, a beloved other person, seems less painful to him. Then he can think about the continuing possibility of Anne-Marie's return, if she does come back some day, become a prey again. Luc also wants to return to the Rue

Téhéran and wait for his father, in case his father decides to visit him, an impromptu visit, a visit decided on the day. Henri will finally ring the door bell. Luc looks out at the night, before him. Bertrand is also waiting, and Claire and Sébastien. One act is missing at the scarlet family's theatre. The awaited act in which they can accuse the murderer of being a murderer, and the victim of being a victim, as if one were not the other, and vice versa. One act so that they can say 'It's the story of' and tell very exactly in a few words what, in fact, escapes summary, has neither a beginning nor an end, nothing but impressions, details, feelings, which call out to life. Turning his back to his friends, Luc says in a very loud voice, facing the night, 'Tomorrow I'll have forgotten all that!'

Luc leans back against the upright of the door, arms crossed, one knee bent. He turns his head toward the interior of the house, the fire, the cups, the table, the decks of cards, the magazines on the chair, the chairs, the flagstones, and the walls about which Antoine says every year 'I'm going to re-paint them myself, but only if Luc backs me up.' Luc observes Christine. She is beautiful. Young. She is silent. She does not believe anymore. He would really like to be convinced of it. He murmurs, 'Every night when I go to bed, I tell myself that tomorrow Anne-Marie won't be here anymore. She will not move around anymore. She will not take up the whole place anymore. We will be able to take the photograph. And I'll be able to throw the photo away as I do when something is finished. Done with.' Christine looks at Antoine, Antoine looks at Eliane, Eliane picks up the broken cup and goes to throw it away in the crate that serves as a trashcan. Antoine says laughing to his wife, 'The garbage collection is tomorrow, we mustn't forget it.' He turns to Luc. 'And every morning, Anne-Marie is still there in your head?' Christine rises. 'I'm going to bed. If you leave, Luc, please don't wake me. I'm staying here,' She looks at Eliane and Antoine, 'until tomorrow. Thanks.' She leaves the room. Her step is heard on the stairs and in the first floor hallway, a door opening and closing again.

Eliane goes up to Luc. 'Why do you always hurt yourself?' Antoine joins them. He announces, 'Tomorrow I'm replacing the canvas on the deck chairs! Tomorrow, the garbage and the canvases!' Eliane murmurs, 'Please, Tony, this isn't the time.'

237

Antoine takes Eliane by the hand. 'It's been a long time since you called me Tony. You'll see!' And he drags her outside. Eliane has just the time to say to Luc, 'Are you coming with us?' Antoine bellows 'No! We don't need him.' Behind the trees so near the house, the buried house, the suspended moon, already sinking, Eliane and Antoine disappear. Antoine yells loudly into the night, 'The right time to laugh is when it's the wrong time!'

Luc is left alone on the doorstep. The fire has died down. Silence on the second floor and silence all around. A dog barks in the distance, then two, then three. They are answering each other, provoking each other, who knows, or simply saying hello? Luc feels neither offended by what has just happened nor proud of what is now going to occur inevitably, his leaving. He even feels better and more in harmony with himself, free to live with his image, the photograph, and his feelings, his oneness, for which he is fighting, that he must defend and which at any price must not become a resentment. The general indifference of others is nothing compared to their attention when they bring it to bear, suggest to you, make you believe in it, only just long enough for it to become the proof and provocation of a confession, so that they can withdraw it again, the way you pull a rug from under someone's feet to make him fall and make fun of him for falling. In this practice friends excel. Scarcely have they given the impression of bending a little, of being ready to listen, than they straighten up, scoff at you, and go away laughing. Luc has just fallen into a trap he has so often set himself, as a boss, and which no doubt was worth his nomination to the Legion of Honour. At least in intriguing for him to receive it, Henri had chosen in this way to tell his son how inevitably he was like him. One who walks rather than one who is walked upon.

Luc lets himself slide along the door's upright. He sees Cécile again, in her final months, in the hospital. She did not want flowers or books or spoiling. She was no longer able to talk. A cotton turban replaced her hair, crowning that unrecognisable head that seemed to be shrinking. Only the look in her eyes was left to recognise her by. Her left arm was bound, outside the sheets, alongside her body. Needles were implanted in her veins. Tubes came out of them, suspended, attached to test tubes and bottles, a whole apparatus for keeping her alive. All she cared about was the cassette recorder for which she had asked Bernadette, still not daring to ask anything of Henri, and which she would request, waving to a visitor or the duty nurse, to be turned on to play some music. Then the headphones would have to be put on, raising the turban a little. With a look Cécile would say thank you. She only wanted symphonies. They would show her various cassettes, Suzy had even brought some show tunes. She always chose symphonies. Only one book excited her. She would leaf through it with her other hand, one knee slightly raised, *The Secrets of the Orchestra*, a book in which everything was illustrated, explained, the oboe, the flute, the English horn, the violin, the way the orchestra was made up, the organisation of massed sound, the secrets of conducting. The whole thing in a language for educating children, which was in fact, a masquerade of simple formulas, only in adult language that demonstrates too much, intent upon rendering everything complicated. Cécile, with the headphones on, when Luc visited her, would choose such and such a page, would indicate the passage and with her finger ask her eldest son to read to her, in a voice loud enough for her to hear the music at the same time and, who knows, understand how all that beauty could be bound together, and melt and lift as it does. Cécile started learning music. Although throughout her whole life she had never expressed any interest other than for her family and in protecting her relations with Henri, Cécile started off with the descriptions of the crescendo, the trombone, the saxophone, the cymbals, the viola, spinet and cello, read to her in turn by Claire, during her two round trips to and from Paris, by Sébastien, on his way between Cherbourg and Rotterdam, more often by Bernadette, in the middle of the day, and by Luc when he left his office, at the hour when the hospital corridors began smelling of soup and boiled fish. Luc would have liked to be able to share this discovery of music with his mother. He would read what she asked him to read but did not hear what she was listening to simultaneously. Because of this detail, he began to suffer his mother's last days still more painfully, for right up to the end they had shared nothing totally together, to the full, like other couples. Cécile's favourite cassette was a recording of Sibelius' Fifth Symphony because, it seemed, she found all the instruments in it and sometimes, listening to it, appeared overwhelmed at recognising a certain timbre or tone.

For her too, everything was happening in her head, an orchestra in place of a husband. It was one way as good as another of packing your bags and leaving on a good impression.

Luc regrets not having talked about Cécile to Christine, Eliane and Antoine. Luc is annoyed at himself for not saying the essential thing about the photograph. The essential is formulated only afterwards, when no one is there anymore to listen. Luc crosses his hands in his lap, braces the top of his head on the door upright. He takes a deep breath. The recorder, the headphones and the cassettes are shut up forevermore in the top of a closet at the Place d'Antioche. Luc heard his father say, 'When I think that your mama didn't even use them. Bernadette and the nurses said she did. But it isn't possible. Your mother never liked music. She never knew what it was all about. Neither did I.' Luc did not dare contradict his father. If he had tried, his father would not have believed him and would have become even more firmly anchored in the idea that all that equipment had only been the whim of a dying woman. After Cécile's death, Henri no longer said, 'Your mother' when speaking of her, but 'your mama.' Too late.

Luc knows he is going to leave. He will have to do it discreetly in the bedroom he shares with Christine. He does not like explanations much and, when guilty, knows that he is capable of the worst insults or absurd reproaches. All those things that, in Uncle Jean's theatre, caused doors to be slammed and scenes and acts to reverberate. Luc would not like to run into Eliane and Antoine either. Unless those two were still more afraid than he of that confrontation and were on the alert watching him from behind the trees, up to his departure. How many times, like this, leaving those who love and surround him, has Luc left on a bad impression, with a wrenching of the heart or the worry of not saying or doing what should have been said or done. Luc says out loud, 'Tomorrow I'll have forgotten everything!' But he knows that is not possible.

He also wants to return to Paris because of his job, to take advantage of summer to inspect, check, prepare the work of others and to be in his office, on the top floor of the glass building with a panoramic view of the Sacre-Coeur on one side, and the Panthéon and the Eiffel Tower on the other. He needs to be there, to be able to tell himself that he is at work while the

240

others are on holiday, whereas his nature makes him take a holiday in himself, twelve months out of twelve, occupied in not understanding what it is that cuts him off from everything and everybody, and his failure with Anne-Marie, his only experience at escape. 'You are incapable of enjoying what you have when you have it. You only have the capacity to suffer from what you have not been or from what you could not be. I leave you a kiss and I love you more than ever. I want to live another life. That's all. A.M.' Luc still keeps this note from Anne-Marie in his wallet. He knows it by heart, an intact emotion, a sign of possible return.

Cécile moves in the photograph. Each time Henri raises his voice, she brings her left hand to her throat, unconsciously, not even realising it, as if someone were going to strangle her. Then, a moment later, aware of the gesture, feeling herself betrayed in her fear, with the same gesture she puts her hairdo back into place, at the nape of the neck, on each side of her face, a fear made-up in a coyness that is not like her. In the photograph Cécile still has her hair. That gesture betrays her, a gesture caused and provoked by Henri's voice.

In the photo there is Pantalon I, Pantalon II or Pantalon III, always a poodle bursting in with his leash in his mouth. He wants to go around the chestnut trees in the Place d'Antioche. He is moving because he is wagging his tail or because he is standing on his hind legs. They give him a hard biscuit when he returns the leash. In the photograph Uncle Jean is always bending over, but over a note-book. He is taking notes. But Suzy doesn't stay still. Her dress squeezes her too much at the waist, like the dresses of the dolls that are invading her bed, her rag children. In the photograph, on the backdrop, there is a fortified farmhouse, in front of a pond. Over the door of the primitively painted house, so compatible with the image one has of a family house, can be read, on painted canvas, '*Qui vivis pacem parabellum*'. In the photo, Sébastien is grimacing because he was not allowed to put on his shirt with the sailor collar. Bernadette does not want to pose. She always finds an excuse, a dish to be watched over or someone who has just rung at the door, for leaving the area. In the photograph, Bertrand is delicately holding a model glider in his hands. He is afraid of breaking it. Claire devours Sébastien with her eyes. In the photograph,

241

Henri poses in the first row, just as he would happily pose on the bottom step of the doorsteps of the Palais Élysée, one day. It is one of the possible photos. They are only waiting now for Ruth, Gérard, Romain and Anne-Marie. Anne-Marie?

Luc closes his eyes. That photograph is taken. But it isn't the best one. It will never be definitive. He gets up. He feels stiff. He sees himself again accompanying the concrete mass, the fake dolmen, but why? He hears himself answering the television reporter, but testifying about what? As of tomorrow, from the office, he will make a note of those who have written to congratulate him on his award of the Legion of Honour and especially make a note of those who have not written. Luc is a bastard and he knows it. He also knows that true bastards never recognise it in themselves. Luc gets up, puts out the lights in the living room, and goes out in the direction of the woods, the trees, the mosses, the ferns. He calls 'Eliane? Antoine?' Then he is silent. He wants to see. He wants to surprise them.

In the photograph, one of the four children is always missing. They go in relay, one after the other, each in turn, to discreetly pillage the father's wallet, because the father never gives them pocket money, because the father claims the children do not need anything. And while Luc, Sébastien, Claire or Bertrand, on the pretext of going to help Bernadette, of going to get a garment, a book or who knows what, slip into the office where Henri has left the black leather briefcase in which his wallet, rich with paper money is found, the other three carry on the conversation, say things that annoy their father and keep him there. Nobody is fooled. Not even Bernadette nor Uncle Jean who is familiar with the scenario, nor Cécile nor Suzy, nor even Henri himself who, pillaged, feels himself even more so the father.

In the photo, as in a child's game, each one is on the alert for the 'little sign' which gives the go signal and, while waiting, each one plays the 'statue', one, two, three, I turn around, no moving. If you move, come back to go, and so on.

In the photo, each one is facing death. Bertrand used to quote Bossuet, the bishop of Condom, 'Who never came to Condom, who has never had to come to Moncrabeau, and yet who says, with a flourish, in the tone of a sermon, "this death, facing us all, which spreads so many shadows from all sides on that which the

242

brightness of the world would like to colour".' Everybody moves in the photograph. Luc begins to run in the woods. He stops. He must not give himself away. He wants to surprise. He wants to see. The light from the moon is still too bright.

Luc calculates his steps, careful to place his foot only on the moss or the grass, and especially not to step on any branch or twig. He advances, stroking the tree trunks, separating the ferns, creating his own path. He wants to see. He knows he is going in the right direction. He knows Antoine could lead Eliane only where he is headed. The pairing of others awakens in the third person an instinct for the precise direction, a sharpened sense of the topography and places where lovers take refuge when he himself has gone astray.

They are there, lying down, naked, against each other, in a bed of hastily pulled-up ferns. They are there, stretched out, knee to knee, face to face, mutually caressing their brows, seizing the backs of their necks so that they can kiss each other better. The kisses are brief, furtive, repeated. They are watching each other with their eyes wide open. Around Antoine and Eliane, clothing is scattered, and sandals tossed a little farther away, no doubt kicked off. There is disorder in the picture. Luc holds his breath. He feels protected by the fascination that is uniting his friends, just by watching them, their knees touching, their rapidly repeated kisses, with the tips of the lips, amazed, delighted, hidden kisses. Luc is happy to see them like that busy in the mutual pleasure of their bodies and in the surprise of their exchange of looks. That's what he has come to see. Often, at the office, Luc reproaches Antoine for his servility and for his meagre ambition. Antoine answers then that he needs nothing more than what he has, fragile as it is, and to keep it 'for the longest time possible'. Seeing them there, side by side, Antoine's brown and Eliane's astonishingly white skin, a skin that catches even more intensely the light of the moon, Luc knows that by mocking smaller happinesses, one can only suffer from never knowing that greater happiness which obsesses, conditions one, and which only really exists in the unhappinesses of break ups, silences, flights or misunderstandings.

This fervour that others use in achieving excellence only or the benefit of their vanity, Luc uses to overcome an inherited incapacity, the set look of the father in the first row. But Luc

243

neither wants to nor can admit this. And if Antoine repeats to him 'From now on, considering what's going on in the world, you mustn't shake the boat,' Luc prefers hearing this warning as an act of resignation or cowardice. He does not want that wisdom. It is a fact of pride. But it is also the lesson of Uncle Jean, the family voyeur, who in complaining too much about the artist in him that no-one recognised, no doubt because he really was one, had finally convinced the new brood of his adopted family that they were all a 'race of gladiators'. Even Henri, finally appointed a minister, had said, drinking champagne, to his brother-in-law, in front of Luc, but without Anne-Marie and Sébastien, without Ruth or Claire, with Gérard, and in the absence of Bertrand who was already at Moncrabeau and before Cécile, 'But I too have struggled!' Uncle Jean had said to him, in his dry way, 'Why but?'

Luc would like not to have to judge or be judged anymore. He wanted to see a loving couple, he has seen it. He wants to leave. But at the first step backward, a twig cracks under his foot and gives him away. Eliane sits up hiding her bosom. Antoine gets up abruptly. Luc takes flight, crazily, having been seen, the blood rising in his head. Never will they understand why he came. And what emotion made him do it. Never.

On the second floor of the house, the light in the guest room is lit. Christine, in silhouette, is leaning on her elbows at the window. Luc, out of breath, emerges suddenly from the undergrowth. He has hurt his forehead on a low branch. He stops short. The ceiling light in the bedroom, a bare bulb, dazzles him. Luc blinks his eyes, holds a hand before his face, the palm toward Christine, for a screen. Christine pulls herself back in, closes the window, puts out the light. Luc turns round. In the direction of the trees, there is no noise and that smell of ferns, even stronger now, is pursuing him. He has seen and he has been seen. He puts a hand to his forehead. He is bleeding. While fleeing, it seemed to him that the trees were setting themselves in front of him to interrupt his flight. He has also hurt his hands, hurt his knees, falling and getting up again, staggering, panic-stricken. He has never seen himself like this, wholly prey to a fear, because he had been caught red-handed. He was someone else, suddenly gone mad. The trees seemed to want to stop the runaway in him, as in a nightmare. Luc rips a piece of his torn shirt, daubs the wound and, his head down, charges into the house, crosses the living room, dashes up the stairs, to the first floor hallway and violently opens the bedroom door. Christine tells him, 'You've done nothing wrong, Luc. Nothing.'

In the dark of the bedroom, Luc gathers his clothes together. Awkwardly, with one hand, he throws everything haphazardly into his suitcase, their suitcase. Christine will manage with the few things she brought. Christine murmurs, 'Are you hurt?' The wallet, the papers, the car keys, the key-ring for the Rue de Téhéran, his watch, jacket and sportcoat. Luc has forgotten nothing. He goes into the hall, slamming the door.

On the table in the living room are the deck of cards, three remaining cups and the coffee pot. The house, suddenly, has developed a smell of life, of embers in the fireplace and outdoor odours. Luc goes out. The car is waiting. He throws his things into the back and the suitcase on top of them. He goes around, opens the front door, sits at the wheel and starts the motor. The headlights. He backs up. He turns. Then he goes forward. In front of him, on the side of the road are Antoine and Eliane. Antoine holds Eliane by the waist. They both make a little farewell wave. The photograph is out of focus. Nothing must ever be said. Not ever.

15

José, seated on the floor against the door, is blocking the only way out of the bedroom. The shutters are hooked and the windows closed. Antonio, lying along the wall, all curled up, his forearms folded over his face, is sleeping. In case of an alert, José, with a move of his hand could wake his brother. Bertrand is seated on the edge of the bed, elbows on his knees, hands joined, he watches José. From time to time, with his hands flattened, palm to palm, Bertrand claps as if he wanted to keep time for a dance, give the rhythm to a round dance. He wants to go home to the big house. He does not understand why they are keeping him here. He claps. José, and Antonio have their father's order not to let 'el Bertrand' go out and to keep him for the night. Juan said to Lucio, 'Tomorrow we'll see what's to be done. *Mañana es otro día!*' Tomorrow, another day, what day, really another? José had looked at his father with anxiety. Antonio had just said in his ear, 'Don't argue. He's right. You never know.' And while Merced and Jeanne were doing the dishes, in the bare silence of that evening, for once, which was unusual, the television not turned on, Juan and Lucio accompanied Léon and Mathilde back to the village. José and his brother put away the dishes, the glasses, the tableware and Bertrand remained seated at his place, at the table, stroking the wood with his fingertip, drawing imaginary figures, a circle for a face, a line for the nose, a line for the mouth, two dots for the eyes, and with the back of his hand would erase it all, starting again, another face or the same face, how can you tell?

Lucio came back first. Everyone heard the clanging of the gate that Juan was closing, on the outside, the squeaking of the hinges, the banging of the metal, even the clinking of the chain and the padlock, a noise José and Antonio had forgotten for years. Juan was closing the gate because of the day's event, why and for what fear? Lucio himself took Merced's apron off her and said, 'Come, it's late, Jeanne and the youngsters will put everything away.' And without a word or even saying goodnight to Bertrand, they went up to bed in José and Antonio's room, leaving their room to Bertrand, for one night.

Juan then closed the shutters in the downstairs room. Bertrand watched him. Juan avoided meeting this look fixed upon him. Jeanne put away the rest of the cake which Bertrand, his fork raised, has refused to taste. Merced had tried to help him, but Bertrand had waved to her not to persist. What should have been a party, in spite of everything, had not been. Everything was clean now, put away. Jeanne washed her hands and wiped them on a dishtowel hung on a wire over the sink. Juan waved to his two sons to get Bertrand up and take him to the bedroom. 'Tomorrow I'll telephone M. Prouillan. This can't go on.' Then, waving to Jeanne to precede him up the stairs, waiting for his wife to get to the first floor, to go into their bedroom and to close the door, speaking to his sons, and also to Bertrand, but without paying attention to him, as if he did not exist anymore, Juan had added, 'Starting from now, it's him or its us. The old man only has to take him back. Léon agrees about that. Do you understand?' Antonio had waved yes, then José, imitating his brother, but the father and his two sons had exchanged a look, in front of Bertrand, a look of doubt, a fleeting anger from one, an obligatory consent from the two others, which said loud and clear the opposite of what had just been asserted. In fact, tomorrow everything would continue just as it had the day before yesterday.

With his back to the door, seated, with his chin on his knees, José knows that Bertrand understood what Juan had said, but had not seen or really read the look exchanged from father to sons, afterwards. Bertrand, vaguely, retained only the threat. No doubt because Juan had waited until Jeanne was gone to speak to his children, no doubt also because of the noise of the gate, the chain, the padlocks, the noise of the closing shutters, and the silence of the turned-off television, an opaque screen showing nothing. José looks at Bertrand. 'It's not true. Papa was joking. He won't say anything to anybody.' And Bertrand, on the blanket on the bed, begins drawing faces, a circle, two lines, two dots, a movement of the hand to erase it all. He begins again the way he was drawing on the table a while before. José murmurs, 'Who are you thinking about?' Bertrand continues drawing.

248

'Who? You can tell me. I know perfectly well you hear me. It's now or never, don't you think?'

Suddenly Bertrand leaps from the bed and throws himself at the door trying to get out. José has just enough time to get up and get in between, holding him around the middle. Antonio, awakened with a bound, as in a rugby tackle, has seized Bertrand by the waist and is holding him too. They push Bertrand back and pin him down on the bed, José holding his wrists and Antonio his feet. José says to Bertrand, 'You're crazy! You're going to wake everybody up. Don't you understand? They're not going to do anything. They get paid for saying that. We're paid for that, see?' Bertrand struggles, groans, opens his mouth as if he were trying to bite. The harder he struggles, the harder the boys hold him. He arches his back, tries to get loose to the right, to the left, hitting then suddenly, as suddenly as he had leapt from the bed, then sighs, with a great breath, gives up and becomes calm, an inert mass. Antonio tells his brother, 'Don't let go. He's going to start again.' José answers 'I don't think so,' then, 'Did you see, he was behaving as he did with the kids, in the clearing, with his mouth open.' Bertrand closes his eyes. He breathes through his mouth. The wound on the eyebrow is beginning to bleed again. José looks at his brother. 'What should I do?' 'Let him piss out all his blood.' 'But it'll get on the bed.' 'Then let me do it. Go and get a towel.' Antonio jumps on Bertrand, straddles him, pins him down at waist level, grabs his wrists which José simultaneously releases. Everything is efficiently done, police-like, suddenly almost funny for the two of them, as in a film they have seen time and again, and yet they are here, with an order to be carried out. Bertrand must stay here and they must do everything necessary to keep him.

José comes back, he wipes Bertrand's wound. Antonio murmurs to his brother, 'He doesn't hear anything, he doesn't see anything and then suddenly he hears everything, he sees everything! In the end I wonder if papa . . .' José claps a hand over his brother's mouth. 'Shut up!' The two, kneeling on the bed, face to face, look at each other. José takes his hand away. Antonio says to him, 'What's getting at you?' 'We're going to take him home.' 'You're crazy!' 'No. He isn't at home here. He wants to go home.' 'But . . .' 'There isn't any but. It's what you think yourself.' José bends over Bertrand's wound. It has stopped bleeding. Bertrand opens his eyes. José says to him, 'We're going to take you back. But promise you won't run away!' Antonio bends over too, pressing down on Bertrand's shoulders. Bertrand, his eyes wide open, watches them, with nothing in his look, nothing but an astonishment. He braces against the edge of the bed, arches his back again. Antonio straddles him harder, José grabs his wrists. 'Calm down. Let us do it.' José jumps off the bed first, the towel in his hand. 'You never know if it'll start bleeding again.' Then he and Antonio, both standing, wait for Bertrand, calmly, to get up, alone and with no help. Bertrand hesitates, his mouth open, dazed. With a gentle gesture that surprises Antonio, José caresses Bertrand's forehead, like an invitation. Bertrand slides off the bed, gets up, staggers and lets himself be led away.

On the stairs, José ahead, Antonio behind, they box Bertrand in. With a finger to his lips, José signals not to make any noise. Bertrand runs his hand, flatly, along the wall as if this contact gave him balance and direction. At the bottom of the stairs José opens the courtyard door. Antonio says to his brother, 'And what if the dogs bark?' 'Don't think about it. This is the only way. You'll see.' But as soon as they were in the yard, Bertrand gets away from them, dashes to the gate, clings to it, shakes it vainly, bangs his head on it. The wound in his eyebrow begins bleeding again. A dog barks, then two, then three. The moon is out. Antonio and José tear Bertrand away from the gate, force him to kneel in front of them, twisting his arm. They are afraid. They watch for the lights on the first floor. 'I told you!' mumbles Antonio, 'we shouldn't have!' José leans over Bertrand, face to face. 'Your father will come! Do you understand? We're going to take you back home. That's what you want, isn't it?' Bertrand looks at them both and makes a small sign with his head, saying a vague yes. José straightens up and tells his brother, 'Hold him, I'm going to get some straps in case he does something stupid.'

Antonio is left alone with Bertrand. If Bertrand tries to move, he twists his arm harder, forces him to put his head down. And if he tries with his whole body, a contraction, at a sudden burst, to get up, Antonio gives him a knee full in the face or a kick in the stomach. Antonio does not like what is happening at Moncrabeau and Antonio has never dreamed of going anywhere else. Antonio enjoys the blows he is giving in secret from his brother, his father and his grandfather. The secrecy and a few blows, that's all. José amuses Antonio because he believes in things, just like that, in a vacuum. He believes in everything. And is able to love. But Antonio, on the other hand, thinks it is not really worth all the trouble. And if, for once, he can do as he likes, he is holding and hitting. Bertrand moans. Antonio, stirred by the groans, slaps and bangs still harder. José comes back with the leather straps that were once used on the horses. Antonio stops. He has hit on behalf of three generations. It doesn't do any good. He knows that. But it does him some good. José says to his brother. 'What happened?' Antonio smiles. 'He was struggling, and besides all he has to do is to eat his cake like everybody else.'

The boys get Bertrand up, tie him, his hands alongside his belt behind his back, they tighten and hold him by both ends of the strap, pushing him forward, making him walk, pushing him even harder and forcing him to run that way, strapped up, toward the big house. The dogs have stopped barking. A silence has fallen again. The moon seems perched, attentive. Bertrand stumbles, sprawls full length in the road, gets up to the 'oh's' and 'ah's' of José and Antonio. Forced by them, he begins running again, held by the leash. An animal. José is happy because he is taking Bertrand back where he belongs. And besides it's fun. Almost a game.

Lying on her back, in José's bed, Merced heard the noises on the stairs and in the courtyard, but she preferred not to alert anyone. In Antonio's bed on the other side of the bedroom, Lucio is sleeping with his tightened fists on his belly, his head turned to the wall. Merced does not remember a single night when they've slept in separate beds. She won't sleep. It's the first time.

In the neighbouring room, in the marriage bed, Juan turns his back to Jeanne. And Jeanne knows that is a bad sign. All curled up, his hands clutched in front of his mouth as if warming his fingers on wintery days, before taking a shovel, a saw or a pitchfork, Juan seems all wrapped up in that deep sleep of troubled times that, with the first look exchanged with his wife in the morning, makes Jeanne feel blamed, guilty. She is afraid. And then if she tries saying good morning with an affectionate gesture, he pushes her away. As soon as he has had his coffee, he leaves for work without a word or a look at anyone. Tomorrow, Jeanne knows Juan will wake up in that mood. Jeanne understood that her sons had taken Bertrand back to the big house and so much the better. Jeanne remembers her mother who never would tell her, if she did something stupid, 'That will teach you a lesson' but 'that will teach you an impression.' Jeanne won't sleep. Juan turns his back to her. Just what is an impression? Something more than a lesson? The dogs barked. The moon is making a funny light through the shutters.

José enters the big house. He turns on the front door light. Antonio points to the inscription carved over the door and taking Bertrand by the arm, says, 'Now can you explain to us what that means up there?' 'Leave him alone, Tonio. He won't say anything. All he wants is someone to talk to him a little.' José, playing with the end of the strap, draws Bertrand to him, then against him, in the vestibule, 'Are you happy, Monsieur Bertrand?' Bertrand, out of breath, looks at them. José tells his brother, 'That's enough hitting! Close the door! Untie the tether! Let him go!' 'So you're the one who decides now?' 'Yes, I am.'

The first sitting room had been emptied of its furniture, on Madame Prouillan's orders, because her son might 'damage them as he goes by.' It is an empty room where steps echo. Then the small sitting room, also bare, but dominated by a locked secrétaire and two leather armchairs. Finally another door and Bertrand's lair, his parents' former bedroom and library. On a tray is the breakfast brought by Jeanne that morning. An untouched tray. Nothing has been touched. The bed is not messed up. José tells Bertrand, 'Here you are at home again. Go to bed. We won't leave till you're in bed and asleep.'

Bertrand takes a few steps, puts a hand to his forehead, pats his elbow, his chest, his knees as if he were taking an inventory of the blows he'd received. Slowly, he heads for the table where, on most days for the last twenty years, he has spent hours on end doing nothing but drawing and leafing through books while staring wide-eyed. He opens the drawer of the table, slips a hand inside and, feels around, messing up the pencils that he only uses for tracing curved signs, spirals, tornadoes, cyclones or square mazes that look like labyrinths and to which the Lucio

252

clan, keeping a close watch, and sometimes inspecting the contents of the waste-paper baskets before throwing them out, give all kinds of explanations: 'It's what goes on in his head,' 'They're the cellars in the big house,' 'It's Paris,' 'They're only scribblings.' When Jeanne goes shopping in Lectoure or Saint-Pardon, she often brings back new pencils, fat ones if possible, the only ones Bertrand really wears down. And once in a while when she is doing the housework, she changes the blade of the pencil sharpener. In the drawer there are also erasers, a pen Bertrand does not use anymore and a bottle of ink. As it dried, the ink has left a deposit, like a tartar blue, on the inside wall, since it was first put away. Antonio stays near the door. The big house intimidates and revolts him, but he won't admit it. He had hit Bertrand behind José's back because he wanted to get a word out of him, even if it were only one real word, something other than one of those noises from the throat he has been hearing since he was little that suggest neither anger nor satisfaction for anything. José has approached the table. At the back of the drawer is a letter in an envelope that Bertrand takes out and holds out in front of him like a blindman. There are also some photographs. With the other hand Bertrand throws them at random onto the table. José mumbles, 'What do you want me to do?'

Bertrand gives him the letter. With a gesture, moving his hand up from the throat to his mouth, he asks him to read it out loud, and with the same movement, his hand flat, a sign for calm, to read it slowly.

With the letter in his hands, José hesitates, looks at his brother. Antonio shrugs and goes to sit on the edge of a chair, at the entrance of the bathroom, as if he were making an obligatory courtesy visit. Juan always says, 'At their place you must never really sit down!' Bertrand picks up a photograph on the table, the photo of a man in a street who is bursting with laughter and looking into the lens, a candid photo of someone walking surprised by a photographer. José catches a glimpse of the photograph. Bertrand goes to the window, opens the two panels, with the reflection of the moon on the lake below, and that slight country wind blowing softly, through the valleys, the groves, the prairies, a night wind, a peaceful wind bearing the odour of thick grass that stings a little and awakens the senses.

Bertrand takes a seat in the armchair, facing the window. He turns his back to the room and to José who reads the envelope 'Monsieur Bertrand Prouillan, 2 Place d'Antioche, Paris 17th.' Antonio smiles in his corner.

The letter is old. The envelope has often been handled and the paper, to the touch, makes one think of a blotter that could not absorb anything more. It is a long letter swollen with folded pages. A soothing letter. As Jeanne used to say when her mother was still writing her 'a letter with a big heart'. Bertrand holds the letter in front of him, very close to his face. José realises he was not seeing anything then, or very little, in the birch clearing and was only vaguely hearing the children's cries. José knows that while Bertrand's whole body still functions normally, something is missing in his head that makes him deaf, blind, and yet, as the years go by, José speaks and looks at Bertrand as if Bertrand were about to answer and see normally. José approaches the armchair. Standing, in a clear voice he reads.

Rue Saint-Benoît, March 21.

'My dear Bertrand. Here it is a little more than a year that we've known each other. Here it is fourteen months that our meeting has tormented me. Here I am not finding the words to write you when *you* find them to send me those messages that, one after the other, harass me, fascinate me, make me flee or return to you. I suffer just as much at receiving them as I do not finding them when I surprise myself waiting for them, whereas I fear them . . .' José stops reading, sits on the edge of the table and looks questioningly at Bertrand. Bertrand places the photo on his knees, turns his head slightly toward José, gives a hint of a smile. Antonio, hidden from Bertrand, points to his temple with the index finger of his left hand, a spontaneous gesture indicating that someone is crazy or mad.

'Here I am finding myself in a situation I have often mocked, no doubt for fear of living it one day, which is called "Love". I don't write simply "love" but indeed "Love", as if it were an essential raw material, a living material, food, fertile soil, water, air or fire. Yes, Bertrand, I am breaking the silence that has kept me for so many months from responding either to your letters or your notes or even to your spirit, breaking it, obstinately, to tell you at one blow, the only truly telling blow, and thereafter more telling, you see, I am imitating you, that I am in "Love" with you and that I am swept away. Let us speak here of "love", if you care to, at the risk of making the persons we were or will be smile inside ourselves, incapable, or capable only of that love which resembles love and is not "Love". Every letter is, alas, a diagnosis. We expect from it, as from all poetry, all theatre, every novel, all music and every painting, a too logical explanation of facts, or an obscure absurdity based on impressions that no longer have any relation to reality. Now, there is no reality except what is extended toward the other person. I am capitulating. I am extending in my turn. I do not want to know anymore that you are miserable at our not being together. I no longer want the things, in me, that separate us nor those people trying to separate us. I met your father yesterday. Everything he said to me enters into the logic of the diagnosis. He wants to save you. But from what? From "Love"? From the love he could not experience himself (in speaking of your mother to me, he said "that woman") or that was refused him by events, by education or even by the social milieu, insane as we have become from not being able to live our lives naturally any more?'

José places the first page of the letter on the table, in the midst of all the photographs. In fact they reveal a whole family that José has never seen and of whom Léon said, after dinner, as he got up from the table, in conclusion, 'As soon as you touch the Prouillans, things start stirring up inside!' This time, in tomfoolery, Antonio points both forefingers on his temples, a double gesture, and sticks his tongue out at José to make him laugh. José pretends not to see him. He does not understand the letter he is reading very well but he feels it strongly, just as he felt strongly his father's determined look on the way back from Auzan. Juan seemed then just as pleased to have found the runaway, without causing a drama, as he was furious at having to drag him back, to look after him. Second page.

'I don't like the word repression, my dear tibi, but it must be admitted that what could have been a supportive encounter in each of our lives has become, through your father's presence, and his type of affection, a story of corruption, involving the police, detectives, in short a tale of morals that distorts your spirit, your willingness to give everything, and of my unease, a primary quality of "Love" when one is about to receive it. I tried

255

explaining to your father, yesterday, that the impelling demand emanated as much from you as from me, that one is always corrupted by the other person, that adulthood was above all a matter of sensuality, and that it might be better for you to fulfil yourself with me than to lose yourself with ten or one hundred. He understood by all that only that I was advancing automatic reasonings and measures meant to trick him. Our cause has not been heard. I doubt very much that it ever will be really, even if one day someone tries defending it openly. We will always be marginal because we're attached to our marginality. Our identity lies, above all, in the mask, the forbidden, and the night. We will always be repressed because we repress ourselves. And writing to you in this way, discussing us both, I feel ridiculous. It all sounds as if I were speaking of all of us and of a future, a homage to you, if there is one. We will always be forbidden a dwelling place. We forbid ourselves a dwelling place. You can call me a hesitant. I have thirteen years of disappointed hopes more than you, the only ones worthy of the name. And that cannot last any longer. I will not hesitate, in a little while, to jump, as I am writing you. It's the same plunge. I expected everything but you. I believed I was armoured and you have taken me over, grubby little soiler of my door.'

The photograph slips from Bertrand's hands and falls to the floor. Bertrand places his hands on his knees, sits up straight in the armchair, closes his eyes. Antonio sits squarely on his chair, his legs crossed. José cautiously places the second page of the letter on the table. The reading continues.

'I then told your father everything that he should not be told, about the reality of my life, the distance of it, "Love" held at a distance, that "Love" which keeps its distance and which as a result, since I have been armed with my body, which is as much capable of having an orgasm as of feeling emotions, because of which I have never been able to prolong the duration of a relationship with anyone, whether loved by my heart, or by my sex organs. Each time, as we were becoming a couple, we became a target. And if, in the games of intrigue which are typical of our milieu, we were not or became no longer a target, then we acted wilfully or despite ourselves as if we were being aimed at. In that, and this time with homage to your images, I have always sacrificed to the principle of farewells. But you are

256

right. But we don't have the right to know these things at your age. The knowledge of failure in love, which follows where love is unsure of itself, is an insult to the tenaciously held ideas made about "Love". So many enemies shows their faces then. When you burst into my life, I had just, what delusion, given up all expectations. I did not want to wait any longer for anyone and then you arrived. So, by means of the theatre and my first produced play, I thought I could, in the performance of my own script, escape from my own life and the memory of Richard, Serge, Christian and Claude-Henri, four names hiding four stories of which I wonder why my memory retains only the painful endings, all curiously alike, but never the moments of richness and sharing. And it is in the theatre where I was taking refuge that I met you. The third look I kept for myself. I told myself right off you were the one who would push me into the void, once and for all. Alley cats don't always land on their feet. They fall from the third or the fourth, never the fifth floor. I was told that by a concierge who likes them a lot. From the day I met you, Bertrand, I don't remember listening to any other language but my fear of seeing you again and letting you come into my life. How did you say it in your second letter from Moncrabeau? No point telling you I love you, so I adore you.'

The third and last page of the letter. José kneels near the armchair. He wants to see Bertrand more closely and, who knows, to hear him say something other than 'Thank you,' 'It's alright' or 'Till tomorrow.' José reads on.

'So farewell. And greetings to your father. There is nothing sadder than an arrogant man who has no ambition and nothing more dangerous than an arrogant man when he becomes ambitious. Be careful of him. He'll know how to convince you of the worst. He will always come back when you expect it least and, be capable of violence, when you expect it the most. When I got back from that confrontation with him yesterday (he showed me evidence that he called "damning" of all our meetings and even a photograph of me taken in the street without my knowledge), and I wanted to build a wood fire, here, in the fireplace. I put some newspaper and pieces of a crate under the log that has been sitting there for a long time, for decoration. Everything flamed up so much I thought I'd set the house afire. I wanted a fire to warm my hands, a fire to look at, a fire for thinking about you, and I was setting fire to the house. I filled a pan with water and, as I'd been told, I poured slowly so that the steam would rise and extinguish itself gradually. I threw water on the fire. A simple act. I was thinking of you. Of course, there was no fire. I had to sponge up a puddle of ashes spreading on the floor. I was still worried. Everything had flamed up so much. I had never heard so many siren noises in the Boulevard Saint-Germain, the Rue Bonaparte and the Rue Jacob, all around me. Then I stood at the window. A fire in a chimney is like a small volcano erupting on a roof. I watched the whole scene. There was nothing happening. The sirens were for other farewells. From the window I watched the street, the pavement, the passers-by. This house is nothing if you no longer come looking for what you put inside me. I prefer to leave. I prefer to leave with a memory of you, in bed, one morning, the only one really. If I re-read this letter, I know I won't leap. I'm finishing. Quick, into the envelope. Tell your father it isn't worth loving anymore the way he loves. Tell him also it isn't worth making a legal complaint. I have just written the envelope and glued on the stamp. This letter — who will mail it? I am choosing silence. Respect it. There is "Love" in the air, I'm going to try to catch it. So right now, dear little gnawing rat. I really must get you out of me. Romain Leval, deceased. Not a hesitant.'

José picks up the photograph and holds it out to Bertrand. 'Is that him?' Bertrand takes it, rises, closes the window, places the photo on the table, with slow movements intended to be precise. He is trembling. José, standing, holds out the last page of the letter. Antonio has approached. 'Why do they keep everything, these people?' José waves to his brother to be still. Bertrand puts the photos and the letter, at random, in the drawer. He looks at the boys and says, 'Thank you,' then 'Very much,' and 'Till tomorrow.'

16

Do you want to take a cold shower?' Suzy, seated on the edge of her bed, takes off her shoes. 'Each time I wear new ones, I can think only about them. I get the impression they're dragging me someplace I shouldn't go.' Suzy looks at her feet, flat on the bedside rug, wiggles them, rubs them together. 'I'm not made for high heels. But I did it for you, Henri, are you listening?' Henri has remained in the living room. Silence. Suzy remembers evenings, late, after a supper, a party or a show, when Jean would stay in the living room, for a long time, midway between his office and their bedroom. He too would be silent, and would listen to her talking about everything and nothing, 'about everything and everything' he would say coming into the bedroom, if he had just taken note of some observation which made him happy, 'about nothing and nothing' he'd confess, sheepish, if Suzy had said nothing out of the ordinary. It was like playing a little at *Hide and Seek*, another title of a play by Jean Martin which had had some success on Broadway. 'An unforeseen success,' Jean used to say, in order to specify immediately 'over-abundance!'

'Riquet? I put myself on stilts for you, so I could be up to the height people ascribe to you and be able to imitate you! I'd have so liked to have gone once to the Elysée with you. Inconspicuously. A little curtsey. Touching the hands of presidents. Sliding on the parquet floor of the salons like a "swan on a frozen lake". Whose simile? Guess. Bertrand's! On the evening of Claire's eighteenth birthday ball! Everybody was bored that night. We couldn't even take refuge in the kitchen, the rolled up rugs blocked half the hallway. The bedrooms, let's not talk about them, the living room furniture was stored in them. The buffet from Berthier fils? Always the same, petits four *ad vitam aeternam*. The tub in your bathroom was full of sacks of ice cubes. For once the Glacières Réunies had come to the house. Everyone left very early. It had to be melted so that you could take the bath you demanded precisely because the tub was full. It didn't melt all that easily, those ice cubes. When they were gone, the hot water had run cold. You were angry. You were funny when you were angry. You're harmless when you get angry, nowadays. You've lost that little bit of terror that used to let you dominate without being able to love. I'm thinking about that because I also had new shoes that evening, for which I paid cash, not like these. I wondered what I was doing at your place. We all wondered, first of all the young men, the girls, who were saying amongst themselves, "Do you know them?" "No. They're the children of my parents' friends." "Why did they all withdraw?" "So we could dance!" "But nobody's dancing." "You can't dance when you don't know each other." What an idea, Henri, choosing that band that played only waltzes, tangoes and, the supreme audacity, the cha cha chas? You can't create a party. It's created by itself. Claire was ill at ease in that long dress, cut from one of Cécile's dresses. They'd simply adjusted the straps and bought a white silk ribbon for the belt, to make it stylish. Claire only danced with her brothers that night. She was happy only then, maybe because they were laughing at what was happening. Cécile and you stayed at the entrance, greeting the people arriving, worrying about those who were leaving so soon, and still waiting for the ones who wouldn't be arriving at all. It was a reluctant ball. Pantalon never stopped barking in the back bedroom because he'd been shut up there. It was only really enjoyable when there was no one left but us, a friend of Luc's, Antoine, I believe, and two of Sébastien's chums, in their naval uniforms. The band was still playing. It was Jean who asked them to stop. And when Pantalon, liberated, made his entrance into the living room, he slid in on all fours "like a black swan on a frozen lake". It was the only time we laughed that evening. And for another good laugh, Bertrand made Cécile waltz without music. The musicians were drinking a glass of champagne. Sébastien asked Bernadette. Luc asked me. We were dancing. And as Jean suggested you ask Claire to dance, the father's honour, you answered "No, I don't dance." Does that remind you of one of Jean's plays? It wasn't a hit, but you saw it. We were together, in the same box. You didn't flinch at the end when everyone was dancing with no music and when the father refused to ask his daughter to dance, saying precisely, precisely what you had said in real life.'

Silence in the living room. Suzy rises, puts the shoes in their box, folds them in the tissue paper. 'I may never put them on again,' she smiles, 'or then for the opening of *Mortmain*.' She laughs. 'It was quite lovely, your house, that night, but only from the outside, from the Place d'Antioche. Everything was lit up. The façade! There was a gendarme in front of the gate and a coatroom at the foot of the stairs. Don't let me talk, Henri, don't leave me alone in my bedroom. Come in here. Or else go home.'

Henri appears in the doorway. 'How can you remember all those details?' Suzy, with a movement, undoes the belt of her dress. 'I don't want to play the supporting role anymore. Jean played too good a trick on us by observing us when you were not observing anything.' Suzy takes her dress off and places it flat, delicately, across the bed, like a theatre costume. She puts the folds back in place, checks for spots and caresses the fabric rose. With one move she lets her hair down and with another, unembarrassed, takes off her tights, finds herself in her bra, facing her brother who does not really dare enter the bedroom, who does not dare return home either, who fears what is being said and cannot not succumb to the curious pleasure of living the day's drama right to the end rather than finding himself playing it out by himself, in a soliloquy at the Place d'Antioche.

Suzy looks at him. 'In the street, coming back here, I believed that you were going to talk at last, to say the necessary words as if that were possible for you. But it wasn't. You relate everything to criticism. You think you have nothing to be criticised for.' She undoes her bra. 'I'm not afraid of cold water, I'll be back.' She disappears into the bathroom leaving Henri planted, surprised at seeing his sister naked, old and naked, aged liked him. At the head of the bed, large and small, made of cloth, of porcelain or celluloid, there were a multitude of dolls that Suzy puts back in place every morning when she makes her bed. There is even one dating from Moncrabeau days when Suzanne, a little girl, promenaded her dolls in a miniature baby carriage. 'I'm going to let them breathe,' she would say, 'they need fresh air.' Among the dolls were stuffed animals, a monkey, a rabbit, a giraffe, a lion, a whole menagerie of mascots turned to the visitor, an attentive, staring public. Time can pass, they are always there for the rendezvous. At the head of the bed.

Suzy calls out from the bathroom, 'If you're staying in the bedroom, turn out the living room light.' She laughs. The sound of water, a thump in the bathtub, another shout, as if giving herself courage, a fearful and delighted cry, as she takes her shower. Henri sits on the edge of the bed. The dolls are observing him, he tells himself, 'without a thought in their heads'. He knows this collective look. It's the look he knows from boards of directors, sessions of the Academy or the Economic Council when it meets, once again, to listen in present time to decisions that have to be made, that are taken, but have been decided in advance, with never any development, never a deviation from the real initiatives, a past that always returns. Dolls and stuffed animals, it is a little as if the whole family were here, a human family that would have capitulated before the father, members of a family without a readable book that turns toward him, Henri, not even to question any more, but simply to remain where they are.

On a wall in a street, one day, Henri read 'Many fall in love'. If his first reaction was amusement at the preposterousness of the slogan, his second had been to pursue his pedestrian's way pretending to have neither seen nor read anything, and checking that no one had seen him reading it. The word 'love' at first had in a way frightened him, so little do we want to see it that way, in huge letters, written in the street and revealed to all like an appeal. In the slogan was also the verb 'fall' which greatly distresses those who, in not asking themselves the love question, believe they are still upright and on their way, upright for no reason and on a barren way. The verb 'fall' had after all a pivot between it and 'love', that 'in' in the way is in a religious order or in battle. That left the 'many', unusual, a multitude, placed there for a more striking effect, a straightforward thrust, when the conformist would have automatically chosen 'numerous are they who' or an evasive 'several'. No, Henri had indeed read 'Many fall in love'. And, seeing the graffiti, he had reacted like a runaway, only to come back the next day, between two appointments, guilty of the crime of reading, and pass by on the opposite pavement to verify that it was a real graffiti and not something he had dreamed. It was there. Stationed on the other side of the street, Henri could read and re-read it. It was shortly after Cécile's death. Henri did not feel that he was in mourning except that he would, suddenly and for almost no reason, give an extraordinary importance to small details as if, as messages, they had begun to multiply, to gnaw and appeal to him continuously. The third day, obstinately, he had come back to read the slogan again but the wall had been cleaned. If one went a little closer, the acrylic ink had left a trace on the surface of the stone, a mark slightly lighter, as if the words written in big letters on the wall of that building on the Rue de Grenelle had drunk the patina and grime of the years. On his third confrontation, Henri had felt resigned to the message, actually happy not to see it pushed at them anymore, deriding the passers-by who only wanted to go on their way, and troubled about the meaning of the message. Had he been the only one who had noticed and understood it a little? Henri undoes the knot of his tie and his collar button. Suzy calls from the bathroom, 'Haven't you anything to say?'

Understanding, understanding everything. Before the dolls and the stuffed animals, near the spread-out dress, seated, hands on his knees, on the foot of the bed, facing the dressing table that is covered with invitations, Henri sees the graffiti again and says to himself that one moment in a life may be enough to think about, on the one hand, but there is a satisfaction, in being armed in spite of everything with a conscience on the other, and above all one has brushed by the worst. An ability to feel and to want to share. Luc may well smile as the eldest, while Sébastien flees, Claire keeps silent and Bertrand remains where he has been put; for them too understanding is refusing to share, it is even no longer feeling. Jean could ridicule, Suzy can still attack, Henri tells himself that falling in love is like nightfall, just a moment when you may be left alone and in tatters, with no landmark for continuing on your way. Henri wanted and still wants to be stopped. Henri knows falling in love is the bump and not the fall, the roadway and rarely the gulley. But never will he admit it. And those who fall hide themselves. Even Cécile.

She was hiding that day, how long, how long ago? Counting time is an abdication. Everything is now, if you listen. Everything is the unfolding day, a passing on, examining a tomorrow that will be congenial to the person, the conqueror, who will lose in the end or a desire for a different kind of future, for those, the conquered, who will win in the end. That day

263

Cécile was hiding. They were on a trip to Niagara Falls, like two lovers, and were both afraid of their twenty years of marriage. In spite of himself, Henri had just worked it out. It was the year of that anniversary. Luc was going into special maths, Sébastien had just been admitted to basic maths, Claire was about to take her first bac and Bertrand was reading too much. Bernadette had had to call him several times for dinner and often he would bring his book to the table so as not, as he'd say, to 'break up with it'. Cécile, on that day!

It was an afternoon at the end of October, one of those brief, Indian summer days that, over there in Canada, exhales an astonishing, warm air although winter was already giving signs of its arrival. A convention, but which one was it and why was it, had brought Henri on an official mission. Once is not a habit: Cécile had come with him when, for years, she had refused every trip to stay at home with the children. Perhaps also because Henri did not really care to have her accompany him on similar occasions, to see and hear him in the exercise of the absurd power that led him to be a pointless delegate. During the few days of the convention, the wives were entertained by touring Montréal and the surrounding areas. But after the closing luncheon they had taken the plane to Toronto. The next day they hired a car to take them to the falls. That jaunt amused Henri. He had repeated several times that 'It wasn't worth the trouble,' the place was 'ruined and touristy,' but he did not want to 'regret not going there.' So both had found themselves in the back seat of a Packard, watching the sunny countryside and the trees of a surprising autumn, yellow, red and, in places in the distance, bluish leaves. Cécile said nothing. She only looked. Once again Henri was compelling her. In his wife's silence there was an anxiety, a questioning, an appeal. For a long time, perhaps ever since their wedding, they had not been left alone, in this way, alone together, in broad daylight and on a trip. Seized with doubt, Henri had not now dared speak. Cécile was holding him by saying nothing. She was amazed. And from Henri's doubt admiration followed, like his desire at their first meeting. Cécile was beautiful. Henri had never really realised it. Cécile was much more beautiful than Jacqueline and the others. Cécile saw him, saw him alone and only him. Henri took Cécile's hand, stroked it, kissed, furtively. The driver was watching them, the fear of the rearview mirror. Cécile did not flinch. It was neither too late nor too soon.

Henri lies back alongside the dress, under the eyes of the dolls. He observes the ceiling, closes his eyes, brings his left hand to his forehead as if he were trying to chase an image away from his memory. The position is uncomfortable. He is lying back, his knees bent, his feet still on the floor. You must not soil the bedspread when you have your shoes on, an instinct of his upbringing. In her bathtub, standing up, naked, Suzy lets the cold water run. She holds out her hand, wets her fingers. She doesn't dare. She has to take another breath. Henri knows, by the noise of the water, that his sister is not taking her shower yet. She is hesitating but, with bravado, she will do it.

The image returns. Henri sees himself again, getting out of the Packard. The chauffeur has opened the door. Henri holds his hand out to Cécile. Cécile gives him a smile without lassitude or tenderness, a vague smile of companionship. Getting out of the car she did not respond to her husband's gesture. Henri remained with his hand in the air. He did not like the chauffeur noticing him. They had two hours before them. The falls were there. Cécile started to go ahead of Henri, belted in a raincoat, a silk scarf knotted around her neck, with that bright red hat in light felt, the only kind of hat that he had ever known her to wear and which she ordered every two years, the same style, from (she too) Berteil's. Memory spins and weaves, continually at the same day's events, a single day, the same day, if one questions oneself.

And the closer they got to the falls, the more the churning air, bathed in sunlight, bore swirls of minute droplets that wet their faces. Before he knew it, Henri had a drop on the end of his nose that tickled. The Niagara River, an immense, wide torrent, seemed to be flowing toward them between the rocks, the foam, the backwashes, turning abruptly at a right angle and plunging, dashing into a void, a screen of some hundreds of metres, of an impressive height. All around were parking lots, hotels, towers, a concrete watch tower. There were even an aquarium and a wax museum, everything Henri feared and had derided in advance. But Cécile, in front of him, pre-occupied just by the spectacle of the falls, drew him along. She stood for a long time against the fence, at the most advanced place on the terrace, nearest the edge and the level of the river, where the water, light, frenzied, falls abruptly, whitened, broken by the void. A rainbow, the play of sunbeams, stretched, implanted and perfect above the basin below. A rainbow fixed, immovable. The river's force in leaping, over such width and height, with such furore, rendered impossible the fear of seeing it effaced and disappear. There was something constant in this play of light, sun, mist, boiling, of icy halo, the spluttering, deafening noise of the water that becomes gentle because it is continuous, continually dropping over the falls, not an anger of nature, an unforeseen event, or a wrenching, but a power unceasingly renewed, the power to leap. Henri did not dare approach Cécile now. Cécile, fascinated, was watching, even leaning forward a little, slightly, as if she were trying to forget the fence and to make an abstraction of everything.

His fists in his coat pockets, Henri was waiting for Cécile to turn around. He was standing slightly apart. He needed the feeling of the fence. He began thinking that this water had flowed a long time before them, would flow a long time after them, and that the organised spectacle of the surroundings, the millions of visitors, the hordes of young marrieds, the geologists' calculations of erosion were nothing in comparison to the river's lesson and the reality of lives. Cécile was long in turning around. He was afraid that she too would leap. He took three steps, grabbed Cécile by the arm. 'Don't stay here.' For a moment she leaned against him as if she were going to kiss him. Henri remembers the contact with the wet raincoat, Cécile's misted face and the distinct smile, a first burst, rending his wife's lips. He had never been able to really love her, no doubt for fear of becoming attached. She was vivacious, reticent, ready to deliver up her reticence. In that he had drawn out the strength of his indfference, his fear of only having less, or of so little, to offer her in sharing. For a brief instant, as their eyes met, Henri understood that Cécile knew everything about him, would never blame him for anything and would protect him, within her, from that minimum amount of curiosity, that watchful, little nothing that would distinguish her and always designate her as unique, and better than others. Henri felt doubly abandoned, left behind and confused.

He wished he could say 'Wait for me,' 'Explain' or even 'Speak to me,' but now she was walking along the fence, this time overlooking the basin. Downstream from the falls, at the point where the water becomes clear again, seagulls were watching out for fish brought up by the eddying water, a meal, a feast, the whirling of those birds also the colour of mist and foam. Cécile put 25 cents in a 'Magic Vision' viewer. With her eyes glued to the metal box, she pivoted it downward, onto the seagulls, then toward the curtain of the falls, a grey, uniform image, and upward, a fringe of sky, finally to seek the base of the rainbow and, slowly, bent over, leaning, drawing its half circle. She waved to Henri to take her place. 'It's beautiful, you know.' Henri did not dare. She said, 'You always deny yourself everything,' and she headed toward the 'Scenic Tunnel' pavilion.

Henri followed so as not to lose her. He wiped his nose again. His shirt collar was all wet, like an animal's collar. At the ticket booth Cécile paid. They went down two flights on foot and at the coat room they were dressed in boots and black oilskins, and, on their heads, wide-brimmed sou'westers tied under the chin. And both, as if done up for a tempest, waited for the elevator to come back up. Henri was cold. Cécile took him by the hand. The elevator doors opened. A group of men and women, all identical in the shiny, mourning clothes, exited silently. It was Henri and Cécile's turn to descend. There were only the two of them. The elevator operator waited for other customers but none came. The doors closed again. A wind whistled in the elevator cage bumping against the metal. As soon as they were delivered below, the elevator rose again. Henri and Cécile were left alone at the end of a sloping, concrete corridor, with electric lights, white, oozing walls, a wet floor. They were under the rock of the falls. Dull vibrations spread through their bodies. Henri cried 'Let's not go.' Cécile let go of his hand, and alone, awkward in her boots, headed toward the rear of the corridor. A first sign, to the left, marked 'The Terrace', then a second, away at the end, 'The Balcony'. There at the corner, she waited for Henri to join her.

The second corridor, to the left, led to a hole dug in the rock, a balcony opening onto the back of the falls. All that could be seen was water falling, thundering, powerful. They were seeing the falls from the back. Henri found the spectacle pointless, disturbing, dangerous. There was now another fence and in particular a sign that Cécile looked at once, which read 'Please do not climb over'. Henri thought that in France in a similar place they would put screens, a barricade against deranged people, everywhere. Cécile stepped back of her own volition and, at Henri's level, turned toward him. She tried to smile but could not. She was pale. The earth rumbled from within. Everything reverberated. A few minutes later, at the end of the first corridor, they came to the terrace. Gusts of spray whipped their faces. Once again they were alone, a chance in which Henri did not want really to believe. Alone, at the pool level, a few metres from breaking, there were churning waters that bounded, surged, a grand disorder at the bottom of the smooth falls. They stayed there a while, looking at the river's plunge and the hole of sky above their heads. A cold wind also came in, nervously, from everywhere. Henri waited for Cécile's signal to leave. The corridor, abstract, white, bare, looked like the beginning of a nightmare. Cécile took his hand. 'I have just understood,' she said, 'a lot of things.' Henri did not dare ask her what they were.

They had tea on the pavilion's first floor. Cécile bought a post card: 'Prouillan Family, 2 Place d'Antioche, Paris 17, France.' As a message she wrote 'I love you' and signed 'Mama'. Henri pointed out that the card would arrive after they returned back. Cécile insisted that he write something too. Henri signed 'Henri' and repeated 'Really, we're going to be home before it does.' Cécile murmured 'No, it's important.'

A setting sun. In the back seat of the Packard, in too large a car, a space separated them. They were looking at the countryside, each to his own side, so as not to talk. Soon Toronto's skyscrapers were outlined on the highway's horizon. Henri asked Cécile 'What was it you understood?' 'I understood that we had forgotten...' She turned toward him 'that we had forgotten , you and I . . .' She closed her eyes 'you and I, to . . .' She took off the felt hat, squeezed it in her hands, opened her eyes and murmured, 'Nothing really started between us. Never. Why?' Henri only shrugged his shoulders as his entire response. Later at the hotel, while they were preparing for dinner, Cécile had added, 'I so wished that you would answer or look at me when I spoke to you, a while ago. What holds you back? I chose you too, you know. I am still waiting for that tiny gesture that will make me believe we are a couple.' Henri had gone up to Cécile and slapped her.

Henri sits up on the bed. Suzy has just called him. He gets up, a wave of dizziness. Suzy calls him again. She is finally in the shower. She wants her brother to see her. The memory of the Niagara River had lasted only a few seconds. Unconsciously, Henri rubs his left hand, the slapping hand. He sees Cécile stretched out between the bed and the armchair in the sitting area of the Toronto hotel bedroom. He dashes toward her. She thinks he is going to hit her again. He grabs hold of her, lifts her up, shakes her, kisses her, presses her so hard against himself that she has to push him away gently. During the entire dinner, she would only speak of Luc, Sébastien, Claire and Bertrand. The next day, at Montréal airport, in transit, they would lose their suitcases. They would wait for a long time beside the moving track that was supposed to return their luggage. Above the opening where the track comes through the wall, there was still a sign that read in two languages 'The luggage will return' '*Les Bagages reviendront.*' Henri had seen Cécile smile at the sign. A few minutes later, beside himself, he complained to many people in the airport, threatening all kinds of legal action. Cécile stood out of the way, calm, almost happy, the tickets to Paris in her hand, watching the time for the second flight. The luggage was not important. It would return. And ten days later, when Air France delivered the strayed suitcases to the Place d'Antioche, Cécile said nothing to Henri but was glad to have him wear the clothes which, in principle, had been lost forever.

Henri approaches the bathroom. Suzy has just come out of the tub. She is rubbing herself with a towel. 'What were you thinking about?' She turns around, looks at her brother. 'Is this the first time you've seen me naked?' She puts on a dressing gown, fastens it at the waist, drapes it and puts the collar in place. 'Jean used to say about old women "A shame and a tribute"!' She turns out the bathroom light, walks by her brother. 'A liqueur? A herbal tea? A taxi? Do you want to sleep here? The bed is made up in Jean's study. It's never used. What do you do with all those bedrooms at the Place d'Antioche? Come on.'

In the bedroom she goes around the bed, opens the window wide. 'It's so nice out' and, kneeling, with the back of her hand, left, right, pushes off the dolls and the stuffed animals, pulls back the spread, loosens the pillows, puts one on the other, stretches out leaning her elbows on them, closing her dressing

269

gown at the knees, her legs bent. She looks at her brother, 'Go away, Henri, go away, quickly!' She opens the drawer of the bedside table, a cigarette, a lighter, an ashtray that she puts on the bed. She looks outside. 'Tomorrow it will be beautiful. Another day. Go away!' Henri knows she will say nothing more. Abrupt. Stubborn. She has always been like that. He has won the match.

He goes into the living room. From the low table he takes the manuscript of *Mortmain*, comes back into the bedroom, places it on the bed, sits at the dressing table, pushes the flasks aside, takes his cheque-book from his inside coat pocket, opens it, looks for something to write with, finds a ball point pen and looks at Suzy. 'Do you have a second copy of this manuscript?' Suzy lights a cigarette and waves no. Henri mumbles, 'So, how much?' Suzy does not answer. On the cheque Henri writes a sum, in numbers, then slowly all the letters. 'To the order of . . . Madame Lehmann?' Silence. He signs the cheque, detaches it, enters the amount on the stub, closes the cheque-book, puts it back in his inside coat pocket, gets up and places the cheque in the manuscript's place on the bed. 'If it isn't enough, Suzanne, you'll have to tell me. I'll warn my bank tomorrow morning, so that they won't be surprised.' He takes the manuscript, leaves the bedroom, turns one last time, 'Good night.'

Henri leaves the building, crosses the Boulevard Haussmann. Suzy's bedroom window is closed, the light is out. Suzy is watching him in the dark, he senses it. In any case, he throws her a kiss, with his fingertips, like in the old days when they used to play together. He will go home on foot. From the corner of the Rue de Courcelles, he turns around a second time and waves the manuscript in farewell.

17

Suzy places the cheque on her husband's desk. Since the dividing up of the Place d'Antioche and Moncrabeau, it is the first time she has had money from her brother. More than is needed, no doubt, to produce three or four shows at the Théâtre des Champs, including the advertising. More than is needed as well to cover the outstanding debts and to be able to go to the bank without fear of meeting one or another of the powers-that-be or that assistant director, a friend of David's, who has been manoeuvring for years to buy the theatre. Suzy re-reads the cheque, verifies that the amount in numbers corresponds correctly with the written figure. The date too, July 9th. And the signature, illegible, a brother's hieroglyphics. In exchange, for this little piece of paper, she will have a little consideration, a forgotten feeling, an assurance, certainty, everything that masks, and restores an air of youth and power. With this little piece of paper she is going to give herself a little consideration. Automatically, after watching her brother, she left her bedroom, crossed the living room in the dark and came to this desk that she respects, a memorial, a little, loving memorial. She wants Jean to witness. She is waiting for approval from him. She must settle that matter with herself. Now, Suzy knows that she will never have a good conscience. She gets only the memory of a disapproving smile from Jean. She will get nothing else. But she sits there, in her husband's chair stroking the cheque, flat on the desk. She is trembling a little, as if she had won the Lottery and were afraid of losing the winning ticket. She has just sold Jean and Bertrand.

To distract herself, she makes plans. Repaint the apartment. Choose a new carpet. Buy flowered sheets. Why not an ultra-modern kitchen with a wall oven and a dishwasher? She would be able to give dinners, have a circle of friends again or even make little dishes for Pilou. Give him a motorcycle. Pilou or another, give him a motorcycle or something else. Suzy also dreams of a new bathroom with a vibrator built into the bathtub and a magnifying mirror for her make-up. A new water heater, of course. And holidays? The theatre? She would have to change the balcony and box seats, replace the stage manager's control panel. And a new sign for the front. For the fun of it, Suzy mixes everything together. Tomorrow morning, first thing, she will take the cheque to her bank. If she wipes away an ironic smile, a debit from so many years, she will be able to find the words necessary to impose the silence of respect, that silence that Jean called 'offensive' in the sense, he would explain, 'of the offensive! In this country where no one will ever again gather together enough trust, only the offensive of money decides the length of the reprieve.'

With bare feet, an open dressing gown, her belt undone, little by little Suzy breathes anew the old days, when her only care was being the wife of a successful author. This cheque gives her back her role. Too bad for Jean if he disapproves and for Bertrand if he is vegetating. Too bad for everybody. The cheque is here. Suzy knows she will never really enjoy it. She also knows that by today's game she has only just been granted a favour. She picks up the telephone, dials a number. 'Luce? Give me David, please . . . No, it isn't urgent.' Silence. 'David? Look, I've just read *Mortmain*. It's for later on. We're reviving *The Collision*. I'm producing it, all by myself. I'm reclaiming my theatre.' 'With what money, Suzy?' 'With mine.' 'Hold on. I want you to explain. I'm going to my office.' Silence. Suzy hangs up. A minute later the phone will ring. She won't answer. When David speaks, you don't know if he is saying 'I want' or 'I won't.'

Henri is approaching the gates of the Parc Monceau. He remembers the Council of Ministers when the 'Cleaning up Paris' plan had been presented to the government. The city had to be given back 'a clean face,' the 'original grain' to monument stones, and sculptures 'their proper space' and gates 'their brilliance'. Paris, for once, was going to regild its balusters and portals. Henri looks at the park, deserted, forbidden at night, closed, with its neat alleys and its signs 'Keep Off The Grass' 'Put Papers in Trashcans', 'Dogs must be leashed'. He smiles, the day's inventory, 'Many fall in love', 'Please do not climb over', 'Luggage will return'. Around the park, the apartment buildings, the private homes, there is not a single light in the windows. Everyone is sleeping. Many shutters are closed too, for the holidays. Cécile is here, in the shadows, with her red, felt hat. She is crumpling it in her hands. Henri tells himself she was only her children's labourer. He should have left her on the floor, after he hit her. Why did he pick her up, hug her against him, kiss her so hard, too hard actually? Cécile had accepted the kisses in the same way she had accepted the slap. They were the same thing.

His face between two bars of the gate, leaning against his temples, as if he were trying to squeeze his face, the bars of the city's cradle, Henri breathes deeply. His hands press the manuscript against his chest. He feels faithful to himself and his hesitation. Now where did he read, one day, 'You can never get over a future love.' On the eve of his departure for Barcelona, Bertrand had told him, 'I simply want to be recognised as different.' Henri had pretended not to understand. Bertrand had also said, 'What good is it claiming your due from the deaf?' then, 'I know where you're sending me. But the reason I'm going isn't to make you finance the trip and the operation. I used to have a glider in my head. Now someone is sleeping within me, his arms in a cross, on a bit of pavement. Bastard!' Bertrand had spat in his father's face. Henri had not flinched. Bertrand had begun laughing, 'You can wipe your face, Papa. Like the man beside you in the car, the night you surprised me at 5, Rue Saint-Benoît. Turn the wrong button. Turn on the windshield wipers!'

Henri takes a step back, rubs his face. Bertrand seemed happy that day. No one is responsible. No one. A slap, a spit, some graffiti, the memory of a red hat, and that remark of Bernadette's when, once, after Cécile's death, Henri had thought he would leave the Place d'Antioche for a smaller apartment near the Invalides, 'But, Monsieur, my slippers are in this neighbourhood.' Henri pulls his head back and taps his forehead against the gate. He shuts his eyes and bumps harder and harder. He feels better, doing that. It is night. No one can see him. He wishes Cécile would disappear forever into the park, with Bertrand, with the others and Jacqueline too. Henri lets the manuscript fall against the gate. He puts a hand to his forehead. He is bleeding. Henri has only seen this blood once before in his life, at the Liberation, on other people's foreheads when he had been appointed to the

273

Committee for the District Purge. No one was responsible, then either. No one. Henri picks up the manuscript.

At the corner of the Boulevard de Courcelles, this time it is a drop of blood that he wipes from the end of his nose. In his left trouser pocket is the handkerchief Bernadette always puts there when she prepares the suit that Monsieur has selected to wear that day, a baptiste handkerchief, well folded and ironed. Henri takes it out with one hand, grasping the manuscript with the other. He pats his forehead. That makes spots on the handkerchief, that's good. Like a child, he feels proud of his wound, ready to blame someone other than himself for being the cause. When he was a minister, he would be wounded also but he was jovial about it. It was 'purification by the smile' when, every morning, Bérard, his executive secretary, would come into his office, at the beginning of the day, to converse with him about the day's agenda, the interviews, the press releases, the official outings, and the performance of his duties. One day, weary of giving way to all those people in the ministry who remain on the job when the ministers have left office, he said to Bérard, 'I have only one dream. I'd have liked to write. I've been thinking for some months now, in this post, that politics is only a form of writing gone astray.' Bérard had smiled for once, and then confessed 'You aren't the first to tell me that, Monsieur le Ministre.'

At the end of the Rue de Chazelles Henri decides to sit on a bench, for a moment, and breathe in sleeping Paris. He opens the manuscript. A million francs on his lap. The first page: 'Mortmain. Play in three acts. Jean Martin.' Second page *The Scene*. A bourgeois living room. Three French doors opening, from the first floor, onto a square. The foliage of chestnut trees can be imagined. A statue in the style of the Third Republic, a woman waving a flag, can be made out. Only the middle French door opens onto a small balcony. Between the French doors, two identical chests of drawers and, on each one, a bronze statuette. Over one of the two bronzes, a wall clock of which the hands have stopped at noon or midnight. Lyre chairs. Wing chairs. Two English armchairs. On the left a double door that gives access to the dining room. To the right of the fireplace, the hall door that leads to the pantry. This setting will be conceived in such a way that, from the auditorium, there will always be a

274

feeling of having entered this living room by breaking in, and that it constitutes the only safety exit. In fact, no access from the outside. The play's characters must give the impression of being prisoners in the apartment. The objects in the living room are indifferent to the unfolding drama. They are the elements added by a family who, for three generations now, have created this proof of success decor for themselves, which has never been anything but decoration.' Third page: '*The characters*. Albert Ceyraque, the father. Lydia, his wife. Lucien, their eldest son. Serge, the second son. Chantal, their daughter. Bernard, their youngest son. Sylvie, Albert Ceyraque's sister. Jacques Rosenberg alias Jacques Rosan, theatre critic, Sylvie's husband. Blandine, an old servant. And a stuffed dog in three poses: standing, seated, lying down.' Fourth page: 'Act I, or the standing dog act. Scene 1. A Sunday afternoon in spring. Voices are heard in the dining room. The stuffed dog, standing version, is near the middle French door which is open. The mantle clock chimes three times. Blandine enters, right door carrying a tray with coffee pot, sugar bowl, cups. She places the tray on a low table near the armchairs. She puts the cups in place, spoons on each saucer, tongs in the sugar bowl, and with a sudden movement meant to cause smiles, raises the lid of the coffee pot, dips a lump of sugar in it, secretively, and crunches it. She puts back the lid noisily, as if someone had surprised her. Laughter, bursts of voices. Blandine approaches the dog, pets his head, closes the French door. Jacques enters the living room first. He is lighting a cigarette. He looks at Blandine. *Jacques*: Do you listen to them when you're serving them at table? What do you think of all their stories? *Blandine*: I don't think anything, sir. I'm paid not to. *Jacques*: Don't you like me? *Blandine*: That's all you like. *Jacques*: Not me, I don't like their stories. I like what's all around them. I clean things up. I'm a cleaning woman. Like you!

Henri closes the manuscript. A car is turning the corner, at the Rue de Chazelles. The tyres squeal. Henri rises. He has only to go back up the Rue de Prony to find himself at home. He is cold. The cold of soft nights, when one is alone and in particular when one wants to be alone. The setting for *Mortmain* is established. Jean speaks first, on stage. Bernadette is just there to set things up. And what's the good of disguising the first names? Henri

275

thinks about various ways to destroy the manuscript. Only one satisfies him. He will burn it in the fireplace, under the clock that will also chime three times, but in the morning, under the clock between the two vases that make up a pair. Henri tells himself he has paid dearly for the right not to read what follows. He has paid. The sweetness of the cheque and the cheque-book always awakens in him the dawning of an emotion resembling pleasure. His forehead hurts. The coagulated wound does him good. Humans attack so they can say they are attacked.

From the kitchen cupboard Suzy has taken several plastic bags, fifty litre bags 'given by the City of Paris' and in which she takes her trash down to the building courtyard. The manager's rules require the service stairs be used but Suzy prefers taking the lift and risking meeting a woman neighbour, whom she looks straight in the eyes, or a male neighbour, when she puts on an indifferent air. One day the third floor tenant, the wife of a 'company director', had reproached her for imposing her 'garbage on others'. Suzy had answered, 'Everything I throw out is clean, Madame. Look!' Suzy recalls it each time she opens a new bag. In the building she is looked upon as mad. In life as well. She knows, and she learned it from her husband, that it is the easiest way for orderly, unthinking people to bring into line neighbours or passers-by who are not like them.

Into the bag Suzy throws the dolls, Léa, Pitchoune, Mimi, Paulo the swimmer, Sandra, Catherine who says mama when her belly is pushed, Carlotta, Queenie whom Jean had brought back from New York, walking Lola whose mechanism is broken, Diva, Chantal, Pierrette and also the nameless ones, folklore dolls, souvenirs from trips. Then it is the stuffed animals' turn, Jumbo, Donald Duck, the monkey with the zipper for a child's pajamas, the leopard, the giraffe. The bag is full. She pushes, packs down, knots the top in one direction, then in the other, and takes a second bag. She is throwing out, wants to throw out, have a clean place and no regrets. She must do it quickly. She is afraid of feeling guilty. How many times, since Jean's death, has she wanted to part with all her rag children? Each time she would stop at the memory of each doll, where, who, when, how, and very quickly she would give up the sacrifice, feeling like an unworthy mother. Into the second bag she throws the rabbit, the teddy bears and the koala, so soft to touch, now shredded, worn out from petting. These little people have loved her.

On her knees, Suzy checks that she has not forgotten a doll or an animal under the bed. She finds only magazines, a book of poems, that pair of scissors she has looked for so long everywhere, scissors that 'cut well', bits of cotton and hair pins. She throws away the magazines, the cotton and pins, keeps the scissors and poems. Uneasy, she goes to see if the cheque is still on the desk. It is. She comes back to the bedroom, pulls the second bag to the dressing table and begins throwing out the nearly empty bottles, the old powder boxes, powder puffs, combs, brushes, costume jewellery, the invitation cards, post cards, overdue mail left lying there, and empties the glass filled with pencils and felt pens. She feels better. She is putting things in order, a disorder in reverse. She is emptying, she is creating an empty space by filling the bag. It's disgraceful. She likes this activity, taken with so little decision. She tastes the impulse in it, the control, the feeling of being in control. She had become the object of these objects. She laughs. She is once again herself. She has money. And if she were not throwing everything away, she would probably begin to shout, really mad this time. She has just sold Jean and Bertrand. And a lot of love with them. She has just sold herself. To her brother. She has just done what they all have been doing, always, neither upper nor lower class, but midway between, to get rich amongst themselves. Treason pays off. She doesn't want to think about it. The second bag is full. She ties it up in one direction, then the other. She lifts it. It is heavier. There are all those bottles. The second bag smells good, a pot pourri of left-over perfumes. The telephone begins ringing.

The third bag is quickly filled with blouses she has not worn for a long time, unmatched stockings, panties, slips and twin sets with the pallor of too many washings. The clothes have an old look that comes from being worn down to the threads. This sorting out Suzy has already been doing mentally for years as she again put on clothes that she no longer wanted. She kept everything for fear of not being able to do otherwise. She throws out the dried up nailpolishes, the out of style pumps, walking shoes with holes or unglued soles, shoes with heels that have been replaced several times. As for shoes, almost nothing remains. The bottom of the closet is empty. For years she has done a lot of walking to save her theatre, explaining, seducing, defending, and never getting others to admit that Jean's success, in order to be second to none, was no less costly for it. A ruin. And if the cheque allows her, so much the better. And knotting the third bag, she says out loud, 'Well, that's something at least!' She answers the telephone. She laughs. 'Listen, David, don't insist. I have the money. Appointment in a little while, around ten, at the theatre. I have to go to the bank before. Watch out, it's a forced landing, I'm going to hang up. I've a lot to do. There are people in the house!' She hangs up. She imagines David in his pajamas and Luce in her bathrobe. Luce is saying to David, 'What's got into her?' Luce hangs up the receiver. David makes a face. He has lost. And *Suzy* has won.

One by one, Suzy carries the three bags out to the landing. In a while she will put them in front of the building. In the bathroom, into a fourth bag, she throws the sink mat, the bidet rug and the bath mat. How could she even put her feet on them again? And in the medicine chest, there are pills for sleeping, digesting, vitamins, thinning creams, old boxes of antibiotics and medicines of which she had even forgotten the names: out!

Two, Place d'Antioche. Henri stops in the middle of the staircase, one hand on the rail. With the other he holds the manuscript. He hurts. Pantalon, Dr. Bermann, Suzy, Bernadette, the starched napkins, Moncrabeau, Barcelona, the Théâtre des Champs, Taillevent, 5 Rue Saint-Benoît, Bérard, Cécile, Toronto, Luc's Legion of Honour, the silences of Sébastien and Claire, a wound on his forehead, and millions for a few pages of manuscript; Henri feels forbidden to stay in Paris, and everywhere else. Henri tells himself it is a first sign of death's approach. Not knowing where to be anymore. Do they wish his death? They won't have it. He catches his breath, climbs the last steps, opens the door. So when has he ever returned home with pleasure? Never.

Suzy empties the drawers of Jean's desk. She does not want these records anymore, these envelopes of letters, articles, indexed file folders of reviews. She even throws out the albums, the box of erasers that Jean favoured, 'there's an eraser for every use', and the pens, blotters, the packages of unused labels, the paper clips, even the notebooks in which Jean put down everything that happened and that he waved sometimes, amusing his entourage by saying 'my memory is here!' Suzy hurries to throw everything away, without much questioning, even if Jean is still speaking in her head, and is not missing, almost to the word, one of his cues in life. Suzy bangs the empty drawers one by one. All that is left is what is on the desk, especially the little frame, with the quotation by Flaubert that Suzy quickly re-reads out loud, declaiming it as if to give herself courage: 'The bourgeois hardly suspect! That we are serving them our hearts! The race of gladiators is not dead! Because every artist is one! He amuses the public with his death throes!' Suzy did not respect the punctuation. Exclamations. She laughs. She throws it away.

On the desk there is nothing but the cheque. On the evening of Claire's eighteenth birthday, when Bertrand got her to dance, Suzy had noticed that the living room mirrors, facing each other over the two fireplaces, reflected an infinite image, ever repeated, an endless corridor, and that they were countless, while she and Bertrand, that night, closed a party that was happy only in name. Suzy knots the last bag. It is the heaviest. Paper and books weigh more than everything else when you are throwing things away. Suzy slides the bag gently on the carpet so it won't tear. Then she carries it by successive lifts to the landing, cluttered up in some ten minutes as if someone were moving. She will take everything down to the front of the building at the last minute and watch that the garbage men throw the bags into the jaws of the compactor. If necessary she will give them a tip.

Suzy closes her apartment door, takes a breath, knots her dressinggown belt, crosses the living room, goes into her bedroom and throws herself on the bed, head first, like a child, her head buried in the pillow. No more is she being watched by anything or anyone in her home. In July workers are easy to find for remodelling an apartment. But before everything else, the trash cans, the cheque and David. She sits up on the bed, wedges a pillow behind her, puts out the light and lies in wait for the city's clamours, the noise of cars on the boulevard, and that light in the sky announcing the day, another day. After all, Henri has only given her the interest on what he knew he was keeping for himself and himself alone. She smiles, lights a cigarette. She is making decorating plans.

Henri closes the French doors in the living room, puts out the lights. Everything is put away, as always. He goes to the pantry. Breakfast is prepared on a tray. Nothing is left out on the work table. The pans are hung in order by size and the dish towels folded beside the sink. An odour of biscuits or biscottes, a light smell, almost sweet. The light was on there too. Henri turns it out. The hall clock chimes three times, then the living room clock and, again, the hall clock. Henri goes back to the entry hall, surprised, disturbed by this one hour that has just chimed three times in a row, as if time were crying an alert. Pantalon's cushion is no longer under the console. The collar and leash are no longer hanging in the coatroom. Henri goes through the apartment, turns out other lights, closes other doors, until he comes to Claire's room. The bed has been undone and the mattress rolled up on the bedstead. Another, distant, odour lingers, the citronella scent of Bernadette's eau de toilette. The bedroom is empty. Bernadette has left. Henri goes to his office. No message. Then to his bedroom. On the bedside table is an envelope. 'To Monsieur Henri Prouillan.' Henri opens the letter. 'Midnight, this July 9th birthday. Dear Sir. I am on my way. I will take the first train to Toulouse and from there I will send word. This is not a holiday I am taking. I am leaving. I am returning Claire's room that I have never truly been able to make my own. I would appreciate it if you would please send the balance of my wages to me in care of Juan. I will stay in touch with you about my visits with Bertrand, as often as possible. They will be better than imaginary ones. Please accept my most devoted sentiments. Bernadette Despouet.'

Henri puts down the letter, looks at the manuscript on the other bed, Cécile's bed. He takes the telephone, calls a taxi. Muzak, a rumba, someone answers, 'Five minutes.' He has just enough time to go to the bathroom and dab his forehead with a little alcohol, to change his shirt and leave for Austerlitz station. That's the only place Bernadette can be. He checks that he has enough money in his wallet. There's enough. Quickly.

18

'I, the undersigned, Claire Henriette Colette Prouillan, Born August 29, 1936 at Lestaque, Gers, daughter of Henri Joseph Roland Prouillan, Born January 28, 1906 at the same place, and of Cécile Noellie Adrienne Bastien-Veyrac, born December 24, 1911 at Lectoure, same department; wife of Gérard Sébastien André Pierrelet, Born July 19, 1932 at Valence, Drôme; mother of Loïc, Yves and Géraldine Pierrelet, living at Sauveterre, near Saint-Michel-l'Observatoire, in the department of Alpes-de-Haute-Provence, hereby decline my identity in my desire to see, in the trunk and branches of this sentence, and to know, through the contours, punctuations and respirations of it, where I am coming from, where I am going, where this night is leading me. Writing now, in this deserted house, does me good, keeps me on my feet, and allows me to give tongue, in the silence of the night and after my children's departure, to what I have not dared cry out. I want to speak of threat. If I get this taste for words that stumble from Bertrand, I will say that in writing, here, I feel alert, exactly because of my fear of alerting. I am choosing the only real cry, the liberated sentence that expresses and grows taut under the bow. What I am seeking on canvas, with the palette, with brushes, palette knives and colours when I mix them, I also get in the sense of what I am finding here, the discovery of an anniversary date, in the inkwell, in the ink and on paper. Words have something powerful that nothing ever totally draws out or encloses. In the body of a phrase they are unceasingly modified. The threat for us Prouillans was Bertrand. He had discovered the words and was getting ready to make use of them. Therefore, nothing was allowed to modify the family. That's why.

'Gérard is here. The image I have of him moves ahead of me. It is out of focus. The only precise image of him moves ahead of me. It is out of focus. The only precise image, a distortion, is forgetfulness. The forgotten is only what has not been seen, or lived. The seen would be the contraction of what has been lived and its movement.

'Gérard is here, as husband, father. He still uproots me. Nothing works. And he is dead. The image I hold of him, jealously, does not have the colours of a stage spectacle. We imagine love too much the way we are obliged to. Our image is in black and white. This is not a bereavement but the framework of a wish, my sensitivity, to touch him again. I have a whole ream of paper here before me, and for him.

'I left Paris because I began to hear all the noises of the city. All of them. I want to sing Gérard. My children have just left, all three of them, together. This time they are escaping from me and Gérard with them. I don't want to find myself again as a Prouillan. Nothing but a Prouillan.

'Gérard is here. The image of him left in me is never complete. Desire truncates and does not make the point. I see only some detail or other. Each part of him, each instant is a dance. Each sequence moves me, rarely. At rarest moments.

'Gérard is here. The image of what was our first meeting is not defined. The definition, a finition, is vexation, the end and a perfection. A nuisance. Gérard is moving forward, back, is escaping me. He is reading over my shoulder. He is holding my breath. I must not turn around. The surprise of seeing him again makes me sway, spins me around, disturbs. He bends over. He is going to touch me. A thousandth of a second would not suffice to fix the image of this meeting. The thing effaced remains. Yes, Bertrand, repetition has a creative power. Slogans from the heart always rebound, becoming stronger and stronger!

'Pages, pages. By writing here, I am running behind my children's car. I want neither to catch them nor to hold them. I just want to tell them that I appreciate being their mother, with the only torment the good shock! But for their father it doesn't work at all that way. We're not sure at all what a father becomes to a child being born. Return to the image, the pages.

'You are here, Gérard. Nothing ever will truly reveal the image I have of you. I know of no snapshot fit to be seen. The photos I keep of you look so little like us. The image I have of you, developed, finished, perfect, ready to be shown to the world, would show your leaving, so much more than your death. You would be elsewhere, for others, another movement. Love is not divided. No one is correcting what I write down here. That's the way love talks. That's the way "Love" is expressed. Don't move, Bertrand. We will always be meeting for the first time. Nothing else justifies a life but that feeling. There it is.

'Your image is here. It is shadowy. I don't trust the brilliance and the flash. Our meeting is true. Nothing will ever hide us. Our image should speak, from the same ink and paper, the look I bear you and your body, examined, surprised. I know nothing about the Pierrelet family and the house at Valence where you grew up. You too used to defend yourself well from understanding the Prouillans and the Place d'Antioche. You would measure the tree. You tore me from their arms. And in your arms I began to grow up. We were beginning a story we hoped would be different. Words, when I speak of you, have a lovely way of shivering. You left too soon, the appearance of you, and we are still together. What Bertrand used to say about the broad and the fine strokes, the sensuality, when we write it comes to mind. Here it is.

'The image of you, Gérard, is multiplying. It will never be the right one, but it is still the best, the moment's final one. You are not leaving me. I'm at my post, I wait and I watch for you. The impression is the single, unique certainty. You are here. Nothing inscribes your image. It is continuously inscribed by itself, the time of a shared glance, outside of time. Us? It is the Rue des Beaux-Arts. I give way for you and you for me. We hesitate. The image is out of focus. The photograph, it is death. But the image lives.'

Claire is delighted. She empties the pen, dips it in the inkwell, fills it again, and wipes the tip with a piece of wrinkled blotter that she throws into the basket under the table, in front of the window. The window is open. There is a clear moonlight over the Lubéron mountain as if drawn in charcoal on the southern horizon. The pen must be full and the night wind must enter this room where for so many years, as if only a day, a single day, she has been staying, sleeping, painting, waiting, watching, containing Gérard within her. She needs this view that Cécile used to call 'the panorama of run-for-your-life.' She needs this house, never visited, never trodden by Henri, as if the father had understood that visiting this place was forbidden him. Claire

283

writes again, 'I love the countryside from here in the Autumn when everything becomes mauve and fawn coloured.'

Two lines, that's all. She had to note the fawn and the mauve, to seize and transcribe these two words that rise in her head every year, an earth odour, to make known what she sees, the beginning of her favourite season. The Turning. The children have just left. It's the start of their summer. Writing and pursuing them.

'A dream. I am becoming bigger than the furniture in the house at Moncrabeau. I am getting bigger than the wardrobes, the sideboards and buffets. I see the tops of everything. I am growing but I never bump the ceilings. And in the beds, now very tiny, I put my loved ones, a family of Lilliputians. With the tip of a finger, with just one, light touch, being very careful, I can pet their whole bodies. I am leaning on my father's bed. But he is so tiny, scarcely a dot, a flea, that he escapes. This dream I've had many times. The more I grew, the more I loved them individually, brothers and mother, one as much as the other, the father, even though I was trying to kill him. There is no real rupture from the family except by determining exactly the extent of the attachment one has for it. It trails along everywhere, especially when we claim to be free of it. Then one day I felt my hips and my front growing. I had a loaf of bread in place of a belly and it was becoming immense, a golden crust, of a crunchy bread and a whole horde waiting to taste it. When I told you this dream, Bertrand, you said I had done some good reading because from now on I was beginning to "read my life well". Here at Sauveterre, it's the opposite. The countryside is studying me, I am its dwarf, a dot, almost nothing. There is never an exact size of being if you want to feel.'

Claire puts the pages in order, makes a pile that she places squared up along the left side of the desk. On the right, within hand's reach, the ream of virginal pages are awaiting her reach. Another page.

'Here, a repetition. I appreciate being the mother whose only torment is the good-shock, as Bertrand used to say. Whereas, for a father, it doesn't work at all that way. There is no certainty of what a father becomes to a child being born. For Henri, our Cronus, that god we never speak of, time is inaugurated with his sons, Luc, Sébastien, Bertrand. Sons. Other beings. Different or indifferent beings who, theoretically, will break time, the father's time, making a history of it, a sequence on a series. Now, Henri does not recognise his desire that comes from another, from Cécile, and that is not even certain. It was an otherness, in any case. And there is Henri Prouillan, facing the same beings, not alike, who bear his name. He wants to annul them all, in one, Bertrand. He wants to meld them, wall them up in the family house. That was twenty years ago. We let him do it. And Bertrand has gone there. That's it, the anniversary. The night of July 9 to 10. The truth of that day escapes all caricatures. Truth strays. One can only keep it company, en route, and share its landscapes as long as possible, at the risk of getting lost.'

Loïc is driving. Géraldine is beside him, Yves in the back. They left Stéphanie at the first station they came to and they hurried on to Italy. Claire wished she could call them, not for them to come back but for them to really leave, if leaving is really possible, with other baggage, other lives, otherwise. She writes.

'Between Gérard and myself there was always the photograph of a father assassin, because he was incapable of any verve, jealous of our embraces, furious of having had my brothers and me, and maddened at losing us. Between Anne-Marie and Luc, between Ruth and Sébastien, between Romain and Bertrand, there was always the father's photograph, like a calling card. I came by, I am here, I will come back, the invitation is threatening. I won't leave you. I will have done. He has us. I am saying here is Gérard, here is Bertrand, here are Luc, Cécile, Sébastien, Bernadette, Pantalon, here are Ruth, Anne-Marie, Pierre, Laura, Paul, Loïc, Yves, Géraldine, here is Lucio, Merced, Juan and I am writing now there is Henri, there is my father. All tried to cross over, one alone holds back.'

Only then, for the first time does Claire understand the still lifes she has been painting for years, imprecise, pale objects, grouped on what is never really a table or windowsill, with no figurative decoration around them, impressions of objects bathing in the light of a rising day and of which the form can be enjoyed without being concerned about the function, objects which Loïc finds moving. Claire has just, suddenly, remembered mornings when she would wake before Gérard. She dared not move. She was held in her husband's arms and legs. Scarcely would she dare to look at him, she had such fear of robbing him

285

of that sleep they had just shared, the smell of sheets, the warmth of the bed, skin to skin, even the breath smell was like a signal, Gérard's exact taste. Then, eyes half closed, all drowsy, Claire would look at the objects in the bedroom standing guard, vases, ceramic dishes, boxes, turned wood objects, baskets, mirrors, which Gérard had chosen solely for their shapes and materials because, he used to say, 'Architecture starts there.' And for years, without knowing why, without really wanting to understand, safeguarding this bit of innocence and unawareness which alone allows the artist to continue creating without fear of the judgement of others, Claire had created these lives, this guard, everything that had surrounded their mornings, the mornings shared with Pierrelet, her abductor. Now she hardly dares look at the pictures that her son Yves turned outward a while ago. She has just understood, and understanding is too much for a creator. Henri is here. Gérard is going away. The children are already far away. Claire is cold. She gets up, closes the window, goes to look for a pullover, puts it on, goes downstairs, drinks a glass of water, locks the door, from inside, something she has never done in this house. She feels threatened. She goes back upstairs. She knows she will never again be able to paint the still lifes as before because she has just understood. Claire goes back to the desk. A page.

'I am left.' She starts drawing a face, neither brother nor son nor husband but, feature by feature, the father's face. She scratches it out. Another page.

'A threat. The more I flee him the more he approaches me. His crime is perfect. No clue, no trace. He simply accomplishes it. We never speak of him except to claim to kill him whereas he is the killer, he the undertaker.'

How do you express that this is not a thesis but an observation, a family, an experience, a situation, a flash of one day? Claire rubs her arms, takes a deep breath. The door is locked. She had a glass of water. It was good. She is writing.

'A threat. They only want to hear causes that have already been heard. Don't leave, Gérard, please. I need you more than ever. I need to feel it was possible once. You didn't want the Pierrelets. I didn't want the Prouillans. The night before your accident, we were angry because I was reproaching you for not seeing them often enough. How thirsty we were for everything.

Are you reading me?' Claire puts the pen crosswise at the bottom of the page. Seated in the chair, she turns around, closing her eyes and raising her chin as if Gérard, standing behind her, were about to place a kiss on her lips . . .

She gets up. The pullover catches on the chair. The chair tips over. The pen rolls on the paper and falls to the floor. The night wind bangs the shutters. The light grows faint as if there was about to be an electricity failure. Claire turns in a circle. She bites her lips. She throws herself on the bed, grabs the other pillow and presses it against her belly. Her children are leaving. She must keep the pain away. She gets up, comes back to the desk, as if on the attack, picks up the pen, takes a page and begins writing again, deliberately, in that broad, round handwriting that Bertrand found 'laughable' because it was 'legible'.

'A threat. The Place d'Antioche. My mother is arranging my hair. I am seated on a stool, in her bedroom. She tells me to sit up straight and not to move. I like her brushing my hair but I don't want her to arrange it. She is going to make braids again the way they did them, no doubt, in Lectoure, in the Bastien-Veyrac family when she was little. Before long, stroking me with the brush, she is no longer really looking at me. She is thinking about the child she used to be. To be sure she is not paying attention, I wink, I stick my tongue out. She does not notice. I wished I could help. I am six, seven, eight years old. She rarely calls me into her bedroom. If she does, it's because she is troubled. Abruptly she needs me, to touch me and to make me pretty. In her way. A need to remember who she was, to think less about what she has become in the shadow of the father, without ever complaining, watching that no one pities her, rebuffing my brothers if they try taking her part, forbidding us to criticise our parents. She arranges my hair. She forgets time. She brushes my hair so long that I finally tell her 'Mama, you're hurting me.' Surprised, she stops. In her look, for a fraction of a second, I read a fright, as if she had just given herself away. She bends over, kisses me on the forehead, mumbles 'Sorry' and begins braiding my hair. I no longer dare say I don't like the braids. Henri holds us. Nothing must change his idea of the family. A society is overturning. It is the last Sunday after the holidays. The expression is Bertrand's. The threat was in Cécile's look, a shadow borne from my father.'

Claire places the sheet on the left hand pile. She wets her finger and takes another white page.

'A threat. Moncrabeau. The game consisted of cutting the newspapers into sheets, all the size of an envelope. A lot were required for the game to last as long as possible, and especially to win. Outside it was raining on the lake and the birch wood. Going out was forbidden. All four of us were around a table. Luc and Sébastien knew how to write, Bertrand and I couldn't yet. We were the "secret service of the mails and telecommunications". We had the "responsibility for the network". Without our stamp, messages "would never get to their destinations". Because he was the smallest, Bertrand's job was only tending the pile. Beside him, I was supposed to take a sheet and by blowing over it verify that there was indeed only one. Sébastien then would snatch it from my hands, stamp it on one side, a thump of the fist on the table, an imaginary stamp. Luc would take it in turn, stamp the other side, another thump, and count out loud. We were supposed to do up to a thousand. Only at a thousand would we save the world and we would be saved with it. Sébastien would say, "They'll finally understand it's thanks to us." The Germans were searching for us. They were shooting resisters. Then, I would quickly take two sheets at a time and hadn't the time to separate them. Sébastien would stamp them anyway and treated me like a saboteur. Bertrand tended the pile, averting his eyes. He was happy because we were letting him in on the game and fearful that we might lose. The table shook. Luc, counting out loud, urged us on. We never reached a thousand. Bernadette would call us, or else Merced, or Cécile. Henri surprised us one day. We had just passed nine hundred. The door opened. "Now, what are you doing?" And as neither Luc, Sébastien nor I answered, he had taken Bertrand away saying, "Don't stay with them." That same evening when I was putting him to bed, Bertrand asked "Is he the German?" I have just remembered this story because of the sheets I am taking from the right pile, pages on which I write, pages stamped with writing, which I place on the left pile. How can I make the assembly line? I am alone. It is still the same network, the same secret service, the same imaginary stamps, the same appeal. How do we get to a thousand? It is still Bertrand's cry, taken away by papa. The first front was us. The game was called "SOS to the whole world". It was during the war. Nothing has changed! I am making the same movements today. Maybe I locked the door of this house, tonight, an exception, so that my father might not enter, alerted, furious at the scratching of the pen on this paper.

'A threat. Henri wanted us to be incapable of enjoying ourselves. Henri kept us incapable of pleasure. Henri still keeps us. The law is there. Law and not excitement.

'I, the undersigned, Claire Henriette Colette Prouillan, born at, the, in, daughter of, and of, sister of, wife of, and mama of three children on their way to Italy and other countries, certify and certify myself, by these lines, that nothing can truly escape the judgement of the father in the exercise of the power he gives himself and that we give him, as much by our silence as by flight or confrontations. He is here. He is always here. Everything not originating from him gets reported back. Everything that does originate from him will never be enough like him.

'Appeal. I claim from Gérard my sensual due.

'Sauveterre. The night of July 9–10. My Gérard. I have just written the drafts of a letter I wish I could dictate to time so that everything would start over again. I am just beginning to miss you. You are no longer behind me, reading over my shoulder, copying for the final exam that will carry me away when my turn comes, sooner rather than later, but you are the ink in this pen and the paper receiving it. I am caressing your belly here. I am listening to your heart beating. I feel your hand in my hair. You are undoing it. You are still undoing my hair. Yours is the only look I liked meeting and against which I collided without fear. Tonight I have just understood that all I did was play the game they dictated to me, they, all of them standing at attention, identical, men, women, people other than ourselves, Henri and, behind him, a society stamped in his exact image. In helping someone at times of misfortune or depression, others push you more towards the void than they hold you back or support you. For that they have two nice methods. The first is to give no importance at all to what happens to you, the second is to give it too much. There is rarely between the two, a genuine emotion, or true help. I have watched carefully, since you left, not to let myself be taken in by either of these two kindnesses. I found only your memory within me, between two people, to keep me on my feet, on my way, and to see our children growing up. They are leaving me and I am beginning to miss you. It does me good writing to you. It contains the cry within me.

'My Gérard. Writing under his name is still suspect. What is discovered then? A voluptuousness taken for love? And we were quick to verify a necessity (I am a necessity to you, you are a necessity to me) and even a due. You are letting me down.

'Gérard, my friend. Why do I put your name at the top of each page since all of me, more than ever, is addressed to you, and no message will ever be delivered to you? For years I have been wearing out your shirts. I wear them for housecoats. I roll up the sleeves. I adore buttoning them. I like feeling too small in them. Not a relic nor a fetish, it is what still clothes you. When I wash them, I caress the fibre. When I iron them, I am careful not to make wrinkles. And when I paint, I take care not to get any spots on them. I am your scarecrow. Right now I am wearing one of your pullovers. You are keeping me warm. Everything forbids us to live a past if it is still present. Everything forces us to think that what is beautiful is ideal and thus an illusion. Why, in the secrets of these pages, these messages, am I still, guilty, asking myself about other people's judgements? It's our love. That's all. It lasts. They foresaw everything but that!

'A story. It was a few days after your death. The day after your burial. Ruth, Anne-Marie and Cécile had accompanied me to the lawyer's on the Boulevard Saint-Germain. Bernadette was looking after the children at the Place d'Antioche. As we were coming out, in the courtyard, Cécile suggested going for tea in the neighbourhood. We would find a pleasant place. I hear her saying "pleasant" in that precise diction, slightly stilted, that betrays doubt and affection. All three of them no longer knew how to treat me, how to speak to me. Everything they could say or do scarcely masked the profound joy, for each of them, at not having to live through the drama I was living. They were keeping busy with me through solidarity. That would last only a few days. They knew it as much as I felt it. As Uncle Jean used to say, "It doesn't deserve being noted down, it is played in advance." It was played in advance, that day. It was sunny. The people in the street seemed happy. Three women were dragging me along, they said, "To distract me a little" and especially "To get me to react." I am telling you, Gérard, because I did not in fact find you again until I arrived here, when I arrived at Sauveterre the day this house was chosen. You don't know this story. I need to free myself of it. With no shame. As it is. Listen.

'I continue. We are having tea. Everything they are telling me is inescapable. In the state I am, cut off from you, fractured, no word can throw up a bridge. Words then slash, stab, rummage about. And still worse are the important looks. There is no tea room in the area. We are in a snack bar on the corner of the Rue du Bac. I remember the name, the Escurial. Cécile asks if there are any cakes. She says "cakes" the way she said "pleasant". The waiter brings us slices of cake in cellophane. Cécile says. "Eat, it'll do you good." Anne-Marie picks up my scarf that has fallen on the floor, shakes it, folds it and holds it out to me, "It's lovely. Where did you buy it?" It was a gift from you, Gérard. I am writing "gift" the way Cécile said "cakes". There are intonations in words if you take the time to read them. Snack bar. Escurial. Bac. Cake. Gift. Ruth suggests that I come to live with her for a while. "I'm alone too, you know. Sébastien . . ." She blushes. She has said something stupid. I stroke her hand, on the table. She withdraws her hand quickly to drink her tea. A pretext. She looks at Cécile and Anne-Marie. The three women watch each other and say nothing more. There is music from a juke box and the murmur of people at the counter. The table is formica. Snack, Escurial, Bac, cake, music, juke box, formica, I'm not playing, Gérard. Everything, abruptly, had an unbearable brilliance. I had just realised that these women had married Prouillans and I was, an enemy, myself a Prouillan, in their husband's lineage.

'Cécile pays. "Aren't you finishing your cakes? You're right. They're dry. Let's go home." I unfold your scarf, knot it around my neck a little too tightly, as if I wanted to strangle myself. Ruth notices and turns her head. She will walk ahead of us to the car. At the lawyer's the clerk had sleeve protectors and the same voice as on the day he had read us the marriage contract. Do you remember? Henri had demanded everything be signed at the lawyer's. In Paris. Not in Valence. Not at your home.

'Valence. The day before. At the cemetery. The entire Pierrelet family is there. At my side, as they say, no one accompanied me. I demanded that. There were beautiful clouds in the sky. Clouds the way you liked them, round and in

291

plumes, snowy mountains, those clouds I sometimes watched passing in your eyes. Your parents were very kind to me. There was no reception line. We lunched in a dining room where I imagined you were. Your oldest sister wanted to show me your childhood bedroom but I refused. They accompanied me back to the train and insisted that I come to "Spend a vacation" with them, with the children. Everything unfolded so fast. Why did I let you be put in your family vault? When does a family begin, then, so it can have a new vault? An absurd question, but nevertheless. Continuation and end of story.

'Anne-Marie is driving. Ruth is beside her. I hold myself straight in the back seat, careful not to touch my mother's arm. Several times she tries to take my hand but I do all I can to avoid this contact. I lower the window. I pass my hand through my hair. I look at the streets, the other cars, the other people. Never have red lights appeared so stubborn. Several times Ruth turns around as if she wanted to speak to me. I look down. From time to time Anne-Marie looks at me in the rearview mirror. We could only be strangers to one another. It's what Bertrand used to call "the end of the ball, when you feel what the dance could have been". I don't like the story I'm going to tell you, Gérard. I am afraid you won't read me again afterwards. This image, long hidden inside me, is unbearable. Here it is.

'Anne-Marie finds a place to park in the Place d'Antioche, right in front of the building. We get out of the car. I smell that scent in the air of coming back from classes on the days when Bertrand would come to meet me after school to "walk along with me". I smelled that vegetable scent, from the tree, the trunk, the earth that, in autumn or spring, blows in Paris, strong gusts that rise in the head. I saw Bertrand again, at that moment, happy for me and me for him. The times in the street, when we were free. We could be anybody at all and we enjoyed it. He expressed his joy by doing everything we were not supposed to do, crossing at the green lights, writing on the walls in chalk, saying hello to just anybody, calling me darling in the bakeries when we were getting a chocolate roll with the stolen money, or giving the wrong direction to someone who would ask us the way, jumping with both feet into the puddles or the gutters, slipping the book he had just read and I was supposed to read into my handbag as if it were a secret. He called Henri "Mario-

Power" and Cécile "Mimi-I-keep-still". He told me detective stories about them. He said they alone had the right to buy arms but that no organised army had ever been able to put down an action by isolated rebels. Getting out of the car I called, "Bertrand!" I had just seen him again, getting out of the taxi, the evening of Barcelona, at that very spot, before that tree. And they, the three of them, looked at me without understanding. I laughed. They were afraid. They had a look of fear. Continuation and end.

'I found with you, Gérard, a use of body and time. We unified everything by always making the same discoveries, together. Around the table at the Pierrelet's, at Valence, they don't really talk to each other either. Your eldest sister insisted on showing me your childhood bedroom because above all she wanted to see it again herself, to experience it. It's always the same story and it's worth the trouble of telling it. The trouble of loving. The only true, irreducible trouble. Politics begins with two, when you are two, when you were, when you are no longer. At the end of the ball the couples are formed. It's too late. Watch out, we're getting out of the car. I cried "Bertrand!" and I burst out laughing.

'Continuation and end. I take a couple of steps, Anne-Marie catches me by the arm and says, "Watch out!" I was about to step in a mess. A dog's mess. Pantalon's mess near his favourite chestnut tree. And as the three women begin smiling nervously, kindly, because I am not paying attention now, I put my right foot in the mess. I flatten it. Then the left foot so as to have it all over my soles. Cécile, Ruth and Anne-Marie are no longer smiling. From one foot to the other I smear my legs, ankles, and calves. I cover myself with the mess, in front of them, in front of the building. I am dirty. Very dirty. I even believe it smells bad. I don't like it but I do it because I don't want anyone to grab my arm anymore and tell me to watch out. I don't want that dialogue of the deaf, an absence of dialogue between women. I don't want those hindrances and silences that are dictated to them just as much as to me. I don't want to be treated like a widow and I have just seen Bertrand again at that spot, he who was also maltreated. I am standing, legs slightly apart, surprised by what I have just done, happy at the omen, aware of the risk I am running, faithful to myself and to you, Gérard. Some people passing by have stopped, looking disgusted. Then, only then, did Anne-Marie and Cécile pounce on me and drag me away. I was about to bend down to put some on my hands and face. But they carried me off. This was not just any mess in front of just any building.

'The end. They push me into the apartment. Cécile orders Bernadette to keep the children in the kitchen. They hide me in the bathroom. They undress me. They give me a shower. They soap me. It is good. I let them do it. Anne-Marie scrubs my feet and legs hard. I am crying, but it is under the shower and they don't see. Cécile, brush in hand, cleans my shoes in the bidet. Ruth hands me a towel and dries my back. They jostle me a little, the three of them, and I grasp the edge of the sink. They want me clean, neat, once again and quickly. Loïc, Pierre and Laura have escaped Bernadette's watchful eye. They are pounding on the door and calling us. Three mamas have just cleaned up a naughty fourth one. They dress me again. Looking at the shoes in the bidet, Cécile says "I'm going to give you mine. I don't want to see them again, please." Everything happened very quickly. Don't hold it against me, Gérard, for hiding this story from you so long. After that, I began hearing all the noises of the city and I took refuge here. To Cécile, Anne-Marie and Ruth, I had become mad. For Suzy too, for Jean, for my father. They washed me but they told the story. There was nothing I could do but leave Paris, like Bertrand. And for another Moncrabeau. The existence of pain teaches me. I am fond of it. I am holding on to it. And I love you.

'I am going to try sleeping with just one pillow. I still have the taste of your mouth in my mouth. That's enough.

'I am crazy because I don't know forgetfulness. The children are far away. I can stop. Much love.'

Claire rises, re-caps the pen, puts the pages she has just written in a neat pile. She slips them into the drawer. She puts the bottle of ink away, opens the window partway and jams the bolt. She goes downstairs, drinks a glass of water, opens the door and takes out the key. She wants to put everything in the house in order. There is a light at the Schulterbrancks'. She will visit them tomorrow if the pain is too sharp. She looks at the time, three in the morning. She puts on some music. She takes a breath. Loïc, Yves and Géraldine are certainly at the border. The cry is curbed.

19

A lighted sign, red, flashing 'Open All Night'. Luc slows down. A second sign 'Last Station Before the Autoroute'. In open country, a parking lot filled with trucks, international transportation, a service station, a rest stop for long distance drivers. Luc unhooks his safety belt, angles to the right, looks for the closest possible parking space near the snack shop. He wants light, noise, people, smoke, voices, other faces and a coffee, black, in a big cup, like the old days when he was preparing for his exams. In the rearview mirror Luc looks at the swelling on his temple. He looks bumped but not suspicious. He can show himself in public. He grabs his jacket, gets out of the car, slams the door, checks to see if the trunk is well shut. In the cabs of the parked lorries the curtains are drawn. In the Paris-to-provinces direction there are numerous cars. But who is going back to Paris tonight? Almost nobody. Luc pushes the door of the snack shop violently but holds it with the same move so it doesn't bang against the wall and signal his entrance. He needs to be here. A break.

All the tables are taken. At a table for four, one man is alone. Luc approaches, takes a chair, 'May I?' The man waves yes. He's bearded, with blue eyes, thirty years old, like the other customers. His luggage is against the wall, two bags stacked, on top of each other and an oilskin raincoat on top of them. He has finished his beer. Judging by the crumbs on the table, he has just eaten a sandwich. Luc orders 'A large coffee and two croissants.' The waitress wipes the table in front of him. There are noises, voices, smoke, other people, but there is also this table, to be shared, and this man looking at him, across from him, leaning forward and saying, as if communicating a secret, man to man, 'Don't forget I owe you a franc!' Luc, surprised, hesitates 'you've made a mistake . . .' The man bursts out laughing, straightens up in his chair and says loudly, as if he wanted everybody to be witness, 'Then it's two francs I owe you!' Luc crosses his arms on the table, lowers his head, waits for the coffee, the croissants. The man insists. 'You're not saying anything? You don't find that funny? Alright then, three francs!' Luc shrugs slightly, hunches down, pulls his chair closer to the table. He tells himself he's fallen onto a nut. Or perhaps not, here in open country, in the middle of the night, in a public place, with people having something to eat, he's sitting across from someone else who wants to talk, that's all. As if he, too, had nothing to say.

'Good! Then it's four francs!' Luc looks at him. The man smiles. 'Don't worry. I'm not going to put the touch on you. The loot is hard to get, but I manage. I was just waiting for someone to come to sit here. Someone to trade a couple of words with. Words to laugh about. But nobody knows how to anymore.' Luc plays deaf. The man pushes his chair away, turns toward the room as if had decided not to say anything else. So much the better.

Antoine and Eliane must have gone right up to their room. Christine stayed in hers. They won't speak to one another until tomorrow morning. While he was driving, Luc no longer saw the road, the side of the road. He was only seeing himself now, devoted to his own loss, breaking everything, once again, at the exact instant when admission prevailed over the moment, when the liaison became possible. An attempted hold-up. Fleeing reassures him. He can then invent all kinds of scenarios for himself, after-the-flight scenarios, as if he could exist only by running away. Luc wants to return to Paris quickly because he is afraid of returning to Christine and saying the simple words he could never say, not even to Anne-Marie. The forbidden words Cécile would have liked to hear, the suppressed words of many generations. Or else Christine ran downstairs, with Antoine holding her back, Eliane calming her. No. That isn't possible.

The coffee, the croissants. Luc says, 'Thanks.' The waitress goes. The man points a finger at Luc. 'You're going back to Paris? I'm coming from there. I can give you the latest news: there's no more room, for anybody. And I owe you five francs. I say that because you have the mug of someone with an injection engine 504 car and lots of corpses in the back!' Luc looks at the man. 'Please . . .' The man smiles, 'So it's six francs? The croissants are good at this hour, aren't they. They're hot!' Luc is furious at himself for getting involved. All he can do now is hurry up, drink his coffee and eat his croissants. The man mumbles, 'I have a debt to you because I don't know you.' He laughs. He wipes off the crumbs, pushes the empty glass aside, places his hands flat on the table. Luc swallows a piece of croissant the wrong way, coughs, drinks a mouthful of coffee. The man continues, softly 'Seven, eight, nine francs. And so to a million! I'm doing you the favour because they did it for me. Don't go to Paris. Go back where you started. Stop hurting yourself. And above all listen to me, because when they told me, I didn't know how to listen. I said to myself, a man talking there, like that, hitting the truth, that he was crazy. It was in a metro station, at midnight. There aren't a lot of trains at that hour. Are you listening?' Luc turns his head, looks at the waitress behind the counter, and at the men, the other men, night travellers. Only one woman, the waitress. Her eyes are made-up, a dark complexion. A button is missing on her blouse. What a bust. An old man passes, a pail in his hand. He is throwing sawdust on the floor. Luc waves to the waitress. He wants to pay. He hasn't even finished his coffee. The man says, 'Leave it, I do owe you that. Or else you can give me a beer. Even if it's because I haven't got anything to pay with. Understand? I'm coming and you're going. You have to listen to me.' The waitress approaches. Luc says, 'A beer, and the bill, please.' The man smiles. Luc watches him. The man looks proud, 'You've been had. And it's up to you to say thanks.'

Luc takes a breath, strokes his temple with his finger tip, unconsciously. In a kind of image, a flash, he sees a forest and trees that are not parting now as he passes. Now he can drink his coffee, calmly, and think about the second croissant he's going to eat. What a need to invent pressing things to be done and enemies everywhere so as never again really 'to take time's time', Bertrand's expression. Luc mumbles, 'Get out of here!' The man is surprised 'Sorry?' Luc smiles vaguely, 'I was speaking to someone else.' The man shakes his head, looks amazed 'I told you! You've got some bodies in your car!'

The waitress brings the beer. Luc pays for everything. The humming of a lorry starting up in the parking lot, the shine of headlights, a beam sweeping the room, a sharp light from outside. The old man is sweeping the sawdust. The waitress pockets the tip, a little purse swollen with coins hanging from the belt of her apron. The high heels of her shoes are worn. Luc observes her, from the back, waddling, jigging from behind, going back to the counter. The man says, 'I really had you!' He raises his glass of beer like a toast. Without thinking, Luc asks him, 'What's your name?' The man answers, 'and you? What's it matter? You're going to fill your tank with super, check the oil level, blow up your tyres. You're also the kind who uses seat belts, it shows on your lips. You don't say what you have to say. Coins for the toll? Dough for everything? People under your orders? Others you're leaving? Some you don't forget? If you make good time, you'll arrive in Paris when they're collecting the garbage. In fact, it's Paris they should throw out with one heave. Only you'd need a big compactor lorry or a big bomb. Some Parisians are incompatible.' The man empties his glass, wipes his lips, 'If you want I'll stop.' He laughs heartily. He has Bertrand's blue eyes. Luc drinks his coffee, slowly, elbows on the table, the cup between both hands, an offertory gesture he doesn't like that reminds him of masses he had to go to at Saint-Ferdinand. Nobody believed, but they went just the same. That made a unified family. He mumbles, 'No, go on,' then more clearly, 'talk, please. Do you want another beer?' The man shrugs his shoulders, turns towards the room. He is silent. Luc feels hooked. A piece of croissant remains, he crunches it. The old man says, 'Sorry' and sweeps under the table. Bursts of laughter at the counter. Someone has found the waitress' blouse button. A voice, 'So I've got a kiss coming!'

Luc feels stiff, exhausted by the physical exercise of the day before. The story of these last days spent playing 'scouts of advanced middle-age', Christine's expression is ridiculous. No matter how much Christine maintained that from then on the 'event' was 'drowned out by the commentary', never did Luc dare lead her to believe that that, too, was a commentary meant to drown out and silence. Luc places the empty cup on the saucer. He likes the bitter taste of the coffee in his mouth. The man is still turning his head. The waitress has kissed everybody, except the two of them, at the table off to one side. The floor is clean. The old man is emptying the ashtrays into the pail of dirty sawdust. Luc is already conjugating Christine in the imperfect tense. She used to know and do everything too well. Like

Bertrand. Like all those who have begun to love him, him, Luc.

The man turns back to the table, leans on his elbow. Luc looks down. The man says, 'Still here? My name's Jacques. Is that okay with you? I used to work for a printing press. I'm unemployed. Does that please you? I've been married, two kids. Happy? I'm going down Biarritz way. I don't know why. Maybe because of the name. It sounds rich. My surname is Jacky. Now you know everything.' The man extends his hand to Luc, over the table, a broad gesture as if saying goodbye. Luc does not move. The man takes his hand back, 'but I'm not asking you anything. When you came in, I just said to myself that I knew damned well that I'd seen you a thousand times. Always sure of yourself. And then not so sure this morning. So, I'm taking advantage of it.' The man smiles, looks Luc straight in the eyes and says slowly, in a low voice, distinctly, 'You are the perfect bastard who passes totally unnoticed until you crack. Crack or break. I, at least, am leaving you the choice.' The man hits the table with his fist. The waitress is watching them. Luc grabs his jacket, gets up. The man tries to keep him. 'Why are there so many of you?' Luc goes out. The man laughs. The waitress heads for the table with a tray.

Outside, there is a smell of tyres and old metal. Like a roadside dump. And all around are fields. Luc wished he could tell himself he had only been dealing with a drunk but the look in the man's eyes was awfully clear. It was Bertrand's look, a few days before he left for Barcelona, when he had said to his eldest brother, 'Are you happy? *You*, too, have everything you want.' Luc had not answered. Bertrand had then acted out someone sawing his skull. Pen in hand, he was drawing dots on his forehead. Luc had hit his brother to make him stop. The pen had fallen onto the living room rug at the Place d'Antioch and had made a spot. Anne-Marie and Cécile were entering, followed by Sébastien and Suzy. Uncle Jean was joking in the dining room. Luc sees Bertrand again cleaning the rug and Pantalon leaning down sniffing. 'One lump, two lumps?' Everyone had pretended not to notice the dots on Bertrand's forehead. Luc hits the hood of his car, kicks a bolt, turns around, dives at the car door, opens it, gets in, grabs the wheel. He feels 'surrounded'. He starts up squealing his tyres, backs up, brakes, goes forward, and a few metres further on stops abruptly in front of a petrol pump. 'Fill it up, please!' Luc looks at the door of the snack shop. The man is coming out, bags slung across his back. He has put his rain-coat on. The two men look at each other from a distance. Luc mumbles, 'Get out of here!' The man crosses the road. He positions himself for hitchhiking, in the opposite direction.

Full tank, oil, tyres, money, tip. The attendant has cleaned the windshield. Luc starts the engine again. On purpose Luc does not look in the rearview mirror, but he has seen the man give a little wave. Entrance to the autoroute, first péage, take a ticket. Then night. Headlights. Like a carpet for returning to Paris. From time to time, automatically, Luc looks in the rearview mirror. Nobody there following him. He's the only one. He will never tell the story of the blue-eyed man, the hot croissants and the button on the waitress' blouse. True stories are never told. For twenty years, they have not spoken of Bertrand.

Luc likes the smell of the apartment on the Rue de Téhéran when he comes back after a few days' absence. A smell of being closed up, then it breathes. He feels safe. He has the sense of starting over again. He has sorting to do. Unimportant sortings. Dirty linens, mail, bills, unpacking his bag or suitcase, bringing his appointments up to date, plans, meetings that he wants and deals he wants to end, a well-informed dose of being alone. In secret from his brothers, Luc always used to 'report' everything to his father. He kept him abreast of the remarks that were made, the tempers, runnings away, games, plots and even the thefts. He was fulfilling his role of eldest brother. Henri is at the end of the autoroute. Luc has always broken sibling loyalty for him, and by him, using the same gestures, the same words, the same spiteful attitude, the same taste for what is immobile and conforming. Luc only pretended to like Claire, Sébastien and Bertrand. He shared their enthusiasms and dreams only so he could be convinced of imitating his father, of resembling him and travelling through life, like him, without changing anything. Luc has only remained a son. Anne-Marie left him just as he was beginning to accomplish his model role.

Luc grips the steering wheel. He is driving too fast. He no longer knows the road. He has failed, as a father, faithful to the model, and he is coming back, as if he were held at the end of a tether, to report again the dreams of those he did not want to be. Sébastien, Claire and Bertrand never suspected anything. Luc excelled at foreseeing the doubts that would have betrayed him and would then do everything to take the necessary initiatives or to make still more violent remarks which ensured him, for an additional time, his brothers' and sister's approval. He did exactly the same thing in his profession. He has failed as a father but he has become president of the company and henceforth a chevalier of the Legion of Honour. Grotesque. Bad conscience will never graze him. And, here at the steering wheel, Luc admits it for the first time, as an observation of himself. The man's wave goodbye, on the roadside, in the opposite direction, was almost affectionate. For distraction Luc turns on the radio. The three a.m. news. A plane crashed at the end of the runway on takeoff at the Cotonou airport in the People's Republic of Benin. One hundred and twenty-seven dead. No survivors. Next news at four. And now the commercial messages.

20

'French composition. Subject: The Zoological Gardens. Form: free. For: Sébastien. By: Bertrand. Written: as a letter, the only real novel, a single author, a single reader. Presented: his wedding day. Will be read: always too soon. Sole copy. Author's note: I ask you, Sébastien, to keep this composition to yourself. It is a sailing ticket which will have no value if anyone else has knowledge of it. It is my wedding gift and your family register.

'1. We only went there once, one Thursday afternoon. Cécile had left for Lectoure, to her mother's bedside, the grandmother we have only known slightly who only came to see us on Epiphany to give us money that, she used to say, "cost her more" than it did our father. Cécile was with her to help her die, as if one could help someone at such a time other than rejoicing at not being in the same boat. Stop. Papa was not here, like everyday at noon. A revenge. For years, every time going there came up, one of us four would always say that it was "stupid", "for the retards" or "no fun at all". Well, that Thursday the idea appealed to us. Claire organised a collection. She would pay for everything. In the kitchen, she also took from the recipe drawer the money Cécile had left for the shopping and the butcher. As if on purpose, Bernadette went at that moment to the other side of the apartment. I think she would have liked to go with us. But she had "a lot to do" and "Madame was going to call for news". Pantalon thought we were going to take him along. He wagged his tail and followed us everywhere, in the bedrooms, in a panic. It was not an autumn nor a winter Thursday. The sun was not warm. We took the no. 43 bus at the Porte des Ternes, three stops, two tickets for each of us, and we got off at Parmentier, in front of the Saint-Croix School. You, Sébastien, gave the finger to the good fathers who had booted you out and who, you used to say, were watching for your "return, hidden away behind the windows and gates". At the Porte Maillot we took the "little train" that goes to the "Gardens". Luc and Claire in front, you and I behind. We were all too big for the benches. Even me. The last one. Stop.

'2. In the pine woods, along the Boulevard Maillot, there were women, nannies, prams, children all bundled up in scarves (I feel like I was born strangled in a scarf, how about you?) and in particular an odour of dry earth, trodden too much, in front of posh apartment buildings. You said, pointing at one of them "that one's pot-bellied." I loved you for those images, Sébastien. Everything was becoming alive, because of you. Because of Claire. Luc too. But for him, only sometimes. We wanted life, everywhere, especially when there wasn't any, or anymore. How many times, for fun, did I see you climb up on a living room chair and turn the hands of the wall clock? Who then always turned them back to noon or midnight? Stop. Not blaming. But observing. I am fond of my Zoological Gardens, a "useful" wedding gift, as mama would say. It is my bridge table. Luc has married. You are getting married. Claire's turn soon. And me then? For me the little train has jumped the track. It was "jumping the track" when I was born. I was already bending too much even before being born. Stop. Never throw this note away, it can sail. You will read it someday. You will live then, at last, the lesson of that Thursday and that garden. You were preparing for the B.E.P.C. exam. Claire had just gone into the fifth class. They were making me repeat the seventh because I had not had special permission to go Sixth and start Latin. Stop. Let's enter the Garden.

'3. Distorting mirrors. The room is empty. There's only us. We're looking at ourselves, dwarfs, giants, fat, skeletal. Our images melt into one another. We pose grouped, before the mirrors. We move forward, backward, we pinch each other, box, staring at our distorted images. We're laughing at the monsters we're becoming. I hear the brightness of our voices in the room. I too laugh heartily, but a fear is taking hold of me. You sense it because you take my hand. You say "It's stupid, I'm dizzy." Luc pushes Claire in front of a mirror that makes her look round, like a balloon. He says "You look pregnant." Claire gets mad "Let's go!" But there are other mirrors and we stop. We laugh anyway. Laughing is always "anyway" and it's "a lot" of fear. "Not by a long way", the moral code at Antioche and Moncrabeau. Luc is making gesticulations in front of us. Step by step we back up and leave him alone. He doesn't realise it until a little later. He joins us. "Did we come to have fun, or didn't we?" Claire murmurs "No." We go out. You say, "I feel sick." I have always known you to feel sick and here you are a naval officer. Claire notices that I'm pale. Luc drags us on. Our laughter has attracted other children, accompanied them and they are pushing to get into the room's entryway. Summary: to acclimatise us, we are deformed. As soon as we enter we are told to laugh about it. And we laugh. Stop.

'4. Black-topped paths lined with arches and lawns we can't walk on. Each bush has a little sign beside it on which can be read a strange, complicated name, with y's and x's and endings in -is or -us. I don't like these names. They misrepresent. Everything is raked, weeded, swept. I see children with candy floss bigger than their heads, and balloons that fly away if they let go of them. I see grumpy children because their balloons have blown away. In this garden there are only thwarted dreams. Running is forbidden. We must not stop either or we might "take root", you're the one who said it when you pulled my arm, and become a bush with a name that doesn't mean anything anymore to people going by. We come to the ghost train. Claire takes me with her this time. The car of a train, a cog rail ramp, then the blackness of backstage and painted drops like behind the scenes at Uncle Jean's theatre. Someone screams to frighten us. And we don't scream because fear is part of the price. A stage set. Some skeletons. A coffin that opens. I tell myself that grandma at Lectoure is dead. Shapes shake around under clothes. Hands touch our heads in a carnival nighttime. They are paid to tickle us, "they", will we ever see their faces? End of the ride, our car bangs into a double door and here we are outside again. Claire has a good grip on me. She was afraid, "a lot" and "all the same". They brake us. We get out. In turn the car comes out with you in it, eyes closed, beside Luc. Luc yells "Come on, we have to do everything else!" Stop.

'5. The figure of eight. Luc gets in front: "I'm not afraid", you behind, your mouth all crooked, Claire and I in the middle. Claire tells me "Hang on tight!" And there we are pulled along, hoisted in that little metal rocket, almost vertically. No need to lift your eyes to see the sky. Things spin a little. The sun gets colder and colder. A bend, fall, climb, fall again, roller coaster hills, vibrations. Claire screamed the whole time. Luc leaned forward like he was going to jump and wanted to impress us. You yelled, "Stop!" Everything happened very fast. I saw lots of buildings around the Bois de Boulogne, numb, sated, and the trees at the square. The end. Stop. We have to hold you up. You say "No, I'm alright. Let's go on!" What are you trying to prove to Luc? Further on there are lions sleeping on a rock, an elephant sticking its trunk over a moat, and some monkeys with pink bottoms, we laugh at them a little, who are waiting for us to throw those biscuits Claire has just bought for them. I lend you my handkerchief so you can wipe your mouth. Stop. You have to pay to enter this garden. You have to pay all the time. In this garden, everything has to be paid for. Luc says, "we should have come more often." I have nothing more to explain. I scarcely dare express myself. Do tell Ruth I think she is beautiful. Today I can only give you this garden where we will always be growing up without knowing it, without wanting to.

'6. The race track. Claire pays for us four and gives us our tickets. We each climb into a little car. The circuit is in the shape of an eight. I don't like this number, the sign of infinity, the number of death. The roadway is rather wide, with concrete slabs loose in places, with jolts at the steering wheel, and metal noises from each of our contraptions. Signs, "No Passing" and "Keep Right". Luc started off first. Then you. Then Claire. Then me. Right in order. Luc tries to leave us behind by taking the curves straight as an arrow. It goes up, down, very gently this time, in the middle of bushes no different from those planted everywhere in this garden where even the air seems to stagnate. We are allowed four times round. You turned around, once, to be assured that I was indeed following you. Claire also, once, smiling. But not Luc. French composition: The Zoological Gardens. Thesis: forces and ways of acclimatising. Antithesis: dangers. Synthesis: we are all born in this garden whether one has the means to pay or not. We always arrive in the same order. But we finally lose one of them. I am lost, Sébastien, and I am losing myself. Travel as much as you can. I hope so much you will read this message-gift someday in the middle of a storm. The elements, *they* are unleashed. The river remains.

'7. The enchanted river. It was getting cold. We were going to go home. Luc said, "No, there's still that one!" A sentry box.

Claire pays. A gate. Tickets taken. A pier. We are waiting for a boat "just for us". A mill makes the water flow in the concrete canal that is just the width of the small boat. Another sign "Do not put your hands on the edge". And we are taken away, a winding way, forced. We pass under a stone bridge. There are Snowwhite and the Seven Dwarfs, Sleeping Beauty's Castle, and *Le Petit Poucet* being chased by an ogre. You shrug your shoulders. Claire has had "enough!" Getting out of the boat, you are shivering. You find the strength to say, "It's the disenchanted river." We've laughed anyway. All the same. Stop. And we went home to the Place d'Antioche. I had a terrible headache.

'7a. Grandmother from Lectoure had died that afternoon. Bernadette was waiting for us with the news. I went to bed, I had a "high" fever. I saw everything, helterskelter, the mirrors, the train, the figure of eight; the track and the river. We have never again spoken, afterward, as we did before. Cécile gave me new pajamas. She said, "It's nothing." Henri would say the day I came back to the table, "There's nothing wrong with you." It was finished, finished in advance. Someday I will write a hundred thousand page novel called *The Immobile Father*. As an inscription, I'll put "This is the story of a murderous father who could find no better way of killing his children than letting them live." The expression is his. Following will be a hundred thousand blank pages that I won't be allowed to write, refused in advance. I dedicate them to you. See you soon, when you read me here. Escape, for everything crosses us out. Your brother, Bertrand. The evening before your wedding. Stop.'

Sébastien, naked, the sheet pulled off the bed, lying on the banquette in his cabin, folds the message he has never had the courage or the curiosity to read. He replaces it in the envelope 'To Sébastien Prouillan, the memory of the forbidden heart' and slips it into the annotated copy of *The Memoirs of Hadrian*. Sébastien gets up, takes the letter he had written to his father that same morning and places it, with Bertrand's message, in the book. So all he has sent is a postcard, to Toronto to his children. 82, Amelia Street. The address sings. Ruth does not dance anymore. Life goes on. Sébastien puts on his trousers, a pullover with nothing underneath and, his feet bare in his shoes, goes out of the cabin, the book in his hand. A few minutes later, he throws it vertically, from the top of the ship, over the side. The book disappears immediately. The two envelopes float a few minutes. Then the waves bumping against the *Firebird* swallow up the messages. Sébastien rubs his arms. A slight chill. He doesn't want to think about anything anymore. To each his place. A hundred thousand blank pages. There are no more storms.

21

Bertrand turns out the light and listens for the noises. The house creaks, at night. Steps on the stairs, keys in the locks, slamming doors, or shutters, cries, voices, so many indistinct rumblings. He frowns, draws lines in space. Then Bertrand approaches the wall, presses against it, his hands flattened, moves along it and bends at the door frame, which he always leaves open, and goes from room to room, surprised, curious to know if someone is waiting for him, if there is anyone, or no one or nothing. He then moves into the next room. He hears better, he sees better there, in the night. The downstairs rooms belong to him, as well as the staircase, the hallways on the second floor and the third, under the roof. Often, when it rains, he stays all the way upstairs. He listens to the pattering on the tiles. The house keeps him company. He caresses the walls. He moves about. Jeanne always asks, 'Did you make your night rounds?' Bertrand, looking surprised, does not understand. What does he hear in this voice, a small reproach and much tenderness, or the reverse each in turn? Jeanne says again, the usual phrases, 'I'm going to cut your hair, you need it,' 'Your father called, everything's alright.' 'You have to put on more than that, you'll catch cold,' 'Juan's in a bad mood,' 'Merced is going to bawl me out for staying too long,' 'I remembered to get your pencils,' 'Your father will surely come one day,' 'There's a good movie on television tonight. Tonio will come to get you.' These sentences Jeanne believes Bertrand will finally understand if she repeats them. Bertrand says 'Thanks,' 'Outside,' 'Them,' 'Lo' for hello, 'wri' for write, and especially 'Clean,' 'Head' if he wants medicine, 'Zee' for dizzy, the doctor must be called. It is always the same tranquillisers then, the same directions. But why does he say 'Them' as often as 'Thanks'? Juan maintains it is 'Thmmmm,' a sigh, a groan, clearing his throat, an animal grunt. Jeanne knows it is 'Them' and that this word means something.

The light out, Bertrand goes into the bathroom. At the sink, his arms outstretched, he washes his hands for a long time. He soaps them, rubs, rinses, soaps them again and holds them, one against the other, a gesture of prayer downward, under the faucet and water. José has often surprised him that way, running the water as hard as possible, holding his hands but not rubbing them now, standing, rigid, his back a little arched, his face slightly thrown back, disgusted or fascinated, eyes half closed. Then José approaches, turns off the water and hands Bertrand a towel. Bertrand takes the towel and, before wiping his hands, brings it to his face as if trying to recapture a smell. Of this mania Merced says, 'So much the better since he is washing.' Juan mocks her. 'We should cut off the water from time to time.' Lucio orders his family to be still. Sometimes, when he comes in from the fields, José makes the same gesture as he washes his hands. He would like to feel what Bertrand is feeling, and to understand. He only makes his hands cold.

Bertrand brings the towel to his face, breathes, buries his head in it, then wipes his hands, folds the towel, puts it back, turns off the faucet and goes out of the bathroom. He turns completely around as if he were being attacked from the sides or from behind. He raises one arm, then the other as if to free himself from the tethers. He stops short. Did he hear a noise? He looks hard at the ceiling. Antonio went to bed calling his brother a 'lackey'. José has posted himself, outside, behind a French door that opens onto Bertrand's bedroom. The shutter serves as a screen for him. He bends down. He watches. He would like to make the rounds with Bertrand. To see where he goes, what he does and why.

Bertrand approaches the desk, opens the drawer, pulls it completely out, holds it high in both hands, in front of him, arms spread wide and with an abrupt move spills the contents onto the floor, photos, letters, exercise books, pencils, papers, notebooks, envelopes, shirts in cardboard, a disorder of pages and objects at his feet and all around him. He puts the empty drawer back, heads for the linen closet, in the corner near the chimney. He tries to open it. But Jeanne keeps it locked. Bertrand hits the lock with his fist, kicks. Then he gives up, goes to the bed, undoes it with a quick move, tears off the sheet, comes back to the desk, spreads the sheet on the floor and, on his knees, throws on it the envelopes, photos, notebooks, everything fallen from the drawer. Sometimes he kisses a pencil or a letter. He looks carefully to see he has not forgotten anything under the desk. He creeps on all fours, feeling around. Then he rises, approaches the bookcase, slides his finger along the edges of the books, takes one here and one there, without hesitation, automatically, and throws them on the sheet with the rest. He also suddenly throws out the contents of the drawer of the bedside table, and some clothes he gets from a closet, a suit, a pullover, a coat. José holds his breath. The sheet makes a spot of light on the floor. José senses only that Bertrand is choosing what he is piling up, there, in a jumble, but he wishes he could see better and closer. Those clothes Bertrand has never worn.

Bertrand ties the sheet, makes a bundle and drags it toward the French door. José steps back and flattens himself behind the shutter. Bertrand does not go out. Silence. José waits, then bends over again. The bundle is there. The French door is open. Bertrand has gone into the house.

José enters and follows him, gliding from room to room until he comes to the entry hall. His hand on the railing, slowly, Bertrand is going up to the second floor. He stops, as if he were anxious at not finding a way, as if he had forgotten a destination, an errand to do, a message to take. He hesitates. Then he makes a large movement of his head, nervously, and climbs the last steps. José waits until he is at the top, takes off his shoes, hides them under the staircase and climbs up in turn, two at a time, close to the railing, making no noise.

The second floor, the hallway, a door at the end. Bertrand tries to open it and, is hitting it, kicking it, like the linen closet, he bangs on it, fidgets around, steps back, charges it with his shoulder, steps back and throws himself at it again. Bertrand falls to his knees, his forehead against the door. José goes to him, gives him his hand, helps him get up, puts him to one side and throws himself in turn, once, twice. The third time the door gives way. It is a bedroom, with a bed without springs or mattress, a chair turned upside down on a table. Bertrand mumbles 'Thanks', enters and goes directly to a small frame hanging across from the bed. He unhooks it, wipes it with his fingers and holds it right against his face as if he wanted to kiss it. Night in the bedroom. Night in the hallway. Bertrand goes away with his booty. Several times, on the stairs, José thinks Bertrand

311

is going to miss a step and fall. But from wall to railing, from railing to wall, Bertrand manages to keep his balance. José follows him, barefoot. He forgets to get his shoes. Bertrand seems in a hurry.

Outside, Bertrand drags the bundle with one hand and holds the frame in the other, very tightly against himself. The moon is down. Day is going to break. Mist is on the lake, a strong odour of earth and dew. At a few dozen metres from the house, Bertrand stops, undoes the bundle, tramples on the frame, breaking it, tears the print in it, then, on his knees, a matchbox in his hand, burns an envelope, a photo, tears a notebook, strikes another match, fans it. The things are not burning.

José runs to the laundry shed, behind the house. Under the sink is a bottle of heating alcohol. When he comes back, dogs in the area start barking. Bertrand stands up, moves away, panics. Holding him, José shows him the bottle. 'It'll burn with this!' José kneels, picks up a small piece of the torn print, slips it into his trouser pocket, sprinkles the sheet, clothes and objects. He rises again. The bottle is empty. With all his strength he pitches it into the pond. He takes the box of matches and lights the sheet. José rubs his hands. Bertrand says 'Clean' and backs slowly toward the house.

At the end of the road, alerted, are Antonio, Juan, then Lucio, Jeanne and Merced. They do not dare approach. The cocks are singing. The mist on the pond is dissipating. A black smoke above the fire. Then soon no more flames and a spot on the grass. Head hanging, arms dangling, Bertrand waits for someone to come to him.

The women have busied themselves with him. They have undressed him, put him to bed and tucked him in. Bertrand let them do it. They were all in the bedroom, the men near the door and the women on each side of the bed. Then, Merced closed the French door and drew the curtains. Juan was watching his sons. Antonio shrugged. José smiled at his father. Lucio made a sign to Juan not to say anything. One last time Merced caressed Bertrand's forehead. He was already sleeping, eyes wide open.

They closed all the doors behind them. José got his shoes from under the stairs, saying, 'There's a door broken on the second.' But everybody was already outside. Nobody heard. Furtively, José looks at the piece of the print: a face in some bushes.

312

A little further along the road, as he was joining the group, José threw the piece of the print into the weeds. Lucio said, '*No paso nada!*' Juan repeated, 'Nothing happened!' Merced took Jeanne's arm. Jeanne placed her hand on Merced's hand. José said to his brother, 'Did anything happen?' Antonio answered, 'Nothing!' Juan stopped and turned around to look at the house, from a distance. Hands in his pockets, shoulders raised, he spat on the ground. Lucio did the same. Antonio and José imitated them. Merced crossed herself. A new day was beginning. Jeanne said, 'Let's go home. I'm cold.'

22

July 10th. Five o'clock in the morning. Austerlitz Station. Henri Prouillan stands, hands crossed behind his back, head slightly tilted, forehead against the window-paned door of the waiting room. The station is deserted. The ticket windows are closed. At each minute the noise of the big hand of the electric clocks can be heard. They all show exactly the same time. Computerised. For nearly two hours he has been watching, waiting, going and coming back to verify that Bernadette has not left her refuge during one of his circuits. Bernadette is seated, hands in her lap, very straight and sedate at the far end of the room. At her feet there are two suitcases. Henri does not dare enter. Three other people are sleeping. Bernadette looks at him. The first train for Toulouse is at 5.57 a.m.

Several times Henri wanted to give up and go home to the Place d'Antioche. He already saw himself tearing up the manuscript of *Mortmain* without even reading it, throwing it into the building's trash cans, half in one, half in the other, poking his hand deep inside to mix the garbage well, a simple precaution. He saw himself taking an unusual, morning bath and going to bed, washed, totally abandoned, perhaps stronger than ever, thinking of everything except the cheque he gave Suzy, except Moncrabeau, except Cécile, Luc, Claire and Sébastien, trying to think of nothing but 'living until he dies', an expression used at lunch at Taillevent's, by his stockbroker, a week ago today, Saturday. Several times Henri found himself in front of the station, on the Seine's quay, departure side, or on the boulevard, arrivals side, waiting for an unoccupied taxi to pass.

But he was retracing his steps, obstinately. Bernadette could not leave like that, doing that to him, to him, there's the rub, now. And here he is again, his forehead against the window glass of the door. With a set look, Bernadette keeps him at a distance and forbids him to enter the waiting room. What can he do against Bernadette since he knows nothing about her, even after

315

so many years, since she knows everything, about everybody and everything, and since she has decided to take back her liberty? By holding his forehead against the glass, his hands behind his back, a childish attitude, pouting, dreamy, overlooking the Place d'Antioche, Henri still thinks, showing off, that he can disturb Bernadette, move her to the point of coming out and speaking to him. If he says the first word, it will only be worse and necessarily awkward. All his life Henri has let others condemn themselves by abandoning to them the initiative of speaking. Didn't Bertrand used to say that he would always have the 'first word'? He had it. Too bad for him. Henri is not thinking of Bertrand now, but Moncrabeau, a pile of stones with someone moving around inside. Henri will have the twin bed, Cécile's bed, removed, he doesn't want more than one bed in his bedroom. Henri will not go to the presentation of Luc's Legion of Honour. He will be 'not free' to Sébastien the next time he comes through Paris. Henri will answer the letters from Loïc, Yves or Géraldine only if Claire writes him. At least one letter. At least that. Where is Pierre? Who is he like? Where are Laura and Paul? They are not like him. Henri no longer wants to see Suzy, ever. Henri will not dare telephone Jacqueline anymore. And if she calls, he will hang up without a word. Henri, his forehead against the glass, creates, invents, makes all kinds of blackmail for himself. He has not come to Austerlitz Station to convince Bernadette to return to the house and resume her duties, but to see her leave, once and for all, like all the others, and to feel there is nothing but a king and four bishops left on the chessboard. Eyes meeting eyes across the distance, a door separating them, Bernadette Despouet and Henri Prouillan scrutinise each other in silence.

Sentences, speeches, Henri had the power once. Sentences, always the same sentences. 'Power is not supposed to choose the moral order against liberty.' 'The blending of security and the security of the established power must not be allowed,' and speeches, always the same speeches, 'The conquest of liberties will always be an unfinished battle. In this struggle, all relaxation is a defeat. Let us look behind us for a moment. The bourgeoisie has created its own feudalism. It is not against it but with it that the first foundations of social democracy should have been built, to overcome collectivism. Too late!' With his voice Henri would then make his cravated, potential-minister's, minister's or ex-minister's 'Too late' ring out. Always the same sentences, the same speeches, ideas, nothing but ideas. This morning Henri hears the noise of the minutes passing, a clang, each time like a final heart beat. Nothing can stop that time.

Henri straightens up. He leaves the mark of his forehead on the glass pane. Several marks, he has soiled the door. To the dull vibrations of the first metro train, a man puts a package in front of the news-stand, two girls, in sandals, with backpacks, bare legs, are looking at the panel of the main line departures. Little by little, there are people, travellers, workers. A military man comes out of the waiting room. The two other people have wakened. Henri goes in. Instantly Bernadette rises, tightens the belt of her coat, checks that her bag is well closed, takes her suitcases and passes in front of Henri, without a word, and without looking at him. Henri holds the door for her. She goes out. He follows her. The suitcases are heavy but she is afraid. She is in a hurry. Henri had never seen her so small, frail, fragile. He sees her again at Auzan, the day of the first visit. She was a beautiful woman. Since then, he has never really looked at her. How could he have said, exercising his rank, that the bourgeoisie had 'created its own feudalism', and from the moment it would be necessary to 'build with it' and not 'against it'? Henri reddens, puts his fists in his suit coat pockets. Hatless, coatless, he feels naked, a target for all eyes. Bernadette is ahead of him. She is feeling a little pain, almost stumbles, and quickens her step. Henri stops at the entrance of platform 7. The weather is fine, the air is fragrant. The train is not yet in the station. The sun has risen. Bernadette is at the end of the platform, well beyond the limit of the glass roof. She stops, puts down her suitcases, puts her handbag on one of the suitcases. She hesitates. She turns around and looks at Henri, from a distance. Henri takes a step backward so as not to frighten her anymore. He tries to give a little wave of goodbye. But Bernadette falls, as if she were broken at the knees, cut down, between the two suitcases. Some people saw her. A woman runs to her. The train enters the station slowly, backing in. An empty train. 5.13 a.m. Henri goes away. Other people have run onto platform 7.

At the corner of Austerlitz bridge Henri waited a long time. He saw the Police Emergency van, and an ambulance. He heard the sirens. He spied the stretcher. Then he hailed a cab. 'Two Place d'Antioche, please.' On the dashboard, a handwritten sign. 'Your route will be mine.' But he said nothing. He lets himself be driven.

On the Champs Elysées the grandstands are being set up for the July 14 parade. On Boulevard Haussmann, at the corner of the Rue de Téhéran, a 504 turns right, Luc is at the wheel. Henri says 'Continue!' The taxi driver, surprised, looks at him in the rearview mirror. A little further on, in front of the entrance to her building, Suzy is pulling some large plastic bags. Henri mumbles, 'Faster, please.' Henri asks the driver to let him out at the corner of the Place d'Antioche 'Here will do.' He pays. He gets out. He waits for the taxi to disappear. Often, with Suzy, they would play at staring at each other, eye to eye. The first to laugh had lost. He always won. Suzy would claim then that it was 'the loser who wins.' Henri walks around the square. The concierge has not yet brought out the trash cans. Henri enters his home, like a thief. He closes the door delicately. The telephone is ringing. He let it ring. Then he answers. Bernadette has been taken to the Pitié Hospital. She is dead. A blood clot. 'No, she had no family,' then, 'I'll come by in the morning to identify the body.' Another day. Another story.

July 10th. 5.30 a.m. At that hour, in the Impasse des Acacias, the Sanitation Department truck backs up and stops in front of the gate to Dr. Bermann's veterinary hosital. A watertight, metal case is taken in which are, on the day's list, the bodies of three dogs, seven cats, a parrot and a poodle, in a jumble, Pantalon III. The crematorium is at Gennevilliers. They take a full case, they leave an empty case. And so on. At that hour, a few elderly women head for the Saint Ferdinand church for the first morning mass, the pavement in front of Berthier fils is heavy with the smell of hot brioche, a water sprayer is wetting the roadway of the Avenue des Ternes, two canvas clad men are cleaning the windows of the United Stores. At that hour, on this summer day, Paris has a look of youth. Paris seduces. Nothing screams. Everything sings. Life goes on and nobody's the wiser. At that hour, Luc is reading the congratulatory telegrams slipped under the door, the names, not the text, just to know who has joined the game. At that hour, Suzy is watching for the garbagemen to pass. She sees her dolls, crushed all at once in the iron jaws of the compactor truck. She goes back inside. A revival of *The Collision*. Money. A reprieve. She is going to make herself pretty to go to the bank. At that hour, the immense, blue sky rings out over Sauveterre. Claire is opening all the windows in the house and unconsciously stares at the Italian horizon. At that hour, in the Overfjellet fjord, a wind is falling from the mountains and the woods, a wind from rocks and peaks that makes the sea shiver. Sébastien does not want to go back to his cabin. He closes his eyes. He is sailing. At that hour, Juan and his sons are leaving for the fields. Lucio is staying at the house. Merced is changing the sheets on the bed in their room. Bertrand has risen to open the French doors. At that hour, Henri is looking at the wall clock in the living room, the bronzes on the chests of drawers on each side of the balcony doors. The lorries from the Glacières réunies are crossing the Place d'Antioche, the morning delivery. Saturday, the day before Sunday. In the pavement cafés the drinks will be iced. It was the July 9th of the year to come. A cry from the heart. A cry restrained. The Prouillans are still here. Henri waits. He has time.

Joucas, June 79
Joucas, January 80
For Marie-Claude and Jean-Jacques